DR. B.R. AMBEDKAR

DR. B.R. AMBEDKAR

Messiah of the Downtrodden

Janak Singh

KALPAZ

Published by

Kalpaz Publications
C-30, Satyawati Nagar,
Delhi – 110052
Ph.: 011-47034999, 9811692060
www.kalpazpublications.com
E-mail: kalpaz@hotmail.com

Distribution Network
gyanbooks.com
India, USA, Canada, UK, Australia, France

ISBN: 978-81-783-5821-5 (HB)

Reprint in India, 2024
First Published, 2010

Printed at: Gyan Press, Delhi.

Dr. B.R. Ambedkar: Messiah of the Downtrodden
Author: Janak Singh

Dr. B.R. Ambedkar was one of the greatest Indians of the 20th century. His ideas have the potential to trigger the biggest revolution in the caste-based Hindu society in the 21st century. Already Hindu orthodoxy and politicians are trying to appropriate Ambedkar to win the support of his one hundred sixty million followers and to forestall any Dalit insurrection, which may cause a social upheaval in India.

Dedicated to my Father,

Sardar Gurbakhsh Singh

Contents

Foreword

This is a warmhearted and laudatory biography of Dr. (Babasaheb) Bhimrao Ramji Ambedkar, written from a personal and passionate standpoint. All areas of Ambedkar's life are tackled, including some omitted from other work. Ambedkar's economic writings, his theories of race and caste and his book on the demand for Pakistan, for instance. On the latter controversial matter, the author writes that "although the book was not entirely flattering to Muslims, the fact that it supported the division of the subcontinent into two nations was like a boon to the hardliners in the Muslim League". He adds that "Ambedkar had correctly anticipated in his book that there would be no alternative to Pakistan."

The chapter on Gandhi, entitled "An Enigma", is as harsh as that of any angry Dalit. The author points out that Gandhi never followed his ancestral calling of Bania, even though he held that one's duty is to the occupation in which one is born. Gandhi appointed an 18 years old Brahmin to "teach the Ashram scavenger cleanliness", surely a misplaced trust. Gandhi and Jinnah both "by their domination... demoralized their followers" and, as an example of the faults of Congress in not giving the Scheduled Caste candidates adequate importance, notes that Nehru's servant Hari was fielded in the 1937 election.

Another of Ambedkar's statements that is not widely known came at the time that the Cabinet Mission was deciding the future political patterns of India's democracy in 1946 and he was concerned that the Scheduled Castes be given their proper degree of power. Ambedkar, disgusted with the Cabinet Mission giving in to Gandhi on the matter of separate electorates, "circulated a pamphlet in which he argued that the Untouchables would not like to suffer the fate of the American Negroes who valiantly fought in the civil war, died in large numbers, but when hostilities ended, were denied equality with other Americans." Although I have studied the ways in which Ambedkar brought knowledge of world history into his advice for India, I had not read this profound truth about my own country. However, both the range and depth of evocation of Ambedkar's life in this book still must be appreciated.

Eleanor Zelliot
Randolph, Minnesota
November 30, 2009

Professor Eleanor Zelliot is the best known international authority on Ambedkar.

Preface

For long after the end of the Mauryan empire in the 2nd century B.C, it was a heresy to talk of Buddhism in India. The Brahminical domination of the Hindu society ushered in by Pushyamitra, who ascended the Magadh throne in 185 B.C. after assassinating Brihadratha, the last of the Maurayan kings, not only put an end to all preaching of Buddhism, but also fixed a price on the head of every Bhikku whose calling was the propagation of Buddhist thought and religion. If emperors of the Gupta period, which followed the Mauryan rule, resorted to religious persecution of the Buddhists, the Muslim invaders who followed them outdid India's previous monarchs: they not only put to sword every Buddhist preacher, they also desecrated and destroyed Buddhist monuments and Viharas. Thus, Buddhism was almost obliterated in the country of its birth. But it prospered and flourished in China, Japan, Thailand, Srilanka and several other countries where Buddhist monks fleeing from India had sought shelter and later started propagating their faith, winning hordes of willing votaries for it.

If Buddhism came across an impregnable wall of resistance in India over 2,000 years ago because it had sought to supplant Brahminical domination of Hindu society, discouraged Vedic rites and rituals involving animal sacrifices and tried to introduce egalitarian social order free from caste stratifications, Bhimrao Ramji Ambedkar, although he was easily one of the greatest Indians of the 20th century, could not gain general acceptance in the Indian society and caste Hindu dominated intellectual circles because he was, as acknowledged by Mahatma Gandhi himself, "the greatest challenge to Hinduism." He roused the depressed classes to rebel against the caste system which confined them to play only mean, subordinate roles and thus by comparison enhance the dignity and prestige of the upper castes. He also asked them to throw overboard their fatalistic outlook that if they were the victims of social inequality and tyranny, it was because of their sins in the previous birth; and if they suffered in silence without any grudge or protest, at least after their death they would be liberated in their next life.

All this, Ambedkar said, was nothing but a Brahminical conspiracy to keep the Shudras on the lowest rung of the social ladder. He made a bonfire of Manusmriti, the Bible of the caste-based Hindu society. As reflected through the books he wrote, the lectures he delivered, the arguments he marshalled in support of the stand on various subjects he took during debates in Parliament or in discussions outside, his thoughts had an incandescent luminosity before which almost everything else paled. Although all his life Ambedkar was hated, baited and discriminated, the fact is that none of his contemporaries could match his intellectual brilliance. He had doctoral degrees from the prestigious Columbia University in New York, the London School of Economics and Political Science in U.K, studied at the Bonn University in Germany, and was even called to the Bar at Gray's Inn in England.

Ambedkar, wearing a hat with blue suit, white shirt and red tie, often looked more like a European than an Indian gentleman despite the fact that he was treated as an Untouchable by the Hindu society. He knew and understood the Indian social system, and he worked within it not to wreck it but change it. He assailed the Indian social system because it did not foster the spirit of critical inquiry and instead expected the masses to accept caste-based stratifications as the will of God. The spirit of inquiry is the *sine qua non* of progress, but since it was not there, India remained stuck to its glorious past and could not progress like the European nations. The desire for monopoly made the priest the most powerful factor in social control. During the Vedic period when worth and not birth determined one's place and occupation in life, Ashoka, a Shudra, emerged as the greatest king remembered to this day. But the rigid division of society by castes made India weak and vulnerable, and an easy prey to foreign invaders. All his life Ambedkar fought for an end to the caste system.

Normally, every Indian should have been proud of Ambedkar, hailed his achievements from the rooftops, sung paeans in his praise and named roads and big buildings after him as is happening today, though rather belatedly. Ambedkar's tragedy was that he belonged to a community of Untouchable Mahars, who were seen as occupying the lowest rung of the caste ladder, and, therefore, forfeited the right to be treated humanely. Mahars, who are atishuddras, were in fact even barred from studying the Vedic scriptures and other religious books. For centuries, they were treated like pariahs, denied entry into temples, not allowed even to draw water from wells or touch water taps lest they should pollute them. The upper caste Hindus would sneer at them the moment they set their sights on Mahars ; they would even shout profanities at them if they dared cross their path. Despite all these handicaps, disadvantages and the appalling poverty at home, Ambedkar, the fourteenth child of a mere subedar-major, went on conquering peaks of academic achievements, first encouraged in his childhood by his father, and later by his sheer determination, to equal if not outshine all caste Hindus who treated him with utter contempt only for the reason that he was born a Mahar.

Growing up in the crucible of poverty and want, adversity and social contempt which he met with at almost every stage in his life, barring the brief period he spent abroad for his education, he was a giant among pygmies who could not see beyond their nose. No wonder, he had no tolerance for people whom he thought unworthy of his attention. To such persons, he was sometime rude to the point of a fault. But the Untouchables never found him wanting in concern for their welfare. His life was a total dedication to their cause. He was like Voltaire, the man who dared expose what he thought to be the misdeeds of the Catholic Church in Europe in the 18th century. Ambedkar not only challenged but also demanded annihilation of the 2,000 years old caste system, the very foundation of the Hindu society. The untouchable leader, who was adored and admired for his intellectual attainments by many abroad, remained neglected in his own country. For long, he was dismissed as a British stooge.

If he could accomplish and attain what was long thought impossible for Mahars and other Untouchables amongst Hindus, what prevented others belonging to the Scheduled Castes and Scheduled Tribes in India from moving up in life instead of remaining confined and resigned to a low status? Their low caste did not diminish their faculties of learning. Such thoughts worried Ambedkar. With his portfolio full of foreign degrees and testimonials by leading educationists of the Columbia University and the London School of Economics, Ambedkar returned home with a steel-like determination to awaken the underdogs and to infuse in them zeal and zest to make a bid for a better life, which was long thought to be the exclusive monopoly of the caste Hindus. Despite the imposing list of degrees and testimonials he had, Ambedkar was denied jobs, would not be touched by the Hindu society even with a bargepole. No wonder, young Ambedkar soon realized that his deliverance and the deliverance of the Untouchables lay only in challenging the very foundation of India's caste system. He wrote books, published pamphlets, edited newspapers and formed powerful organizations of the Scheduled Castes to fight for their due place under the sun and not remain confined to ghettos marked for them.

Despite the handicaps, Ambedkar's brilliance continued to attract attention. In the pre-Independence days, when Untouchables lived on the mercy of the caste Hindus, Ambedkar caught the attention of the then British rulers and was invited to attend the Round Table Conferences in London held to discuss and prepare a ground for the transfer of power from Britain to India. He had the sole distinction of being made a member of the Viceroy's Executive Council during the Second World War. Notwithstanding deep prejudice against him, Ambedkar was made chairman of the panel set up by the Constituent Assembly to frame the Constitution for Independent India. He was appointed Law Minister in India's first Cabinet formed by Nehru. Yet there always existed a deep chasm, between him and the upper caste Hindu society, which he could never bridge.

Although Quaid-e-Azam Mohammed Ali Jinnah initially did not want Pakistan, Ambedkar sensed the necessity for a separate Muslim nation and in 1940 wrote a book, "Pakistan or the Partition of India." He said that a Muslim state must be formed because Muslims were convinced that they were a separate nation. Although many Muslim intellectuals praised the book, it was not taken seriously by the decision-makers. Had there been peaceful transfer of populations in Punjab and Bengal as Ambedkar had suggested, rivers of blood all resulting from communal violence would not have flowed on the Indian subcontinent as it happened in 1947. Several million Hindus, Muslims and Sikhs fell victim to the animus of communal hatred which gripped India when the subcontinent was divided into two nations, India and Pakistan. Many trainloads of refugees moving from one country to another perished in the communal frenzy let loose by fanatics.

Eleanor Zelliot, an American scholar, who has been in India for long and who has written extensively on the problems of the downtrodden in this country, says Ambedkar's life and work should be better known in the West for he was a leader who believed that the leadership of a people must come from within the group; religion must meet the needs of a people and reflect their greatness; education must be stressed and must reach the lowest. Those who have achieved elite status must remain concerned about their depressed brethren and courage is the essential element among those who wish equality; also, those who lead must be moral and pure of heart.

Losing all hope of redemption of the Untouchables by the Hindu society, a disgusted and frustrated Ambedkar started examining other religions to help his fallen brethren save themselves from the stranglehold of caste which had kept them in virtual bondage for centuries. If Ambedkar led his followers to embrace Buddhism and not, say, Christianity, it was because he felt that Christianity was not only foreign, it did not emphasize enough the social aspects of life. He could have embraced Islam or Sikhism. But he chose an older religion, one with a longer, creative, literary and artistic past, one which had blossomed in Maharashtra, the state to which he belonged.

Although a victim of caste hatred all his life, his death on December 6, 1956, plunged in grief the entire Bombay city where his body was cremated amid tumultuous scenes of sorrow witnessed on the streets through which the cortege passed on the way to the cremation ground in Dadar. Thanks to political jealousies he had aroused because of his surpassing brilliance, those who always thought him to be a thorn in their side felt somewhat relieved. But his countless followers became more restive. By way of homage and tribute to Ambedkar, many of his admirers wrote hagiographic books after his death. His birth anniversary on April 14 began to be celebrated by myriads of his followers. Swept by a consuming passion to pay homage to their Babasaheb, as millions of his votaries call him, they dance and raise slogans every year on this day, glorifying Ambedkar on the streets of Pune, Nagpur and several other cities in Maharashtra.

Ambedkar rose on the horizon of the depressed classes like a lodestar who went on guiding them to fight for their human rights. But once the lodestar was gone, the zeal and zest to challenge India's caste-system, which holds more than half the country's population in perpetual bondage, started losing momentum. There was at least a symbolic concern for the Untouchables so long as Gandhi lived. But Untouchability against which Ambedkar fought all his life never became an article of faith with the civil society in India. That is why Ambedkar wanted to reorganize civil society by disbanding the caste system: he wanted worth, but not birth, to determine one's place in society. No wonder against this background of social reality, Ambedkar's stature has grown and continues to do so after his death. The downtrodden, irrespective of their social and political cleavages, are showing a proclivity to swear by Ambedkar's legacy.

Because of a studied attempt by the government not to allow the emergence of Ambedkar as a great leader of the depressed classes even posthumously, several trunks loaded with his writings remained unopened for over three decades after his death. Such callous treatment meted out to the written legacy of the greatest leader of the Scheduled Castes in the 20th century is without parallel. When some of his followers protested and demanded publication of these papers, their protest was dismissed on the ground that pending decision on a court case about the ownership of these documents, the government could not do anything. The matter was allowed to be dragged in litigation for long. As a result, Ambedkar, the greatest leader of the depressed classes, remained for long in oblivion.

Was this nonchalance the result of a conspiracy by governments ruling the Centre and Maharashtra? It is difficult to answer this question with certainty, but the fact is not much attention has been paid to discussion and debate on the thoughts and deeds of Ambedkar. Recognizing him as a great leader of Dalit resurgence in India, Columbia University in the USA has opened a website on him. Not only that his bust is there in the university library. Although his statue stands in the Parliament House in New Delhi, the fact is that the greatest leader of the downtrodden still continues to be marginalized in his own country. If he is being remembered here, it is only as a maker of the country's Constitution. His sterling contribution towards arousing the depressed classes from their slumber of resignation to their fate does not seem to merit even notice in intellectual circles.

It was only when India's main political parties, which had been leading the downtrodden up the garden path only to secure their votes, became alive to the increasing erosion of their popularity that they thought of Ambedkar. It occurred to them that reviving Ambedkar's memory might help them in winning again the support of the depressed classes whom Ambedkar had led in his lifetime like the Pied Piper of Hamlin. It was in this context that Ambedkar's centenary was celebrated in 1991. Not only that, the Bharat Ratna award was also conferred on him posthumously. It was only then that his writings were published in a multi-volume edition by the Maharashtra government. Scholars are belatedly realizing the importance of the greatness of Ambedkar.. Now it has become an almost annual ritual for leaders of various political parties to pay homage to Babasaheb on the occasions of his birth and death anniversaries.

What kind of man was Ambedkar? Long after his death he is being projected as a great personage by all those who in his lifetime were eager to haul him over the coals because he wanted annihilation of the caste system. What went into the making of this Untouchable, born in a military cantonment quarter at Mahow in Madhya Pradesh, as one of the greatest leaders of India in the 20th century? In fact, in the turmoil caused in the Hindu society by Ambedkar, who challenged the very basis on which its caste hierarchy rests, Dalit militancy is on the rise. Whether it will succeed in revolutionising the Hindu society or not only time will tell.

Janak Singh

1

A Hero in Distress

Late in the afternoon on July 14, 1956, Delhi was lashed by a heavy dust storm. Dark clouds raced across the sky. Soon, it started raining. People ran helter-skelter, looking for shelter in shops, buildings, bus stops or under road bridges. Many trees were uprooted, blocking traffic. Those returning from offices caught in the hailstorm, got completely drenched. In low-lying areas, roads were waterlogged. Even driving cars became difficult. It was a typical monsoon day. Notwithstanding the fury of the weather, people heaved a sigh of relief for it had been very hot and humid earlier.

But the stormy weather made no difference to the normal routine of Bhimrao Ramji Ambedkar He lived in a large bungalow on Alipur Road. Although it was pouring outside, he remained preoccupied reading and writing in his study. When hailstones started pounding the windowpanes of his room, Ambedkar paused, began to watch the nature's fury. After sometime, when the rain had stopped and the weather became somewhat pleasant, a violin hung on the wall in a corner of his room attracted his attention. He lovingly dusted it and with the bow in his hand began playing the musical instrument though he was not very adept at it. However, this was very unusual. Although he had started taking violin lessons rather late in life, he had rarely indulged in this kind of leisurely activity. He was always in solitude, preoccupied day and night with reading books or writing chapters of the books he planned to finish soon.

When his part-time personal assistant, Nanak Chand Rattu, returned from his office, he was completely soaked to the skin. Abandoning his bicycle in the verandah, he wrung the water out of his clothes and wiping his face quietly went towards Ambedkar's study. He was somewhat nervous for having been summoned to come over by 5 p.m., he had got late because of the rain. He feared that Ambedkar would be angry with him. But when he peeped in, Rattu was surprised over what he saw: Ambedkar was playing on the violin and humming some tune along with it! This was a most unusual sight for Rattu. There was a special reason for Rattu to be happy. Caught in the hailstorm he had paused at many places on the way. At a bus stand shelter, when the rain had somewhat slackened, he heard the mournful barking of a dog probably caught under a fallen tree or injured by some speeding vehicle. It was not a good omen, thought Rattu. It had made him gloomy not so much on account of anything in his personal life but on account of his master to whom he was deeply attached, often typing pages of his books until late in the night.

Ambedkar had not been keeping good health. This worried Rattu. He had lost weight, looked depressed and shrunken. His summer and winter suits which now looked baggy when he wore them, were altered to fit him properly. His lean legs could not bear the weight of his heavy frame. Even while performing routine tasks like bathing or walking in the verandah or the lawn of his bungalow, Ambedkar needed someone's help. Sometimes he was not able even to shave himself. He would remain lying in bed with no inclination to eat anything. He had to be persuaded to have some grub. The change of climate did not improve his health either. Because of his failing eyesight, his eyes were tested and spectacles changed several times. Yet there was no improvement. All this irritated Ambedkar and one day making a casual remark, he said: "In the event of losing my eyesight, life would not be worth living as I would not be able to read and write and accomplish the monumental task of completing my books." In fact he was so weak and gloomy these days that whoever came to see him felt worried about his deteriorating condition.

No wonder, finding Ambedkar at peace with himself playing on the violin dispelled Rattu's gloomy thoughts and he heaved a sigh of relief. Mesmerized, he kept on watching his master for sometime. But since what he saw was so unusual and breathtaking, he quietly retreated from the scene and told everybody in the house that "Babasaheb", as he used to address his master, "is playing on the violin today." Every member of the household peeped in Ambedkar's room from outside and saw him lost in his own musical reveries. That their master who had not been keeping good health lately could find time to amuse himself thus, was indeed a real source of joy and relief to them all.

Although Ambedkar had achieved much in life and could derive satisfaction from the fact that he had been able to arouse the Untouchables in the Hindu society not to take it all lying down any more and instead strive hard for their rights, he was not altogether a happy man. He was more worried about the publication of the books he had written and often wondered whether anybody after his death would ever be able to publish his books he had written after a great deal of research and labour. The book, "Riddles of Hinduism," that he had started writing in January 1954, was completed by the end of November 1955, with four press copies typed out on fine strong paper. When his attention was drawn to the fact that preparing four copies of the manuscript was uncalled for, he said: "Look, what is the title of the book – Riddles of

Hinduism – which is itself a reply to this question. I haven't got my own press and naturally it has to be given to some Hindu press owner for printing. Anything can happen to it because of the explosive contents of the manuscript. It can be lost, burnt or destroyed and my several years' hard labour could thus go waste. Doesn't matter what the cost involved is, I must have some spare copies with me." Actually, Ambedkar feared that if some Hindu fanatic got wind of what was in the book, he would stealthily try to destroy it.

But the printing of the book was held up due to other reasons. He wanted to include in it two very important pictures. One was of the then President of India, Dr. Rajendra Prasad. The picture was taken when he went to Benares, worshipped the Brahmins, washed their toes and drank the water he had used for washing. The second picture was that of India's Prime Minister, Pandit Jawaharlal Nehru. It was taken on August 15, 1947, when he sat at the Yajna, performed by the Brahmins of Benares, who had been specially summoned for the purpose, to solemnize the rare event : a Brahmin becoming the first Prime Minister of free India. In this picture Nehru was wearing some special dress called Raj Danda befitting this occasion. It was specially brought by the Brahmins. The picture also showed Nehru drinking the holy water of the Ganges, which was brought for him by the Brahmins. While Dr. Rajendra Prasad's photo was traced, Nehru's picture could not be found.

The other books he wanted to write were: "The Riddle of Rama and Krishna," "The Riddle of Trimurti" and "The Riddle of Women." He had compiled material for these books in the form of rough notes, written in small notebooks and loose sheets, some typed extracts, markings and references put together in file covers and paper bags, under different headings. His growing inability to tackle this task on account of his failing health saddened him. Ambedkar was a great observer with an analytical mind. Certainly he got interested in what was happening in the Hindu society, which is one of the oldest civilizations of the world, claiming linkage to the great Aryan invaders, who many historians believe ventured to come across Europe and seek their fortune in the Indian subcontinent over 2,500 years ago.

Ambedkar challenged Hinduism as he had been at the receiving end all his life because of his low caste. Also, possibly because he had read Voltaire who also had raised questions about the functioning of the Catholic Church. Fired like the great French writer, Ambedkar could not bear such social inequalities as bestowed the status of a superman on a Brahmin and condemned the Shudra as a virtual slave of society born to do menial tasks. The pity is that while Voltaire is acknowledged to be one of the greatest intellectuals produced by France, Ambedkar is not only being denounced by hired and paid agents of Hindu orthodoxy today, but questions are also being raised about whatever he wrote regarding Chaturvarna system governing the graded inequality of the Hindu society. Some of the pseudo-intellectuals have gone to the extent of saying that Ambedkar was nothing but a British stooge used by the colonial rulers to run down India. No lie could be more monstrous!

India's Voltaire was a frustrated man in the last phase of his life. Rattu was aware of it. His master wrote several other books, attacking the caste-dominated Hindu society and set the intellectual world on fire. Sanskrit scholars questioned his competence to write on social subjects without the knowledge of Sanskrit, the language which is the key to the proper understanding of the Vedas, Shastras, Smritis. In fact, all that is contained in the Hindu religious books is in Sanskrit. Ambedkar admitted that he did not know Sanskrit because the Brahmin teachers of the language in the schools where he had studied refused to take him as a student. Ambedkar was frank enough to admit that it was not only the religious tomes, all written in Sanskrit, he was not even competent to speak on Indian politics.

He said: "I admit the deficiency that I cannot claim mastery over the Sanskrit language. But I do not see why it should disqualify me altogether from operating in this field. There is very little of literature in the Sanskrit language which is not available in English. The want of knowledge of Sanskrit need not therefore be a bar to my handling of a theme which is ancient in origin. I venture to say that a study of the relevant literature, albeit in English translation, for 15 years ought to be enough to invest even a person with such moderate intelligence like myself, with sufficient degree of competence for the task. It may be argued that my attempt at delving in ancient treatises is an illustration of the proverbial fool rushing in where the angels fear to tread. But I take refuge in the belief that even the fool has a duty to perform, namely, to do his bit if the angel has gone to sleep or is unwilling to proclaim the truth. This is my justification for entering the prohibited field."

Ambedkar was very unhappy to see that the All India Scheduled Castes Federation he had launched in 1942 as the mouthpiece of the depressed classes had become faction-ridden. He was utterly dissatisfied with the functioning of the Federation. It had become the hot-bed of intrigue and disruptive forces, group rivalries, growing indiscipline and insubordination. Although the Untouchables were ready to shed their last drop of blood for him, they could not make him win the elections he had fought. A sizable chunk of them had been won over and made not to vote for Ambedkar. The beneficiaries of the concessions he had secured for the downtrodden not only became indifferent to the plight of their brethren, they also deliberately kept themselves aloof so that they might gain greater acceptance in respectable social circles where normally there was no room, not even tolerance, for the Untouchable Shudras.

Dadasaheb B.K. Gaikwad was his chief lieutenant in the Federation. On July 29, 1954, deeply frustrated Ambedkar wrote to Gaikwad: "The disease of disunity in the Federation has gone very deep. The saddest thing to say is that if you take action against any one, this organization will break up. I do not propose to be head of the Federation. I am too old and too sickly to play any effective role in politics. You people can now run the party." But what Gaikwad said in his reply was the most shattering blow to Ambedkar. He said: "Matters have come to such a pass that it is an occasion not only for sorrow but also for introspection. You do not fully realize the level of discontent against you. There are letters with me which make all sorts of accusations against you. It seems there is a conspiracy to oust you from public life. I wanted time to speak to you privately. But you have never allowed me any opportunity to do so."[2]

In the last few years of his life when his health was deteriorating fast due to diabetes, gout, arthritis, and blood pressure, some of his trusted lieutenants when they sought to meet him were prevented by his wife, Dr. Savita Ambedkar. No doubt, they were angry and wrote to Ambedkar, accusing his wife for becoming a hurdle not easy to cross. But he could not accept this accusation. Whatever he had been able to achieve for the depressed classes through provisions in the Constitution was enjoyed by the educated few. The lot of vast number of illiterate masses remained the same. He wanted to do something for them, but now there was no time. Life seemed to be short and there was no other depressed class leader who could rise to the occasion and shoulder the responsibility. Most of his lieutenants were engaged in squabbles or fights for leadership and power.

The growing anxiety about his own failing health despite prolonged treatment weighed on his mind. The fact that he had not been able to complete so far some of the books he was writing, was a source of major anxiety to him. All this depressed him and all those who were close to him felt very sorry over his plight. Rattu who used to do most of the typing work in preparation for the books his master wanted to publish was really at a loss, seeing his dear master gloomy and lost in his own thoughts. Rattu himself was born in an Untouchable caste but he deeply adored Ambedkar because of the battles he had fought single-handedly for better treatment of the Untouchables in the Hindu society. Rattu was a government servant, but daily after his office hours came to Ambedkar's bungalow to do the typing work.

Although he would meet Ambedkar every day, Rattu could not muster enough courage to ask his master the real cause of his agonizing depression lately. Rattu could not fathom the reason why Ambedkar was sometimes seen weeping when he was all alone with books in his study. Even his loving wife, Savita Ambedkar, who also acted as doctor and nurse for him, refrained from asking him about his repeated shedding of tears. Since any inquiry about his growing depression would only irritate him, she rarely touched upon the subject and instead sought to comfort him with her loving care for what he ate, or what medicines he needed daily to fight his worsening condition and kept a check on his visitors many of whom kept on sitting with him for long periods, often discussing trivial matters, something which irritated her. Although he was still a member of the Upper House, the Rajya Sabha, his visits to Parliament had become rather infrequent.

On one occasion, just when he was participating in a debate in the House, he started feeling uncomfortable. Instead of making a point forcefully, he started speaking somewhat incoherently, mumbling words and gasping for breath. Dr. Radhakrishnan, who was presiding over the House, directed the attendants to rush to Ambedkar's help as he dropped heavily on his seat. He was taken out of the House and made to sit in the open. Radharkrishnan retired to his chamber and phoned Savita to rush to Parliament. Soon she was there and with the help of the watch and ward staff of the House took Ambedkar out to his waiting car and returned home. Radhakrishnan, who later became the President of India, had great respect and admiration for Ambedkar. On many occasions when important debates were on the agenda he would himself phone Ambedkar to come to the House for participation. But even Radhakrishnan had stopped calling him in view of his failing health. Now Ambedkar mostly remained home. Yet he did not regret his inability to be more active in public life. All that was bothering him was his obsession to finish his incomplete books.

On many occasions, when Rattu had left him sleeping and gone home after completing his typing work, he was surprised to find Ambedkar on the following morning still sitting before the table lamp in his study, surrounded by sheets of paper he had been writing on for long. It was obvious that Ambedkar had woken up very early and kept on reading and writing in preparation of his books. But it was clear that his infirmity, his anxiety about getting his books published, were taking a heavy toll on him. Once, after seeing Ambedkar weeping alone, Rattu could not help enquiring from Mrs. Ambedkar the real cause of his sorrow. She simply grinned and said: "Not a new thing. This goes on every day. I just don't know what to do. Medicines are not helping him. He is your Babasaheb. Go and ask him. I don't know."

This made Rattu more determined to ask Ambedkar himself about the cause of his increasing depression some day when he would be in good spirits to respond to such a query. The very heavy load of work, especially from July 18 to 28, all relating to the books he was writing, further weakened Ambedkar's health. So strong was his urge to get the work done that he had his meals and tea wherever he was working, whether it was in his study or in his bedroom. At last, at about 6.30 p.m. on July 29, when Ambedkar was lying in bed, and getting his legs massaged, Rattu very humbly enquired: "Sir, why do you look so sad, worried and distressed these days, and even weep at times." But instead of replying to the query, Ambedkar gave him a stern look and snorted: "Go and do your typing work. Don't disturb me." Undaunted, Rattu again posed the same question the following day when he was massaging his legs while Ambedkar was lying on the sofa. "Sir, why do you look so sad and depressed, and even weep, at times. Excuse me, Sir, for asking this question, but pray kindly let me know what is eating you up?" Ambedkar looked at Rattu and feeling convinced about the sincerity of his personal assistant, who had been working for him for over five years without taking any remuneration. At last he sat up and said:

"You people do not know what is troubling me and what makes me so sad. The first worry is that I have not been able to fulfill my life's mission. I wanted to see my people as a governing class sharing political power in terms of equality with other communities. I am now almost crippled and prostrate with illness. Whatever I have been able to achieve is being enjoyed by the educated few, who, with their deceitful performance, have proved to be a worthless lot, with no sympathy for their downtrodden brethren. They have belied my expectations, they live only for themselves and their personal gains. Not even one of them is prepared to do any social work. They are only treading the path of their ruination. I now want to divert my attention towards the vast illiterate masses in the villages who continue to suffer and remain almost unchanged economically. But I don't seem to have many more days to live.

"I also want all my books to be published during my lifetime. The very idea of my being helpless to complete the monumental task of publishing my books, "Buddha and Karl Marx", "Revolution and Counter-revolution in Ancient India", and "Riddles of Hinduism" distresses me terribly as nobody will be able to publish them after me. I also want someone from among the Depressed Classes to come forward in my lifetime and take the heavy responsibility of running the movement after me. There, however, seems none who would rise to the occasion. My lieutenants, in whom I had full faith and confidence to run the movement are fighting among themselves for leadership and power, unmindful of the heavy responsibility that is going to fall upon them. I also wanted to serve this country and its people. But can I? It is a sin to take birth in a country whose people are so caste-ridden and prejudiced. In the existing set-up, it is very difficult to maintain one's interest in the affairs of this country as people are not prepared to listen to any other view which does not concur with that of the Prime Minister Jawaharlal Nehru. To what extent the country is sinking!" He exclaimed with a sigh and collapsed on the sofa.

As he said this Ambedkar couldn't control himself. Tears welled up in his eyes. When he realized that because of his illness he would not be able to complete the books he had planned, he was heartbroken. He really wanted to do more for his country. After a pause, he wiped his tears, raised his hand a little above his glowing eyes and said: "Tell my people, Nanak Chand, that whatever I have been able to achieve for them, I have done it single-handed, passing through crushing miseries and endless troubles, in the midst of abuses hurled at me from all sides, more so from the Hindu press, fighting with my opponents, all my life, as also with a handful of my own people who deceived me for their selfish ends. But I will continue to serve the country and my downtrodden people till my end. With great difficulty, I have brought the caravan where it stands today. Let the caravan march on and further on, despite the hurdles, pitfalls and difficulties that may come in its way. They must rise to the occasion, if they want to live an honourable and respectable life. If my people, my lieutenants are not able to take the caravan ahead, they should leave it where it stands today, but must not, under any circumstances, allow the caravan to lag behind. This is my message, probably my last message given in all seriousness, which I am sure will not go unheeded. Go and tell them. Go and tell them. Go and tell them," sighed Ambedkar in a guttural voice.

After this emotional outburst, tears started rolling down his cheeks. With such unbearable sorrow and anguish writ large on his face, he was really sunk in despair getting out of which seemed difficult at this stage in his life. Although he was mentally agile and alert, he was a physical wreck. He could not move even to bathroom without staff in his hand or somebody's help. But what was Ambedkar, what had gone into the making of this intellectual giant who spent his lifetime only to get a better deal for the Untouchables? The story of the wars he waged, the struggles he was engaged in, the victories he won and the setbacks he suffered is recalled in the chapters that follow.

References

1. The entire paragraph quoting Ambedkar is from page 11 from the book, "Who Were the Shudras" published by Thacker and Co. in 1964, reproduced in Vol. 7 of Ambedkar' Writing and Speeches published by Maharashtra Government in 1990.
2. Nanak Chand Rattu was Ambedkar's personal assistant who remained with him until his death on December 6, 1956. The quotation here is on page 38 of the book Last Few Years of Dr. Ambedkar by Rattu published in 1997 by Amrit Publisher, Delhi.

2

A Messiah is Born

Although Ramji Sakpal belonged to an Untouchable caste called Mahar, he had risen to be Subedar-Major because of his devotion and hard work in the Bombay Army of the East India Company. Mahars are believed to be the original inhabitants of Maharashtra. Some scholars say the state derives its name from them, for Mahar-Rashtra means land of Mahars. It is said that in the remote past, when Aryans invaded the subcontinent, they drove Mahars into the jungles. Whenever they ventured out away from the jungles in search of food or livelihood towards places where the invaders had settled, and came in contact with the Aryans, they made them do dirty, menial jobs. Gradually, doing dirty jobs became their profession and with the passage of time, they came to be known as Untouchables.

With the arrival of the East India Company in Bombay, their occupation changed. Many of them were recruited to serve in the British Army when the Company embarked on the conquest of the subcontinent. Having lived in jungles, often at the mercy of the elements, the Mahars proved themselves as a brave and robust people. They were recognized by the British as good fighters. Consequently, joining the British Army became a sort of regular profession with them. Following the family tradition, Ambedkar's grandfather, Maloji Sakpal, had joined the British Army and had retired as Havaldar.

Ramji Sakpal had followed in his father's footsteps. Ramji Sakpal was the headmaster at an Army School in Mhow Cantonment near Indore when one of his uncles, who had renounced the world and taken to religious pursuits long ago, happened to visit the town along with a group of hermits. A woman relation of Ramji recognized his uncle among the hermits squatting on the banks of the canal near the cantonment. Immediately, she rushed to convey the news to the family. Ramji came to the canal, met his uncle and entreated him to visit his house. But the uncle did not accept the invitation, saying that having renounced the world he was a Sanyasi and could not go to his house. However, he was happy to meet his nephew. In the conversation that followed, the Sanyasi made a prediction that soon a son would be born to Ramji whose name would go down in India's history as a great saviour. Ramji could not imagine even in his wildest dreams that his fourteenth child about to be delivered by his wife, Bhimabai, was destined to play such a role.

Exactly the date the child, who came to be known as Bhimrao Ramji Ambedkar, was born was not remembered even by his father. The date of birth recorded in the primary school at Dapoli in Ratnagiri district of Maharashtra where he was first admitted, was April 14, 1891. Whether April 14 had any significance or not is difficult to say. But according to historians, Gautam Buddha was also born on April 14 (Vaisakha Purnima) in BC 523. Later in life, while giving a talk on October 28, 1954, on the eve of his Diamond Jubilee celebrations held at Purandare's Stadium in Naigon, Ambedkar recalling the event of his birth, said: "My father did not care to maintain a record of my date of birth and the exact date of birth is not known. I might be above sixty or below sixty. However, it was true that I was born about midnight, and my mother suffered great pains at the time of my birth. When I was born, the stars were thought to be inauspicious. An astrologer had predicted that my mother would die soon. Because of this foreboding, I was hated by my brothers and sisters. After the death of my mother I was brought up by my aunt."

Although Sidharth and Ambedkar were born around two and a half millenia apart on the same day, as is generally believed, there was not much similarity between them; the former was a prince, the latter was virtually a pauper who struggled all his life because of the stigma of Untouchability which was his cross to bear. Gautam's mother died seven days after his birth and she left her son, Siddharth, in the charge of her sister, Prajapati. But Ambedkar's mother died when he was six years of age. His aunt Mirabai who took charge of his upbringing was Ramji Sakpal's sister. She used to treat Ambedkar with great love and affection. All that can be said as being of some significance concerning Gautam and Ambedkar is that later in life Ambedkar embraced Buddhism along with thousands of his followers and is now said to be mainly responsible for the revival of Buddhism in India, the country where this religion was first propagated by Gautam but from where it had almost disappeared until Ambedkar came on the scene as an emancipator of the downtrodden and a strong believer in Buddhism.

As an infant, Ambedkar was bonny and playful. His proud mother, Bhimabai, named him after her. First, he used to be called Bhima and sometimes lovingly, Bhiva. Of the 14 children of Ramji and Bhimabai, only three sons and two daughters survived. Not only because he was a lovable child, but also because he was the youngest, Ambedkar gradually became the darling of the family. Sometimes when Ambedkar's mother got angry, irritated by his pranks, and was about to slap him, Ramji would admonish her and say: "See! Bhiva's ears and stomach are like our God Ganapati's. How fortunate he is can be seen from the lines on his palms. You should be happy that he is your son. He is going to be a great and famous man. You should be tolerant of his mischiefs which are like Lord Krishna's when he was a boy. You have no business to be harsh to him." His father's love and concern for him in the early years of his life might have sown the seeds of the feeling in Ambedkar's mind that he was extraordinary, different from other boys, and that he should try to live up to his father's expectations.

In 1893, two years after Ambedkar's birth, Ramji retired from military service on a monthly pension of fifty rupees. He left Mhow and settled down at his ancestral village Dapoli in the Konkan region of Maharashtra. In 1896, Ambedkar was admitted to the primary school in Dapoli. Ramji Sakpal managed to secure a job in the military office in Satara and moved there along with his family. According to the school records, Ambedkar's original name was Ambavadekar, the ancestral village of the family close to Dapoli. In Maharashtra, sometimes children born in the state are named after the village they belong to. Ambavadeker, however, was changed to Ambedkar by a school teacher in Satara, whose name was Ambedkar, and who was very fond of his pupil.

Notwithstanding the prophecy made before his birth that he would be a great man, Ambedkar's childhood was not very happy. Experiencing indignities and discriminations both at school and in the play fields because he was the son of a Mahar, an untouchable caste in Maharashtra, made him bitter. Although he was never clad in rags, was free from any unclean habit, he was not accepted as an equal by other children. Discrimination dogged him wherever he went. Later, recalling the experiences of childhood, he wrote: "I knew that in the school I could not sit in the midst of my class mates according to my rank. I used to sit in a corner by myself. I knew that in the school I was to have a separate piece of gunny cloth for myself to squat on in the class room and the servant employed to clean the school would not touch the gunny cloth used by me. I was required to carry the gunny cloth home in the evening and bring it back the next day. While at the school I knew that children of the touchable classes, when they felt thirsty, could go out to the water tap, open it and quench their thirst. All they needed was the permission of the teacher. But my position was different. I could not touch the tap and unless it was opened by a touchable person, it was not possible for me to quench my thirst. In my case, the permission of the teacher was not enough. The presence of the school peon was necessary, for he was the only person whom the class teacher could ask to open the tap for me."

No wonder, when he was meted out such contemptuous treatment at school not only by his classmates but also by his teachers, Ambedkar had very little interest in his studies. Returning home from school, he loitered about showing little or no inclination to do his homework. But he was ceaselessly indulging in all sorts of hobbies and fancies, like the tending of the cattle and rearing of the goats.

Gardening fascinated him to such an extent that he would spend whatever little money he could lay his hands on upon purchasing new varieties of plants. Most of the time he was away from his home, not bothered about his books or homework. Utterly disappointed and frustrated, one day he went to the Satara railway station where he did 'hamal' work (act as a coolie) but with a little bit of reservation. Somehow, his aunt, who was his guardian at home after the death of his mother just when he was six years old, got wind of what he had done. She was very upset. "My aunt (he later recalled) terribly felt humiliated over my conduct, but she loved me so much that she had no heart to punish me."

Acutely aware of the treatment that would be meted out to his children by a step-mother, Ambedkar's father was not even toying with the idea of marrying again after the death of his wife. However, with the passage of time he had second thoughts and married again. Ambedkar was very upset over this development. What irritated him most was the fact that his stepmother had started functioning like Bhimabai and began wearing even her ornaments. He didn't like it at all, but could do nothing about it. Thoughts that he should no longer remain in the house and instead start living elsewhere sometimes crossed his mind. He had often heard his elder sisters gossiping that several boys from Satara had got jobs in the Bombay mills. Being unhappy with the presence of the stepmother at home, he started fancying that he should also be like the other boys his sisters had mentioned, flee from home and try his luck as a winding boy in some mill in Bombay. But his problem was how to reach Bombay. He did not have enough money to pay for his fare.

Frustrated, he made a plan that he should steal the purse of his aunt and thus get some money to pay for the fare. He conspired to sleep with his aunt on the floor to try his luck. "For three consecutive nights," he later recalled, "I tried to remove the purse tucked at the waist of my aunt but to my disappointment I could not do so, fearing that my aunt might be awake. However, on the fourth night I seized it but only found half an anna in it. And with half an anna, I could not go to Bombay. The four nights' experience was so nerve-racking that I gave up the idea of collecting money in this shameful manner and I came to another decision - a decision that I must give up my truant habits, that I must study hard and get through my examinations, so that I could start earning my livelihood and thus become independent of my father."

From that day onwards he gave up his slovenly habits and became so diligent and attentive that even his teachers who were first disappointed with him one day summoned his father and advised him that Ambedkar was an exceptionally devoted student and therefore he should give the best possible education to his promising son in whom they saw something extraordinary. Much to the delight of his father, Ambedkar not only started concentrating his attention on his school text books but also developed a passion to read other books and devote much of his time going over from place to place in search of such books. His insatiable thirst for knowledge could be compared to that of Tilak and Savarker, well-known freedom fighters of those days, who being Brahmins had no problems and had full access to all the literature they wanted. But young Ambedkar could not always buy the books he wanted: he did not have money.

Seeing the growing craving for knowledge in his son, Ambedkar's father tried his best to get the books his son wanted to read. As a dutiful and loving father, he went to the extent of borrowing money from his married daughters to buy books for Ambedkar. So much was his anxiety and concern for his son that sometimes he made his daughters sell their ornaments he had given them at the time of their marriage. However, the loving father returned to his daughters the money they arranged by selling their ornaments whenever he could from his meagre pension of only fifty rupees per month. Obviously convinced by the advice of the school teachers and from his own inner voice, Ambedkar's father did everything to make his son a man of letters, name and fame.

In keeping with the family tradition of gallantry, Ambedkar was a brave and daring boy right from his childhood. Nobody could frighten him if he wanted to do something. Once a classmate challenged him to walk to the school in heavy rain. He walked to the school in a downpour and reached there with his dhoti and shirt soaked in water. Since it was quite cold, his Brahmin class teacher took pity on him and asked his son to take him to his house for a hot water bath and change his clothes lest he should fall sick. He returned to the classroom and sat as usual in a corner, half-naked because his clothes were still wet. Writing about his early childhood, Ambedkar recalled: "Owing to the poverty I used to attend school wearing nothing more than a loincloth. I could not get water to drink in the school. I had to go without water for many days. My mother instructed me to address the strangers with respect. There was in our family discipline or 'vinaya.' Accordingly, I used to address the postman as 'postman mama.' There was a lady peon, Maratha by caste, in our school. Even my satchel was untouchable for her. When thirsty, I was not allowed to touch the tap myself. Once when I thought nobody was watching me, I opened the tap to drink water. But I was beaten black and blue by upper caste boys who abused me and said I had polluted the tap with my touch."

Ramji Sakpal knew that the treatment meted out to his children for no fault of theirs, but only on account of the fact that they were Mahars, could have a damaging effect on their psyche. He sought to minimize this effect by imparting them religious education. He offered prayers to gods morning and evening, sang devotional hymns of Kabir and the other great saints. Having served in the Army all his life, he was a strict disciplinarian and expected his children to follow his habit of reciting shlokas and hymns, glorifying gods and goddesses. Sometimes pretending that they were busy making preparations for going to school, the children would not join their father in his prayers. But in the evening, they could not escape whatever their devoted and religious father wanted them to do. When he was still in Mahow, there was another problem. The cantonment regulations required that lights should be switched off early in the evening. Ramji would ask his wife to close the windows and doors and go on reciting sholakas until late in the night. He used to recite and read out to his children great national epics, the Ramayana and the Mahabharata, the two unfailing sources of divine inspiration for all Hindus. Ramji also sang the spiritual songs written by Marathi saint-poets like Moropant, Mukteshwar and Tukaram. Daily recitations and explanations of what these songs meant helped develop a taste in the holy books among Ramji's children. Every morning after the Puja, Ramji would bless his beloved son, Ambedkar, along with others, and give him prasad, saying: "Bhiva, you are going to learn a lot. You are going to be a great and learned man. You are going to get great fame and make the name of your family shine in the world."

Later on, writing about his childhood experiences with his father, Ambedkar stated: "When he started saying with devotion the 'Abhangas' of saints and couplets of Kabir then a very serious and sacred atmosphere was created. When my sister started saying the 'Abhanga' in a sweet voice I too began feeling that religion and religious education are extremely necessary in the life of man. From the recitations of my father, I had also learnt by heart, the religious poetry of saint-poets like Tukaram, Mukteshwar, etc. Not only that, I also started thinking over this religious poetry in my mind. Few people might have made such a deep study of Marathi saint poets as I have done." There is no doubt that Ambedkar's interest in religion and theological discussions was mainly due to the influence of his father who was himself keenly interested in theological and religious debates. Ambedkar made a deep study of the various religions and developed a firm belief in the necessity of religion in life. He said that a poor man mad with hunger did not resort to theft not because he feared the legal consequences but because of the healthy pressure religion exercised on his mind.

Ambedkar's father not only cared for the spiritual development of his children but was also anxious for their temporal advancement. Having been a teacher in the Army schools most of his life, he had acquired a mastery over Marathi and English and could easily teach his children these languages. In his reminiscences, Ambedkar wrote: "It was my father who taught me how to find out a good English word for an equivalent Marathi word and how to use it in the right place. I feel that I do possess some fame for writing and speaking good English. But how to use the right word in the right place so that it would carry the greatest weight has been taught by my father in the manner in which no other teacher has ever taught me. He always used to ask me words at random in Tarkhadkar's book and thus test my knowledge of the English language. Similarly idioms and how to use the right language style has also been taught by my father."

A friend and great admirer of Mahatma Phooley, the acknowledged father of the Indian social revolution in the nineteenth century, Ramji also took interest in the social problems of his day which concerned his community. Although Mahars were among the first group of people to join the Bombay Army of the East India Company and had valiantly fought battles for their British masters when they were engaged in India's conquest, their importance in the eyes of the British began to decline after the first war of Independence in 1857. The colonial rulers became conscious of the fact that the caste stratification of Indian society was so rigid and strong that people from upper castes would never like to sit together, much less mix with people from lower castes. In order to win the loyalty of Brahmins, Rajputs, Kayasthas, they felt it would be wrong to encourage the lower caste Mahars to join military service. Therefore in 1892, the colonial British government issued orders banning the recruitment of Mahars in the Indian Army.

Subedar Ramji Sakpal played a leading role in protesting against this decision of the government. He approached Justice Mahadev Govind Ranade to draft a petition appealing to the government to rescind its order against the recruitment of Mahars in the Army. Ramji also met the British Governor of Bombay and appealed to him to take greater interest in the development of the Untouchables. When Ambedkar grew up he read the old papers left behind by his father after his death. He was inspired to dedicate his life in the service of the Untouchables just as his father had done in his lifetime.

Recalling the hardships he had to face in school, Ambedkar once told Mahadev Desai, a close associate of Mahatma Gandhi, that "I got what little education I could as a child in Dapoli. But you can imagine how much I could learn when I tell you that I had to sit with boys of my community outside the school-house. Depressed class boys of all standards had to be seated together. No one cared to teach them, the teacher would simply ask if we had read our lessons. My father moved me to Satara. I was admitted to Satara High School. Here I had to sit on a separate bench. Fain would I have studied Sanskrit, but the Sanskrit teacher would not have me. So I had to take up Persian. My father was a retired military pensioner, getting a pension of rupees fifty. Thus he was much more respectable than many middle class Hindus, but I tell you, we could not get the services of a barber. My sister used to shave five or six members of the family. The hard conditions in Satara compelled us to leave for Bombay where after admission first to the Maratha High School and later to the Elphinstone High School I found the plight of the Untouchables as bad as elsewhere in schools in other towns in Maharashtra."

But frequent brushes with Untouchability left a lasting impression on young Ambedkar's mind. Later on he wrote: "At home I knew that the work of washing clothes was done by my sisters. Not that there were no washermen in Satara. Not that we could not afford to pay the washermen. Washing was done by my sisters because we were Untouchables and no washerman would wash the clothes of an untouchable. The work of cutting the hair or shaving the boys including myself was done by our elder sister who had become quite an expert barber by practicing the art on us. Not that there were no barbers in Satara, not that we could not afford to pay the barber. The work of shaving and hair cutting was done by my sister because we were Untouchables and no barber would consent to shave an untouchable. All this I knew. But the incident that gave me a shock, such as I had never received before, happened in 1901, when my father was away on service as a cashier at a place called Koregaon in Khatav Taluka in the Satara district where the government of Bombay had started the work of excavating a tank for giving employment to famine-stricken people who were dying by thousands. The incident was so stunning that it made me think about untouchability which, before this incident happened, was with me a matter of course as it was with many Touchables as well as the Untouchables."

Describing what had happened Ambedkar recalled: "When my father went to Koregaon he left me, my brother, who was older than myself, and two sons of my eldest sister who was dead, under the charge of my aunt and some kind neighbours. My aunt was the kindest soul I knew, but was of no help to us. She was somewhat of a dwarf and had some trouble with her legs which made it very difficult for her to move about without the aid of somebody. Often, she had to be lifted. I had sisters. They were married and were away living with their families. Cooking our food became a problem with us especially as our aunt could not, on account of her helplessness, manage the job. We, the four children, had to go to school and also cook our food. We could not prepare our breakfast. So we lived on pulav which we found to be the easiest dish to prepare, requiring nothing more than mixing rice and mutton. Being a cashier, my father could not leave his station to come to Satara to visit us; therefore, he wrote to us to come to Koregaon and spend our summer vacations with him. We were thoroughly excited over the prospect especially as none of us had up to that time seen a railway train."

The family was very happy. They started making great preparations for the journey. New shirts of English make, bright bejeweled caps, new shoes, new silk-bordered dhoties were ordered. Ramji, Ambedkar's father, had given them all particulars regarding the train journey and had left instructions to be informed about the day of their journey so that he could send his peon to the railway station to receive the children and take them to Koregaon. According to this arrangement, Ambedkar, his brother and one of his sister's sons left Satara. As the railway station was ten miles away, they engaged a tonga to take them to the station. Since the children were dressed in their Sunday best, specially made for the occasion, they left home in a jubilant mood with a great anticipation of enjoying their train journey, though amidst cries of Ambedkar's aunt who was almost prostrate with grief at the parting of the children.

Continuing the story, Ambedkar wrote: "When we reached the station my brother bought tickets and gave me and my sister's sons two annas each as pocket money to be spent at our pleasure. We at once began our career of riotous living and each ordered a bottle of lemonade at the start. After a short while the train whistled in and we boarded it as quickly as we could for fear of being left behind. We were told to detrain at Masur, the nearest railways station for Koregaon The train arrived at Masur at about five in the evening and we got down with our luggage. In a few minutes all the passengers who had got down from the train had gone away to their destinations. We four children remained on the platform looking out for my father or his servant whom he had promised to send. Long did we wait but no one turned up. An hour elapsed and the station master came to enquire. He asked us for our tickets. We showed them to him. He asked us why we tarried. We told him we were bound for Koregaon and that we were waiting for my father or his servant to come but neither had turned up and that we did not know how to reach Koregaon. We were well-dressed children. From our dress or talk no one could make out that we were children of the Untouchables. Indeed the station master was quite sure we were Brahmin children and was extremely touched at the plight in which he found us.

"As is usual among Hindus the station master asked us who we were. Without a moment's thought I blurted out that we were Mahars. He was stunned. His face underwent a sudden change. We could see that he was overpowered by a strange feeling of revulsion. As soon as he heard my reply he went away to his room and we stood where we were. Fifteen to twenty minutes elapsed; the sun was almost setting. My father had not turned up nor had he sent his servant, and now the station master had also left us. We were quite bewildered and the joy and happiness which we felt at the beginning of the journey gave way to a feeling of extreme sadness. After half an hour the station master returned and asked us what we proposed to do. We said that if we could get a bullock-cart on hire we could go to Koregaon, and if it was not very far off we would like to start straightway. There were many bullock-carts plying for hire. But my reply to the station master that we were Mahars had gone round among the cartmen and not even one of them was prepared to suffer being polluted and to demean himself carrying passengers of the Untouchable class. We were prepared to pay double the fare but we found that money did not work. The station master who was negotiating on our behalf stood silent not knowing what to do. Suddenly a thought seemed to have entered his head and he asked us: "Can you drive the cart?" Feeling that he was finding out a solution of our difficulty we shouted, "Yes, we can." With that answer he went and proposed on our behalf that we were to pay the cart-man double the fare and drive the cart and that he should walk on foot along with the cart on our journey. One cart-man agreed as it gave him an opportunity to earn his fare and also saved him from being polluted.

"It was about 6.30 p.m. when we were ready to start. But we were anxious not to leave the station until we were assured that we would reach Koregaon before it was dark. We therefore questioned the cart-man as to the distance and the time he would take to reach Koregaon. He assured us that it would be not more than three hours. Believing in his words, we put our luggage in the cart, thanked the station master and got into the cart. One of us took the reins and the cart started with the man walking by our side. Not very far from the station there flowed a river. It was quite dry except at places where there were small pools of water. The owner of the cart proposed that we should halt there and have our meal as we might not get water on our way. We agreed. He asked us to give a part of his fare to enable him to go to the village and have his meal. My brother gave him some money and he left promising to return soon. We were very hungry and were glad to have had an opportunity to have a bite. My aunt had pressed our neighbours' women folk into service and had got some rice preparation for us to take on our way. We opened our tiffin basket and started eating. We needed water to wash things down. One of us went to the pool of water in the river basin nearby. But the water really was no water. It was thick with mud and urine and excreta of the cows and buffaloes and other cattle who went to the pool for drinking. In fact that water was not intended for human use. At any rate the stink of the water was so strong we could not drink it. We had therefore to close our meal before we were satisfied and wait for the arrival of the cart-man. He did not come for a long time and all that we could do was to look for him in all directions."

Ultimately he came and we started on our journey. For some four or five miles we drove the cart and he walked on foot. Then he suddenly jumped into the cart and took the reins from our hands. We thought this to be rather a strange conduct on the part of a man, who had refused to let the cart on hire for fear of pollution, to have set aside all his religious scruples and to have consented to sit with us in the same cart, but we dared not ask him any questions on the point. We were anxious to reach Koregaon, our destination, as quickly as possible. And for some time we were interested in the movement of the cart only. But soon there was darkness all around us. There were no street lights to relieve the darkness. There were no men or women or even cattle passing by to make us feel that we were in their midst. We became fearful of the loneliness which surrounded us. Our anxiety was growing. We mustered all the courage we possessed. We had traveled far from Masur. It was more than three hours. But there was no sign of Koregaon. There arose a strange thought within us. We suspected that the cart-man intended treachery and that he was taking us to some lonely spot to kill us. We had lot of gold ornaments on us and that helped to strengthen our suspicion. We started asking him how far Koregaon was, why we were so late in reaching it. He kept on saying, 'It is not very far, we shall soon reach it.'

"It was about 10.00 at night when finding that there was no trace of Koregaon we children started crying and abusing the cart-man. Our lamentations and wailings continued for long. The cart-man made no reply. Suddenly we saw a light burning at some distance. The cart-man said, "Do you see that light? That is a light of the toll-collector. We will rest there for the night." We felt some relief and stopped crying. The light was distant, we could never seem to reach it. It took us two hours to reach the toll-collector's hut. The interval increased our anxiety and we kept on asking the cart-man all sorts of questions, as to why there was delay in reaching the place, whether we were going on the right road, etc. Ultimately by midnight the cart reached the toll-collector's hut. It was situated at the foot of a hill but on the other side of the hill. When we arrived we saw a large number of bullock-carts there all resting for the night. We were extremely hungry and wanted very much to eat. But again there was the question of water. So we asked our driver whether it was possible to get water. He warned us that the toll-collector was a Hindu and that there was no possibility of our getting water if we spoke the truth and revealed that we were Mahars. He said, 'Say you are Mohammedans and try your luck.' On his advice I went to the toll-collector's hut and asked him if he would give us some water. "Who are you?", he enquired. I replied that we were Musalmans. I conversed with him in Urdu which I knew very well so as to leave no doubt that I was a real Musalman. But the trick did not work and his reply was very curt. 'Who has kept water for you? There is water on the hill, if you want to go, get it, I have none.' With this he dismissed me. I returned to the cart and conveyed his reply to my brother. I don't know what my brother felt. All that he did was to tell us to lie down.

"The bullocks had been unyoked and the cart was placed sloping down on the ground. We spread our beds on the bottom planks inside the cart, and laid down our bodies to rest. Now that we had come to a place of safety we did not mind what happened. But our minds could not help turning to the latest event. There was plenty of food with us. There was hunger burning within us; with all this we were to sleep without food; that was because we could get no water and we could get no water because we were Untouchables. Such was the last thought that entered our mind. I said, we had come to a place of safety. Evidently my elder brother had his misgivings. He said it was not wise for all four of us to go to sleep. Anything might happen. He suggested that at one time only two should sleep and two should keep watch. So we spent the night at the foot of that hill. Early at 5 in the morning our cart-man came and suggested that we should start for Koregaon. We flatly refused. We told him that we would not move until 8 o'clock. We did not want to take any chance. He said nothing. So we left at 8 and reached Koregaon at 11. My father was surprised to see us and said that he had received no intimation of our coming.

We protested that we had given intimation. He denied the fact. Subsequently it was discovered that the fault was of my father's servant. He had received our letter but failed to give it to my father. This incident had a very important place in my life. I was a boy of nine when it happened. But it left an indelible impression on my mind. I could not forget how the attitude of the station master changed when he discovered that we were Mahars. I could not forget how we were denied even drinking water because we were Untouchables."

Realising that for the better education of his darling son, he must move to a bigger city, Ambedkar's father took his family to Bombay. He rented a small room in a chawl (a kind of slum settlement for the poor) called the Dabak chawl at Lower Parel. The chawl was a multi-storey building with one-room tenements for mill workers, all of them sharing a toilet and bath provided on each floor. The Lower Parel was situated in a labour area with an environment of the underworld. Ambedkar's sisters having been already married also lived in Bombay with their families. Ambedkar and his brother were admitted to the Maratha High School. After a few months, they were shifted to the Elphinstone High School which was one of the best high schools in Bombay those days. Apparently, with a determination to outshine his classmates and also to justify the trust and confidence reposed in him by his father to be an outstanding student, Ambedkar began working very hard. But the small room where the family lived was full of domestic articles and utensils with no place for any one to occupy and concentrate on his work. The room was not only overcrowded but also smoky. How to create an environment which would facilitate his son to read and write as long as he could, was the problem which started worrying Ambedkar's father. He solved the problem by asking his son to go to bed early. Ambedkar slept on a quilt with a grind stone pushed against the wall and a she-goat tied in the small place close to his legs. His father remained awake till two in the night. Then he would awaken his son to study and himself retire. Ambedkar would sit before a flickering kerosene lamp without a chimney and go on reading and writing, doing his classwork. After having a little sleep in the morning, he would take his bath and go to school.

Since it was a better school with many enlightened teachers on staff, Ambedkar no longer had to face frequently the humiliations which were the lot of Untouchables those days in India. But the atmosphere in the school was not altogether free from casteism. There were the same prejudices and the same hatreds against the Untouchables. Ambedkar's class teacher one day asked him to come to the blackboard and solve an example. But as Ambedkar rose from his seat to go to the blackboard, there was an uproar in the classroom. Most of the students started shouting that Ambedkar's proximity to the blackboard would pollute their tiffins lying behind it and therefore he should not be allowed to go nearby. Some of the boys rushed to remove their tiffin boxes before Ambedkar could reach there. The clanging sound of the metallic tiffin-boxes pierced Ambedkar's heart and although the incident was over soon, it left a lasting wound on his mind, which could not be healed even when he was hailed as a great leader.

Harbouring a deep-seated prejudice against the Untouchables – and probably expressing his own feelings – one of his teachers one day plainly told him that he was wasting his time in school for education would not get him anywhere because he was an Untouchable by caste. Although he was always very polite and deferential to his teachers, Ambedkar could not help expressing his anger over the observations made by this teacher and plainly told him to mind his own business. Notwithstanding the unhappy experiences which continued to be his lot in school, Ambedkar tried to make the most of his life. Sometimes he played cricket and football and often outshone other players. Thanks to hard work and dedication, he always did well in his examinations.

But his saddest experience was when the Sanskrit teachers denied him the right to sit in their class, saying that Untouchables were not entitled to learn this sacred language, according to the Shastras. Both Ambedkar and his elder brother were not allowed to take Sanskrit as the second language as it was the key to the study of the Vedas which were neither to be read nor to be heard by the 'Shudras' and 'Atishudras'—the Untouchables—according to the Shastras. Great Hindu leaders of the day like Tilak would proudly proclaim their knowledge of the Vedas. Although the Scheduled Castes were said to be part of Hindu society, they were forbidden the study of Sanskrit so that they could not get to know what only the upper castes were entitled to learn. Denied the right to study Sanskrit, Ambedkar and his brother were forced to take Persian as the second language against their will. Later in life, Ambedkar studied Sanskrit partly by himself and sometimes with the help of some Pandits who did not suffer from any inhibitions and were impressed by the desire of a student to gain knowledge whatever his caste or status in society. Expressing his view about the languages he studied, Ambedkar said Persian stands no comparison with Sanskrit as it is the golden treasure of epics, the cradle of grammar, politics and philosophy, and the home of logic, drama and criticism.

Although he had to suffer intolerable insults from narrow-minded teachers, Ambedkar remained undaunted and concentrated on his studies. Since his father could not meet the expenses of his two sons studying in school together, Ambedkar's elder brother was withdrawn from school. He started working and contributing in whatever way he could to the education of his younger brother. With the blessings and devotion of his father to see him do well in life Ambedkar passed the Matriculation Examination from Eliphinstone High School in 1907 and thus became the first Untouchable boy ever to attain such a distinction. Ambedkar obtained 282 out of 750 marks, with his highest score in Persian, in the high school leaving examination. Since this was an uncommon achievement for an Untouchable, the event was celebrated by his community. A meeting was called in Bombay under the presidentship of S.K. Bole, a well-known social reformer, to honour Ambedkar. The meeting was also attended by a famous Marathi writer and social reformer, Krishnaji Arjun Keluskar, who was an assistant teacher at Wilson High School and had chanced to meet Ambedkar first in a garden where both of them used to spend their evenings in reading books. Deeply impressed by the achievement of Ambedkar, Keluskar took a fancy to him, lent him books and presented him with a copy of his new book, *Life of Gautam Buddha*, the book which Ambedkar studied thoroughly and which later on became a turning point in his life. He was so much fascinated by Gautam Buddha's life story that towards the end of his life he embraced Buddhism along with thousands of other Untouchables who looked up to him as their Messiah.

Partly as a concession to his father's wishes and partly to satisfy his yearning for knowledge which was growing day by day, Ambedkar enrolled himself as a student at the Elphinstone College in Bombay despite the fact that it was very difficult for the family to pay his fees. No Untouchable had ever before entered the portals of this great institution. Having known untouchability since his childhood and having gradually come to understand what it was, Ambedkar was consumed with a burning passion to excel in life and prove that Untouchables, although denigrated by the caste system, were in no way inferior to any other caste. He took to his studies with all earnestness at his command. But due to his ill health he could not take the annual examination which was due after his first year in college. While Ambedkar was struggling to pass his intermediate examination his father, Ramji, felt that due to increasing family responsibilities, he could no longer afford to keep his son in college.

Since Gods wanted Ambedkar to play a great role in the emancipation of the Untouchables, Krishnaji Arjun Keluskar again appeared on the scene and intervened to save Ambedkar as if he had been sent by God. Keluskar met the Maharaja of Baroda and explained to him the unfortunate circumstances in which Ambedkar was placed. The benevolent Maharaja agreed to interview Ambedkar to satisfy himself about the genuineness of his needs and soon thereafter promptly sanctioned a scholarship of Rs. 25 per month for him. Now Ambedkar was on a sound footing to pursue his studies in college notwithstanding the inability of his father to pay for his education any more.

Seeing his dedication to academic pursuits, one Mr. Irani, who taught him Persian, and Professor Muller, who taught him English, were deeply impressed by the Untouchable student and helped him with books he needed to study. But the stigma of untouchability continued to dog him even when he had noble professors to help him and a stipend granted by a benevolent Maharaja to pay his fees and meet other expenses. He was not served tea or water in the college canteen because he was an Untouchable. The treatment meted out to his dearest son in college was another cruel blow to Ramji Sakpal. In order that his son was not identified with the Untouchables, Ramji changed his place of residence and shifted to No. 1 chawl of the Trust Board buildings at Parel. Here he secured two rooms, numbered 50 and 51, so that his industrious son could study in peace without interference from any quarter. As Ambedkar would sit studying inside the room, Ramji would while away his time sitting outside. In these circumstances, no wonder reading became the greatest joy and passion of Ambedkar's life. He wanted to arm himself with knowledge so that he could equip himself for higher attainments. Notwithstanding enormous difficulties arising out of the fact that he belonged to an Untouchable caste, Ambedkar focused all his attention on his studies and succeeded in passing B.A. examination in 1912. No Untouchable had ever achieved such a distinction before.

Ambedkar was pained to see the attitude of the British government towards freedom fighters. The government had slowly extinguished the freedom of discussion. Complaints, protests and appeals made in regard to these rights were denounced as sedition. The champions of these rights were freedom fighters, but all were arrested, tortured and deported. There was a volcanic political unrest in the country, caused by ruthless measures being adopted by the colonial government. Bal Gangadhar Tilak's deportation to Mandalay, the transportation of the Savarkar brothers to the Andamans, imprisonment of many other leaders and editors and the execution of some of the patriotic youths agitated Maharashtra so violently that there was nothing but a deluge of disappointments and frustration with the colonial rulers. Ambedkar saw all this but struggling with his own problems of untouchability, he could not say or do anything at this stage.

That Ambedkar's patriotic mind could not remain content without giving vent to his feelings was clear from his famous historic thesis, "The Evolution of Provincial Finance in British India." Without making any bones about it, Ambedkar clearly stated in this thesis that the British Government was resorting to repressive measures. He wrote: "Not satisfied with the aid of power with which the Executive was endowed by the provisions of the Criminal and Penal Codes to anticipate offences by preventive acts, it besmeared the Indian Statute Book with a set of repressive laws hardly paralleled in any other part of the world." He condemned the then ruling bureaucracy as conservative, repressive, irresponsible, and observed that it poured its money on the services and not on education and industry. He frankly stated that the Indian Press Act of 1910 put a complete muzzle on the press, the right of public meetings was suppressed in the same measure and with the same sternness as was the right to personal freedom and the right to freedom of discussion. Few front rank authors of those times described this period of Indian history as pithily as Ambedkar did.

Ambedkar's thesis thoroughly exposed British hypocrisy when he said that the colonial government's legislative enactments were not intended to ensure freedom to people to decide the issues brought before them but only to keep them in check. Drawing attention to the provisions of the Act of 1853, the Act of 1861, the Act of 1892 and the Act of 1909, he said the underlying purpose of these measures was not to make the legislature independent but to muzzle it. No wonder, he said, the Indian Parliamentary system was only an empty form because this Parliamentary system was without a Parliamentary Executive, in which the legislature could neither make nor unmake the Executive. The power to do so was retained by the colonial rulers. The Executive in India was not concerned about the progress of the country because it did not sympathize with the living forces operating in Indian society. It was not bothered about wants, pains, carvings and desires of the people; it was inimical to aspirations, did not worry about the poor state of education, always viewed with suspicion anything that was Swadeshi and snapped at anything that smacked of nationalism. This was Ambedkar's verdict on the British bureaucracy in India. The pity is that in the post-independence India and even at times before that, right from the beginning of the Round Table Conferences held in London in the early thirties, attempts were made to run down Ambedkar and meanly describe him as a British stooge.

With the passage of time, Ambedkar became more observant and curious about the discriminatory treatment meted out to the low caste people. Until then, all that he had learnt about social discrimination against the Untouchables was confined to his experiences in school. He discovered that the population not only in his own town but in every village in India was divided into two sections (1) the Touchables and (2) the Untouchables. Just as was the case of his own family, the Untouchable lived outside the village in separate quarters whereas the Touchables lived inside the village. Socially, the Touchables were a ruling class whereas the Untouchables were poor and lived like a dependent community. The inquisitive Ambedkar was shocked to learn that it was considered an offence if the Untouchables started living close to the Touchables or in the north, east or western direction; they could only live towards the south of the village. It was considered an offence for the Untouchables to acquire wealth, such as land or cattle or build a house with a tiled roof. Not only the wearing of a clean dress or shoes or putting on a watch or gold ornament by an Untouchable was an offence, these unfortunate people could not sit on a chair in the presence of a caste Hindu. Untouchables could neither ride on a horse or a palanquin nor could take out a procession in a village. An Untouchable must conform to the status of an inferior and must carry a sign so that he could be easily identified as belonging to an Untouchable caste.

Ambedkar was astonished to see that almost every Hindu in the village regards himself as an overlord; he feels it absolutely essential to maintain his prestige. This prestige he cannot maintain unless he has at his command a retinue of servants to dance attendance on him. It is in the Untouchable that he finds a convenient servant who can be made to do whatever he desires without any payment because of the low status he occupies in the caste hierarchy governing the Hindu society. In the Hindu society, the Untouchables must always conform to a code of conduct which required them to always act as a sort of messenger for the upper caste Hindus to convey to their relations in some distant village their messages relating to death or marriage. When the whole village community is engaged in celebrating a general festivity such as Holi or Dasara, the Untouchables must perform all menial acts which are preliminary to the main observance. On the occasion of certain festivities, the Untouchables must submit their women to members of the village community to be made the subject of indecent fun. The code also laid down that an Untouchable must accompany a caste Hindu girl when she is going from her parent's house to her husband's village no matter how distant it is. There was no remuneration for these duties.

Even if they had money the Untouchable could not purchase land as the caste Hindus would resent it, for it would amount to acquiring the same status as that of the Touchable class. In some parts of the country, the Untouchables were disabled by law from purchasing land. For instance, in the province of Punjab there was a law called the Land Alienation Act. It specified the communities which could purchase land and the Untouchables were excluded from the list. As a result of such provisions, the Untouchables in most of the country were mere landless labourers. As labourers they could not demand reasonable wages. They had to work for the Hindu farmer for such wages as their masters chose to give. The Hindu farmers often combined to keep the wages to the lowest level possible for it was in their interest to do so. On the other hand the Untouchables had no holding power. Later in life, describing the conditions in which the Untouchables lived, Ambedkar wrote: "The wages paid to the Untouchables are either paid in cash or in corn."

In parts of Uttar Pradesh the corn given to the Untouchable was called "Gobaraaha", which meant privy corn or corn contained in the dung of an animal. In the month of March or April when the crop was fully grown, reaped and dried, it was spread on the threshing floor. Bullocks were made to tread over the corn in order to take the corn out of husk by the pressure of their hooves. While treading over the corn, the bullocks swallowed up the corn as well as the straw. As their intake was excessive, they found it difficult to digest the corn. Next day, the same corn came out of their stomach along with their dung. The dung was strained and the corn was separated and given to the Untouchable workmen as their wages which they converted into flour to make bread.

The condition of the Untouchables in other parts of the country was so bad that it made a searing impression on Ambedkar's mind. There was no trade in which they could engage themselves for earning their livelihood once the agricultural season was over. He could not imagine that for landless labourers there were no other means of earning livelihood except to subsist by cutting grass and firewood from the jungle and selling it in a nearby town. Even when the forest was open they had to grease the palms of the forest guards to collect firewood for their survival. Only if he was bribed he would let them take some grass and firewood from the government forest. When it was brought to the town they had always to face a buyer's market. The caste Hindus who were the main body of buyers would conspire to bring down the prices. Having no power to hold out, the Untouchables had to sell their stuff for whatever was offered them.

Ambedkar discovered that all the sources of earning for the Untouchables were precarious and fleeting. There was no security. There was only one source of livelihood open to the Untouchables in some parts of the country. It was the right to beg food from the Hindu farmers of the village. Every village had its administrative set-up. The Untouchables of the village were hereditary menials employed in the village administration. As part of their remuneration the whole body of the Untouchables would get a small parcel of land assigned in the ancient past which was fixed and was never increased and which the Untouchables preferred to leave uncultivated because of its excessive fragmentation. The right to beg for food from the upper caste Hindus was the principal means of livelihood for 60 million Untouchables in India. Swarms of Untouchables moving about the village, begging for food, could be seen any time of the day, but mostly after nightfall. The statutory beggary as a means of livelihood for the Untouchables had been reduced to a system. The Untouchables families were attached to different Touchable families in the village as were the serfs and villeins to the Lords of the Manors in medieval Europe. The Untouchables attached to the Touchable families were at the command of the latter. This relationship had become so personal that one always heard a Touchable speaking of an Untouchable as "my man" as though he was his slave. This relationship helped systematize this matter of begging food by the Untouchables from the caste Hindu households.

The Untouchables had no rights. For them, there was no equality, no justice. Whatever little justice they could get depended upon the sweet will of the caste Hindus, who were their masters, lords and virtual gods. Nothing was due to them except what the Touchables were prepared to grant. The Untouchables in those days could not insist on fair play. They could only pray for mercy and favour and rest content with what was offered to them. The established order was a hereditary order both in status and in function. Once a Touchable, always a Touchable. Once an Untouchable, always an Untouchable. Once a Brahmin, always a Brahmin. Once a sweeper, always a sweeper. Under such an order those who were born high, remained high; those who were born low, remained low. The established order was based on the inexorable law of Karma or destiny which was fixed once for all and could not be altered. Destiny had no relation to the merits of the individual living under it. An Untouchable, however superior he might be mentally and morally, was always below a Touchable in rank, no matter how inferior the latter might be mentally or morally. A Touchable, however poor he might be, must always take rank and position above an Untouchable, howsoever brilliant, or deserving he might be.

No wonder after hearing such atrocious stories Ambedkar steeled himself to plunge into a do or die struggle for the liberation of the Untouchables, the victims of a ruthless caste system governing the Hindu society for over 2000 years. The shocking observations pertaining to the plight of Untouchables in Uttar Pradesh and several other states relate to a situation in India which prevailed until the country gained Independence in August 1947. Thanks to Ambedkar's crusading zeal to improve the lot of Untouchables, the situation is different in most of the country now. Nowhere would one find the Untouchables being treated so inhumanly as to be made to eat corn coming out of the dung of oxen or act as perpetual messengers of caste Hindus for sending messages relating to births or deaths.

The Indian Constitution drafted by Ambedkar granted them equality before law. They cannot be denied the right to buy property if they have means for it. Franchise has enhanced their status. Even the caste leaders are often at pains to woo them for electoral support Nor do they go begging for food from caste Hindu families as was the practice in the past. Earlier, they used to have separate tolas (colonies) outside the main settlements so that they could not pollute anybody by their touch or presence. Now they mix and mingle with the upper castes without any one raising even a little finger of protest. This is not to say that caste discrimination has altogether disappeared from India. It is still there. The Untouchables are not allowed to enter temples in many places. But discrimination against them in a virulent form as was the case earlier has ended.

The Untouchables are making a blow for restoration of their human rights now, just as they enjoyed during the Vedic period. They are demanding worth and not birth as criteria for social advancement. As Hindu society still remains wedded to the caste system, Dalit resurgence is on the rise in India. Thanks to Dalit upsurge in the country, Untouchables are being allowed to occupy positions of importance. The late K.R. Narayanan, an Untouchable from Kerala, rose to be the President of India. Leaders like Mayawati, although belonging to the Dalit stock, are becoming a force to be reckoned with in the country's polity. But still lot of ground remains to be covered before 160 million Dalits, living in grinding poverty and social deprivation, can be reconciled. Otherwise, such a big mass of humanity seething with discontent can only spell trouble for India. Because they want to end whatever caste discrimination is there against them, over 160 million Dalits are determined to revolutionise the Hindu society. "Jai Bhim!" (reference is to Dr Bhimrao Ambedkar) is their catchword now.

References

1. Waiting for a Visa, in the Collection of People's Education Society-Published in 1990, reproduced in Vol. 12 of Ambedkar's Writing and Speeches Published by Maharashtra Government in 1993.
2. Ambedkar's thesis, "The Evolution of Provincial Finance in British India." Vol. 6 of Ambedkar's writings and speeches published by Maharashtra Government in 1990.
3. Untouchables on the Children of India's Ghetto and other essays in Vol. 5 of Ambedkar's Writings and Speeches published by Maharashtra Government in 1989.

3

Fleecing India

Ramji Sakpal had high hopes about the future of his son. He wanted Ambedkar to continue further studies after his graduation. But the lack of resources with the family left Ambedkar no choice; he had to look for a job now. Ambedkar was in a dilemma: he didn't want to apply for a government job for he feared that because of his anti-British views, he would not be tolerated by the colonial rulers. Also, in the government, he could be called upon to work in an office where orthodox Hindus might be in top positions. In such a situation, he would again have to suffer discrimination. Under the circumstances, he got in touch with his old benefactor, the Maharaja of Baroda, and requested for employment in the Baroda state government. He was appointed Lieutenant in the Baroda State Forces. But before he could settle down in his new job he received a telegram informing him that his father was seriously ill. He took leave and immediately left to see his father.

On his way home he got down from the train at Surat to buy some eatables. As it took some time for him to return from the shop, the train meanwhile had left the station. Reaching Bombay the following day he stood aghast to see the condition of his father. He was fast sinking. The searching eyes of the dying Subedar-Major looked at his darling son who embodied all his hopes and aspirations. He touched his son's back with his feeble hand and, perhaps, wanted to say something. But due to congestion in his throat he could not utter even a word and breathed his last. Ambedkar's sorrow knew no bounds. He burst into tears, his loud lamentations drowning the wails of the members of his family. It was February 2, 1913, the saddest day in Ambedkar's life.

Plunged into gloom, Ambedkar really did not know how to come to terms with life. His father had been the main source of strength and support for him in a world full of hatred, contempt and discrimination. Now his father also was gone. But instead of succumbing to despair and despondency he resolved that he should go on working hard to fulfill the great desires and dreams of his father for the uplift of his community. He was not inclined to return to the job he held in Baroda. He thought he might study more to attain a higher status in life which could enable him to fight the curse of untouchability. But where were the means to study further?

As he was pondering over these problems he chanced to meet again his old friend and well-wisher, Krishnaji Arjun Keluskar, with whose intervention he was granted scholarship for his college studies by the Maharaja of Baroda. Keluskar again asked him to meet the Maharaja and talk to him about his problem. Consequently, a meeting was arranged and Ambedkar met the Maharaja at his palace in Bombay. Impressed by his sincerity, the Maharaja asked Ambedkar to apply for a scholarship to the Baroda state government. Already Baroda state had invited applications from students for higher studies abroad. Ambedkar was one of the four students selected for this scholarship. He visited Baroda to sign an agreement with the state government that he would be prosecuting his studies at the Columbia University in New York and on his return serve the state for 10 years. On June 4, 1913, he signed this agreement and started making preparations for going abroad.

Ambedkar arrived in New York in the third week of July, 1913. He was the first Untouchable ever to get an opportunity to study in one of the best American universities. He was pleasantly surprised to find that life there was quite different. Unlike the practice in colleges or offices in India, no one bore any ill-will or malice against him. He could freely mix with his classmates without anyone talking about his low caste. Like other students he sat at the dining table covered with a table-cloth and napkins lying before each chair. Experiencing such things for the first time in his life, Ambedkar was greatly relieved. Although food served to students in the Hartley Hall, a dormitory of the University, where he was first asked to lodge, was mostly ill-cooked beef, which he did not like, he started feeling that he had been transported to a new world altogether. Soon he shifted to the Cosmopolitan Club, where some of the Indian students lived, and where he thought he could perhaps get food of his liking. Later he moved to the Livingstone Hall dormitory and began living with Naval Bhathena, a Parsi student, who remained his lifelong friend.

But what impressed him most on the Columbia University campus was that no one treated him as an unequal despite the fact that he was a Mahar. However, unlike most other students who were enjoying themselves, dating girls, going to theater, attending parties, gadding about in their automobiles, Ambedkar was altogether a different student. He had no time for such things. He resolved to make the best use of his stay at the university. He knew that he could not afford to take the opportunity he had got of studying at the Columbia University lightly. Therefore, he decided to go on studying day and night. In India he had a vigorous appetite, but here he started restricting himself to a cup of coffee, two muffins and a single meat or fish dish, which cost him one dollar and ten cents. He could not spend all the money he received as stipend because every month he had to save something to send to his family which was without any source of income after the death of his father.

In India Ambedkar's subjects in the Bachelor of Arts examination were English and Persian. But in the Columbia University he sought to widen the scope of his knowledge by aiming to be the master of science, politics, sociology and economics. He took up Political Science, Moral Philosophy, Anthropology, Sociology and Economics as the subjects of his study. Prof. Edwin R.A. Seligman, a member of the University's faculty, made a deep impression on Ambedkar because of his knowledge and impressive way of teaching. Ambedkar was so much taken up by this teacher that he used to run after him on the campus to attend all his classes. The Professor taught well and guided his students with affection. Asked by Ambedkar about the methods of research he should follow, the Professor advised him to go on studying earnestly so that he could evolve his own method. Encouraged by his teachers in his ceaseless pursuit of knowledge, Ambedkar started spending most of his time in the university library, engrossed in his studies.

Once he was spotted in the library by the Indian freedom fighter, Lala Lajpat Rai, who was also a friend of Prof Seligman. Impressed by his dedication, Lajpat Rai asked Ambedkar to join the political party he was organizing to help India. But Ambedkar politely declined, saying that he had come to Columbia University to study only and therefore he could not engage himself in any political activity. Eventually, Ambedkar passed the M.A. examination of the University. He was awarded the degree of Master of Arts for his thesis "Ancient Indian Commerce" on June 2, 1915. In June, 1916, his Ph.D. thesis "National Dividend for India : A Historic and Analytical Study" was also accepted by the Columbia University.

The focus of his thesis was that India was a great trading nation in the past despite the fact it was severed from China and Tibet in the north by the Himalayan ranges, from Burma by the Tenasserim hills and from Afghanistan by the Karakoram and the Hindukush mountains. The country had a long waterfront. Hemmed in from all sides, the early Indians demolished all impediments, natural or otherwise, and launched into the Indian ocean, establishing trading contacts with remote countries and places. If the economic activity of the ancient Hindus found no exponents and no mention in the literature, it was mainly because education in the country was monopolized by upper caste Brahmins who were more or less "drones in the hive, gorging at a feast to which they had contributed nothing." The Brahmins or the intellectual caste of India enjoyed conspicuous leisure and conspicuous consumption. They wrote religious treatises but paid no attention to commerce or economic activity. Hence we are compelled to depend entirely on foreign authorities and their scanty reference to India's commerce. The Buddha Jatakas – the birth-stories of Buddha – are the earliest source on the subject and contain literary references to the economic organization of the Indian society which may be supposed on the basis of the dates of these Jatakas to have existed from times very remote in the past. In the olden days, there was a tendency towards hereditary occupation. But the caste system in all its hideousness was not present and even Brahmins had to earn their living through low and mean professions sometimes, especially if they were not well-versed in the Vedic literature or the Shastras.

Ambedkar's theses were remarkable because they threw light on the fact that India was a great maritime nation in the past, having trading links not only with the Roman empire but also with other countries. What he wrote in his doctoral thesis debunked the British version of history that India was a poor country, ruled by ruthless Muslim potentates in the past. By making comparisons, he demonstrated that the predecessors of the British rulers in India were more concerned with the welfare of the people than the masters of the East India Company who supplanted them. The British sought to create the impression that India had neither any culture nor any heritage of which it could be proud. On the contrary it fell to the British conquerors of the subcontinent to educate the people, and teach them what civilization was. Ambedkar's painstaking research denounced the British claim that India was a "white man's burden." He thoroughly exposed how ruthless the British rule was in bleeding the country white. Unlike historians and scholars of yesteryears, who won laurels from the British by their sycophancy, Ambedkar made no bones about the fact that the British policy right from the very day they set foot on Indian soil was aimed at fleecing the country. No wonder the American dons were greatly impressed by Ambedkar.

Dealing with India's past, Ambedkar's thesis stated that it was a matter of great controversy whether or not the Egyptians had direct trade with India. Gardiner Wilkinson in his book, *The Ancient Egyptians* says: "Whether they (the Egyptians) had a direct communication with India or were supplied through Arabia with the merchandise of that country, it is not possible to determine. But even as indirect trade, it was capable of opening to them a source of immense wealth; and the productions of India did actually reach Egypt. We have positive testimony from the tombs of Thebes that the productions of India came to Egypt at the early period of Joseph's arrival in the country. This is evident from the spices which the Ishmaclities were carrying to sell there; and the amethysts, hacmatile, lapis-lazuli, and other objects found at Thebes at the time of the third Thothmus and succeeding Pharaohs indicate that the intercourse was constantly kept up."[1]

According to Ambedkar's thesis, the rise of Babylonia was the high watermark in the commercial activity of ancient India. Situated at the confluence of the Euphrates and Tigris joining the Persian Gulf with the Mediterranean and being a meeting place of upper and lower Asia, Babylon was destined to be the great emporium of the eastern and western trade. It was the meeting place of routes from all parts of the ancient world. Quoting from the book by Kennedy, Ambedkar says that there is ample evidence which "warrants us in the belief that maritime commerce between India and Babylon flourished in the seventh and sixth and more especially in the sixth century B.C. It was chiefly in the hands of the Dravidians, although Aryans also had a share in it. Indian traders settled in Arabia and on the eastern coast of Africa. As we find them settling at this very time also on the coast of China, we cannot doubt that they had settlements in Babylon also.."[2]

The policy of Roman Empire during the two centuries following the Christian era was "to encourage direct sea trade with India, cutting out all overland routes through Parthia and thus avoiding the annoyance of fiscal dependence on that consistent enemy of Rome. Under the Pax Romana, trade between India and Rome was greatly fostered and grew so much in importance that guides to the ports of India and itinerary of land travels and caravans were begun to be written for the benefit of the merchants. It was during the middle of the first century A.D. that Hippolus, a Greek Egyptian, discovered the regularity of the Indian monsoon and thus facilitated the voyage of the traders. It was also about this time that a Greek merchant wrote "The Periplus of the Erythrean Sea" or guide to the Indian ocean. It is the most authentic document we have for the study of the Indian commercial activity. During the Roman empire Indian goods were greatly sought after and snapped up in markets all over the world. Because of widespread maritime activity, there was prosperity not only in coastal towns and cities but even in remote areas of the country.

As Ambedkar wrote, some of the Tamil poets beautifully described the commercial ports and towns in Southern India. According to one of them, the thriving town of Muchiri, where the beautiful large ships of the Yavans, bringing gold, would come splashing the white foam on the waters of the Periplus which belonged to the Cherala, and return loaded with pepper. Another poet described how the fish was bartered for paddy, which was brought in baskets to the houses. Sacks of pepper were brought from the houses to the market: the gold received from ships, in exchange for articles sold, was brought to shore in barges at Muchiri, where the music of the surging sea never ceased and where Kudduvan (the Chera king) would present to visitors the rare products of the seas and mountains.

That India was a great prosperous nation in the past was proved by Ambedkar not only with quotations from the world famous classic, *The Decline and Fall of Roman Empire* by Gibbon, but also from books by several other famous writers of yore. The rot started with the arrival of the English in India. The East India Company's trading began the process of exploitation of the country for the benefit of the British industries, markets and people. As had never happened before, the process started gathering momentum day by day. The prosperous subcontinent where starvation and hunger were unheard of became poorer with the march of the British from coastal areas to interior regions. In support of his argument that the British policy right from the beginning of the East India Company operations was aimed at fleecing India,

Ambedkar quoted excerpts from the proceedings of the British Parliament and the accounts given by many other objective and sensitive writers who could not hide their shame over the way their countrymen were robbing India without any qualm or scruple.

In his introduction to Ambedkar's thesis, "National Dividend for India: A Historic And Analytical Study," for which he was awarded a Ph.D. degree by the Columbia University, New York, in 1917, Prof. R.A. Seligman stated: "Nowhere to my knowledge has such a detailed study of the underlying principles been made. The chapters on Budget in the thesis were in fact found very valuable in their educative and illustrative aspects with regard to the nature and enlargement of the Provincial Finances." No wonder, the book was found useful by the Indian legislatures at the time of the budget discussions, and it became a ready reference for men in authority and a guide to students of Indian economy.

In his earlier M.A. dissertation, "Ancient Indian Commerce," Ambedkar stated that the British sought to justify their imperial policy in India by claiming that they were a people of superior race with a culture too high to be compared with any other; that they had a better system of administration and were well-versed in the arts of life. The British also proclaimed that the Indians were people of an inferior race with a very low culture and were absolutely devoid of the arts of life. As a logical consequence of this, the British started arguing that it was not only their divine mission to civilize their low lying brethren, but also to conquer them and superimpose on them their culture in the name of humanity. Logically reacting to the denunciation of India by the British, Ambedkar wrote that the optical vision of British historians of India somehow or the other magnified the vice, not the virtues of the predecessors of the British in India. Not only were they loud in their denunciation of the Mughal and the Maratha rulers as despots or brigands, they cast a slur on the morale of the entire population and their civilization. Historians of British India have often committed the fallacy of comparing the British rulers with their immediate or remote predecessors. In deference to historical methodology, they ought to compare the rulers of India with their contemporaries in England.

The British historians often dwelt at length on the abject condition of the Hindu under the subjugation of the Mohamedans but conveniently forgot their own past. The condition of the Anglo-Saxons under their Norman conquerors was so atrocious that even to be called an Englishman was considered a reproach. Those who were appointed to administer justice were the fountains of all iniquity. Magistrates, whose duty it was to pronounce righteous judgments, were the most cruel of all tyrants. They were greater plunderers than common thieves and robbers. The Normans were mad about money; they did not care by what means it was acquired. Licentiousness was so great that a Princess of Scotland found it necessary to wear a religious habit in order to preserve her person from violation. The British historians have written extensively about Mohamedan cruelty, forgetting that it could hardly exceed that committed by the first Crusaders in their conquest of Jerusalem. The garrison of 40,000 men was put to the sword without distinction; arms protected not the brave, nor submission the timid: nor age or sex received mercy; infants perished by the same sword that pierced their mothers. The streets of Jerusalem were covered with heaps of the slain, and the shrieks of agony and despair resounded from every corner.

Ambedkar's thesis stated that it was plainly the biased attitude of British historians that prompted Sir Thomas Munro to warn English historians of India and say: "When we compare other countries with England, we usually speak of England as she now is, we scarcely ever think of going back beyond the Reformation and we are apt to regard every foreign country as ignorant and uncivilized, whose state of improvement does not in some degree approximate to our own, even though it should be higher than our own as at no distant period." Former rulers of India were dismissed by British historians as "Despots and Brigands". But the fact is that the condition of people was far better when the "Despots and Brigands" ruled the country than was the case under the British rule. As Munro continues "The magnificence of Canouj and the wealth of the temples of Somnath bear witness to it. It is a mistake to suppose that the Muslim sovereigns of India were barbarous and despots. On the other hand the majority of them were men of extraordinary character. Mohommed of Ghuzni showed so much munificence to individuals of eminence that his capital exhibited a greater assemblage of literary genius than any other monarch in Asia has ever been able to produce. If rapacious in acquiring wealth, he was unrivalled in the judgment and grandeur with which he knew how to expend it."

Of all his illustrious successors (one of whom was a Razia Sultana) Feroze Shah is very well known for his administration. His public works consisted of 50 dams across rivers to promote irrigation, 40 mosques and 30 colleges; 100 inns, 30 reservoirs, 100 hospitals, 100 public baths, 150 bridges, besides many other edifices for pleasure and ornament; and above all, the canal from the point in the Jamuna where it leaves Karnal to Hansi and Hissar, a work which was partially restored by the British government. The historians and travelers of the period when this monarch ruled India, expatiated on the happy state of the ryots under his government, on the goodness of their houses and furniture and the general use of gold and silver ornaments amongst their women.

The general state of the country must have been flourishing, for Milo de Conti, an Italian traveler, who visited Indian about A.D. 1420, spoke highly of what he saw in Gujarat, and found that the banks of the Ganges were covered with towns amidst beautiful gardens and orchards. He passed four famous cities before he reached Maarazia, which he describes as a powerful city, filled with gold, silver, and precious stones. His accounts are corroborated by those of Barbora and Bartema, who traveled in the early part of the sixteenth century. The former in particular describes Cambay as a remarkably well-built city, situated in a beautiful country, filled with merchants of all nations, and with artisans and manufacturers like those of Flanders. Caesar Frederic gives a similar account of Gujarat and Ibne-Batuta, who traveled during the anarchy and oppression of Mohammed Tuglak's reign, in the middle of the fifteenth century, when insurrections were rife in most parts of the country, enumerates many large and populous towns and cities and gives a high impression of the state in which the country must have been before it fell into disorder. Babar, the founder of the Mughal dynasty in India, found the country in a prosperous condition and was surprised at the immense population and the innumerable artisans everywhere. He was a benevolent ruler and public works marked his statesmanship. Sher Shah who temporarily wrested the throne from the Mughals, was the greatest of the Mohamedan rulers excepting Akbar and like Babar executed many public works.

Ambedkar's thesis also speaks about the condition of the people in the dominions of the Marathas in glowing terms. The Marathas were the contemporaries of the later Mughals and a traveler says about their rule in these terms: "From Surat I passed the Ghats, and when I entered the country of Maharattas, I thought myself in the midst of the simplicity and happiness of the golden ages where nature was yet unchanged, and war and misery were unknown. The people were cheerful, vigorous, and in high health and unbounded hospitality was a universal virtue; every door was open, and friends, neighbours and strangers, were alike welcome wherever they went."

With regard to the economic conditions of the people in Southern India which was under the rule of Tipoo Sultan, a historian says: "When a person travelling through a strange country finds it well cultivated, populous with industrious inhabitants, cities newly founded, commerce extending, towns increasing, and everything flourishing, so as to indicate happiness, he will naturally conclude it to be under a form of Government congenial to the minds of the people. This is a picture of Tipoo's country, and this is our conclusion respecting its government. His country was found everywhere full of inhabitants and apparently cultivated to the utmost extent of which the soil was capable. His government though strict and arbitrary, was the despotism of a strict and able sovereign, who nourishes, not oppresses, the subjects who are to be the means of his future aggrandizement, and his cruelties were, in general, inflicted on those he considered as his enemies." Even Clive described Bengal as a country of "inexhaustible riches". Macaulay said, "In spite of the Mussalman despot and the Maratha freebooter Bengal was known through the East as the Garden of Eden – as the rich kingdom. Its population multiplied exceedingly; distant provinces were nourished from the overflowing of its granaries, and the noble ladies of London and Paris were clothed in the delicate produce of its looms."

Ambedkar's thesis, the original copy of which is still lying in the archives of the Columbia University along with the contributions of outstanding scholars of this campus, frankly stated that the economic welfare and contentment of the people of India went in the reverse gear with the advent of the British. Prosperity forsook India and perched itself on the Union Jack. The saddest commentary on the situation was that although the East India Company and the Crown Government which succeeded it following the first War of Independence in 1857 began to preach the myth that the "uplift of India was a white man's burden" which the British had to bear to justify their rule, nothing could be further from the truth. It is borne out not by the writings or propaganda of the Indian revolutionaries who fought for the independence of their country but by the writings of Englishmen themselves.

Unfortunately, there is no record of how many books Ambedkar read to prepare his thesis except that he spent more than 16 hours a day in the Columbia University library during the two years he was enrolled for his Master of Arts degree. But there is no doubt that the thesis he produced blew the lid off the cauldron of British atrocities against Indians. What Ambedkar wrote about the injustice done to India by the British masters has not been matched to this day by any scholar, Indian or foreign.

The administration of the East India Company, it was frequently claimed by its protagonists in London, was a prototype of the Roman provincial administration, under the Roman Empire. The Roman provincial constitution, in substance, only concentrated military powers in the hands of the Roman governor, while administration and jurisdiction were, or at any rate were intended to be, retained by the communities. But quite unlike the Romans of 1800 years ago, the British suppressed everything, sought to bleed India white, struggling in poverty, starvation and backwardness of the worst type. In fact, even more than 50 years after India attained Independence, the British legacy continues to dog India's planners and really one doesn't know how long it will take the country to regain its past glory.

How the British went about their business of depleting the country's resources was vividly stated by Frederick John Shore of the Bengal Civil Service. Very pathetically he said; "But the halcyon days of India are over. She has been drained of a large proportion of the wealth she once possessed, and her energies have been cramped by a sordid system of misrule to which the interest of the millions have been sacrificed for the benefit of the few." The gradual impoverishment of the people and the country, under the mode of rule established by the British Government has no precedence in human history. The grinding extortions of the British Government have effected the impoverishment of the country and its people to an extent unparalleled in human history. The fundamental principle of the English had been to make the whole Indian nation subservient in every possible way to the interest and benefit of themselves.

Had the welfare of the people been their object, a very different course would have been adopted and very different results would have followed. But such was not to be the case. In fact, it would have been unnatural had it been otherwise. As Mill says: "The government of a people by itself has a meaning and a reality; such a thing as government of one people by another does not, and cannot exist. One people may keep another for its own use, a place to make money in, a human cattle-farm to be worked for the profits of its own inhabitants."

Under such a system of government, the native inhabitants had no voice under the rule of the East India Company. They were barred from all high paid offices and had no scope beyond the position of a petty clerk. The internal administration was so devised that the Governors and the official staff in their capacity as advisers did or were compelled to do all the thinking for the inhabitants of the country. They enact, true to a word, the part of Sir John Bowley or the "Poor man's friend" so ably drawn by Charles Dickens: "Your only business, my good fellow, is with me. You need not trouble yourself to think about anything. I will think for you; I know what is good for you; I am your perpetual parent. Such is the dispensation of all-wise Providence... what many can do, I do. I do my duty as the Poor man's Friend and Father, and I endeavour to educate his mind, by inculcating on all occasions the great lesson which that class requires, that is entire dependence on myself. They have no business whatever with themselves." The Bowleys no doubt did the thinking as a divine mandate but unfortunately, nonetheless naturally, their thinking and enacting proved decisively favourable to England though fatal to India. How England prospered while India declined may be well ascertained if we recall the economic conditions of England immediately before and after A.D. 1600, and also the nature of India's tribute to England.

According to Sir Josiah Child, who gives a very interesting and comparative description of the rising prosperity of England, the trade of England in A.D. 1545 was inconsiderable and the merchants very mean and few. But subsequently there were more men to be found upon the exchange with ten thousand pound estates, than were there of one thousand pounds. The fact remains that India contributed or rather was made to contribute to the prosperity of England in many ways; direct as well as indirect.

Besides several indirect ways, England adopted more direct and drastic measures to harm India. This was effected through the protective system. England was in no way able to compete with Indian goods and as a manufacturing country, India was England's superior. To destroy the competition of Indian goods which in spite of the cost of transportation ousted the English goods from their home markets, England adopted a strong protectionist policy, imposing very high tariffs on Indian imports. But even that was not the end of discouraging Indian imports. England went a step further and made an invidious discriminatory move against Indian goods which bore import duty much higher than that on the same goods from other parts of the world. The English tariff on Indian goods was not only discriminatory but differed with the use to which they were put to in England.

Writing about high tariffs imposed on Indian imports in England, Sir W.W. Hunter said: "Europe, just emerged from mediaevalism, was then making her first experiments in Asiatic rule. Mediaeval conceptions of conquest imposed themselves on her exploitation of the Eastern world. Mediaeval types of commerce were perpetuated in the Indian trade. Portugal, Spain and Holland established their power in Asia when these conceptions and types held sway. The English ascendancy in India came later and embodied the European ideals of the eighteenth century in place of the European ideals of the sixteenth. It was the product of modern as against semi-mediaeval Christendom. Yet even for England it was difficult to shake off the traditions of the period ....of monopoly in the Indian trade, and of Indian Government for the personal profit of the rulers." In his book, *The Old Colonial System*, G.B. Hertz stated: "Self-interest certainly swayed the corrupt and oligarchic legislature, and politics were always discussed on a plane from which principles were banished. Men fought avowedly for the most material objects only. Gold ruled the aspirations of the greatest, and India afforded many examples of its fatal power at the time."

After winning the battle of Plassey in 1757, Clive became really the king-maker. He sold his support to the Nawabs who promised him better terms. He not only got great bribes from the Nawabs and Jagirdars and controlled the salt monopoly in spite of the wishes of the Home authorities but gave perfect liberty to the civil servants to indulge in private trade to monopolize certain trades to the utter exclusion of the natives. As a result of this the people were greatly oppressed and reduced to poverty. The wealth of Clive and the poverty of the people are well described by Macaulay. He says: "As to Clive, there was no limit to his acquisitions but his own moderation. The treasury of Bengal was thrown open to him. There were piled up, after the usage of the Indian princes, immense masses of coins, among which might not seldom be detected the florins and byzants with which before any European ship had turned the Cape of Good Hope, the Venetians purchased the stuff and spices of the east. Clive walked between heaps of gold and silver, crown rubies and diamonds, and was at liberty to help himself. Enormous fortunes were thus rapidly accumulated at Calcutta, while thirty millions of human beings were reduced to the extremity of wretchedness. This misgovernment of the English was carried to a point such as seems hardly compatible with the very existence of society. The Roman proconsul, who in a year or two squeezed out of a province the means of rearing marble palaces and baths on the shores of Campomia, of drinking from Amber, of feasting on singing birds, of exhibiting armies of gladiators and flocks of camelopards; the Spanish viceroy, who leaving behind him the curses of Mexico or Lima, entered Madrid with a long train of gilded coaches and of sumpter-horses trapped and shod with silver, were now outdone by Clive and many other English plunderers of his ilk."

Ambedkar stated in his thesis that Clive ruined the Bengal populace and Hastings, the first Governor-General, turned to the potentates. His ill-treatment of and exactions from the Raja of Benares and the Begums of Oudh, his massacre of the Rohillas excited the catholic sympathies of that great 18th century political philosopher Edmond Burke who by impeachment of Warren Hastings re-enacted, so to say, the memorable impeachment of Verres by Cicero for similar reasons. Burke espoused the cause of the oppressed and strained all his nerves to redress their wrongs and punish their offender. The impeachment, in spite of his vigour and the active participation of Sheridan, failed but not without its salutary effect. It was one of those failures that was worth a hundred victories. Lord Morley in his *Life of Burke* says,[3] "That Hastings was acquitted was immaterial. The lesson of his impeachment had been taught with sufficiently impressive force – the great lesson that Asiatics have rights, and that Europeans have obligations that a superior race is bound to observe the highest current morality of the time in all its dealings with the subject race. Burke is entitled to our lasting reverence as the first apostle and great upholder of integrity, mercy and honour, in the relations between his countrymen and their humble dependents."

As a result of Hastings' impeachment and other disclosures in British Parliament, the direct mode of administrative exploitation was nipped in the bud. But certain other indirect modes of exploitation were either imposed or allowed to remain by the same administration. These indirect modes of exploitation were the inland transit duties. The servants of the Company in their capacity as private traders enjoyed perfect immunity from these duties but they were levied with all strictness upon the natives whose economic betterment was thereby greatly hindered.

There was no dearth of means adopted to kill Indian industries. As Lord Ellenborough has pointed out, there were gross anomalies in the transit duties imposed on goods of English manufacture imported into India and duties imposed on goods of Indian manufacture. For example, cotton goods manufactured in England were levied only two and a half percent duty when imported into India as against nearly seventeen and a half percent duty levied on cotton goods manufactured in India (for Indian consumption). Similarly, a 15% duty was levied on Indian leather goods used in India. In this way nearly 235 separate articles, which included almost everything of personal or domestic use, were subjected to disproportionate inland duties.

Many historians have commented upon the way the English exploited India. H.H. Wilson is very emphatic in saying that the British policy was to completely throttle India's economy. He wrote: "It is also a melancholy instance of the wrong done to India by the country on which she has become dependent. It was stated in evidence (in 1813) that the cotton and silk goods of India up to the period could be sold for a profit in the British market at a price from 50 or 60 per cent lower than those fabricated in England. It consequently became necessary to protect the latter by duties of 70 and 80 per cent of their value, or by positive prohibition. Had India been independent, she would have retaliated, would have imposed prohibitive duties upon British goods, and would have thus preserved her own productive industry from annihilation. This act of self-defence was not permitted her. She was at the mercy of the stranger. British goods were forced upon her without paying duty, and the foreign manufacturer employed the arm of political injustice to keep down and ultimately strangle a competitor with whom he could not contend on equal terms." The land revenue policy of the British in India destroyed agriculture and their prohibitory protectionist policy ruined industries of the country whose wealth attracted these swarms of flies that drained her to the last dregs.

No wonder, the British attempts to kill Indian industries and leave people no other avenue except agriculture only resulted in the misery and poverty of India's masses. Bishop Heber, who travelled in India about 1830, wrote: "In Hindustan (Northern India), I found a general feeling among the Kings's officers and I myself was led from some circumstances to agree with them, that the peasantry in the Company's Provinces are, on the whole, worse off, poorer, and more dispirited, than the subjects of the Native Princes; and here in Madras, where the soil is, generally speaking, poor, the difference is said to be still more marked. The fact is, no Native Prince demands the rent which we do, and making every allowance for the superior regularity of our system, etc., I met with very few men who will not, in confidence, own their belief that the people are over-taxed, and that the country is in a gradual state of impoverishment. The Collectors do not like to make this avowal officially."

The land tax levied by the British Government was not only excessive, but, what is worse, it was fluctuating and uncertain in many provinces. In Bengal the land tax was fixed at over ninety per cent of the rental, and in Northern India at over eighty percent of the rental between 1793 and 1822. It is true that the British Government only followed the precedent of the previous Mohamedan rulers who also claimed an enormous land tax, with the difference that what the Mohamedan rulers claimed they could never fully realize, what the British rulers claimed they realized with rigour.

An astounding fact of history, as stated in Ambedkar's widely acclaimed thesis, was that the British acquired India, came to rule this vast subcontinent, without the expenditure of a single shilling on the part of Great Britain, but India regularly paid to Great Britain a heavy tribute, an almost incredible sum of a hundred millions sterling in the course of the 19th century. "The Indian tribute, whether weighed in the scales of justice or viewed in the light of our own true interest, will be found to be at variance with humanity, with common sense, and with the received maxims of economic science." If the affairs of the nation continue to be guided by considerations of people who dwell there, it is mainly because conscientious people are to be found all over the world. One such person was Major Wingate, who immediately after what is known as the first war of Indian Independence in 1857, asked questions that could embarrass the politicians in the British Parliament.

He asked: "Has our policy in India been determined out of pure, unselfish, and benevolent regard for the welfare of the people of that country, and without the smallest regard for the manner in which it may affect our own way? Was this the principle which guided us in imposing prohibitive duties upon Indian manufactures imported into this country, and merely nominal duties upon British manufactures imported into India? Was it out of pure regard for India that cotton exported to great Britain from India, is exempt from duty, while it is taxed on exportation to all parts of the world besides? Were native interests solely concerned in the exemption by which native redress for British wrong-doing has been made a practical impossibility in ninety-nine cases out of a hundred? Was it out of consideration for the tax paying Hindoo and Mohamedan that the official European in India was provided with a costly ecclesiastical establishment before anything else was done for their education or enlightenment? Was it an unselfish regard for the natives that dictated the policy of obtaining, upholding and extending British dominion in the East by means of taxes raised in India in opposition to the ruling obtaining in all other British dependencies, of providing for the costs of their military defence from the British Exchequer? And lastly, were the arrangements for defraying what is styled 'the home charges' out of the Indian revenues, under which nearly one hundred million sterling of taxes collected in India have been transferred to Great Britain in the course of the present century, devised for the purpose of benefiting the people of India alone?"

Because of increasing level of poverty and suffering in the country, the natives submitted a petition to the British Parliament saying: "While every encouragement is held out to the exportation from England to India of the growth and produce of foreign as well as English industry, many thousands of the natives of India who, a short time ago, derived a livelihood from the growth of cotton and the manufacture of cotton goods, are without bread, in consequence of the facilities afforded to the produce of America, and the manufacturing industry of England." But the appeal for justice fell on deaf ears and the interests of England always remained in the forefront in the eyes of those who were called upon to rule the destinies of India.

The Court of Directors of the East India Company on May 7, 1766, wrote: "We have the sense of the deplorable state ..... from the corruption and rapacity of our servants, and the universal depravity of manners throughout the settlement ...We think that the vast fortunes acquired by servants of the company are the result of the most tyrannical and oppressive conduct that ever was known in any age or country." Sir Thomas Munro was so indignant at the misrule of the Company that he said, "It would be more desirable that we should be expelled from the country altogether, than that the result of our system of government should be such an abasement of a whole people."

Ambedkar's doctoral work was so well-researched and illuminating that the academicians who read it were deeply impressed. But in his own country, because Ambedkar was a Shudra, nobody could accept his brilliance or accord him the recognition due to him because of his unmatched scholarly work, the reading of which even today, more than half a century after the British quit India, makes one's flesh creep over the misdeeds of the people who got away by denouncing India as a "white man's burden."

Reference

1. The quotation is on page 13; 2-Page 17 and 3-last paragraph on page 65 of Ambedkar's Writing and Speeches Vol. 12 published by Maharashtra government in 1993.

4

Struggle Begins

After completing his Ph.D thesis at the Columbia University, Ambedkar left for the U.K. to continue further studies at the London School of Economics. Already having an American doctorate on a subject which was a topic of discussion in academic circles at important centres of learning, he had no difficulty in catching the eye of the faculty members at the LSE. Here he enrolled for another doctorate under the guidance of Prof. Edwin Cannan, an eminent economist and illustrious teacher, and again started working day and night on his new thesis. Simultaneously with his studies at the LSE, he joined the Gray's Inn to arm himself with legal qualifications for practicing at the Bar in India. During his stay in England, he read a paper on "Responsibilities of a Responsible Government in India" at a function organized by the Students Union. But it caused such a furore in the academic circles in Britain that he came to be suspected as an Indian revolutionary. Even Prof. Herald J. Laski said that the views expressed in the paper were "frankly of a revolutionary nature."

Just when he was pursuing his studies in England, Ambedkar was informed that the period of scholarship he had been given by the State of Baroda was over. The news was like a bolt from the blue. Deeply immersed in his work he wanted to complete his new thesis. But he didn't know what to do. He could not prolong his stay as he did not have any resources to fall back upon. When he explained his difficulties to his guide, he was assured not to worry and come back whenever he had funds to complete his unfinished work. Before packing his bags he resolved to return to London soon. He booked his luggage, which mainly consisted of piles of books he had purchased, with Thomas Cooke and Sons, and embarked the S.S. Kaiser-i-Hind for return home. As the World War I was still raging, the steamer carrying his books was torpedoed in the high seas. When the news reached India, his family fearing that he was aboard the same steamer, was plunged into gloom. But when they came to know that Ambedkar was on another ship, they heaved a sigh of relief.

Many of his friends and well-wishers held a reception to felicitate him on his achievements in the academic world soon after his return to Bombay on

August 21, 1917. His publications on the origins of caste and the discrimination meted out to Shudras, besides his doctoral thesis accepted by the Columbia University in New York had already made a big splash. But Ambedkar was publicity-shy, as a result of which he did not attend the reception arranged for him by an organization of the Scheduled Castes. His admirers went to his residence to congratulate him on his achievements. Thereafter, Ambedkar decided to proceed to Baroda, for in accordance with the agreement for scholarship the state government had granted him, he was required to serve Baroda state for 10 years. But he had no money even for the train fare. Luckily the ocean carrier which had booked his luggage paid him compensation for the loss of his belongings. Giving a part of the amount he had received to his wife for household expenditure, he went to Baroda. The Maharaja of Baroda had ordered his staff to receive him at the railway station. But reports that he was an Untouchable made many caste Hindu employees of the State Government sit up and wonder over this move. Making flimsy excuses none turned up to receive Ambedkar at the railway station for they all felt it would be a disgrace for them to receive a Mahar.

Notwithstanding the fact that he belonged to an Untouchable caste, the Maharaja wanted to appoint Ambedkar as Finance Minister of the State. But to give him time to get acquainted with various departments of the state government, he was first designated as Military Secretary to the Maharaja. Strangely, the staff in the office, far from showing respect befitting his rank, soon began to treat him with contempt. The peon would fling files on his table. Nobody cared to serve him even drinking water. The staff rolled the mats when he got up to go. It was a mortifying experience, but he could do nothing to change the situation, for he knew that all this was happening because of the Mahar caste label he carried. Instead of spending all his time in office, he sought refuge in a public library with the tacit consent of his immediate superior.

But the treatment meted out to him in the Parsi inn where he had taken accommodation under the pretence of being a Hindu was a shattering blow. A group of Parsis wielding lathis descended on the inn and asked him who he was. When he said that he was a Hindu, they shouted: "You arrant knave, you are a despicable Untouchable, we know." They ordered him to vacate the room he was occupying immediately. Ambedkar begged for eight hours' leave to do so. Neither any Hindu nor Muslim would take him as a tenant in the city. When the Maharaja was informed about his problem, the State Diwan was instructed to help him. But even the Diwan could not do anything. Deeply despondent Ambedkar, who was treated very courteously abroad but was hated in his own native land, sat under a tree and burst into a flood of tears. In such circumstances, he could not help returning to Bombay.

Hearing about his unfortunate experiences in Baroda, his old friend and well-wisher, Keluskar, informed the Maharaja about the insufferable treatment meted out to him. A professor at Baroda, who was well-known to Keluskar, when approached for help, agreed to accommodate Ambedkar in his flat as a paying guest. Ambedkar returned to Baroda, but right at the station he met a messenger sent by the professor with a note saying that he could not agree to take Ambedkar because his wife was strongly opposed to the idea. Ambedkar again returned from Baroda, as disgusted and disappointed, as he was on his first visit there. In Bombay, he found his step-mother seriously ill. She passed away after a few days. Although by her turbulent nature, she had alienated the whole family, Ambedkar performed her last rites in accordance with his filial duties. But there was no end to suffering and want which had been dogging him since his return from England.

Just when Ambedkar was grappling with the problem of adjustment in a society where nobody cared for him despite the fact that he was a highly qualified person with a Ph.D degree from Columbia University, the Indian National Congress passed a resolution at its annual session in Calcutta, expressing concern over the treatment meted out to the Untouchables. Following this, the Depressed Classes Mission Society of India held its first All-India Depressed Classes Conference on March 23 and 24, 1918. The conference presided over by the Maharaja Sayajirao Gaekwad of Baroda was attended by prominent Indian celebrities including Vithalbhai, M.R. Jayakar, Bipin Chandra Pal and many others. The organizers made it clear that the main purpose of the conference was to appeal to the conscience of the country, awaken its reasoning, its heart to remove the blot of Untouchability.

The Maharaja said that old prejudices and fanaticism could not bear scrutiny of the scientific thought and forces of social regeneration which were remoulding the outlook and temper of thousands of countrymen. Bal Gangadhar Tilak said that he could not deny that some day in the ancient past the autocracy of Brahmins had created the scourge of Untouchability, which was a disease and must be removed. The conference concluded with an All-India anti-Untouchability Manifesto signed by prominent leaders. But Tilak did not sign it, either on account of pressure from his followers or because he felt that being an upper caste Hindu it would cause him embarrassment. Apparently, seeing through the hypocrisy of some of the participants, Ambedkar did not associate himself with the conference. He was convinced that he must first have a sound footing before launching his crusade against Untouchability.

Ambedkar could not get a job. Wherever he tried, he was rejected because of his caste. About this time, there was a vacancy for the post of a professor at Sydenham College of Commerce and Economics in Bombay. He applied for it but he knew that his caste would again be held against him. In order to forestall rejection, he got in touch with Lord Sydenham, former Governor of Bombay, who was his London acquaintance and requested him to recommend him for the post. Edward Cannan, Professor of Political Economy at the University of London, who had been mentioned by Ambedkar as a referee, when asked to give an opinion on him, wrote to the Principal of Sydenham College, saying: "I don't know anything about Ambedkar except that he came to do a thesis and attacked it and me in a way which showed he had quite extraordinary practical ability. I rather wonder if he is a pure Indian; his character is rather Scotch-American." With such a recommendation, Ambedkar had no difficulty in impressing the Sydenham College principal. He succeeded in getting this appointment on a temporary basis as his main concern was to collect some funds so that he could return to London to complete his interrupted doctoral work.

Because of his caste label, the students did not take him seriously in the beginning. But by and by, Ambedkar's deep study, exhaustive exposition of the subject and thoughtful style started impressing the students. With his fine dress, profound studies, serious glowing eyes, the young professor became popular among students of economics, and students from other colleges also began flocking to his classes. But his success as professor could not help him ward off the caste stigma which made some Gujarati members of the faculty take objection to his drinking water from the pot kept in the staff room. Such repeated insults goaded him to go deep into the problem of Untouchability. He began to feel the pulse of the Untouchables by silently contacting and meeting all those who sympathized with them.

As a Professor in Bombay, however, he had started getting a handsome salary. But he lived frugally and gave some money to his family for household expenditure. He wanted to save as much as possible so that he could again go back to London to complete his doctoral work. But when the Baroda State authorities came to know that he had a good income as a Professor in Sydenham College, they initiated proceedings to recover from him the scholarship amount which they said was due from him because he had not served the state as per the original agreement when he was sent abroad for higher studies. This created new problems for poor Ambedkar. But the Baroda state officials were doing all this without the knowledge of the Maharaja and much to the chagrin of Ambedkar, they kept on sending him repeated reminders about repayment. Ambedkar felt absolutely helpless and suffered these pinpricks silently. However, when Ambedkar met the Maharaja later in London, the Maharja intervened and ordered that the recovery proceedings initiated against Ambedkar should be dropped. Ambedkar heaved a sigh of relief.

While searching for people sympathetic to Untouchables, Ambedkar came to know that the Maharaja of Kolhapur was also taking great interest in the uplift of the depressed classes. He was trying to promote education among them to eradicate the prejudice and barriers created by the caste system and to liberate them from the tyrannous priesthood and the unjust dominance of the Brahmins. Ambedkar's meeting with the Maharaja of Kolhapur took place in 1919 and, seeing his credentials, the Maharaja was greatly impressed by him. With financial assistance provided by the Maharaja, Ambedkar launched a fortnightly paper called the 'Mook Nayak' 'leader of the dumb' the first issue of which came out on January 31, 1920. Outlining the aims and objectives of the paper, Ambedkar wrote that India was a home of inequality thanks to the caste system. The Hindu society was just like a high structure which had several storeys without a ladder or an entrance as a result of which one died in the storey in which one was born howsoever able or brilliant he might be. According to the Hindu philosophy, there existed god in the animals as well as in inanimate things. As such, the same god existed even for the depressed classes. But the Hindus treated the depressed classes, who were also their co-religionists, as Untouchables.

On March 21, 1920, Ambedkar presided over a conference of the Untouchables at Mangaon in the Kolhapur state. It was attended by the Maharaja of Kolhapur. Speaking on the occasion the Maharaja declared in a prophetic vein: "You have found your saviour in Ambedkar. I am confident that he will break your shackles. Not only that, a time will come when, so whispers my conscience, Ambekdar will shine as a frontrank leader of all India fame and appeal." The Maharaja was right in his prediction, as is obvious from the fact that 50 years after his death, Ambedkar is being projected as their leader by the Untouchables, and also by the Congress, as is clear from his photograph now being used in posters along with that of Nehru, Indira and Rajiv. The Maharaja of Kolhapur himself presided over another all-India conference of Untouchables held at Nagpur in May 1920. In a fighting speech, Ambedkar said at this conference that any organization started by the caste Hindus for the uplift of the depressed classes should be opposed because there was no guarantee about their sincerity for the cause of the Untouchables. The affection and admiration of the Maharaja of Kolhapur for Ambedkar grew as he came to know more and more about him. One day Ambekar was taken by surprise to find at his doorway the Maharaja of Kolhapur who had personally come to see him at his humble abode in Bombay.

Ambedkar began to propagate that in order to save the depressed classes from the disabilities they suffered from, they must be made aware of the stranglehold of the priestly classes. Referring to the demand for Home Rule in the country, Ambedkar said it would have no meaning for the depressed classes until and unless they were accorded social equality. Home Rule was as much the birthright of a Brahmin as that of a Mahar. If the Brahmins were justified in their attack upon and opposition to the unjust power of the British Government, the depressed classes were justified a hundred times more so in their opposition to the over-lordship of the Brahmins in case the transfer of power took place. If the protection of the British was withdrawn, those who did not condescend even to look at the Untouchables lest their very sight should pollute them, would continue to trample upon them. Ambedkar wrote that the Swaraj in which there were no fundamental rights guaranteed for the depressed classes, would not be a Swaraj. It would be a new kind of perpetual slavery for them.

Although Ambedkar was getting increasingly involved in activities aimed at arousing the depressed classes to start fighting for equality in the caste-based Hindu society, the idea of returning to England to complete his interrupted academic pursuits was never far from his mind. With some financial help from the Maharaja of Kolhapur and a fresh loan of Rs 5,000 from his old Parsi friend, Naval Bhathena, he again left for London to complete his studies in Law and Economics. His wife, Ramabai, who had been facing hardships for long, did not say a word against Ambedkar's plans to go abroad again. On the contrary, she prayed for the success of his mission and resolved to look after her little son, Yashwant, and the family of her husband's elder brother. Two of Ambedkar's sons had earlier died in infancy for lack of proper medical care.

Although Ambedkar was regularly sending some money to his wife, Ramabai, from abroad, the family always suffered from want and lived in abject poverty in the hope that one day Ambedkar would start earning well and put paid to their suffering. When the Maharaja of Kolhapur came to know of this, he showed his readiness to protect and maintain her at Kolhapur. But Ambedkar refused. The Maharaja, however, started sending her some financial assistance so that she could take care of herself and her child. Ambedkar told his wife that the hardships she was passing through was a temporary phase and would be over as soon as he got back after completing his studies. He asked her to dispose of all her jewellery which her father had presented to her on their marriage to tide over the financial problems. Dutiful Ramabai could not help selling off her jewellery just as her husband had directed her from London, so that she could live without looking for charity from Ambedkar's friends and well-wishers. Ambedar had promised that he would buy her everything she sold on his return to India.

Ambedkar resumed his studies at the London School of Economics and the Gray's Inn from September, 1920. Also, he started visiting the London Museum, and in order to gain more knowledge about India's past often pored over books from 8 a.m. to 5 p.m. In view of his limited financial resources, he started living as frugally as possible. He had taken his lodgings at a semi-boarding house run by a stringent, old lady; the breakfast she offered her boarders consisted of a piece of fish, a cup of tea, a piece of bread with a sprinkling of jam. Since he wanted to save money in order to prolong his stay in London, he would go without lunch sometimes. He was often the first man to arrive at the Museum in the morning and the last to leave it. He did not confine his research work to the Museum alone. He also spent a lot of time at the India Office Library, the London University library, and in the other city libraries. He took voluminous notes on the subjects of his study. Returning to his room in the boarding house, he would again go on reading until late in the night.

Just as he finished his thesis, he was also called to the Bar at the Gray's Inn. Since he had some money and time on his hands until his thesis was accepted by the London University, he decided to enhance his qualifications further and went to the Bonn University in Germany where he enrolled as a student. But before proceeding there, he requested his friend Naval Bhathena to send him a remittance of Rs 2,000 so that he could buy German currency needed for going to Bonn. Soon after receiving the money he left. But his thesis, "The Problem of the Indian Rupee; its origin and its solution," provoked a storm of protest. Several deans and dons of the London School of Economics strongly reacted against the conclusions he had drawn. They denounced Ambedkar as an "Indian revolutionary in a sheep's clothing." But his guide did not see eye to eye with them. He sent word to Ambedkar to return to London soon. This made Ambedkar cut short his stay at the Bonn University before completing his education there. When Ambedkar returned, Professor Cannan asked him to redraft a chapter or two in the thesis so that no one could raise even a little finger protest when his name would be placed on the roll of honour of distinguished alumni of the London School of Economics. Ultimately the thesis was accepted and Ambedkar awarded a D.Sc degree by the University of London in 1923.

It was published with a foreward by Professor Cannan, saying: "Even when I have thought him quite wrong, I have found a stimulating freshness in his views and reasons. In the practical conclusion Ambedkar was right." In his final observations on the thesis, Prof. Cannan stated: "'The Problem of the Rupee' was an exceedingly instructive treatise on a terribly controversial subject. Ambedkar tackled the problem of the rupee in all its details. He traced its history, analyzed all sorts of opinions, and finally gave us his verdict that the problem had arisen on account of the neglect, by those in power, of the truth that it was internal purchasing power of the rupee which was of primary importance and not its exchange value as has been assumed and worked upon by them."

In December 1923, when Ambedkar's thesis was published in London, he was hailed as an outstanding scholar. Reviewing the book, *The Times* said: "Excellent piece of work. The English style is easy and his knowledge of his subject obviously very full. "*The Economist* commented: "It is a clear and ably written book. Certainly none of the other numerous works on one or the other aspect of the monetary problem have anything like the readability of this tract." *The Scotsman* observed: "His work throughout shows the utmost care and is clearly the fruit of painstaking research..... The book (to which Professor Cannan contributes a foreword) is, on account of the originality of its treatment, to be commended to all students of the finances of India." *The Financier* said: "Ambedkar deals with the problem in a very lucid and praiseworthy manner and puts forward not merely its origin but also valuable proposals for a solution, which should be studied by bankers and those merchants whose business depends upon the exchange."

References

Ambedkar's Writing and Speeches Vol. 3, 5, 12, Dhanjay Keer's, book, Ambedkar's Life and Mission, 1962, Published by Popular Prakashan.

5

Caste Puzzles

Worried as he was day and night about the contemptuous treatment meted out to him, Ambedkar began to wonder about his fate. He had distinguished himself by getting doctorate degrees from the Columbia University in New York and the prestigious London School of Economics. He had also studied at the Bonn University in Germany. Few of his contemporaries could boast of such a brilliant academic record. Had he been lacking in anything, a charming Irish girl, who could have no dearth of suitors amongst her own people, would not have fallen for him. She was so much infatuated with him that she wanted to marry Ambedkar. Although he belonged to an untouchable caste, this fact did not disqualify him from being the object of her adoring passion. Outside India, he was loved and respected. Within his own country, he was hated, denigrated and discriminated because of his low caste.

Was it always like this that the people belonging to low castes were treated with contempt in India or was it a recent phenomenon? Such questions began to assail his mind. With a view to finding answers to the caste puzzles in India, he undertook an intensive study of the Vedas, Shastras, Mahabharata, Ramayana, Gita and other religious and historical books. He was surprised to find that India's greatest emperor Ashoka who ruled the entire subcontinent in the third century B.C. was a Shudra by caste. Not only the Mauryan emperor Ashoka, but several other Shudras also had ruled in the ancient days. They all commanded awe and respect just like Brahmin, Kshatriya or Vaishya rulers. What had turned people against Shudras? Why were they being treated like pariahs now?

Delving deep into the ancient religious books and history, Ambedkar discovered that the ancestors of people in India were a mixture of Aryans, Dravidians, Mongolians and Scythians. All these races came from various directions with different cultures centuries ago when they were still in a tribal state. They all elbowed their entry into the country by fighting with the Dravidians, the original inhabitants of the subcontinent, and after a long spell of fights and skirmishes had settled down as peaceful neighbours. Thanks to constant contacts and mutual intercourse they evolved a common culture. As there had not been a complete and thorough amalgamation of the various stocks, people living in the eastern region presented a marked contrast in physique and complexion to those settled in the west. Similarly the physical profile of the people living in the north and the south of the country is very different. But there is no doubt about the common cultural streak running across the subcontinent.

The Indo-Aryan society which was formed with the amalgamation of various races had been practicing caste-based graded inequality for over 2,000 years. According to the Hindu social order, though it is true that all men are children of Prajapati, the creator of the universe, they are not equal on that account, as they were created from different parts of Prajapati's body. The Brahmins were said to have been created from the mouth, the Kshatriyas from the arms, the Vaishyas from the thighs and the Shudras from the feet. As the limbs from which they were created each performed functions of unequal value, the men thus created were also seen as unequal. Initially the Indo-Aryan society governed by the Chaturvarnya system lived happily. It was worth and not birth that determined one's position in life when the Chaturvarnya system was prevailing. Varna was not hereditary either in status or occupation in the original dispensation.

Unity of culture became the basis for homogeneity all over the land. The various races occupying definite territories fused into one another. On the whole, the Hindu society, in common with other societies, was composed of several classes and the earliest known classes were Brahmins, the priestly class, the Kshatriyas, the military class, the Vaishyas, the merchant class, and the Shudras, the menial class. The Chaturvarnya system governed the Hindu society. According to it, the Brahmins should cultivate knowledge and guide the people, Kshatriyas should bear arms and fight if the tribal society existing then was attacked, the Vaishyas should engage in trade and the Shudras should serve the other castes by building their houses and doing such other things which needed to be done so that all could live together happily. There was no bar on acquisition of Vedic knowledge. Even a Shudra could learn the Vedas and thus become Brahmin and if a Shudra could excel in martial arts, he could become a Kshatriya. Indeed, in those days, the Chaturvarnya system decided one's caste by worth and not by birth. If a born Brahmin was not well-versed in Shastras and other religious books, he forfeited the right to belong to the Brahmin Varna.

Although they were created from the feet of Prajapati, the Shudras did not suffer from any disability or discrimination. That they were treated like other castes is proved by the description given in the Mahabharata of the coronation of Yudhishtra, the eldest brother of the Pandavas. Shudras took part in the consecration of the king. In ancient days, there used to be a group of the representatives of the people called Ratnis who played a significant role in the investiture of the king. The Ratnis were so called because they held the

Ratna (jewel) which was a symbol of sovereignty. The king acquired his sovereignty only when the Ratnis handed over to him the jewel of sovereignty and on receiving this the king went to the house of each of the Ratnis and made an offering to them. It is significant that Shudras used to be among the Ratnis.

Whatever their origin, the Shudras in the ancient Aryan society had attained a high political status. They could even become ministers of state as mentioned in the Mahabharata. Enumerating the different classes of ministers the writer of the Mahabharata mentions a list of 37 ministers of whom four were Brahmins, eight Kshatriyas, 21 Vaishyas, three Shudras and one Suta. The story of Shudras given in the Rig-Veda confirms that they could even be kings those days. There was a fierce contest between Vashishtha and Vishvamitra as to who should become the purohit or royal priest of King Sudas who was a Shudra. Vashishtha, a Brahmin, was already the officiating priest of Sudas. He claimed that a Brahmin alone could become the King's purohit. Vishvamitra, a Kshatriya, contended that a Kshatriya was equally competent for that office. Vishvamitra won and became the purohit of King Sudas. The story shows that both the Brahmins and Kshatriyas not only saw no humiliation in serving a Shudra king but they even fought with each other to secure his patronage and were ready to perform Vedic ceremonies for him.

During the Mauryan period when Ashoka ascended the throne of Magadh, Buddhism became the state religion. That Ashoka was a great ruler is a fact acknowledged by historians all over the world. But the unity of the Chaturvarnya system, which had held the then Indian society together, came under much strain. The country remained very powerful and united but the Varnas which governed the Indo-Aryan society earlier were pushed into the background. Ashoka was so much fascinated by the new Buddhist religion that he started giving it more importance than the Hindu doctrines propagated by the Brahmin priests in the past. The earlier Vedic rituals, which were propagated by Brahmins, were relegated to the background. The holding of Yajnas and other religious ceremonies which allowed Brahmins to wield considerable influence and prestige and also amass riches by way of their fees for performing these rites came to be frowned upon.

Since Buddhism had become the religion of the state in the country, Brahmins suffered the greatest blow to their power and prestige. But they could not do anything except to suffer in silence. Ashoka prohibited all animal sacrifices which constituted the very essence of Brahminic religion. Brahmins not only lost state patronage but they also lost their occupation which mainly consisted of performing sacrifices for a fee which often was very substantial and which constituted their main source of living. The Brahmins, therefore, lived as the suppressed and depressed classes for nearly 140 years under the Mauryan rule.

A rebellion against the Buddhist state was the only escape left to the suffering Brahmins. No wonder, Pushyamitra, who was a Sunga by Gotra conspired against the last Mauryan king, committed regicide in 183 B.C. and proclaimed himself the new ruler. The Sungas were Samvedi Brahmins, who believed in animal and Soma sacrifices. To demonstrate that the Maurayan empire was now under Brahmin rule, Pushyamitra, on ascending the throne, first of all performed Ashvamedha Yajna or the horse sacrifice, the Vedic rite which could only be performed by a paramount sovereign. The exaggerated regard for the sanctity of animal life which was one of the most cherished features of Buddhism, thus came to an end. Pushyamitra launched a violent and virulent campaign of persecution against Buddhists and Buddhism. That Pushyamitra's persecution of Buddhism was pitiless can be gauged from the fact that a royal proclamation issued then set a price of 100 gold pieces on the head of every Buddhist monk. Drawing attention to the plight of Buddhists under Pushyamitra's reign, Ambedkar quoted Dr. Haraprasad Shastri who wrote:[1] "The condition of the Buddhists under the imperial sway of the Sungas, orthodox and bigoted, can be more easily imagined than described. From Chinese authorities it is known that many Buddhists still do not pronounce the name of Pushyamitra without a curse."

Pushyamitra overthrew Buddhism and re-established Brahmanism in its place. Even Manusmriti was promulgated as a code of laws during Pushyamitra's rule. As stated in ancient Indian history, Manu had great prestige. With a view to investing the new caste code with authority and prestige, its authorship was attributed to Manu. Actually, according to the Naradasmriti which was written about the 4th century A.D., the Manusmriti was composed by a scholarly Brahmin, Sumati Bhargava. Historians whose authority cannot be challenged said that Sumati Bhargava must have composed between170 B.C. and 150 B.C. the code which he deliberately called Manusmriti. That the new regime of Pushyamitra was flagrantly anti-Buddhist is betrayed by the provisions enacted in the Manusmriti against the Buddhists and Buddhism. Manusmriti accorded Brahmins the highest position, making them the lord of the whole creation. The Manusmriti contained provisions, according to which Brahmins are the supreme head of all castes and whatever exists in the world is the property of the Brahmins. It is obvious that the deification of the Brahmins, placing them even above the king, would have been impossible unless the king Pushyamitra himself was a Brahmin.

Under the reign of Pushyamitra, Manusmriti became a Bible of the Hindu society. In order to consolidate their position the Brahmins introduced practices aimed at ensuring their supremacy. Gradually, the priestly class detached itself socially from the rest of the people and through a covert policy became a separate and elitist entity enjoying royal patronage and powers to rule the lives of other castes. Scriptures did not throw much light on the fact how the Brahmins became a powerful exclusive group wielding enormous influence. Judging from the Brahmins' anxiety to remain an exclusive and powerful group, Ambedkar concluded that they must have resorted to endogamy, for it is a fact that nothing but endogamy can ensure purity of any caste or tribe. As endogamy forbade marriages outside one's caste, the Brahmins took measures to strengthen the system in such a way that they could keep their individual caste identity intact. It was since then that the custom of marriages within one's own caste must have become a social practice.

Endogamy stipulated that both sexes were evenly distributed and neither a man nor any woman was left without their conjugal partner. Otherwise, endogamy could not be maintained properly. Often, in tribal societies, there were nearly as many men as women; and unless this was so, endogamy or the purity of the caste could not be maintained. But parity between the sexes could be kept only if a couple died simultaneously. This could happen but rarely. The presence of a young widow or a widower in society could pose danger to endogamy and even the morals of the tribal society. Naturally, the young widow being a temptation for other males could incite violation of the moral code. If she sought a mate outside from amongst other tribes, endogamy could easily endanger the purity of the caste. The widower could weaken the moral code by having illicit sexual relations with wives of other men or seek gratification by marrying somebody from outside the caste.

Although no religious or historical book gives any account of how the Brahmins succeeded in solving the problem, and thus maintained purity of their race, Ambedkar made his own interpretation and analysis and arrived at conclusions which cannot be contradicted by any argument[2], and seem to suggest what actually might have happened in the past. The Brahmins wanted to maintain the purity of their race at any cost. So they introduced the practice of burning their young widows on the funeral pyres of their deceased husbands. Thus began the practice of Sati in Hindu society. As this practice involved cruelty and could not be easily imposed in case the widow was past her prime and, therefore, could pose no danger either of corrupting the moral social code or contracting marriage from outside the tribe, the Brahmins must have allowed her to live degraded to a condition in which she could not easily corrupt anyone and pass her days in peace. Thus, it was most probably in this way that the Brahmins who sought to segregate themselves and resorted to endogamy, maintained the purity of their race and could solve the problem of surplus widows amongst them.

While they burnt their young widows, they could not do so in the case of widowers, young or old, mainly because from time immemorial man as compared to woman always has had the upper hand. But if he was allowed to remain single in society he could violate the social code of endogamy by picking up a wife from outside the class or engage in illicit relations with members of the opposite sex, within the Brahmin class. As imposition of celibacy on the widower could thus fail, it must have been thought proper that he could be provided with a wife only by recruiting a bride from the ranks of those not yet of marriageable age. This was the only option to tie him down to the group. And they resorted to it. Even if a girl was of very young age, she was married to a widower. Thus the Brahmins ensured that there was no numerical depletion from amongst their ranks through outflow from their class.

No religious treatise or history book mentions what happened to the other classes when the Brahmins decided to segregate themselves and maintain their purity. But the practice of burning young widows on the funeral pyres of their husbands became common even among Kshatriyas. This made Ambedkar conclude that they also adopted the same customs and practices which were favoured by Brahmins to maintain the purity of their race. And the widows who could pose no danger to the morals of the group were allowed to pass their days in a degraded condition. For the widowers, they adopted the same practices which were introduced by the Brahmins. The Brahmins being the highest caste were the trend setters as the Vaishayas and Shudras also followed suit and endogamy became a flourishing practice among the tribal societies of those days.

Ambedkar was not wrong in his conclusions. The practice of Sati continued uninterrupted until modern reformers like Raja Ram Mohan Rai came on the scene and the Governor–General William Bentinck banned it by law. Thanks to the hangover of the Sati custom, which continued in India for over 2,000 years, stories of widows being burnt on the funeral pyres of their husbands are sometimes reported by newspapers even to this day. Obviously, the practice of sending widows to Ashrams built close to the river ghats in Benares and several other holy places in the country started as a follow-up measure of the decisions taken by tribal societies to let the old widows live. In Bengal and several other states, where the Sati custom had acquired very hallowed traditions, the surviving widows were sent in unusually large numbers to live in Ashrams in holy places until they departed from this world. Even today large number of widows can be seen passing their days in Ashrams in Benares (now called Varanasi) and other holy places on the banks of rivers in India.

But the emergence of Brahmins as rulers following the end of the Maurayan empire and their overriding desire to maintain their superiority and racial purity ushered in an era of marked hostility among different castes. The Shudras became the worst sufferers, a fact confirmed and borne out by recorded history. Degeneration of social harmony was precipitated with the rigorous implementation of Manusmriti. Was it a divine occurrence, as Hindu priests and fundamentalists claim, or was Manu a scheming and calculating Brahmin who felt that the Brahmins would not be able to maintain their pre-eminent position merely on the basis of their knowledge of the Vedic lore unless something more concrete could be done to ensure their social superiority. He felt that the privileges enjoyed by the Brahmins due to the belief that they were created from the mouth of Prajapati must be codified. Anyone who violated the code should not only suffer excommunication from society but also come to grief in other ways. In short, punishment for violating social laws was to be such as to inspire awe and respect for the highest caste of Brahmins.

But who were the Shudras originally and how did they become the fourth Varna in the Indo-Aryan society before the promulgation of the Manusmriti? In an interesting book that he wrote, Ambedkar advanced a new hypothesis about the origin of the Shudras. He said contrary to the general impression that the Shudras were menials right from the period the Aryans and the other tribes arrived on the Indian subcontinent, they were originally part of the Kshatriya clan and thus having been created from the arms of the Prajapati were well versed in martial arts. After painstaking and exhaustive research, Ambedkar found that originally only three Varnas comprised the Indo-Aryan tribal society. These were Brahmins, Kshatriyas and Vaishyas. All the Shudras were part of the Kshatriya clan. They looked like Kshatriyas and were expert in warfare. But due to tribal rivalries, there were frequent clashes between the Brahmins and the Kshatriyas. In these encounters Brahmins often had to bite the dust or be on the run for they were not a martial tribe. However, in order to wreck vengeance on their oppressors, the priestly class of Brahmins stopped performing Upnayana ceremony for some sections of the Kshatriyas whom they regarded as their enemies. Gradually, the number of Kshatriyas who had not been sanctified by the Upnayana ceremony as ordained by the Vedas grew so large that they came to be identified as Shudras. Not purified by religious Mantras, they were forced to do menial jobs.

Manu set about making necessary provisions for ensuring Brahmin supremacy. He called Brahmins the "lords of the earth" and framed the law with such care that they shall remain so. The transformation of Varna into caste was the most stupendous and selfish task in which Brahmanism after its triumph became primarily engaged. Varna and caste, however, are not the same. Varna is not hereditary either in status or occupation. On the other hand caste implies a system in which status and occupation are hereditary and descend from father to son. The Manusmriti made the high status enjoyed by the Brahmins from ancient times the privilege of every Brahmin and his progeny without reference to merits or qualifications. To put it differently, the object was to elevate and ennoble every Brahmin, however mean and worthless he may be, to the high status occupied by them. It was a blatant attempt to ennoble the whole of the Brahmin community without exception. Manu knew that by making caste hereditary, even the most ignorant Brahmin will be elevated to the status occupied by the most learned, which was the aim of this attempt at ennoblement of the whole class of Brahmins.

The Hindu scheme of divine governance, as is claimed by priests and pujaris, according to Ambedkar, was enshrined in a written constitution in the Manusmriti, believed to be a sacred book and a divine Code which lays down the rules concerning governance of the religious, ritualistic and social life of the Hindus in minute detail. Thanks to the dominance of Brahmins not only because of their caste but also because of the fact that Manusmriti was conceived and propagated under Brahmin kings, this religious treatise came to be regarded as the Bible of Hindus, containing the philosophy of Hinduism.

But what Manusmriti preached and propagated divided the Hindu society into water-tight compartments. Earlier, under the Chaturvarnya system, the caste was determined by the worth of the person. Even if a lower caste man like a Shudra acquired the knowledge of Shastras, he could become a Brahmin. But Manusmriti changed all that. Now the caste could be determined only by birth. Whether any Brahmin knew the Vedas or not, he could enjoy the privileges granted to people of his caste. Howsoever good, talented and intelligent a Shudra might be, he would remain at the bottom of the social ladder, as ordained by Manu in the codification of castes in Manusmriti. This was an eye-opener for Ambedkar as he read these ancient books. No wonder armed with this knowledge, he saw no future for Untouchables in the Hindu society unless the caste system was abolished and the Manusmriti consigned to the dustbin.

As Ambedkar discovered in the Shastras, the laws of Manu relating to the status of the Shudras moulded the psychology of the Hindus. Manu laid down strict laws according to which Brahmins, Kshatriyas and Vaishyas could not dwell in a country where the rulers were Shudras. A Brahmin could never beg any property from a Shudra for performing a religious rite. All marriage ties with the Shudras were proscribed. Marriage with a woman belonging to any of the three other castes was forbidden. A Shudra was not to have any connection with a woman of the higher caste and an act of adultery committed by a Shudra with her was declared by Manu to be an offence deserving capital punishment. Even the provisions of the Criminal Procedure Code of the Government of India for dealing with social offenders pale before what Manusmriti had prescribed for them.

According to the ancient Hindu law code, a Shudra who had an intercourse with a woman of the higher caste, guarded or unguarded, was to be punished in the following manner. If she was unguarded, he escaped the offending part. If she was guarded then he was to be put to death and his property confiscated. A Brahmin who had neither studied nor performed any other act required by the Vedas could, at the King's pleasure, interpret the law to him, i.e. act as the judge, but not so a Shudra, howsoever learned he might be. The kingdom of a monarch who looked on while a Shudra settled the law must sink low like a cow in a morass. If a Shudra arrogantly presumed to preach religion to Brahmins, the king was to have burning oil poured in his mouth. A Brahmin was never to read the Vedas in the presence of the Shudras. No superfluous collection of wealth was to be made by a Shudra, even though he had the power to make it, since a servile man, who had amassed riches, was likely to become proud, and, by his insolence or neglect cause affront to Brahmins.

Ambedkar's flesh began to creep when he read the abhorrent provisions of the Manusmriti according to which a Shudra could have only one occupation: to serve meekly the other three castes – the Brahmins, the Kshatriya and the Vaishyas. If a Shudra unable to subsist by serving Brahmins sought a livelihood, he might serve the other two castes. The service of Brahmins alone was declared an excellent occupation for a Shudra as whatever else besides this he might perform would bear him no fruit in the next birth. If a Shudra refused to serve there was a provision for conscription in the Manusmriti. A Brahmin might compel a Shudra, whether bought or unbought, to do servile work; for he was created to be the slave of a Brahmin. Manu called upon Shudras to be always servile in their speech, humble in manner and lowly in conduct, surviving only on the leftovers of food from upper caste households. Could there be anything more degrading than the prescriptions of Manusmriti treated for over 2,000 years as divine charter governing the Hindu society?

Unless he was a tyrant who held all the population in subjugation, it cannot be imagined that Manu could have been allowed to dispense his patronage in this grossly unjust manner, wrote Ambedkar. It is a fact that the Varna system existed long before Manu. He was an upholder of the system and turned it into a sort of inflexible caste system as embodied in Manusmriti. But he could not have philosophized about it and ordained the present stratification of Hindu society. His work ended with the codification of existing caste rules and the preaching of the Caste Dharma. There is a strong belief in the minds of the orthodox Hindus that the Hindu society was somehow moulded into the framework of the caste system and that it is an organization consciously created by the Shastras which came to be written by Brahmins subsequently after Manu. Not only does that belief exist, it is being justified on the ground that it cannot but be good, because it is ordained by the Shastras and the Shastras cannot be wrong.

Ambedkar felt that due to the division of Hindu society into various castes, Brahmins have been the most inveterate enemy of the menial classes (the Shudras and the Untouchables) who together constitute about 80 per cent of the total Hindu population. If the common man belonging to the menial classes in India is today so fallen, so degraded, so devoid of hope and ambition, it is entirely due to the injunctions of Brahmins and their philosophy. The cardinal principles of this philosophy of Brahmanism are: (1) graded inequality between the different classes; (2) complete disarmament of the Shudras and the Untouchables; (3) complete prohibition of the education of the Shudras and the Untouchables; (4) ban on the Shudras and the Untouchables on occupying places of power and authority; (5) ban on the Shudras acquiring property; and (6) complete subjugation and suppression of women.

Ambedkar stated inequality is the official doctrine of Brahminism and the suppression of the lower classes aspiring to equality has always been their creed, and carried out by them without remorse as their bounden duty. There are many countries in this world where education did not spread much and most of the people there remained illiterate. But India is the only country where the intellectual class, namely, the Brahmins, not only made education their monopoly but also declared acquisition of education by the lower classes a crime punishable by cutting off their tongue, or by the pouring of molten lead into the ear of the offender. Having read about such monstrosities committed against the lower castes, no wonder Ambedkar wanted to annihilate the caste system.

In the olden days, the disarmament of the Shudras and the Untouchables was the rule of law promulgated by the Brahmins. Indeed, so strongly did the Brahmins believe in the disarmament of the Shudras and the Untouchables that when they revised the law to enable the Brahmins to arm themselves for the protection of their own privileges, they maintained the ban on the Shudras and the Untouchables, as was the case earlier. If the large majority of people of India appear today to be thoroughly emasculated, spiritless, and with no manliness, it is the result of the Brahminic policy of wholesale disarmament to which they have been subjected for over 2,000 years. There is no social evil and no social wrong to which the Brahmin does not give his support in order to perpetuate his supermacy. Man's inhumanity to man, such as the feeling of caste, Untouchability, unapproachability, etc. is a religion to the Brahmin.

According to Ambedkar, the Brahmin has also given his support to the worst wrongs that women have suffered in any part of the world. The Brahmin gave his fullest support to Sati, the burning alive of a widow. Widows were not allowed to remarry. Girls were required to be married before eight and the husband had the right to consummate the marriage at any time thereafter; whether she had reached puberty was immaterial. The record of the Brahmins as law-givers for the Shudras, the Untouchables and women, is the blackest as compared with the record of the intellectual classes in other parts of the world. For no intellectual class prostituted its intelligence to invent a philosophy to keep the uneducated countrymen in a perpetual state of ignorance and poverty as Brahmins had done in India.

Looking at his own life and the odium and hatred doled out daily not only to people of his own caste called Mahars but also all the castes collectively classified as Shudras, Ambedkar realized that Manusmriti was the worst social code. In retrospect, he could see that castes codified in this religious document could never work for the prosperity of India. He became acutely aware of the injustice done in India mainly as a result of Manusmriti which not only specified the kind of work people born in a particular caste could do but also spelt out severe punishments for those who violated the code. The caste system was not only a division of labour but also a division of labourers; it is a hierarchy in which the divisions of labourers are graded one above the other. In no other country exists the division of labour by this gradation of labourers. Social and individual efficiency requires us to develop the capacity of an individual to the point of competency to choose and make his own career. The caste system violated this principle insofar as it was an attempt to appoint tasks to individuals in advance, even before they are born.

The caste system will not allow Hindus to take up occupations suited to them if they do not belong to those occupations by heredity. If a Hindu is seen to starve rather than take to new occupations not assigned to his caste, the reason is to be found in the caste system. By not permitting readjustment of occupations not assigned to a caste in which one is born, the caste became the cause of much unemployment. The division of labour brought about by the caste-system is not a division based on choice. Individual sentiment or individual preference had no place in it. Based on the dogma of predestination, it is responsible for many problems faced by India in the past and by people in most of the backwards areas of the country even today. There are many occupations in India which, regarded as degraded by the Hindus, provoke those who are engaged in them to aversion. What efficiency can there be in a system under which neither the men's hearts nor their minds are involved in their work? As an economic factor caste is therefore a harmful institution, inasmuch as it involves the subordination of man's natural powers and inclinations to the constraints of social rules.

The caste-system cannot be said to have grown as a means of preventing the admixture of races or as a means of maintaining purity of blood. As a matter of fact, the caste system came into being long after the different races of India had commingled in blood and culture. To hold distinctions of caste or, in reality, distinctions of race, and to treat different castes as though they were so many different races is a gross perversion of facts. The caste-system is a social division of people of the same race. Assuming it, however, to be a case of racial division one may ask, what harm could there be if a mixture of races and of blood was permitted to take place in India by intermarriages between the different castes? Even scientists who believe in purity of races do not assert that the different races constitute different species of men. They are only varieties of one and the same species.

The caste-based Hindu social order as ordained by Manu is exactly what Hitler guided by the philosophy of Nietzsche wanted to create in Germany. Nietzsche's philosophy had become identified with the will to power, violence and denial of spiritual values, the idea of the superman and the sacrifice, servility and debasement of the common man. The Nazis traced their ancestry from Nietzsche and regarded him as their spiritual parent. Hitler had got himself photographed beside a bust of Nietzsche; he took the manuscripts of his philosophical master under his own special guardianship; extracts were chosen from Nietzsche's writing and loudly proclaimed at the ceremonies of Nazism, as the New German Faith. Nor was the claim by the Nazis of spiritual ancestry with Nietzsche denied by his near relations. Nietzsche's own cousin, Richard Ochler, approvingly said that Nietzsche's thought is Hitler in action and that Nietzsche was the foremost pioneer of the Nazi accession to power. In his book *Anti-Christ*, Nietzsche had plainly stated, among other things, that:[3] "When I read the law book of Manu, an incomparably intellectual and superior work, it would be a sin against the spirit even to mention it in the same breath with the Bible. You will guess immediately why; it has a genuine philosophy behind it; it is not merely an evil-smelling Jewish distillation of Rabbinism and superstition, it gives something to chew even to the most fastidious psychologist."

In a treatise on castes in India, Ambedkar wrote: "It is nothing but nonsense to talk about heredity and eugenics, in defence of the caste system. Few would object to the caste system if it was in accordance with the basic principle of eugenics because there can be no objection to the improvement of the race by judicious mating. But one fails to understand how the caste system secures judicious mating. Caste system is a negative thing. It merely prohibits persons belonging to different castes from intermarrying. It is not a positive method of selecting which two among a given caste should marry. If a caste is eugenic in origin then the origin of sub-castes must also be eugenic. But can any one seriously maintain that the origin of sub-caste is eugenic? If sub-castes cannot be eugenic in origin there cannot be any substance in the contention that caste is eugenic. And if caste is eugenic in origin one can understand the bar against intermarriage. Actually, caste has no scientific origin; those who are attempting to give it an eugenic basis are trying to support by science what is grossly unscientific. Professor Bateson in his "Mendel's Principles of Heredity" says: "There is nothing in the descent of the higher mental qualities to suggest that they follow any single system of transmission."

Just as a tree should be judged by the fruits it yields, the caste system should be judged by what it has done to the Hindu society, argued Ambedkar. Physically speaking, the Hindus are a race of pygmies and dwarfs stunted in stature and wanting in stamina. It is a nation nine-tenths of which is declared to be unfit for military service. This shows that the caste system does not support the eugenics of modern scientists. It is a social system which embodies the arrogance and selfishness of a perverse section of the Hindus who were superior enough in social status to set it in fashion and who had authority to force it on their inferiors. The fact is, caste cannot and has not improved the race. Of course, each caste is conscious of its existence and not only dines among itself and marries among itself, but each caste also prescribes its own distinctive dress. Caste has, however, done one thing. It has completely disorganized and demoralized the Hindus.

In Ambedkar's opinion, the Hindus conveniently forget that this anti-social spirit is the worst feature of their own caste system. One caste enjoys singing a hymn of hate against another caste as much as the Germans did in singing their hymn of hate against the English in the past. The literature of the Hindus is full of caste genealogies in which an attempt is made to give a noble origin to one caste and an ignoble origin to the other castes. The anti-social spirit is not confined to caste alone. It has gone deeper and has poisoned the mutual relations of the sub-castes as well. An anti-social spirit is found wherever one group's interests clash with and prevent it from full interaction with the other groups, so that its primary purpose is protection of what it has got. This anti-social spirit of protecting its own interests is as much a marked feature of the different castes in their isolation from one another as it is of a nation in their isolation. Often, the Brahmin's primary concern is to protect his interest against those of the non-Brahmins and the non- Brahmin's primary concern is to protect their interests against those of the Brahmins.

The Hindus are not merely an assortment of castes but they are so many warring groups each living for its local and its selfish interests. The present-day non-Brahmins cannot forgive the present-day Brahmins for the insult their ancestors gave to Shivaji. The Brahmin priests had declined to preside over the coronation of Shivaji, saying that he was a Shudra, who had never been sanctified by the Upnayana ceremony. The present-day Kayasthas will not forgive the present-day Brahmins for the infamy cast upon their forefathers by the forefathers of the latter. To what is this clash of interests due? Obviously to the caste system. The existence of caste and caste consciousness has served to keep the memory of past feuds between castes green and has prevented the necessary solidarity. Whatever Ambedkar wrote about castes is true even today. For instance, young boys and girls belonging to different castes have to pay with their lives if they fall in love and decide to marry, thanks to the mutual hostility of castes. Almost every week, such disgusting murders are taking place in backward areas still suffering from the stranglehold of the Manusmriti.

Thanks to the Hindu caste-system, about 13 million (now their number must be much more) continue to live in their primitive uncivilized state in a land which boasts of a civilization thousands of years old. They are wandering communities, moving about in search of a livelihood. Not only are they not civilized, some of them have pursuits which have led to their being classified as criminals. Many of the people living right in the midst of civilization are still in a savage state and are leading the life of hereditary criminals. But the Hindus have never felt ashamed of this fact. Why has no attempt ever been made to civilize the aborigines and to lead them to take to a more honourable way of making a living? Is caste his precious possession which he must save at any cost? It seems he can never agree to lose it by establishing contact with the aborigines.

The fact remains that the Hindu has let the savage remain a savage in the midst of his 'glorious' civilization without any feeling of shame or any sense of remorse mainly due to the caste-system. No wonder, tribals in large numbers are embracing Christianity as their religion. Cries raised by the Rashtriya Swamsevak Sangh workers against conversion of tribals in Chattisgarh or remote areas of the North-Eastern states make no sense when they themselves do nothing to win over the tribals and bring them into the Hindu fold. Poor and neglected aborigines surviving on the mercy of elements for generations tend to treat as messiahs all those who help them when they fall sick or when they starve because of the failure of their crops caused by the failure of seasonal rains. In some areas attempts are now underway to convert them to Islam. No wonder Islamic missionaries are also succeeding in swelling the ranks of their followers. It is a fact that several villages of the oldest living survivors of the Aryan race, living on the banks of the Indus, close to the line of control dividing India and Pakistan near Kargil in Ladakh are now Muslim pockets. The population of Muslims is going up at a faster rate than that of any other community in India. Already, Muslims in India outnumber Muslims in Pakistan.

The Hindu religion was also once a missionary religion, but ceased to indulge in proselytizing activities mainly when the caste system started dominating the society. Caste is inconsistent with conversion. To find a place for the convert in the social life of the community is another and a much more important problem that arises in connection with conversion. Where to place the convert, in what caste? Unlike in a club, the membership of a caste is not open to all and sundry. The law of caste confines its membership to persons born in the caste. Castes are autonomous and there is no authority anywhere to compel a caste to admit a new in to its fold. Hindu society being a collection of castes and each caste being a close corporation there is no place for a convert in it. Thus it is the caste-system which has prevented the Hindus from expanding and from absorbing other religious communities. So long as the caste-system prevails, the Hindu religion cannot become a missionary religion.

From where does the Sikh or the Mohammedan derive his strength which makes him brave and fearless whereas in contrast the Hindu often feels timid and coward? Answering this question Ambedkar says it is certainly not due to the strength arising out of the feeling that all Sikhs will come to the rescue of a Sikh when he is in danger and that all Mohammedans will do likewise in the case of a Muslim. The associated mode of life practiced by the Sikhs and the Mohammedans produces fellow-feeling. The associated mode of life of the Hindus does not to the same extent. So long as caste remains, there will be no social cohesiveness among Hindus and consequently the Hindus will remain socially fragmented.

Ambedkar felt that the Hindu claim that they are a very tolerant people is a misconception. On many occasions they can be extremely intolerant and if on some occasions they are tolerant that is, perhaps, because they are socially too weak and divided, or too indifferent, to oppose. Morris described Hindu society thus: "The great treading down the little, the strong beating down the weak, cruel men fearing not, kind men daring not, and wise men caring not." Why, indeed, is the Hindu so indifferent? Surely because of the caste-system which has made social cohesiveness and co-operation even for a good cause nearly impossible.

Among the Hindus, a caste has an unquestioned right to excommunicate any man who is guilty of breaking the rules of the caste. As excommunication involves a complete censure of social intercourse, as a form of punishment there is really little to choose between excommunication and death. No wonder individual Hindus have not had the courage to assert their independence by breaking the barriers of caste. This is because they cannot do without society. A caste is ever ready to take advantage of the helplessness of a man and insists upon complete conformity to its code in letter and spirit.

The names Brahmin, Kshatriya, Vaishya and Shudra, are names which are associated with a definite and fixed notion in the mind of every Hindu. The notion is that of a hierarchy based on birth. So long as these names continue, Hindus will continue to think of the Brahmin, Kshatriya, Vaishya and Shudra as hierarchical divisions of high and low, based on birth, and act accordingly. The Hindu must be made to unlearn all this, argues Ambedkar. But how can this happen if the old labels remain and continue to recall to mind old notions. If new notions are to be inculcated in the minds of people it is necessary to give them new names. To continue with the old name is to make the reform futile. To allow this Chaturvarnya system, based on birth and indicative of social divisions, is a snare.

According to Ambedkar the division of society on the basis of Chaturvarnya was as erroneous as the division of society into three classes in Plato's *Republic*. To Plato men fell by nature into three classes. In some individuals, he believed mere appetites dominated. He assigned them to the labouring and trading classes. Others, he found, had a courageous disposition, over and above their appetites. He classed them as defenders in war and the guardians of internal peace. Still others showed a capacity to grasp the universal reason underlying things. He made them the law-givers of the people. The criticism to which Plato's *Republic* is subject is also the criticism which must apply to the Chaturvarnya system, insofar as it also envisages the possibility of a precise classification of men into four distinct classes. The chief criticism of Plato is that his idea of lumping of individuals into a few sharply marked-off classes is a very superficial view of man and his powers. Plato had no perception of the uniqueness of every individual, of an individual's incommensurability with others, of each individual forming a class of his own.

Modem science has shown that lumping together of individuals into a few sharply marked off sections is a superficial view of man not worthy of serious consideration. Consequently, the utilization of the qualities of individuals is incompatible with their stratification by classes, since the qualities of individuals are so variable. The Chaturvarnya system may fail for the very same reason for which Plato's *Republic* must fail, namely because it is not possible to pigeonhole men into neat categories. That it is impossible to accurately classify people into four well-defined classes is proved by the fact that the original four classes have now become four thousand castes. Moreover, it would not be easy to maintain the system of Chaturvarnya, even supposing it was established. For the successful working of the Chaturvarnya system, there is the need for a penal system which could maintain it by its sanction. The system must perpetually face the problem of the transgressor. Unless there is a penalty attached to the act of transgression, men will not keep to their respective classes. Being contrary to human nature, the whole system will thus eventually break down.

No wonder Ambedkar came to realize that there is no code of laws more infamous regarding social rights than the Laws of Manu. There have been social revolutions in other countries of the world. Why have there not been social revolutions in India? There is only one answer. The lower classes of Hindus have been completely disabled for direct action on account of this wretched system of Chaturvarnya. They were ploughmen, or rather condemned to be ploughmen, and they never were allowed to convert their ploughshare into sword. On account of the Chaturvarnya system, they were deprived of any education. They could not find the way to their salvation. They were condemned to be lowly and not knowing the way of escape and not having the means of escape, they became reconciled to eternal servitude, which they accepted as their inescapable fate.

Ambedkar knew that there cannot be a more degrading system of social organization than the Chaturvarnya. It is a system which deadens, paralyses and cripples the people from helpful activity. There is no exaggeration. History bears ample evidence of this. There is only one period in Indian history which is a period of freedom, greatness and glory: the period of the Mauryan Empire. At all other times the country suffered from defeat and darkness. But the Mauryan period was a period when the Chaturvaryna system was completely annihilated, when the Shudras, who constituted the mass of the people, came into their own and became the rulers of the country. As against this the period of defeat and darkness is the period when Chaturvarnya flourished to the damnation of the greater part of the people of the country.

The strength of a society depends upon the presence of points of contact, possibilities of interaction between different group which exist in it. But the ties which make people hold together are non-existent in Hindu society. There is no integrating force among the Hindus to counteract the disintegration caused by caste. While among the non-Hindus there are plenty of these organic filaments which bind them together. Although there are castes even among the non-Hindus, as there are among the Hindus, but caste has not the same social significance for the non-Hindus. A Mohmmedan or a Sikh, if asked who they are, could tell you that he is a Mohammedan or a Sikh as the case may be. He does not tell you his caste although he has one. But if a person tells you that he is a Hindu, you feel bound to inquire into his caste. Because so essential is caste in the case of a Hindu that without knowing it you do not feel sure what sort of a being he is. Religion compels the Hindus to treat isolation and segregation of castes as a virtue, but it does not compel the non-Hindus to take the same attitude towards caste.

What is really wrong with people in India, Ambedkar felt, is their Hindu religious system, which has inculcated and thus perpetuated this notion of caste. Today, there are not only four castes – Brahmins, Kshatriyas, Vaisyas and Shudras – but many many more of them. What is the origin of this phenomenon, according to the Hindu law giver, Manu, who says leaving aside the four original castes the rest are simply baseborn! They are the progeny of fornication and adultery between men and women of the four original castes. The immorality and looseness of character among men and women of the four original castes must have been limitless to account for the rise of innumerable castes consisting of innumerable souls! Manu makes the wild allegation without stopping to consider what aspersions he is casting upon men and women of the four original castes. In his mad lust for debasing different castes by ascribing to them an ignoble origin, Manu seems deliberately to pervert historical facts. Giving his interpretation of this phenomenon, Ambedkar wrote that Manu was bent on debasing the whole Chaturvarnya system. One wonders why, while religion everywhere else was engaged in the task of raising and ennobling mankind, Hinduism was busy debasing and degrading it.

According to the Laws of Manu, Brahmins, Kshatriyas and Vaishyas can study the Vedas. But the Shudras can neither study the Vedas nor can be allowed even to hear it read. Manu is the only divine law giver who has denied the common man the right to knowledge. Unfortunately the prohibition against the study of the Vedas for the mass of the people gave rise to illiteracy and ignorance in secular life. Those who had no right to study the Vedas were deprived of the right to read and write. It can be rightly said that according to the laws of Manu reading and writing became the privilege of the high class few, and illiteracy became the destiny of the low class many. Thus thanks to the caste system ordained for it by Manu, Hinduism, far from encouraging the spread of knowledge, became a gospel of darkness. Taking these facts into consideration it is easy to see how. Hinduism is opposed to the conditions in which liberty can thrive and is thus a denial of liberty.

Criticizing and ridiculing people for not inter-dining or inter-marrying or only occasionally holding inter-caste dinners and celebrating inter-caste marriages, is a futile method of achieving the desired end. Ambedkar wrote that the real remedy was to destroy the belief in the sanctity of the Shastras. How do you expect to succeed, if you allow the Shastras to continue to mould the beliefs and opinions of the people? Not to question the authority of the Shastras, to permit the people to believe in their sanctity and their sanctions and to blame them and to criticize them for their acts as being irrational and inhuman is an incongruous way of carrying on social reform. Reformers working for the removal of Untouchability do not realize that the acts of people are merely the result of their beliefs inculcated upon their minds by the Shastras and that people will not change their conduct until they cease to believe in the sanctity of the Shastras on which their conduct is founded.

It is no use seeking refuge in quibbles. It is no use telling people that the Shastras do not say what they believed them to say, grammatically read or logically interpreted. What matters is how the Shastras have been understood by the people. One must take the stand that Buddha took or Guru Nanak took. One must not only discard the Shastras, deny their authority, as did Buddha and Nanak. You must have courage to tell the Hindus that what is wrong with them is their religious system which has inculcated in them this notion of the sacredness of the caste-system.

Ambedkar emphasized that the destiny of a country depends upon its intellectual class. But intellectual class in India is simply another name for the Brahmin caste, which has regarded itself the custodian of the its own caste interest, rather than that of the country. All this is indeed very regrettable. Brahmins, who form the intellectual class of the Hindus, are held in great reverence by the rest of the Hindus. The Hindus were taught that the Brahmins are Bhudevas (Gods on earth). The person of the Brahmin was thought to be sacred. As a sacred person he had immunities and privileges which were denied to the servile class. He was entitled to the first fruits. As Ambedkar points out in Malabar, where the Sambandham marriage prevails, the servile classes, such as the Nairs, regard it an honour to have their females kept as mistresses by Brahmins. There was a time when no person of the servile class could take his food without drinking the water in which the toes of the Brahmins were washed.

Sir P.C Ray once described how in his childhood, rows of children belonging to the servile classes used to stand for hours together in the morning on the roadside in Calcutta with cups of water in their hands waiting for a Brahmin to pass, ready to wash his feet and take the water to their parents waiting to sip it before taking their food. Under the British rule, though the immunities and privileges of the Brahmins ceased to exist. Yet, the advantages they enjoyed still remain and the Brahmin is still pre-eminent and sacred in the eyes of the servile classes, still addressed by them as "Swami" or 'Lord".

Writing about the social conditions, Ludovico Di Varthema, the traveller, who came to India in the middle of the 16th century and visited Malabar, stated: "It is proper and at the same time a pleasant thing to know who these Brahmins are. You must know that they are the chief persons of the faith, as priests are among us. And when the king takes a wife he selects the most worthy and the most honoured of these Brahmins and make him sleep the first night with his wife, in order that he may deflower her. Do not imagine that the Brahmin goes willingly to perform this operation. The king is obliged to pay him four hundred to five hundred ducats." Another traveller, Hamilton, in his *Account of the East Indies* says: "When the Samorin marries, he must not cohabit with his bride till the Nambourie (Nambudri) or chief priest, has enjoyed her, and if he pleases he may have three nights of her company, because the first fruits of her nuptials must be a holy oblation to the God she worships and some of the nobles are so complacent as to allow the clergy the same tribute."

Ambedkar was candid enough to say that when an intellectual class, which holds the rest of the community in its firm grip, is opposed to the reform of the caste-system, the chances of success in a movement for the break-up of the nefarious system appear very remote. The caste-system divides men into separate communities in a graded order, one above the other, in social status. Each caste takes pride and consolation in the fact that within the scale of castes it is above some other caste. As an outward mark of this gradation, there is also a gradation of social and religious rights technically spoken of an Ashtakhikaras and Sanskaras. The higher the grade of the caste, the greater the number of these rights and the lower the grade, the lesser their number.

In Hindu social system all are slaves of the caste-system. But all the slaves are not equal in status. To excite the proletariat to bring about an economic revolution, Karl Marx said: "You have nothing to lose except your chains." But the artful way in which the social and religious rights are distributed among the different castes whereby some have more and some less, makes the slogans of Karl Marx quite useless to excite the Hindus against the caste-system. Castes form graded system of sovereignties, high and low, which are jealous of their status and which know that if a general dissolution came, some of them stand to lose more of their prestige and powers than others do.

But can Hindus use reason to discard the caste-system? Manusmriti lays down sanctions to which every Hindu must conform in matters of behaviour. Here there is no place for reason to play its part. A Hindu must follow either Veda, Smriti, or Sadachar. He cannot follow anything else. According to Manu, rationalism as a canon of interpreting the Vedas and Smritis is absoluately condemned. Thus, where a matter is covered by the Veda or the Smriti, a Hindu cannot resort to rational thinking. Even when there is a conflict between the Vedas and the Smritis on matters on which they have given a positive injunction, the solution is not left to reason. Both are to be regarded as of equal authority. When there is a conflict between Shruti and Smriti, the Shruti must prevail.' Caste and Varna are matters which are dealt with by the Vedas and the Smritis and consequently, appeal to reason can have no effect on a Hindu. All around there are fetters on the reasoning faculty of the Hindus. Actually, the Shastras have given caste a perpetual lease of life and have smothered reflective thought which would have otherwise led to destruction of the notion of caste.

Ambedkar further believed that the Hindu religion as contained in the Vedas and Smritis, is nothing but a mass of sacrificial, social political and sanitary rules and regulations, all mixed up. What is called religion by the Hindus is nothing .but a multitude of commands and prohibitions. Religion, in the sense of spiritual principles, truly universal, applicable to all races, to all countries, to all times, is not to be found in them, and if it is, it does not form the governing part of a Hindus's life. That for a Hindu, Dharma means commands and prohibitions is clear from the way the word Dharma is based on the Vedas and the Smritis and understood by the commentators. The word Dharma as used in the Vedas in most cases generally means religious ordinances or rites. To put it in plain language, what the Hindus call religion is really a formidable set of laws or at best legalized class-ethics. It would be wrong to call this code of ordinances as religion. In it there is no loyalty to ideals, only conformity to commands. But the worst aspect of this code of ordinances is that the law it contains must remain unchanged forever. They are iniquitous also in that they are not the same for one class as for another.

The pertinent question raised by Ambedkar is how can humanity endure this code of eternal laws, without being cramped and crippled forever? It is only when the minds of the people are cleared of this misconception and realization dawns on them that what they are given as religion is not religion but only a set of laws, that there will be calls for its amendment or abolition. So long as people look upon it as religion they will not be ready for a change, because the idea of religion is, generally speaking, not associated with the idea of change. But the idea of law always admits of change and when people truly realize that what is called religion is only a set of law, old and archaic, they will be ready for a change, because people know and accept that law is continually subject to change.

Ambedkar was of the view that once ancient rules of life are annulled, their place shall be taken by a religion of principles, which alone can lay claim to being a true religion. He listed the cardinal items in the new religion as follows: (1) There should be only one and a standard book of Hindu religion, acceptable to all Hindus and recognized by all Hindus. All other books of Hindu religion such as Vedas, Shastra and Puranas, which are treated as sacred and authoritative must by law cease to be so and the preaching of any doctrine, religious or social, contained in these books should be penalised. (2) Prieshood among Hindus should be abolished. But as this seems to be impossible, the priesthood must at least cease to be hereditary. Every person who professes to be a Hindu must be eligible for being a priest. It should be provided by law that no Hindu shall be entitled to be priest unless he has passed an examination prescribed by the state and holds a sanad from the State permitting him to practice pristhood. (3) No ceremony performed by a priest who does not hold a sanad shall be deemed to be valid in law and it should be made penal for a person who has no sanad to officiate as a priest. (4) A priest should be the servant of the state and should be subject to the disciplinary action by the State in matters of his morals, beliefs and worship, in addition to his being subject along with other citizens to the ordinary law of the land. (5) The number of priests should be limited, according to the requirements of the state. All this must be aimed to check abuses of the religious institutions.

At present the profession of a Hindu priest is the only profession which is not subject to any code. A priest may be mentally or physically suffering from a disease, morally he may be a wreck; but he is always found fit to perform at solemn ceremonies, to enter the sanctum sanotorum of a Hindu temple and worship the Hindu god. All this becomes possible because for a priest it is enough to be born in a priestly caste. The whole thing is extremely irrational and is due to the fact that the priestly class among Hindus is subject neither to any code of conduct nor to morality. It recognizes no duties. It gives only rights and privileges. The priestly class must be brought under control by some such legislation. Only then can people be saved from mischief and misguidance. Ambedkar is fully justified in suggesting imposition of controls on priesthood because quite often these so-called intermediaries of God are found indulging in moral turpitude.

Ambedkar wrote the Hindus must examine their religion and morality in terms of their survival value. They must consider whether they should keep worshipping the past as that is not likely to help us to understand the present. A knowledge of the past and its heritage is of great significance when it revitalizes the present, but not otherwise. And the mistake of making the ruins and remains of the past the main material of education in the present is that it tends to make the past a mirror for the present and the present a rather futile imitation of the past. The Hindus must consider whether the time has not come for them to recognize that there is nothing fixed, nothing eternal, nothing sanatan; that everything is changing, and change is the law of life for individuals as well as for the society. In a changing society, there must be an ongoing revolution of old values and the Hindus must realize that there must be standards to measure the acts of men, as there must be a readiness to revise those standards.

The contemptuous treatment meted out to him was the driving force for Ambedkar to dig into the roots of the Hindu society, which is one of the oldest civilizations of the world, claiming linkage to the great Aryan invaders, who many historians believe ventured across Europe to seek their fortune in the Indian subcontinent over 2,500 years ago. Ambedkar could not bear such social inequalities as bestowed the status of a superman on the Brahmins and condemned the Shudras as nothing but virtual slaves born to do menial tasks. Questions are being raised about whatever he wrote regarding Chaturvarnya system governing the graded inequality of the Hindu social order. Some of the pseudo-intellectuals have gone to the extent of saying that Ambedkar was a British puppet conveniently used by colonial rulers to run down India. Nothing could be more monstrous than this lie.

In his pamphlet on the "Annihilation of Caste," Ambedkar said: "The effect of caste on the ethics of the Hindus is simply deplorable. Caste has killed public spirit. Caste has destroyed the sense of public charity. Caste has made public opinion impossible. A Hindu's public is his caste. His loyalty is restricted only to his caste. Virtue has become caste-ridden and morality has become caste-bound. There is no sympathy to the deserving. There is no appreciation of the meritorious. There cannot be a more degrading system of social organization than the Chaturvarnya. It is a system which deadens, paralyses and cripples the people from vital activity. The Hindus observe caste not because they are inhuman or wrong-headed. They observe caste because they are deeply religious. Hence, the enemy, one must grapple with, is not the people who observe caste, but the Shastras which teach them this religion of caste. Therefore, the real remedy is to destroy the belief in the sanctity of the Shastras."

Ambedkar further stressed: "Make every man and woman free from the thralldom of the Shastras. The Hindu religion, as contained in the Vedas and the Smritis, is nothing but a mass of sacrificial, social, political and sanitary rules and regulations, all mixed up; it is nothing but a multitude of commands and prohibitions. And the worst part of this code of ordinances is that the laws it contains are iniquitous in that they are not the same for one class as for another. But this inequity is made perpetual in that they are prescribed to be the same for all generations. Such a religion must be destroyed." "The Annihilation of Caste" was logic on fire, pinching and pungent, piercing and fiery, provocative and explosive. After reading it, Mahatma Gandhi said: "Ambedkar is a challenge to Hinduism."

References

1. The quotation is on page 269, Vol. 3 of Ambedkar's Writings and Speeches published by Maharashtra Government in 1987. Ambedkar has been taken the quotation from Shastri's book, Buddhistic, Studies, page 820, Chapter XXXIV.
2. Annhilation of Caste in Vol. I of Ambedkar's Writings and Speeches Published by Maharashtra government in 1987.

6

Aryan Society

Ambedkar had grown up in a religious environment. Every morning his parents would bow with folded hands before idols of gods in the Hindu pantheon placed on a raised platform and ask their children to do likewise. His father, Ramji Maloji Sakpal, who had retired as a Subedar-Major, brought to bear upon his family the discipline of barracks insofar as worship of the gods was concerned. He would sing devotional songs of Kabir and the great saints of Maharashtra, recite from the great epics, the Ramayana and the Mahabharata. He would expect his children to sing all that he had intoned day after day and in case they forgot the lines or fumbled, he would punish them. With bells ringing, conch-shell blowing and incense burning when religious hymns praising gods were sung, the house looked like a temple. No wonder, exposure to so much devotion to gods early in life made Ambedkar religious-minded.

But in spite of the devotion of his parents to gods and his own ardent desire to do whatever his father told him about worship of idols, he was saddened to note that he could not enter any temple outside his house. The upper castes would bar his entry, would not tolerate even his presence and the presence of any other Shudra even in the shadow of a Hindu holy place. Brahmin priests would not deign to bless him if he wanted to make an offering to gods. He could worship gods only in his own house. After saying prayers before idols, he would become more determined possibly with the blessing of the gods he had worshipped to attain whatever he had set his sights on.

The attitude of the upper castes against entry into temples by Shudras pained him. Sometimes, he and his friends had to listen to harangues by priests or caste Hindus that gods themselves had forbidden Shudras not to pollute them by their entry into the holy precincts. Was it really so? All this made him plunge into a deep study of the Vedas and Shastras to find out if gods and other celestial personages mentioned in the epics his father was so fond of reading really treated Shudras the way caste Hindus were doing now. He made a thorough study of the Hindu mythology and arrived at conclusions which were nothing but anathema to the upper castes. No wonder, there were few takers for the book he wrote, Riddles in Hinduism. He had not made any guesses or jumped to conclusions which could not be justified by close examination of what he found in the Vedas and Shastras about gods and the life of the Aryan society in the olden times.

Reading the old texts and manuscripts and going through the books written by scholars, Ambedkar found the Brahmins had always maintained that the Hindu civilization was Sanatan, that is, unchanging. Some European scholars had also concurred with this view. On the basis of what he himself had read and found in the ancient books and treatises, he was convinced that the perception of scholars who said that the Hindu society was unchanging was not borne out by facts. The truth was that the Brahmins had changed and chopped scriptures in accordance with their own whims and fancies the underlying purpose of which was to project themselves as the highest caste and virtual arbiters of Hindu society. Since they were at the apex of the caste pyramid governing Hindu society, their word was always the law. There was time when they worshipped the Vedic gods. Then came a time when they abandoned their Vedic gods and started worshipping non-Vedic gods. One may well ask them – where is Indra, where is Varuna, where is Brahma, where is Mitra – the gods mentioned in the Vedas. They seldom figured in the sermons the priests gave.

The religious literature of the Hindus included (1) The Vedas, (2), The Brahmanas, (3) The Aranyakas, (4) Upanishads, (5) Sutras, (6) Itihas, (7) Smritis and (8) Puranas. At one time these reiligious books occupied the same status; there was no distinction of superior or inferior, sacred or profane, fallible or infallible. However, later on the Vedic Brahmins proclaimed the Vedas not only superior to other classes of literature but also sacred and infallible. The Upanishads are also called Vedanta, which has got two meanings. In one sense, it means the last parts of the Vedas. In the second sense, it means the essence of the Vedas. The word Vedanta being another name for the Upanishads, the Upanishads have come to acquire these meanings.

The Hindu theology regarding the world is based upon the doctrine of Trimurti. According to this doctrine, the world undergoes three stages. It is created, preserved and destroyed. The three functions which comprise the cycle are discharged by three Gods - Brahma, Vishnu and Mahesh. Brahma creates the world, Vishnu preserves and Mahesh destroys it for the purpose of creation. These gods are spoken of as forming what is called Trimurti. Unlike members of other religions, Hindus worship not one but many gods. The existence of so many gods is due to the fact that the Hindu society has been formed by the conglomeration of many tribes and many communities each of whom had their own separate gods.

Some Hindus are monotheists, some are polytheists and some are pantheists. Even those Hindus who are monotheists are not worshippers of the same gods. Some worship Vishnu, some Shiva, some Ram, some Krishna.

Some do not worship the male gods. They worship goddesses. Even they do not worship the same goddesses. They worship different goddesses. Some worship Kali, some Parvati, some Laxmi. A Hindu will fast on Shivaratri, because it is sacred to lord Shiva. He will fast on Ekadashi day because it is sacred to Vishnu. He will plant a Bel tree because it is sacred to Shiva and he will plant a Tulsi because it is dear to Vishnu. Maybe all this is a legacy of tribal customs for each tribe had its own totem to worship.

Although the Hindu pantheon has the largest number of gods, most of the Hindu temples have idols of only four gods. They are Shiva, Vishnu, Ram and Krishna. At the time of the Rig Veda, there were innumerable gods the Hindus worshipped. At least at two places, the Rig Veda speaks of three thousand three hundred and nine gods. However, with the passage of time the number of gods Hindus worshipped came down to thirty-three. There is a verse in Rig Veda, which seems to suggest that these thirty-three gods were divided for purposes of honours and precedence into two classes, one being great and small and the other being young and old. This view seems to be against an earlier interpretation, also contained in the Rig Veda, which said

"None of you O Gods ! is small
or young; You are all great."

Quoting Prof. Max Muller, who had done extensive study of Hindu Shastras, Ambedkar said:" When these individual gods are invoked, they are not conceived as limited by the power of others, as superior or inferior in rank. Each god is to the mind of the supplicants as good as all the gods. He is felt, at the time, as a real divinity, as supreme and absolute, in spite of the necessary limitations which, to our mind, a plurality of gods must entail on every single god. All the rest disappear for a moment from the vision of the poet, and he only, who is to fulfill their desires, stands in full light before the eyes of the worshipper. Nowhere is any of the Gods represented as the slave of others."

A change seems to have come in the old angle of vision towards the gods. For one finds numerous hymns of the Vedas in which some gods are represented as supreme and absolute. In the first hymns of the second Mandala, Agni is called the ruler of the universe, the lord of men, the wise king, the father, the brother, the son, the friend of many; nay, all the powers and names of the others are distinctly ascribed to Agni. Then a second god came to be elevated above Agni; he is Indira. Indira is spoken of as the strongest god in the hymns as well as in the Brahmanas, and the burden of the one of the songs of the Tenth Book of the Vedas is: Visavasmad Indira Uttarah (Indira is greater than all.) Then, according to the writings in the Vedas, the god at the highest level is Soma. He was not only the maker of heaven and earth, but also of gods – Agni, Surya, Indira and Vishnu. Then Soma was forgotten and a fourth god, Varuna, was elevated to the highest position.

In no other religion, gods were elevated and then ignored as happened in the Hindu mythology. The more Ambedkar studied the ancient books, the more he was stunned to learn about the morals of the early Aryans and their gods and goddesses. Nothing summed up the inter-relation between gods better than the story of the birth of the god Dattatraya. One afternoon when Saraswati, Laxmi and Parvati, the wives of Brahma, Vishnu and Mahesh respectively, were sitting together, chit-chatting, Narada, the sage on eternal tour in the mythology, came to visit them. In the course of the conversation a question arose as to who was the most chaste woman in the land. Narada held out that Anusuya, the wife of rishi Atri as the purest and most chaste woman . This was violently disputed by the three, each one of whom claimed to have that title. Narada disproved their claim by recounting the many acts of adultery which each one of them was guilty of. They were silenced but they became very angry. They wanted to retrieve their position vis-à-vis Anusuya. In their wisdom they decided that the only way by which this could be done was to have Anusuya seduced to illicit intercourse.

In accordance with a plan of action they had made, they told their husbands when they returned in the evening what Narada had said about them and scolded them by saying that they were the cause of their wives' humiliation. For if they had committed adultery with Anusuya she and they would have been on the same level and Narada would not have found cause to humiliate them. They asked their husbands whether they cared for wives and if they did they were duty bound to proceed forthwith to invade the chastity of Anusuya and to pull her down from the high pedestal of purity and chastity on which Narada had placed her. The gods were convinced that what was suggested by their wives was their duty and therefore they could not shirk the task.

It was against this background that the three gods started on an expedition to rob Anusuya of her honour and marched on to the hutment of rishi Atri. The three gods disguised themselves as three Brahmin mendicants. When they arrived Atri was away. But Anusuya welcomed them and prepared food for them. When it was ready she asked them to sit and partake of the meal. The three gods replied that they would take food at her house only if she agreed to serve them food in a naked condition. Bowing to the rule of hospitality in ancient India that Brahmin guest must not depart dissatisfied, Anusuya agreed to disrobe and serve them naked. While she was serving food to them in this naked condition, rishi Atri arrived. Lest he should be aghast to see his wife nude before Brahmin guests, the three gods took the form of new born babes. The three gods in the form of babes were placed by Atri in a cradle. In the cradle, their bodies having become integrated into one and their heads having remained separate there arose god Dattatraya who, as the mythology says, has one body and three heads representing the three gods – Brahma, Vishnu and Mahesh.

The story had a stink of immorality in it. It may have been deliberately designed by Brahmin priests so as to cover the actual fact of Brahma, Vishnu and Mahesha having outraged Anusuya to lower her down to the level of their wives. Be that as it may, the story illustrates the view once prevalent among the Hindus that three gods - Brahma, Vishnu and Mahesh - were co-equal in status and their functions were complementary and not competitive. They were spoken of as forming Trimurti – three in one and one in three, all sustaining the world: Brahma by creating it, Vishnu by preserving it and Shiva (another name of Mahesh) by destroying it. But the state of harmony did not last long. The Brahmins who were the propagandists of these three Gods divided themselves into three camps, each becoming devoted to one to the exclusion of the other two. The result of this was a systematic campaign of vilification and degradation by the Brahmins devoted to one god of the other gods.

Ambedkar was stunned to discover that the religion of the Vedic Aryans was full of barbaric and obscene practices. Human sacrifice formed a part of their religion and was called Naramedhayagna. Most elaborate descriptions of the rite are found in the Yajur Veda Samhita, Yajur-Veda Brahmanas, the Sankhyana and Vaitana Sutras. The worship of genitals or what is phallus worship was quite prevalent among the ancient Aryans. The cult of the phallus came to be known as Skambha and was recognized as part of Aryan religion as may be found in the hymns in Atharva Veda X 7. Another instance of obscenity which disgraced the religion of the ancient Aryans is connected with the Ashvamedha Yajna or the horse sacrifice. A necessary part of the Ashvamedha was the introduction of the Sepas (penis) of the Medha (dead horse) into the Yoni (vagina) of the chief wife of Yajamana by the Brahmin priests. A Mantra in Vajasaneya Samhita (xxiii. 18) shows that there used to be a competition among the queens as to who was to receive this high honour of being served by the horse.

The Aryan community was steeped in the worst kind of debauchery. Gambling had become as widespread as drinking. Every king had a hall of gambling attached to his palace and had an expert gambler in his employment as a companion to play with. King Virat had in his employment Kank as an expert gambler. Gambling was not merely a pastime with kings. They played with heavy stakes. King Nal staked everything in gambling and lost whatever he had. The only thing he did not stake was himself and his wife Damayanti. Nala had to go and live in the forest as a beggar. There were kings who went beyond Nala. The Mahabharat tells how Dharma the eldest of the Pandavas gambled and staked everything, his brothers and also his and their wife Draupadi. Gambling was a matter of honour with the Aryans and any invitation was regarded as an injury to one's honour and dignity and therefore had to be accepted whatever consequences might follow. Not only gambling, even drinking and debauchery was widespread.

No wonder, trying to practice what their gods exhibited as lofty ideals and deeds, the morals of the ancient Aryans degenerated. That the Aryans were a race of gamblers is brought out stunningly by what happens in the

Mahabharata. Actually, gambling was developed by them into a science in very early days so much so that they had even devised the dices and given them certain technical terms. The luckiest dice was called Krit and the unluckiest was called Kali. Treta and Dwapara were intermediate between them. Not only was gambling well developed among ancient Aryans they did not play without stakes. They gambled with such abandon that there is really no comparison with their spirit of gambling. Kingdoms and even wives were offered as stakes, as witnessed in the Mahabharata. King Nala staked his kingdom and lost it. The Pandvas went much beyond. They not only staked their kingdom but they also staked their wife, Draupadi, and lost both. Gambling was not the game of the rich those days, as is the case in Indian society now. It was a vice of the many.

Drinking too was very common. Wine formed a most essential part of their religion. The Vedic gods drank wine. The divine wine was called Soma. Since the gods of the Aryans drank wine, the Aryans had no scruples in the matter of drinking. Indeed to drink it was a part of an Aryan's religious duty. There were so many Soma sacrifices among the ancient Aryans that there were hardly any days when Soma was not drunk. Soma was restricted to only the three upper classes, namely, the Brahmins, the Kshatriyas and the Vaishyas. That does not mean the Shudras were abstainers. Those who were denied Soma drank Sura which was ordinary, unconsecrated wine sold in the market. Not only the male Aryans were addicted to drinking the females also indulged in it. The Kaushitaki Grihya Sutra 1.11.12 advises that four or eight women who are not widowed, after having been regaled with wine and food should be called to dance for four times on the night previous to the wedding ceremony. This habit of drinking intoxicating liquor was not confined to the non-Brahmin women. Even Brahmin women were addicted to it. Drinking was not a sin, nor a vice. It was quite a respectable practice.

The Rig Veda says:

"Worshipping the Sun before drinking Madira (wine)."

The Yajur Veda says:

"Oh, Deva Soma! Being strengthened and invigorated by Sura sacrificer and vigour to Brahmanas and Kshatriyas."

The Mantra Brahmana says:

"By which women have been made enjoyable by men, and by which water has been transformed into wine (for the enjoyment of men), etc."

That Rama and Sita both drank wine is admitted by Ramayana. Uttar Khand says:

"Like Indira in the case of (his wife) Shachi, Rama Chandra made Sita drink purified honey- made wine.

Servants brought for Ram Chandra Meat and sweet fruits."

So did Krishna and Arjuna.

In the Udyoga Parva of the Mahabharata, Sanjaya says:

"Arjuna and Shri Krishna drinking wine made from honey

And being sweet-scented and garlanded, wearing splendid clothes and ornaments, sat on a golden throne studded with various jewels. I saw Shri Krishna's feet on Arjuna's lap, and Arjuna's feet on Draupadi and Satyabhama's lap."

In the beginning there was no law of marriage among the Aryans. It was a state of complete promiscuity both in the higher and lower classes of the society. There was no such thing as a question of prohibited degrees as the following instances will show: Brahma married his own daughter Satarupa. Their son was Manu, the founder of the Pruthu dynasty which preceded the rise of the Aiksvakas and Ailas. Hiranyakashu married his daughter Rohini. Other cases of fathers marrying daughters are Vashishtha and Shatrupa, Janhu and Jannhavi, and Surya and Usha. That such marriages between fathers and daughters were common is indicated by the usage of recognizing Kanin son. Kanin sons mean sons born to unmarried daughter. They were in law the sons of the father of the girl. There must be son begotten by the father on his own daughter.

Reading of Indian mythology enlightens one about the stories of father and son cohabiting with the same woman. Manu is the son of Brahma and Satarupa is his mother. This Satarupa is also the wife of Manu. Another case is that of Shradha. She is the wife of Vivasvat. Their son is Manu. But Shradha is also the wife of Manu thus indicating the practice of father and sons sharing a woman. It was open for a person to marry his brother's daughter. Dharma married ten daughters of Daksha though Daksha and Dharma were brothers. One could also marry his uncle's daughter as did Kasyapa who married thirteen wives all of whom were the daughters of Daksha and Daksha was the brother of Kasyapa's father Marichi. The case of Yama and Yami mentioned in the Rig Veda is a notorious case, which throws light on the question of marriages between brothers and sisters. Because Yama refused to cohabit with Yami, it must not be supposed that such marriages did not exist.

The Adi Parva of the Mahabharata gives a geneology which begins from Brahmadeva. According to this geneology Brahma had three sons, Marichi, Daksha and Dharma and one daughter whose name the geneology unfortunately does not give. In this very geneology it is stated that Daksha married the daughter of Brahma who was his sister and had a vast number of daughters variously estimated as being between 50 and 60. Other instances of marriages between brothers and sisters could be cited. They are Pushan and his sisters Acchoda and Amavasu. Purukutsa and Narmada, Viprachiti and Simhika, Nahusa and Viraja, Sukra-Usanas and Gao, Amsumat and Yasoda, Dasaratha and Kausalya, Rama and Sita, Suka and Pivari, Draupadi and Prasti are all cases of brothers marrying sisters.

There was no bar against son cohabiting with his mother. There is the case of Pushan and his mother, Manu and Satrupa and Manu and Shradha. There were two other interesting cases of Arjuna and Urvashi and Arujuna and Uttara. Uttara was married to Abhimanyu, son of Arjuna when he was barely 16. Uttara was associated with Arjuna. He taught her music and dancing. Uttara is described as being in love with Arjuna and the Mahabharata speaks of them getting married as a natural sequel to their love affair. The Mahabharata does not say that they were actually married but if they were, then Abhimanyu can be said to have married his mother. The Arjuna- Urvasi episode is more positive in its indication. Indra was the real father of Arjuna. Urvashi was the mistress of Indira and therefore in the position of a mother to Arjuna. She was a tutor to Arjuna and taught him music and dancing.

Urvashi was enamoured of Arjuna and with the consent of her father, Indira, approached Arjuna for sexual intercourse. Arjuna refused to agree on the ground that she was like mother to him. Urvashi's conduct was historically more significant than Arjuna's denial and for two reasons. The very request by Urvashi to Arjuna and the consent by Indira show that Urvashi was following a well-established practice. Secondly, Urvashi in her reply to Arjuna told him in a pointed manner that this was a well recognized custom and that all Arjuna's forefathers had accepted precisely similar invitations without any guilt being attached to them.

There was complete disregard of consanguinity in cohabitation in ancient India. It was clear from a story told in the second Adhyaya of the Harivamsha. According to it Soma was the son of ten fathers – suggesting the existence of polyandry – each one of whom was called Pralheta. Soma had a daughter Marisha. The ten fathers of Soma and Soma himself cohabited with Marisha. This is a case of ten grand-fathers and father married to a woman who was a grand-daughter and daughter to her husbands. The same Adhyaya mentions the story of Daksha Prajapati. This Daksha Prajapati who is the son of Soma is said to have given his 27 daughters to his father, Soma, for procreation. In the third Adhyaya of Harivamsha the author says that Daksha gave his daughter in marriage to his own father Brahma on whom Brahma begot a son who became famous as Narada. All these are cases of cohabitation of Sapinda men with Sapinda women.

There was no rule of chastity for maidens. A girl could have sexual intercourse with and also progeny from anybody without contracting marriage. This is evident from the root meaning of the word Kanya which means a girl. Kanya comes from the root Kam which means a girl free to offer herself to any man. That they did offer themselves to any man and had children without contracting regular marriage is illustrated by the case of Kunti and Matsyagandha. Kunti had children from different men before she was married to Pandu and Matsyagandha had sexual intercourse with the sage Parashara before she married Shantanu the father of Bhishma.

That women used to be sold in the Aryan society is also mentioned in ancient books. According to the Arsha form of marriage, which was in vogue those days, the father of the boy gave Gao-Mithuna (a cow and a bull) to the parents of the girl and took her away. This is another way of saying that the girl was sold for a Gao-Mithuna, which in those days was regarded as a reasonable price for girl. Not only daughters were sold by their fathers, but wives also were sold by their husbands. The Harivamsha in its 79th Adhyaya describes how a religious rite called Punyaka-Vrata should be the fee offered to the officiating priest. It says that the wives of Brahmins should be purchased from their husbands and given to the officiating priest as his fee. It is quite obvious from these descriptions that Brahmins freely sold their wives for a consideration.

The Aryan society treated their women like goods and chattels. According to the scriptures, they would let out their women on rent for cohabitation to others. In the Mahabharata there is an account of the life of Madhavi in Adhyayas 103 to 123. Madhavi who was the daughter of King Yayati, was given to Galawa, a rishi, as a fee to a priest. Galva rented her out to three kings in succession but to each for a period necessary to beget a son on her. After the tenancy of the third king terminated, Madhavi was surrendered by Galva to his Guru Vishvamitra who made her his wife. Vishvamitra kept her till be begot a son on her and gave her back to Galva. Galva returned her to her father Yayati.

Polygamy and polyandry were raging not only among gods and goddesses but also their Aryan devotees. Promiscuity in matters of sex becomes quite apparent if one were only to examine the rules of Niyoga, a system prevalent in the Aryan society according to which a woman who is wedded can beget on herself progeny from another man who is not her husband. Since there was no control on the system, it resulted in a very promiscuous society. There was no limit to the number of Niyogas open to a woman. Madhuti had one Niyoga allowed to her. Ambika had one actual Niyoga and another proposed. Pandu allowed his wife Kunti four Niyogas. Vyusistasva was permitted to have seven and Vali is known to have as many as 17 Niyogas, 11 on one, and six on his second wife. Just as there was no limit to the number of Niyogas so also there was no definition of cases in which Niyoga was permissible.

Niyoga took place in the lifetime of the husbands and even in cases where the husband was not overcome by any congenital incapacity to procreate. The initiative was probably taken by the wife. The choice of a man was left to her. She was free to find out with whom she would unite a Niyoga and how many times, if she chose the same man. The Niyogas were another name for illicit intercourse between men and women which might last for one night or twelve years or more with the husband a willing and a sleeping partner in this trade of fornication. These were the manners and morals of common men in the ancient Aryan society. Looking at what is happening in societies all over the world today especially with regard to promiscuity, it does seem that our Aryan ancestors were very modern in outlook and behaviour.

The looseness of the morals in ancient Aryan society was not confined to commoners. The Brahmins were not only willing to sell their wives for a price, but also voluntarily indulged in it and allowed promiscuity. As mentioned in the Mahabharata, Utanka is a pupil of Veda. The wife of Veda calmly requests Utanka to take the place of her husband and approach her for the sake of virtue. Another example that may be referred to in this connection is that of Uddalaka's wife. She is free to go to other Brahmins either of her own free will, or in response to invitations. Shwetketu is her son by one of her husband's pupils. These are mere instances of laxity or adultery. There are cases of recognized latitudes allowed to Brahmin women. Jatila Gautami was a Brahmin woman and had seven husbands who were rishis. The Mahabharata says that the wives of citizens admire Draupadi in the company of her five husbands and compare her to Jatila Gautami with her seven husbands. Mamata is the wife of Utathya. But Brahaspati the brother of Utathya had free access to Mamata during the lifetime of Utathya. The only objection Mamata once raises to him is to ask him to wait on account of her pregnancy. But she does not say that approaches to her were either improper or unlawful.

Ethics and morals had no place even among rishis in the ancient days. The Adhyaya 100 of the Vana Parva of the Mahabharata states that a rishi called Vibhandaka cohabited with a female deer and the female deer bore a son to him who subsequently became known as rishi Shranga. In Adhyaya 1 as well as in 118 of the Adi Parva of the Mahabharata there is a narration of how Pandu the father of the Pandavas received his curse from a rishi named Dama. Rishi Dama was engaged in the act of coitus with a female deer in a jungle. While so engaged Pandu shot him with an arrow before the rishi was spent, as a result of it Dama died. But before he died Dama uttered a curse saying that if Pandu ever thought of approaching his wife, he would instantly die. Vyas, the author of the Mahabharat, tries to gloss this bestiality of the Rishi by saying the Rishi and his wife had both taken the form of deer in fun and frolic.

The ancient literature is full of rishis cohabiting with women in the open within the sight of the public. In adhyaya 63 of the Adi Parva of the Maahabharata a description is given of how the rishi Parashara had sexual intercourse with Satyavati, alias Matsya Gandha, a fisherman's daughter. Another similar instance is to be found in Adhyaya 104 of the Adi Parva, which stated that the Rishi Dirgha Tama cohabited with a woman in the sight of the public. There are many such instances mentioned in the Mahabharata. Another practice which illustrates the revolting immorality of the rishis is mentioned in Chandyogya Upanishad. According to this Upanishad, the rishis had made a rule that while they were engaged in performing a Yajna if a woman expressed a desire for sexual intercourse with the rishi who was approached, he should immediately without waiting for the completion of the Yajna and without caring to retire to a secluded spot proceed to commit sexual intercourse with her in the Yajna Mandap right before the public present there. This immoral performance of the rishi was elevated to the position of a religious observance and given the name of Vamadev-Vrata which later on came to be known as Vama-Marg.

There was no end to the immorality of the rishi in the ancient sacerdotal literature of the Aryans. The Aryans were often possessed with the desire to have better progeny which they accomplished by sending their wives to others and it was mostly to the rishis who were regarded by the Aryans as pedigree cattle. The rishis who figure in such cases form quite a formidable number. Indeed the rishis seemed to have made a regular trade in this kind of immorality and they were so lucky that even kings asked them to impregnate their queens. Thanks to the legacy of the rishis, which many Brahmins inherited without qualm, the practice of letting the Namboodri Brahmins in several southern states have the hansel of new brides continued until middle or perhaps even longer period of the 20th century in India. Just as Shia community's Aghas, regarded as descendants of the prophet Mohammed, in Kargil in Ladakh and many other places would have the newly married bride spend the first night with them, Brahmins invoking the authority of the Shastras also made people in India do likewise.

Life of Aryans as revealed in Vedic literature also mentions the existence of the Devas, who were a powerful and most licentious community. They even molested the wives of the rishis. The story of how Indra raped Aahalya, the wife of rishi Gautama, is well-known. But the immoralities they committed on the Aryan women were unspeakable. The Devas as a community appear to have established an over-lordship over the Aryan society in very early times. This over-lordship became so degenerated that the Aryan women had to prostitute themselves to satisfy the lust of the Devas. The Aryan took pride if his wife was in the keeping of a Deva and was impregnated by him. The mention in the Mahabharata and in the Harivamsha of sons born to Aryan women from Indira, Yama, Nasatya, Agni, Vayu and other Devas is so frequent that one is astounded to note the scale on which such illicit intercourse between the Devas and the Aryan women was in vogue.

Being a powerful community the Devas protected the Aryans in their fight against the Rakshasas, Daityas and Danavas. In return for this service they exacted two boons from the Aryans. The first boon was the Yajnas, which were periodic feast given by the Aryans to the Devas. The Yajnas were feudal exactions by the Devas. The second boon claimed by the Devas against the Aryans was the prior right to enjoy Aryan woman. This was systematized at a very early date. There is a mention of it in the Rig Veda in X. 85.40. According to it, the first right over an Aryan female was that of Soma, second of Gandharva, third of Agni and lastly of the Aryan. Every Aryan woman was hypothecated to some Deva who had a right to enjoy her first on becoming puber. Before she could be married to an Aryan she had to be redeemed by getting the right of the Devas extinguished by making him a proper payment.

The description of the marriage ceremony given in the 7th Khandika of the Ist Adhyaya of the Ashvalayan Grahya Sutra furnish the most cogent proof of the existence of the system. A careful and critical examination of the Sutra reveals that at the marriage three Devas were present - Aryaman, Varuna and Pushan - obviously because they had a right of pre-libation over the bride. The first thing that the bridegroom does, is to bring her a stone slab and make her stand on it telling her,"Tread on this stone, like a stone be firm. Overcome the enemies; tread the forest down." This means that the bridgroom does it to liberate the bride from the physical control of the three Devas whom he regards as his enemies. They get angry and march on the bridegroom. The brother of the bride intervenes and tries to settle the dispute. He brings parched gram with a view to offering it to the Devas to buy off their rights over the bride. The brother then asks the bride to join her palms and make a hollow. He then fills the hollow of her palm with the parched grain and pours clarified butter on it and asks her to offer it to each Deva three times. This offering is called Avadana.

While the bride is making this Avadana to the Deva the brother of bride makes a statement which is very significant. He says: " This girl is making this Avadana to Aryaman Deva through Agni. Aryaman should therefore relinquish his right over the girl and should not disturb the possession of the bridgroom." Separate Avadanas are made by the bride to the other two Devas and in their case also the brother utters the same formula. After the Avadanas follows the Pradakshana round the Agni which is called Saptapadi after which the marriage of the bride and bridegroom becomes completely valid. All this of course is very illuminating and throws a flood of light on the utter subjection of the Aryans by the Devas and moral degradation of Devas as well as of the Aryans.

Even to this day Saptapadi is the most essential ceremony in a Hindu marriage. But very few know why Saptapadi has so great an importance. It is a test whether the Deva who had his right of pre-libation over the bride was satisfied with the Avadana and was prepared to release her. If the Deva allowed the bridegroom to take the bride away with him up to a distance covered by the Saptapadi it raised an irrefutable presumption that the Deva was satisfied with the compensation and that his right was extinguished and the girl was free to be the wife of another. The Saptapadi cannot have any other meaning. The fact that Saptapadi is necessary in every marriage shows how universally prevalent this kind of immorality had been among the Devas and the Aryans.

Inspiration for promiscuity and licentiousness prevalent in the Aryan society came from their gods. Lord Krishna who played the most important role in the Mahabharata belonged to the Vrasni (Yadava) family. The Yadavas were polygamous. The Yadava kings are reported to have innumerable wives and innumerable sons - a trait from which Krishna himself was not free.

Krishna's own house was not free from the stain of parental incest. The case of a father marrying daughter is reported by Matsya Purana to have occurred in the Yadav family. According to Matsya Purana, King Taittiri, an ancestor of Krishna, married his own daughter and begot on her a son named Nala. Samba, the son of Krishna, cohabited with his mother. The Matsya Purana tells how Samba lived illicitly with the wives of his father, Krishna, and how Krishna got angry and cursed Samba and the guilty wives on that account.

The Mahabharata also mentions that one Satyabhama asked Draupadi the secret of her power over her five husbands, who were five Pandva brothers. According to the Mahabharat, Draupadi warned her against talking or staying in private with her step-sons. This corroborates what the Matysa Purana has to say about Samba. Samba's is not the only case. His brother Pradyumna married his foster mother Mayavati, the wife of Samba. Such was the state of morals in the Aryan society before the death of Krishna. But there was progressive reform. This fact cannot be denied. The worst cases of immorality occurred in the earliest age i.e., the Krita age, the less revolting in the Treta age and the least revolting in the Dwapara age. The Kali Yug, which is the present period, is the most reformed. Of course aberrations are there as in every society. But licentiousness of the days when the Aryans were a tribal society is a thing of the past.

With the passage of the time, elders in the Aryan society started getting worried about the looseness of the morals. The immoralities which were prevalent in the Aryan society were largely the result of the imitation by the common man of the immoral acts and deeds of the Devas and the rishis. The leaders of the Aryan society introduced a reform of the greatest significance. They declared that acts and deeds of the Devas and the rishis are not to be cited or treated as precedents. Other reforms were equally drastic. The Mahabharata refers to two reformers, Dirghatama and Shwetaketu. Shwetaketu laid down that the marriage is indissoluble and there was to be no divorce . Dirghatama stopped polyandry and declared that a woman can have only one husband at a time. He also laid down conditions for regulating Niyoga, the practice which allowed women to live and sleep with men other than their husbands.

Elders of the Aryan society decreed that (1) The father or brother of the widow (or of the widow's husband) or the wife who has not been able to beget a child from her husband shall assemble the Gurus to decide what she could do, especially if she was young and still procreative.(2) The Gurus should allow her to raise the issue of her husband; (3) The person appointed to help her procreate must be either the husband's brother or a sapinda or sagotra of the husband or sapravara or a person of the same caste. (4) The person appointed and the widow or wife without an issue must be actuated by no lust but only by a sense of duty. (5)The person appointed for the task must be anointed with ghee or oil, must not speak with or kiss her or engage in the sportive dalliance with her. (6) This relationship was to last till one son was born (or two according to some). (7) The widow must be comparatively young, she should not be old or sterile or past child-bearing or sickly or unwilling or pregnant. (8) After the birth of son they were to regard themselves as father-in-law and daughter-in-law. It is further made clear by the texts that if a brother-in-law has intercourse with his sister-in-law without appointment by elders or if he does so even when appointed by elders but the other circumstances do not exist, he would be guilty of the sin of incest.

The ancient Aryan society carried out other reforms also to improve their morals. One was to establish the rule of prohibited degrees for purposes of marriage to prevent recurrence of father-daughter, brother-sister, mother-son, grandfather-grand-daughter marriages. The other was to declare sexual intercourse between the wife of the Guru and the pupil a heinous sin. Attempts to control gambling were also made. Every treatise in the series called Dharma Sutras contains references to laws made, throwing to the king the duty and urgency of controlling gambling by State authorities under stringent laws. All these reforms had taken effect long before the Kali Yuga started and it is natural to hold that from the point of view of morality the Kali Yuga is a better age. To call it an age in which morals were declining is not only without foundation but is an utter perversion of truth.

The descendants of the Aryans who account for the bulk of population in India today are free from immorality and looseness of their great tribal ancestors. Polygamy, polyandry are still there, but mostly these practices are confined to denizens of forests who continue to live like tribals in the past. Niyoga, which permitted women to have different husbands with the consent of their husbands in a tolerant society, is not there though the practice of married or unmarried women sleeping with different partners on the sly, without any one getting wind of their intimate relationship, is coming into vogue thanks largely due to the increasing influence of European societies and cultures which cannot be checked by any means now that the whole world is becoming a global village.

Hindus today, just as they had been for over 2,000 years since Manusmriti became the bible of Indian society, remain trapped in caste stratifications which divide society, create walls of ill-will, suspicion and misunderstanding. The upper castes do not make a grievance of this fact that they have to swear by centuries-old caste system, for they are prospering just as they were in the past. The Shudras, who are at the bottom of the social ladder, continue to suffer from inequalities, discrimination and prejudices of the upper castes despite the fact that inequalities have been prohibited by law.

References

- Philosophy of Hinduism in Vol. 3, 7 of Ambedkar's writings and speeches published by Maharashtra Government in 1987.
- Riddles in Hinduism in Vol. 4 Published in 1987 by Maharashtra Government.

7

Untouchability

Initially, when the Congress Party was launched in 1885, untouchability did not figure on its agenda. The party was a gathering of intellectuals whose main interest was political. Whatever they discussed was aimed at gaining importance or recognition for their broader national cause from the then British rulers. Despite kicking up dust about its concern for the downtrodden, the party was not bothered about the removal of untouchability. However, when the demand for the removal of this social menace grew louder, the party decided to start a parallel organization, which could serve as a forum for discussion of social problems including untouchability. The forum, called Indian National Social Conference, started meeting after every Congress session under the same shamiana which was put up for discussion of the party's political agenda.

In 1895, when the Congress met in Poona, a sizable section in the party led by Bal Gangadhar Tilak rebelled and threatened to burn the Congress pandal if the party allowed itself to be used for the discussion of problems being faced by the Untouchables. Being a Brahmin, Tilak could not tolerate that the party to which he belonged should get bogged down over such issues. However, in 1917 under the presidentship of Mrs. Annie Besant, the Congress adopted a resolution saying: "This Congress urges upon the people of India the necessity, justice and righteousness of removing all disabilities imposed by custom upon the Depressed Classes, the disabilities being of a most vexatious and oppressive character, subjecting the downtrodden to considerable hardship and inconvenience." Annie Besant's contributions to the social field in India would be remembered for a long time even if she had not started with a great zeal for the uplift of the people who had been crushed by the caste stratifications for ages. Mrs. Besant's views on the subject of the downtrodden were reflected in the article, "The Uplift of the Depressed Classes," she wrote in the *Indian Review* in February 1909.

Dealing with the question of equality for all, she stated: "In every nation we find, as the basis of the social pyramid, a large class of people, ignorant, degraded, unclean in language and habits; people, who perform many tasks which are necessary for society, but who are despised and neglected by the very society to whose needs they administer. What can be done for them by those who feel the barbarity of the treatment meted out to them, by those who feel that the Indians who demand freedom should show respect to others and give to others a share of the consideration they claim for themselves? A man in England, who proposes that ragged school-children should be admitted to Eton and Harrow would not be argued with, but laughed at. Here when a similar proposition is made in the name of brotherhood, people seem ashamed to point out frankly its absurdity, and they do not realize that the proposal is a merely violent reaction against the cruel wrongs which have been inflicted on the depressed classes."[1]

The resolution passed by the Congress about the depressed classes in 1917 was an unexpected development. The party had never done such a thing before. What made the Congress wake up was the fact that the depressed classes had also started becoming active and at separate rallies had adopted resolutions, expressing their loyalty to the British government and praying for victory to the Allies in the First World War. Their resolutions also appealed to the Congress to exert its weight and influence for getting a better deal for the depressed classes. One of the resolutions passed at a meeting of the depressed classes in Bombay after expressing loyalty to the British, demanded that "if the British government decided to give political concessions to the Indian public, this meeting prays that Government should grant the Untouchables their own representatives in various legislative bodies." Lest leaders of the depressed classes should gain any advantage from the British, the Congress, as a strategy, had passed its resolution in order to demonstrate that it was concerned with the welfare of the downtrodden, and if there was to be any consideration of the problems of the depressed classes, the Congress was not to be ignored in any such consultation.

Gandhi's return from South Africa in 1919, with a reputation as a great mass leader determined to fight the British, made the Congress dance attendance on him. This enabled Gandhi to get a firm hold on the party soon and he directed his efforts towards making it a broad-based countrywide organization. The Congress which was till then, by and large, only a party of like-minded people, became a mass organization under Gandhi's leadership. The policy of non-cooperation and civil disobedience made Gandhi soon a household name up and down the country and started ringing alarm bells for the British. Since the depressed classes constituted a vast bulk of the Indian populace, Gandhi could never tire of expressing his concern for them.

In the *Young India* dated 20th November 1920, Gandhi wrote: "No physical inconvenience can warrant abandonment of one's own religion. If the inhuman treatment of the Panchamas were a part of Hinduism, its rejection would be a paramount duty both for them and for those like me who would not make a fetish of religion and condone every evil in its sacred name. But I believe that untouchability is not part of Hinduism. It is rather its excrescence to be removed by every effort. And there is quite an army of Hindu reformers who have set their heart upon ridding Hinduism of this blot. Conversion therefore, I hold, is not a remedy whatsoever. Then, there remains, finally, self-help and self-dependence with such aid as the non-Panchama Hindus will render of their own volition, as a matter of duty. And herein comes the use of non-cooperation. Therefore, by way of protest against Hindus and Hinduism, the Panchamas can certainly stop all contact and connection with the other Hindus so long as they have special grievances about which no one seems to be bothered. But this means organized intelligent effort. So far as I can see, there is no leader among the Panchamas who can lead them to victory through non-cooperation." On November 3, 1921, he wrote in the Young India, "Untouchability cannot be given a secondary place on the programme. Without the removal of this taint, Swaraj is a meaningless term. Workers should welcome social boycott and even public execration in the prosecution of their work. I consider the removal of untouchability as a most powerful factor in the process of attainment of Swaraj."

Ambedkar always wondered why people doing the greatest service to society in keeping villages, towns and cities clean, free from human wastes, refuse dumps and carcasses of dead animals, all of which give stinking smells, are treated as Untouchables in India. After all, Harijans, the children of God, as Mahatma Gandhi called them, contribute a great deal to the welfare of society. Without removal of garbage, there would be outbreaks of epidemics. And yet people who protect the society from such baleful influence become the object of the worst form of hatred, discrimination and humiliation. Unclean jobs which the Untouchables in India do are done in all countries. But people engaged in keeping the environment clean and healthy are not treated as Untouchables in any other part of the world. On the contrary, they live like other citizens, entitled to all rights and privileges. What is so peculiar in Indian society that damns the do-gooders to a sub-human existence of misery, hatred and want?

While trying to find an answer to this question, Ambedkar studied social customs in other countries to see if untouchability or some similar practice resulting in the isolation of people on account of their occupation or condition was being practiced there also. Examining the social life of people he found that although there was no evidence elsewhere of untouchability as practiced in India, the notion of defilement being caused by certain occurrences was there. For instance, the primitive man believed in the transmission of evil from one person to another, and the events the occurrence of which was regarded as certain to cause defilement included birth, initiation, puberty, marriage, cohabitation and death. Pregnant mothers were regarded as impure and a source of defilement to others. The impurity of the mother extended to the child also. Initiation and puberty are stages which mark the introduction of the male and the female to full sexual and social life . They were required to observe seclusion, have a special diet, frequent ablutions, and use pigments for the body, and undergo bodily, mutilation as circumcision. Among the American tribes not only did the initiates observe a special dietary control but also took an emetic at regular intervals.

The primitive society was cautious about marriage lest it should cause defilement. In some cases the bride was required to have intercourse first with men of the tribe as in Australia, or with the chief, or the medicine man of the tribe, as in America, or with the friends of the groom as among the East African societies in the past. Among the Mundas, a girl is first married to a tree before marriage with the bridegroom. All these marriage observances are intended to neutralize ill effects and prepare the individual against the impurity of the marriage. To the primitive man the worst form of pollution was death. Not only the corpse, but the possession of the belongings of the deceased was regarded as infected with pollution. The widespread custom of placing implements, weapons, etc. in the grave along with the corpse indicated that their use by others was deemed dangerous and unlucky.

Of course the rites and ceremonies connected with birth, death, marriage, etc. do not positively and unequivocally suggest that they were regarded as sources of pollution. But pollution is one offshoot among many others as indicated by the fact that in every case there is segregation. There is segregation and isolation in the event of birth, initiation, marriage, death and in dealing with the sacred and the strange. Contact with strange people was discouraged and the primitive societies observed a sort of untouchability with regard to strangers. Among the Bathongas, a tribe in South Africa, it is believed that those who travel outside their own country are exposed to danger from the influence of foreign spirits and in particular from demoniac possession. Strangers are tabooed because, worshipping strange gods, they bring strange influence with them. They are, therefore, fumigated or purified in some other way. In the Dieri and neighboring tribes in South Africa even a member of the tribe returning home after a journey was treated as a stranger and no notice was taken until he sat down. Ambedkar discovered many other sources of defilement and on the basis of his study concluded that although belief about pollution or defilement was there among the primitive and ancient people all over the world, nowhere did it lead to the kind of untouchability practiced in India.

Ambedkar delved deep into the Vedas, Shastras and other ancient and historical treatises in order to find the origin of untouchability, the curse from which over 60 million people suffer in India. Did the Dravidians, believed to have been the first inhabitants of India, have a revulsion against such a calling as practiced by Untouchables or against persons engaged in them? The Shastras did not throw light on the subject. But there was evidence to show that the Aryans were like the Dravidians and their notions of purity and impurity did not fundamentally differ from those of the early inhabitants. According to the

Naradasmriti, the Aryans did not at all mind engaging themselves in filthy occupations. But these were usually assigned to slaves in the Aryan society. No matter to what Varna an Aryan belonged he could be a slave of another Aryan. A Kshatriya could be a slave. So could be a Vaishya. Even a Brahmin was not immune from the law of slavery.

When Chaturvarnya came to be recognized as the law of the land, a change was made in the system of slavery. What this change was is indicated in the following extract from the Naradasmriti:[2] "In the inverse order of the four castes, slavery is not ordained except where a man violates the duties peculiar to his caste. Slavery (in that respect) is analogous to the condition of a wife." Thus, according to Chaturvarnya, a Brahmin could have a Brahmin, Kshatriya, Vaishya and a Shudra as his slave. A Vaishya could have a Vaishya and Shudra as his slave. A Shudra could have a Shudra only as a slave. It means that Brahmin, Kshatriya or Vaishya, if he or she was a slave, did the work of a scavenger. Only a Brahmin, being the highest caste, would not do scavenging in the house of a Kshatriya, Vaishya or a Shudra. But he would do scavenging in the house of a Brahmin. It is, therefore, obvious that the Brahmins, Kshatriyas and Vaishyas did scavenging, the filthiest of filthy jobs, but they did not become Untouchable in those days.

The notion of defilement, pollution and contamination, which can be caused, according to Manu, the ancient law-giver of Hindu society, by birth, death and menstruation underlies untouchability. That anyone engaged in scavenging could also cause defilement might have been the perception in ancient days also, but there is no documentary evidence as such to prove it. As for death, defilement was very extensive in its range. Death caused defilement to members of the family of the deceased technically called, Sapindas, and 'Samanodakas'. It not only included maternal relatives such as the maternal uncle but also remote relatives. It extended even to non-relatives such as teacher, teacher's son, teacher's wife, pupil, fellow student, friend, members of the household and those who carried the corpse and those who touched it. The taint of impurity, however, does not fall on kings and those engaged in the performance of a vow or of a 'Sattra'; for the first sits on the throne and the last two are equal to the Brahmins in purity. A king is an incarnation of the eight guardian deities of the world – the Moon, the Fire, the Sun, the Wind, Indra, the lords of Wealth and Water, and Yama. Because the king is pervaded by these deities, no impurity is ordained for him, for purity and impurity of mortals is caused and removed by these lords of the world.

According to Manu, the period of defilement varies, for the death of a Sapinda, it is ten days; for children, three days; for fellow students, one day. At the end of the period there must be a purification ceremony. For the purposes of purification, Manu treats the subject of defilement in its three aspects: physical defilement, notional or psychological defilement and ethical defilement. The rule for the purification of ethical defilement which occurs when a person entertains evil thoughts are admonitions and exhortations. The rites for the removal of notional and physical defilement include the use of water, earth, cow's urine, the Kusha grass and ashes. Earth, cow's urine, Kusha grass and ashes are prescribed as purificatory agents for removing physical impurities caused by the touch of inanimate objects. Water is the chief agent for the removal of notional defilement. It is used in three ways: (1) sipping (2) bath and (3) ablution. Later on Panchagavya became the most important agency for removing notional defilement. It consists of a mixture of five products of the cow, namely, milk, urine, dung, curd and butter. Manu also prescribed a procedure for getting rid of defilement by transmission through a scapegoat. According to it, keep touching the cow or looking at the sun after sipping water and the defilement will be gone.

But Untouchables in India have a peculiar lifestyle which has not evolved overnight. It is the result of many factors which gradually shaped and influenced the evolution as man progressed from a nomadic tribal society to a settled existence or what may be called a civilized way of living. It is a deplorable fact that Untouchables all over India live outside the village. In Bihar and several other states, their ghettos are often called Harijan Tolas. The nomenclature for colonies of the Untouchables in other states may be different, but infrequently they are found living in segregated colonies away from the settlements of people whom they serve and thus earn their livelihood. But unlike Untouchables in other parts of India, the position of Mahars in Maharashtra has changed ever since they embraced Buddhism under the leadership of Ambedkar. Now they freely mix with the rest of the population and build their dwellings wherever they like without any check or hindrance. Also, the Mahars have stopped claiming dead animals by and large, and certainly none of those who have embraced Budhism do that duty now.

Shortly before his death on December 6, 1956, Ambedkar led several lakh Mahars and embraced Buddhism at a function in Nagpur. Most of the Mahars in Maharashtra answered the call of their leader and became Buddhists. The change of religion has not only spared them from the curse of untouchability of which they had been victims for generations, but also instilled in them a self-confidence and respect. Although many Mahar families are still scavengers, they dress well, send their children to schools, and look like respectable citizens. They celebrate the Ambedkar Jayanti, which falls on April 14, with great enthusiasm. Dancing on streets, they move in processions to spots which have become famous following the installation there of the statues of Ambedkar or are associated with his name due to important events that took place there during Ambedkar's lifetime. For instance, the spot where Ambedkar embraced. Buddhism along with his followers in Nagpur attracts lakhs of erstwhile Untouchables who are Buddhists now on the occasion of his birth or death anniversary.

After a thorough study of ancient books and minutely examining available evidence, Ambedkar was convinced that Untouchables originally were not people cast away by Hindu society just because they did not belong to the four castes of the Chaturvarnya system – Brahmin, Kshatriya, Vaishya and Shudra. They were Broken Men who might have belonged to the castes in the Chaturvarnya system but who had been reduced to their present status by factors beyond their control. These Broken Men came on the scene as a result of the continuous tribal warfare which was the normal occurrence when life was primitive. In a tribal war it often happened that a tribe instead of being completely annihilated was defeated. In many cases a defeated tribe broke into bits. As a consequence of this, there always existed in primitives times a floating population consisting of groups of broken tribesmen roaming in all directions. Since every individual in a primitive society belonged to a tribe, no individual outside a tribe had any existence worth its name.

In a primitive society where tribal warfare was a common feature of life a stray group of Broken Men was always in danger of being attacked. They did not know where to go for shelter. They did not know who would attack them and to whom they could go for protection. Obviously, shelter and protection became the main problem for the Broken Men.[3] Although there is no historical evidence, it seems safe to assume that the Broken Men agreed to do the work of watch and ward for the settled tribes and the settled tribes consented to give them food and shelter. Since the interest of the one required the cooperation of the other, the two separate communities of settled tribes and Broken Men would have come to a perfect understanding. But where were the Broken Men to live? In the midst of the settled community or outside the settled community? According to primitive notions, only persons of the same tribe, i.e., of the same blood, could live together. An alien could not be admitted inside the area occupied by the homestead belonging to the tribe. The Broken Men were aliens since they were an admixture of various tribes who had been defeated and who in any case were different from tribes whose cooperation they had sought. Apparently, tribal leaders must have decided that these Broken Men should live on the border of the village so as to remain alert against raids by hostile tribes. The consideration to keep Broken Men outside the tribe and use them for watch and ward purposes must have influenced the decision to let them live outside the village.

Earlier, when society was governed by Vedic norms and injunctions, Hindus insofar as their food habits were concerned were either Mansahari (those who eat flesh) or Shakahari (those who are vegetarians). The class of Hindus called Mansahari was further divided into two sub-classes: those who eat flesh but do not eat cow's flesh and those who eat flesh including cow's flesh. The edicts of Emperor Ashoka, called upon people not to slaughter animals and birds, but did not prohibit the killing of the cow for sacrificial or ceremonial purposes. Ashoka was interested in the sanctity of all life, human as well as animal. He felt it was his duty to prohibit the taking of life where taking of life was not necessary. Even Manusmriti did not urge people to be vegetarian. Manu did not prohibit the slaughter of the cow. On the other hand he made the eating of cow's flesh on certain occasions obligatory. While dwelling on practices followed during Yajnas, the ancient treatise called the Atreya Brahmana places two things beyond dispute. One is that the Brahmins had monopolized the whole of the flesh of the sacrificed animal. Except for a paltry bit they did not even let the sacrificer share it. Brahmins themselves played the part of butchers in the slaughter of the animal. Shastras make it clear that in the Vedic days, Brahmins were not merely beef-eaters but they were butchers also.

But the situation changed with the emergence of Buddhism as the religion of the majority of people in India. With the spread of Buddhism[4], the Brahmins lost all power and prestige at the royal court and among the people. Buddhism made so deep an impression on the minds of the masses and had taken such a hold on them that it was not easy for the Brahmins to meet this challenge, counter Buddhist influence and thus regain importance and prestige they used to enjoy in the earlier Vedic period. The Buddhists had rejected the Brahminic religion which consisted of Yajna and animal sacrifices, particularly of the cow. The objection to the sacrifice of the cow had appealed to the masses especially as they were an agricultural population and the cow was a very useful animal. Actually, when Buddhism became a popular religion during the Mauryan period, the Brahmins came to be hated because they preached animal sacrifices. The practice of animal sacrifice which was the essence of Brahmanism and to which Buddhism was deadly opposed gave further setback to Hinduism. No wonder, the Brahmins could do nothing to improve their position against the Buddhists except giving up the Yajna altogether as a form of worship as well as the sacrifice of the cow. In fact, they gave up beef-eating and in order to score over Buddhist monks started preaching cow-worship. To recover the lost ground, Brahmins not only stopped the killing of animals but also started proclaiming vegetarianism as their article of faith.

Guided and encouraged by Brahmins, the Gupta kings in the post-Maurayan period went to the extent of making a law against cow-killing, although this was contrary to what Manu had preached. Brahmins had to suspend or abrogate this requirement of the Vedic religion in order to overcome the supremacy of the Buddhist Bhikshus. The worship of the cow is the result of the struggle between Buddhism and Brahminism. It was a means adopted by the Brahmins to regain their lost ground. After the death of Buddha his followers had started setting up images of the Buddha and building stupas. The Brahmins in their turn built temples and installed in them images of Shiva, Vishnu, Ram and Krishna, all with a view to drawing crowds which were otherwise being attracted by the image worship of Buddha. That is how temples and images, which had no place in Brahmanism earlier, became a part and parcel of Hinduism.

Earlier, beef-eating was a common practice among all the castes. But with the emergence of Buddhism as a challenge to the Brahmins, the situation changed. The stoppage of beef-eating by Brahmins and the non-Brahmins and its continued use by the Broken Men, although they were dependent for their survival on settled tribal colonies, produced a situation rife with misunderstandings, division and consequent hatred. It split society as nothing else had done before. Nevertheless, it could not give rise to such an extreme division of society as is marked by untouchability. There must, therefore, be some special reason why in India the difference between the settled community and the Broken Men in the matter of beef-eating created a bar of hostility between the two. If beef-eating had remained a secular affair, a mere matter of individual taste, such a bar between those who ate beef and those who did not, would not have arisen. Unfortunately, with the cow-worship by Brahmins, beef-eating gradually became a very sensitive issue of religion. The Brahmins went to the extent of making cow a sacred animal. This made beef-eating a sacrilege.

Sacred things are always associated with interdictions otherwise called taboos. Religious interdicts take multiple forms. Most important of these is the interdiction on contact. It rests upon the principle that the profane should never touch the sacred. Contact may be established by a variety of ways other than touch. A look is a means of contact. That is why the sight of sacred things is forbidden to the profane in certain cases. For instance, women are not allowed to see certain things which are regarded as sacred. The profane are forbidden to address the sacred things or to utter them. The Vedas must be uttered only by the Brahmin and not by the Shudra. The interdictions relating to the sacred are not open to discussion. They must be accepted without question. The working of the laws of the sacred, wrote Ambedkar, which is the core of religion, should enable anyone to see that the habit of beef-eating should make the Broken Men Untouchables. Since the cow had become a sacred object, breach of the interdiction against the eating of the sacred animal, cow, led to untouchability. "Once the cow became sacred and the Broken Men continued to eat beef, there was no other fate left for the Broken Men except to be treated as unfit for association, i.e., Untouchables", wrote Ambedkar.

But one may ask about the evidence that the Broken Men did eat the flesh of the dead cow. Another question is why did the Broken Men not give up beef-eating when the Brahmins and non-Brahmins had done it? The fact is even during the period when beef-eating was common to both, the settled tribesmen and the Broken Men, a system had grown up whereby the settled community ate fresh beef, while the Broken Men ate the flesh of the dead cow. The Broken Men were a community of paupers with no means of livelihood and were entirely dependent upon the settled community. The principal item of food for both was beef. The settled community could kill an animal for food because it had land to plough and cattle for meeting their other needs. The

Broken Men could not do so as they had none of these assets. The settled community could have agreed to give to the Broken Men its dead animals as part of their wages for their watch and ward duty. It can therefore be taken for granted that in the ancient past when both the settled tribal community and its dependent settlement of Broken Men, did eat beef, the former ate fresh beef and the latter only the flesh of the dead cow, and the system represented a universal state of affairs throughout India.

The law made by the Gupta emperors against the killing of cows could apply only to those people who killed cows. The Broken Men could claim exemption from the law because they never killed cows. They only ate the dead cow. Their conduct did not contravene the law against cow-killing. The practice of eating the flesh of the dead cow therefore must have been allowed to continue. Nor did their conduct contravene the doctrine of Ahmisa, assuming that it has anything to do with the abandonment of beef-eating by the Brahmins and the non-Brahmins. Killing the cow was Himsa. But eating the dead cow was not. The Broken Men had therefore no cause for feeling qualms of conscience in continuing to eat the dead cow. Neither the law nor the doctrine of Himsa could taboo what they were doing, for what they were doing was neither a violation of law nor of the doctrine.

Imitation of the customs and practices of the upper castes was the normal practice in the tribal society. But so far as the question of following Brahmins and the non-Brahmins with regard to their decision to stop eating the flesh of cows was concerned, the Broken Men could not do what their neighbours had decided. The flesh of the dead cow was their principal sustenance. Without it they would starve. In any case, carrying the dead cow from wherever it was lying in the settled community, had become an obligation, though originally it was a privilege. As they could not escape carrying the dead cow they did not mind using the flesh as food in the manner in which they were doing previously. But wittingly or unwittingly the Broken Men thus became Untouchables. Of course, things have changed now. Owing to the reform movement among the Mahars, the position has become just the reverse. The Mahars now refuse to remove the dead animal. However, at some places the Hindu villagers force them to take it. Often in his speeches at the conferences of Untouchables during his lifetime, Ambedkar would urge them to stop eating carrion for the practice only made them Untouchables.

With the passage of time the Broken Men who literally depended for survival on the support of the settled communities, were made to do other tasks involving the removal of garbage, cleaning of settlements by sweeping, and removing of excreta to earn their livelihood. In fact, all sorts of dirty tasks were given to them so that the settled communities could live comfortably. Gradually, settlements of Broken Men became ghettos of the downtrodden who could earn their living only by doing menial jobs or dirty work which the Brahmins and other castes refused to do. No wonder, they turned into colonies of

Untouchables, who were never treated as equals by members of the settled communities. But their situation started improving when social reformers like Mahatma Jotiba Phule came on the scene. Mahatma Jotiba Phule was the greatest Shudra of modern India who made the lower classes of Hindus conscious of their slavery to the higher classes, and who preached the gospel that for India social democracy was more vital than independence from foreign rule. Of course, the movement for reforming the lot of the Untouchables started making rapid strides with the arrival on the scene of Ambedkar, the real messiah of the downtrodden who had taken birth only to redeem the Untouchables.

But when did untouchability first come into existence? The orthodox Hindus insist that it is very ancient in its origin and its observance is enjoined not merely by the Smritis which are of a later date but also by the Dharma Sutras which were written only some centuries before the beginning of the Christian era. An examination of the Dharma Sutras no doubt shows that there was a class of people called Asprashya, which means Untouchables. But the puzzling question is whether the Asprashya of the Dharma Sutras are the same as the Asprashya of modern India. This question becomes important when it is realized that the Dharma Sutras also use a variety of other terms such as Antya, Antyaja, Antyavasi and Bahya. These terms also appear in the later Smritis. But it is not clear if the classes indicated by the terms Antya, Antyaja, Antyavasi and Bahya are the same as those indicated by the term Asprashya. Are they only different names for the same class of people? It is difficult to answer this question because Dharma Sutras do not clarify this point. Neither the Dharma Sutras nor the Smritis help us to ascertain or identify those who were included in the category of Asprashya.

As in the past, the villages today in India consist of a settled community and a settlement of Broken Men. Though both always lived apart, the former inside the village and the latter outside it, there was no bar to social intercourse between the members of the settled community and the Broken Men. When the cow became sacred and beef-eating a taboo, society was divided into two – the Settled Community became a Touchable community and the Broken Men an Untouchable community. It is obvious that the Broken Men came to be regarded as Untouchable not initially but after a long lapse of time. Untouchability is an aspect of social psychology. It is a kind of social revulsion of one group against another. Being an outgrowth of social psychology, which must have taken some time to acquire its present form and shape, it is difficult to fix a precise date to a phenomenon which probably began as a molehill and grew on till it took its present all-pervading shape of a mountain as we know it today.

Untouchability began to strike roots in India only as a result of the intolerance of Brahmins towards a class of people whom they regarded inferior either because of their religious beliefs, eating habits or on account of other reasons. Occupying the highest position in the Chaturvarnya system governing the Hindu society, Brahmins could neither be challenged, slighted nor ignored during the Vedic period. They began to feel threatened only with the emergence of Buddhism during the Mauryan period of Indian history. As such it is clear that the untouchability phenomenon must have made its appearance only after the end of the Mauryan rule, which was in 185 B.C., when the Buddhist emperor Brihadratha of the Maurya dynasty was assassinated by his Brahmin Commander-in-Chief Pushyamitra Sunga. The end of the Mauryan rule marked the re-emergence of Brahmins as a dominant class in Indian society. But it is safe to assume that untouchability was not there even when Manusmriti was written.

The Chinese traveller Fah-Hian who came to India in 400 A.D. wrote in his travelogue: "The Chandalas are named evil men and dwell apart from others; if they enter a town or market, they sound a piece of wood in order to separate themselves; then, men know who they are, and avoid coming in contact with them." But this passage cannot be taken as evidence of the prevalence of untouchability at the time of Fah-Hian's visit because the Chandalas were hated by Brahmins not due to their occupation, which was cremation of the dead, but because they were believed to have been the offspring of a Shudra father and a Brahmin mother. Another Chinese traveler, Yuan Chwang, came to India in 629 A.D., and in his accounts mentioned: "Butchers, fishermen, public performers, executioners and scavengers have their habitations marked by a distinguishing sign. They are forced to live outside the city and they sneak along on the left when going in the hamlets." The description of Yuan Chwang makes it clear that he was referring to the settlements of the Broken Men. It is safe to assume on the basis of this description, wrote Ambedkar in his book on the Untouchables, that untouchability was prevalent in 600 A.D. Taking the ban on beef-eating, imposed in the fourth century A.D. by Gupta rulers, it follows that the beginning of untouchability must be intimately connected with the ban on cow-killing. Since cow-killing was made a capital offence by the Gupta kings some time in the 4th Century A.D., it is safe to assume that Untouchability, which continues to be the curse of Indian society to this day, must have appeared around 400 A.D.

When Peshwas ruled the Maratha country, the plight of Untouchables was miserable. They were not allowed to use the public streets if a Hindu was coming along lest they should pollute the Hindu by their shadow. The Untouchables were required to have a black thread either tied on their wrist or hung in their necks as a sign to forewarn the Hindus from getting themselves accidentally polluted by their touch. In Poona, the capital of the Peshwas, the Untouchables were required to carry, strung from their waist, a broom to sweep away from behind, the dust they trod on, so that a Hindu walking on the same dust should not get polluted. In Poona, the Untouchables were also required to carry an earthen pot, hung round their neck wherever they went, for holding their spit, lest falling on earth the spit should pollute a Hindu who might unknowingly happen to tread on it.

Ambedkar said that, as part of the practice of untouchability, preventing an Untouchable from taking water from a well is worse than dacoity. He told his followers: "Never regard yourselves as Untouchables. Live a clean life. Dress yourselves like the Touchables. Never mind if your dress is full of patches, but see that it is clean. None can restrict your freedom in the choice of your garments and in the use of the metal for your ornaments. Attend more to the cultivation of the mind and the spirit of self-help. You must abolish your slavery yourselves. It is disgraceful to live at the cost of one's self-respect. Self-respect is a most vital factor in life. Without it man is a mere cipher. To live worthily with self-respect one has to overcome difficulties. It is out of hard and ceaseless struggles alone that one derives strength, confidence and recognition."

Following a countrywide survey of the Scheduled Castes, Ambedkar found that as many as 429 communities in all, comprising about 60 million people, were treated as Untouchables whose mere touch is believed to cause pollution to the Hindus in India. The phenomenon of untouchability among primitive and ancient societies pales into insignificance before this phenomenon of hereditary untouchability for these sixty million people. This type of untouchability stands in a class by itself. It has no parallel in the history of the world. It is unparalleled not merely because of the colossal numbers involved which exceed the populations of a great many nations in Asia and in Europe, but also on other grounds. The isolation prescribed by non-Hindu societies as a safeguard against defilement is understandable. It is for specific reasons such as birth, marriage, death, etc. But the isolation prescribed by the Hindu society is apparently for no cause.

Defilement as observed by the primitive society was of a temporary duration which arose during particular times such as the performance of natural functions, eating, drinking, etc. or a natural occurrence in the life of the individual such as birth, death, menstruation, etc. After the period of defilement was over and after the pureficatory ceremonies were performed, the defilement ended and the individual became pure and sociable. But the impurity of the sixty million people in India is permanent. The Hindus who touch them become polluted and can become pure only by undergoing certain elaborate purificatory ceremonies. But there is nothing which can make the Untouchables Touchable or pure. The non-Hindu societies only isolated the affected individuals. They did not segregate them totally in separate quarters. But the Hindu society insists on the total segregation of the Untouchables. The Hindus will not live in the quarters of the Untouchables and will not allow the Untouchables to live inside the Hindu quarters.

Who can deny that the Hindu system of untouchability is altogether different from what is found to exist among non-Hindu societies? That untouchability among Hindus is a unique phenomenon is beyond question. Individuals were treated by non-Hindu communities as impure, but never was a whole class treated in this manner. Also their impurity was of a temporary duration and was curable by the performance of some purificatory rites. There has never been a case of permanent impurity based on the maxim "once impure always impure." Persons were treated as impure by non-Hindu communities and they were cut off from social intercourse. But there has never been a case of persons having been driven into permanent segregation camps. A whole body of people have been treated as impure by non-Hindu communities. But they were strangers outside the fold of the kindred. There has never been a case of a people treating a section of their own people as permanently and hereditarily impure. Untouchability among Hindus is thus a unique phenomenon, unknown to humanity in the other parts of the world. Nothing like it is to be found in any other society – primitive, ancient or modern.

Addressing the meetings of Untouchables, Ambedkar would say: "The sooner you remove the foolish belief that your miseries were pre-ordained, the better. The thought that your poverty is an inevitability, and is inborn and inseparable is entirely erroneous. Abandon the line of thought that you are slaves. The appearance of Tulsi leaves round your neck will not relieve you from the clutches of money-lenders. Because you sing the songs of Ram you will not get a concession in rent from the landlords. You will not get salaries at the end of the month because you make pilgrimages every year to Pandharpur. I, therefore, appeal to you to act and utilize what little political power is coming into your hands. If you are indifferent and do not try to use it properly, your worries will have no end. Fear lurks in my mind that the slavery which we are fighting may overtake us again. Will this awakening of ours be short-lived? The surest way for your salvation lies in higher education, higher employment and better ways of earning a living. Once you become well-placed in the scale of social life, you would become respectable and the religious outlook of the orthodox towards you is sure to undergo a change, and even if this does not happen it can do no injury to your interest.

"Give up eating carrion. Learn to live in this world with self-respect. You should always cherish some ambition to do something in this world. They alone rise who strive. All things are now possible because of your being able to participate in the politics and legislatures of this country. You must abolish your slavery yourselves. Do not depend for its abolition upon God or a superman. Your salvation lies in political power and not in making pilgrimages and observances of fasts. My final word of advice to you is educate, agitate and organize, and have faith in yourself. With justice on our side, I do not see how we can lose our battle. The battle to me is a matter of joy. The battle is in the fullest sense spiritual. There is nothing material or social in it. For ours is a battle not for wealth nor for power. It is a battle for freedom.

"Devotional scriptures would not free you from your bondage, want and poverty. Your forefathers have been doing it for generations but there has been no respite nor even a slight difference in your miserable life in any way. Like your forefathers, you wear rags. Like them, you subsist on thrown-out crumbs; like them you perish in utter slums and hovels; and like them you fall easy victims to disease with a death rate that rages among poultry. Your religious fasts, austerities and penance have not saved you from starvation. You must be always watchful, well educated and self-respecting to attain and maintain success. Untouchability is a curse that has ruined your worldly existence, honour and name.The Hindus must consider whether the time has not come for them to recognize that there is nothing fixed, nothing eternal, nothing sanatan; that everything is changing, that is the law of life for individuals as well as for society. In a changing society, there must be constant revolution of old values and the Hindus must realize that there must be standards to measure the acts of men, there must also be a readiness to revise those standards."

Ambedkar did not accept the view that the Hindu society could be made tolerable and even happy without making any fundamental change in its structure if all the high caste Hindus could be persuaded to follow a high standard of morality in their dealing with the low caste Hindus. "I am totally opposed to this kind of ideology" said Ambedkar. "I can respect those of the caste Hindus who try to realize a high social ideal in their life. Without such men India would be uglier and a lesser happy (sic) place to live in than it is. But nonetheless anyone who relies on an attempt to turn the members of the caste Hindus into better men by improving their personal character is in my judgment wasting his energy and hugging an illusion. Can personal character make the maker of armaments a good man, i.e. a man who will sell shells that will not burst and gas that will not poison? If it cannot, how can you accept personal character to make a man loaded with consciousness of caste a good man, i.e. a man who would treat his fellows as his friends and equals? To be true to himself he must deal with his fellows either as a superior or inferior as the case may be; at any rate, different from his own caste fellows. He can never be expected to deal with his fellows as his kinsmen and equals."

Ambedkar emphasized that campaigns launched against untouchability could not succeed because of the presumption that the Shudras are preordained even before their birth to do menial tasks in accordance with their birth in a low caste. Howsoever good or talented a Shudra might be, he should not refrain from doing what was ordained by gods for him. All this will perpetuate among Hindus the caste-system, the annihilation of which is the only solution by which some semblance of justice and fairness could be introduced in the Hindu social order. Hindu society is in an immediate need of moral regeneration. The question is who can determine and control this moral regeneration. Obviously, only those who have undergone an intellectual regeneration and those who are honest enough to have the courage of their convictions born of intellectual emancipation. But according to Ambedkar there were no such Hindu leaders who had undergone such intellectual regeneration.

Ambedkar was greatly disappointed to note that even the colonial government which had no apparent stake in the caste stratifications of the Hindu society had failed to do anything for the Untouchables, who continued to suffer from disabilities prescribed by the Manusmriti. For instance, their children could not get admission to schools; they could not draw water from a public well; they were even barred form traveling by a public conveyance; and they could not get into any public service. It was the duty of the British government to legislate at least to the extent necessary to protect their civil rights. But nothing of the sort had been done. Although legislatives bodies were established in India in 1861 and had been passing law on every social question and freely discussing public problems, yet the problems of the Untouchables were not even mentioned there except on two occasions. The first occasion they were mentioned was in 1916 when one Parsi gentleman, Sir Maneckji Dadabhoy, moved a resolution in the Central legislature for the formation of a committee of officials and non-officials for an amelioration in the moral, material and educational conditions of the depressed classes and urging the local governments and the administration to formulate schemes for their welfare.

But the Hindu members of the legislature were angry with the mover of the resolution. Pandit Madan Mohan Malviya said: "In moving this resolution the object of which I may at once say, has my whole-hearted support, the mover has gone out of the way to make remarks against the Hindu community which he ought to have avoided. I am not here to defend everything Hindu that exists. I am not here to apologize for the many prejudices or superstitions which are to be found among one portion or another of our community. But it is not the Hindu community alone which finds it difficult to get rid of prejudices. As has been already pointed out, the government have in pursuance of a wise and liberal policy, laid it down that they shall not interfere in matters of a religious or socio-religious character and accusations of the character in question ought, therefore, be avoided." When several other Hindus members also protested against the resolution the government dropped it.

Ambedkar wrote that the British government just neglected the Untouchables and believed that as a government they were not called upon to do anything to help improve the lot of the Untouchables. How did the British justify this neglect of so helpless and so downtrodden a class of their subjects as the Untouchables? They did it by taking the view that the evil of untouchability was not of their making. They argued that if they did not deal with the evil of untouchability they were not to be blamed for it because the system did not originate with them. This was clearly enunciated by the Government of Bombay in 1856 when a Mahar boy had submitted a petition to the government complaining that though willing to pay the usual schooling fee he had been denied admission to Dharwar Government School. But the government declined to do anything, saying that to interfere with the prejudices of ages in a summary manner, for the sake of one or a few individuals, would probably do a great damage to the cause of education. The government had the power to set things right, but it did not use it because for long it did not think that there was anything wrong in the social system of the Hindus. But when it became convinced about the wrong, it was overpowered by a sense of fear.

In a petition submitted to the Indian Statutory Commission on 29th May, 1928, on behalf of the Bahishkrita Hitakarini Sabha, Ambedkar demanded safeguards for the protection of the depressed classes in the Bombay Presidency. The petition stated that an Untouchable cannot escape his fate howsoever hard he may try. He cannot pass off as a Touchable. In the village where he resides he is of course known and there is no room for impersonation while he is there. But if he leaves the village and comes to town there is a strong chance of his passing off as a Touchable. Yet he knows what would be his fate if he were discovered. Ambedkar mentioned several cases of Untouchables suffering barbarities at the hands of caste Hindus. Among other things Ambedkar's recalled the story of two unfortunate Mahars as reported in the Bombay Chronicle on 25th February, 1928, under the heading "Orthodoxy Run Mad." Two young boys, Damoo and Laxuman used to take part in the Bhajan parties of the Marathas without anyone pointing an accusing finger at them. In fact, they were quite chummy with upper caste youngsters of their age. But when the Maratha elders discovered that both Damoo and Laxuman were Mahar by caste, they were furious and assaulted them mercilessly.

One of the boys had a gold ring on his person. It was forcibly removed and sold for Rs. 11. Out of this amount Rs. 6 was paid as reward to persons who had identified the boys as Untouchables. Unfortunate Damoo and Luxman vainly pleaded with their tormentors to let them go home. But the Maratha elders asked them to pay Rs. 500 as fine before being released. Since the unfortunate boys were unable to raise such a huge sum, they were subjected to even severer punishment. Their moustaches on the left side and eyebrows on the right side were shaved, their bodies besmeared with soot mixed in oil and also with dirt. Garlands made of old shoes were put around their necks. One of them was asked to hold a broom in his hand and the other to carry a placard on which it was written that the punishment was meted out to them for venturing to touch the high caste people. The Mahar brothers were taken in procession consisting of about 75 people with a drum-beater in the front. Later, when the Mahar boys made a complaint to the police, the accused persons took the stand that Mahar boys had voluntarily taken the punishment to atone for their sins.

The case of the Untouchables stands on a quite different footing altogether. Their disabilities are imposed upon them. Their isolation is really a segregation which is enforced upon them. There does not seem to be much hope for the emancipation of the Untouchables. At any rate their emancipation is far more problematical and distant than the emancipation of, say, the primitive tribes. If the problem of the Untouchables was one of denial of political and economic rights, it could be solved by legal and constitutional methods. But the denial of political and economic rights is the result of the social psychology of the Hindus. Untouchability will vanish only when the Hindus will change their mentality. The problem is how to make the Hindus unlearn their way of life. It is no small matter to make a whole nation give up an accustomed way of life. Besides the way of life the Hindus are accustomed to is a way which is sanctified by their religion; at any rate they believe it to be so. To change their way of life is almost to change their religion. How can this happen? Only when it is realized that the tragedy of the Untouchables is the crime of none but the Hindus. The question is how long shall the Untouchables have to wait for the change in the religious psychology of the Hindus?

Thanks to the caste-system in the Hindu society, Nayadis are the worst sufferers. Untouchables are those people who cause pollution by physical touch. According to the Malabar Manual, Nayadis are people who are believed by caste Hindus to cause pollution by their very sight. They are the lowest caste among the Hindus. They subsist on eating dogs. They are the most persistent in their clamour for charity and are said to follow for miles together any person walking, driving or boating only in the hope that he will take pity on them and give some charity. If anything is given to them, it must be put down, and only after the person offering it has gone some distance can the recipient come timidly forward and remove it. In the Tinnevalley district of the Madras Presidency, there is a class of unseeable people called Purada Vannas. Of them it is said: "They are not allowed to come out during day time because their sight is enough to cause pollution. These unfortunate people are compelled to follow the nocturnal habits, leaving their dens after dark and scuttling home at the false dawn like the badger and hyaena do in the dark." Describing their plight, Ambedkar wrote: "What must be the hardships of the un-approachables and un-seeables? How must they be passing their lives? If their sight or even their approach is not tolerated, what work can they find? What else can they do except to beg and live on dog's meat? Surely no civilization can be guilty of greater cruelty! It is indeed a great mercy that the population of the unapproachable and the unseeable is so small. But are 60 millions of Untouchables entitled to any civilization?" When Ambedkar pondered over these questions, his heart was burning with vengeance against the caste system which condemned people to the most degrading life.

The policy of non-intervention though understandable was, insofar as the Untouchables were concerned, mistaken in its conception and disastrous in its consequences. It was the duty of the government to educate the Untouchables and place them in a position of authority. The government could even make untouchability a penal offence. But the British Government was prepared to do neither. It would not give to the Untouchables any preferential treatment in public service. It would not undertake to reform the Hindu society. The Untouchables remained what they were before the British rule began in the country. They were its citizen but were not given the rights of a citizen. They paid taxes out of which schools were maintained but their children could not be admitted into those schools. They paid taxes out of which wells were built but they had no right to draw water from them. They paid taxes out of which roads were built, but they had no right to use them. Under the British Raj, the Untouchable was a subject but not a citizen. The Untouchables stood most in need of education and supply of water. They stood most in need of an office to protect themselves. What good did the British conquest do to the Untouchables? There was only one thing which the Untouchable gained and that was equality in the eye of the law. The Law of Manu did not recognize the principle of equality. Inequality was the soul of the Law of Manu. It pervaded all walks of life, all social relationships and departments of state. It had fouled the air and the Untouchables were simply smothered. The principle of equality before law under the British raj served as a great disinfectant. It cleansed the air and the Untouchables were permitted to breathe the air of freedom.

The Untouchables continued to suffer without any one raising even a little finger of protest. In villages and towns they could not sell vegetables, milk or butter – ways of earning a living open to all and sundry – because the caste Hindus would not buy from them. A caste Hindu would buy these things from a non-Hindu, but he would not buy them from the Untouchables. In the matter of employment, their condition was the worst. In the government departments the bar-sinister operated and they were denied the place of even a constable or a messenger. In industries, they fared no better. Like the Negro (now called Black) in America they were the last to be employed in days of prosperity and the first to be fired in days of adversity. And even when they got a foothold, what were their prospects? In the Cotton Mills in Bombay and Ahmedabad they were confined to the lowest paid departments where they could earn only Rs. 25 per month. More paying departments like the weaving department were permanently closed to them. Even in the low paid departments they could not rise to the highest rung of the ladder. The place of the boss was reserved for the caste Hindu while the depressed class workers must slave as their underdog, no matter how senior or how efficient. In departments where the earning depended on piecemeal work, they failed to earn as well as caste Hindu employees because of social discrimination.

Ambedkar was of the view that if untouchability has continued down the ages it was more on account of economic rather than religious considerations. Actually, the system of untouchability is a gold mine for the Hindus. Under this system 240 millions of Hindus have sixty million Untouchables to serve as their retinue to enable the Hindus to maintain pomp and ceremony and to cultivate a feeling of pride and dignity befitting a master class. The sixty million of Untouchables are to be used as forced labourers, to do the dirty work of scavengers and sweepers which the Hindus are debarred by their religion to do. Such lowly work must be done by the non-Hindus who could be no other than the Untouchables. Untouchability is not a religious system but an economic system which is worse than slavery.

References

1. The quotation is on the bottom line of page 3, Vol. 9, of Ambedkar's Writings and Speeches published by Maharashtra Government in 1990 which deals with the question what Congress and Gandhi have done to the Untouchables. Ms. Annie Besant was the founder of the Theosophical Society.
2. The quotation is taken from Page 107, Vol. 3 of Ambedkar's Writings and Speeches published by Maharashtra government in 1987.
3. See paragraph 4, Page 274, Vol. 7 of Ambedkar's Writings and Speeches published by Maharashtra government in 1990.
4. See third paragraph page 268, Vol. 3 of Ambedkar's Writings and Speeches published in 1987.

- Essay on Untouchables and Untouchability in Vol. 5 of Ambedkar's Writings and Speeches Published by Maharashtra government in 1989.

8

Burning of Manusmriti

When he finally returned to India in 1923 after completing his education Ambedkar had M.A., Ph.D., D.Sc., Barrister-at-Law degrees from the Universities of America and England and the rare distinction of having studied even at the Bonn University in Germany. Although among his contemporaries, he was a very highly qualified person in the country, yet the world was not his oyster. Being a Mahar, an Untouchable caste in the Hindu society, he had to suffer discrimination and intolerance bordering on contempt, and studied indifference on the part of the people he met for jobs. His failure to find godfathers in influential circles, and his reluctance to beg or borrow from people who were not even a patch on his otherwise outstanding personality hailed by academicians abroad, made Ambedkar's struggle an uphill task.

But having learnt from his childhood that he could conquer whatever he willed with labour and dedication, he was not the one to give up; instead he resolved to fight for his place under the sun in his native land with all the determination and dedication he was capable of. As he could not secure any government job, his Parsi friend, Naval Bhathena, got him appointed as a tutor to two students in Bombay. Unemployed Ambedkar also started looking after the correspondence and accounts of the business of his Parsi friend. Simultaneously he started a business office, offering advice to the dealers in Stocks and Shares. This was a good move. But as soon as it became known that he was an Untouchable, this project also flopped.

Finding the doors of the academic and the other institutions he could serve with distinction shut against him, he decided to try his luck in the legal profession in the hope that it would enable him to acquire the means to devote himself wholeheartedly to the main aim of his life: the uplift of the Untouchables. But poor Ambedkar had no money to apply even for a *sanad* which alone could entitle him to appear in the courts in the then Bombay Presidency. Once again, he approached his unfailing Parsi friend, Naval Bhathena, for money so that he could register himself as a lawyer. Thus he got his *sanad* and began life as a barrister in June, 1923. As success in the legal profession depended more upon one's influence with solicitors than upon one's ability, Ambedkar joined the Appellate side of the Bombay Bar. The leading members of the Bar would not condescend to have any contact with him mainly because of his low caste. Thus he had to plod his way with whatever brief he could manage to get.

Just when Ambedkar was struggling to find his feet in the legal profession, there were surprising developments in India. Upper caste Hindu leaders who had always dismissed the depressed classes as of little consequence or taken them for granted, started having second thoughts. Possibly because of this perceptible change on their part, the Untouchables who had long been treated as pariahs, began receiving some attention not only from the Indian National Congress and the Arya Samajists but also from the fundamentalist organizations such as the Hindu Mahasabha. But all this was not due to any realization on their part that the Hindu society had long been unfair to the Untouchables. What had brought about a change in their outlook was the propaganda started by the Muslim leaders that since the majority community did not accord equality to the Untouchables, they could not be treated as part of the Hindu society; they were a separate community and as such should not be clubbed with the Hindus for electoral purposes. Since this could reduce their majority, Hindu leaders were naturally alarmed. They were also getting disturbing reports about the proselytizing activities of the Christian missionaries and the Muslim clerics for the conversion of the Untouchables into Christians and Muslims. All these moves were dangerous from the Hindu point of view. No wonder the upper caste Hindu leaders woke up and started what can only be described as shedding crocodile tears for the injustice done to the Untouchables for ages. The exercise was aimed at keeping the Untouchables in the Hindu fold.

It was against this background that several institutions and organizations devoted to the uplift of the depressed classes sprang up in India. The Prarthana Samaj, the Brahmo Samaj and organizations enjoying the patronage of Princes like Chhatrapati Sahu Maharaj of Kolahpur and Sayajirao Gaekwad of Baroda became active in the welfare of the Untouchables as a mollifying gesture of humanitarianism. Suddenly, those areas where the depressed classes had greater concentration began swarming with ardent reformers, pompous rationalists and propagandists, expressing their lip sympathy in eloquent diction for the depressed classes. But it was not for the first time in India's history that such extravagant concern was being expressed for the sufferings of the underdogs. The country's history bears witness to the fact that attempts were made earlier also to set caste imbalances right. But no one had probed the problem deeply and consequently the sufferings of the depressed, victims of the caste-system, had not abated.

Although haranguing demagogues had started raising their fingers of protest against the injustice to the depressed classes, the conservative sections in the country were as unmoved as before. With their ardent faith in Manusmriti, the conservative Hindus could see nothing wrong in the unequal treatment meted out to Untouchables. They were not bothered about the depressed classes. In spite of the fact that the Hindu Mahasabha had passed a resolution in 1923 appealing to the Hindus to throw open temples, schools and their public places to them, the Untouchables remained barred from entry into holy places. The resolution could not be implemented because the majority of Hindus who were members of the Mahasabha viewed it with disfavour. Actually, in the then prevailing atmosphere, everybody seemed more concerned with throwing out the colonial rulers than with the necessity of social reform howsoever urgent or important.

About this time Mahatma Gandhi had also become active in leading agitations against the British who repeatedly put him in detention for stirring trouble for the government. Following his release from jail on health grounds in 1923, Gandhi started advising the caste Hindus and the Congressmen in his individual capacity to abolish the evil of untouchability from the Hindu society. But his words of advice mostly fell on deaf ears. Ambedkar did not approve of Gandhi's method or approach to the problem. He felt that whatever Gandhi was doing for the depressed classes was nothing but an eyewash. Ambedkar was convinced from the very beginning that social reforms flying in the face of caste Hindus could never gain support in society. With educational and economic uplift, the depressed classes could make their own case for social equality denied to them for ages. Although Ambedkar himself, on his return to India from abroad, was not a leader with mass following, he never had a desire to have a meeting with Gandhi or any other Congressman. Just as he was watching attempts both by the Hindus and the Muslim to woo and win over the depressed classes, many associations of the depressed classes mushroomed and started impressing upon their followers that they were not inferior to caste Hindus in any way. There was an all-India organization of the depressed classes also. But all these bodies were there in name only, their contribution in mitigating the suffering of the masses whose cause they espoused was almost insignificant.

When Ambedkar came on the scene, Gandhi and Veer Savarkar, another great leader of those days, were trying to win over the depressed classes by drawing attention to their neglect by the Hindu society. But Gandhi believed in the Varna system, which, according to Ambedkar, was the root cause of untouchability. Gandhi was a humanist, his efforts to improve the lot of the Untouchables stemmed from a genuine sympathy for them. His aim was to keep the castes intact but raise the depressed classes to such a level that the stigma of untouchability could be washed off for good. Perhaps, he could not advocate anything more radical because he was unwilling to hurt the susceptibilities of his orthodox capitalist supporters who were the main prop of his independence movement.

Gandhi was a reformer, but Savarkar and Ambedkar were revolutionaries. Savarkar's stand was nationalistic and realistic. He aimed at transforming different castes into a casteless Hindu society in which all Hindus would be socially and politically equal. But Ambedkar, having been born an Untouchable, was thinking more on radical lines. He could feel the pulse of the depressed classes better than any other leader for all his life he had suffered because of the low caste stigma. Unlike the other social reformers, Ambedkar could feel more the woes and miseries of the Untouchables for he himself belonged to the same class. In his heart of hearts Ambedkar wanted to make the Untouchables self-respecting citizens. But how would he be able to do that without actively campaigning against the caste-system was what worried him most.

As a barrister practicing in the Bombay High Court, Ambedkar gradually began to make his mark. He got over his financial troubles to a great extent. Harassed by caste Hindus, people belonging to the depressed classes came to him from far and near. Moved by their plight, he would hear their grievances and do whatever was possible for him to get them justice without charging any fee. Meeting groups of Untouchables at his house or addressing their meetings in different localities, he remonstrated that they should not take their inferior social status lying down. Very often he cried out: "My heart breaks to see the pitiable sight of young faces and to hear your sad voices. You have been groaning from time immemorial and yet you are not ashamed to hug your helplessness as an inevitability. Why did you not perish in the prenatal stage instead? Why do you worsen and sadden the picture of the sorrows, poverty, slavery and burdens of the world with your deplorable, despicable and detestable life? You had better die and relieve this world if you cannot rise to a new life and if you cannot rejuvenate yourselves. As a matter of fact, it is your birth right to get food, shelter and clothing in this land in equal proportion with every individual, high or low. If you believe in living a respectable life, you start believing in self-help which is the best help!"

Preoccupied as he was with the problems of untouchability, Ambedkar had no time for agitations and protests against the British government for political independence of the country. And no wonder he rather kept aloof from the Independence movement, concentrating all his attention and energies on ending social inequality imposed by the Hindu caste-system. He could clearly see that the caste Hindus were leading the freedom movement in the hope that the ouster of the British from India would enable them to regain power and rule the country just as they had been doing it for long in the past. Ambedkar had no faith in the caste Hindus saying that upon coming to power they would not question Manusmriti which gave them an absolute sanction to rule society, as they had been doing since time immemorial. He could see that under the rigid caste system which was governing Hindu society, the depressed classes could never heave a sigh of relief. The Untouchables who were segregated, discriminated, hated and exploited had no civic, religious and political rights, nor would the situation change with Independence. He knew that he would have to fight with caste Hindus and urge the British government to grant political rights to the people living on the outer fringe of the Hindu society.

Ambedkar launched his movement for the uplift of the Untouchables on March 9, 1924, by convening a meeting of the Untouchables at the Damodar Hall, Bombay, to consider the desirability of establishing a central institution to fight for the rights of the Untouchables and for placing their grievances before the Government. The deliberations of the meeting paved the way for the establishment on July 20, 1924, of an organization called the "Bahishkrita Hitakarini Sabha." The aims and objects of the Sabha were (a) to promote the spread of education among the depressed classes by opening hostels or by employing such other means as may seem necessary or desirable (b) to promote the spread of culture among the depressed classes by opening libraries, social centers or study circles (c) to advance and improve the economic condition of the depressed classes by starting industrial and agricultural schools and (d) to present memorandums listing the grievances of the depressed classes to the government. Sir Chimanlal Harilal Setalvad was made President of the Sabha. Its vice-presidents were Meyer Nissim, Rustomji Jinwala, G.K. Nariman, Dr R.P. Paranjpe, Dr V.P. Chavan and B.G. Kher. The Chairman of the managing committee was Ambedkar, its Secretary, S.N. Shivtarkar and its treasurer, N.T. Jadhav. Under the auspices of this new organisation he opened hostels for students from the Untouchable classes in Sholapur, Panvel, Thane and elsewhere with a view to awakening the Untouchables and bringing about improvement in their social conditions through education.

Simultaneously, with the launching of the Sabha, Ambedkar intensified the campaign for the entry of the Untouchables into temples from which they had been barred for ages. He participated in the Satyagrah at the Kalaram temple, Nasik, Parbati temple, Pune, and Ambadevi temple at Amaraoti. He led a procession to enter the Thakurdwar temple in Bombay. But the caste Hindus did not remain silent spectators to what they regarded as deliberate acts of profanity and pollution in their holy places being committed by the Untouchables under Ambedkar's leadership. An irate mob hounded out Ambedkar and his followers from Thakurdwar temple, although he had gone there after an appointment with the religious head of this place. He was injured and sought refuge in a police van when he was targeted with a stone. While launching these agitations Ambedkar was distressed to note that there was no unity among the Mahars and the Chamars. The Mahars who considered themselves to be superior to the Chamars by birth, always treated the Charmars as their low caste brethren among the depressed classes. The other castes among the poor and neglected sections of the society did not come into the picture as they were very small minorities. Ambedkar was always advising the leaders of both the important castes to dispel the feelings of superiority or inferiority among themselves as all of them were treated as Untouchables by the caste Hindus.

In the fallout of the World War I, there was an emergence of democratic ideals which gave impetus to social reform movements all over the world. Even in India the then British government saw to it that representatives of lower classes were accommodated in legislative bodies in states all over the country. In the reformed legislative council of Bombay S.K. Bole, a discreet social reformer, took a bold stand for promoting the interests of the depressed classes. On August 4, 1923, he moved a resolution in the council, saying that untouchability was a stigma on the good name of India and steps must be taken to eradicate it. He said: "We resent the segregation policy of the South African colonies and therefore we must set our own house in order. It is in our interest and in the interest of the country that the depressed classes should be given better treatment."

In 1925 the post of the Principal of Sydenham College of Commerce and Economics in Bombay fell vacant. But in spite of the fact that Ambedkar had served the college as a popular Professor from 1918 to 1920 and was easily the most qualified person for the post, he was not appointed. Dr R.P. Paranjpey, the then Member of Education, who was known for his progressive views declined to appoint Ambedkar, saying that the college staff and the students being prejudiced against the Untouchables might not tolerate an Untouchable sitting over all of them in the college. Instead, an offer of professorship in Elphinstone College was made to Ambedkar. But he did not accept it. Ambedkar was invited to take over as Principal of the Arts College at Kolhapur. But again he refused, saying he could not leave Bombay, his headquarters. However, he accepted a part-time post of a lecturer in the Batliboi's Accountancy Training Institute in Bombay, where he continued teaching Mercantile Law up to the end of March 1928.

Meanwhile, Bole sounded a warning in the Bombay Legislative Council that if steps were not taken to improve the lot of the Untouchables, they would some day start an agitation for a better deal. Bole moved a resolution to this effect, which among other things stated : "The council recommends that the Untouchable Classes be allowed to use all public watering places, wells and dharmashalas which are built and maintained out of public funds or administered by bodies appointed by government or created by statute, as well as public schools, courts, offices and dispensaries."[1] As the resolution was adopted, the depressed classes of Bombay were overwhelmed with gratitude and at a meeting held under the presidentship of J. Addyman, M.L.C., they awarded Bole a gold medal for his concern for the downtrodden as embodied in the resolution which was placed on the statute book now. Following the adoption of the resolution, the Bombay government issued directives to the heads of all departments, calling for the implementation of the resolution. Although the resolution seemed a turning point in the struggle for equality being waged by the Untouchables, by and large, it remained a dead letter. Not only leaders of the caste Hindus but also their kith and kin in the administration betrayed no eagerness or anxiety in securing its implementation.

Just when he was pondering over the pros and cons of the moves he could make to get a better deal for the Untouchables, an interesting incident of far-reaching importance took place in South India and made a deep impression on Ambedkar. A prominent non-Brahmin Hindu leader, E.V. Ramaswami Naicker, who belonged to the Shudra Varna, offered Satyagraha at Vaikam in Travancore state for vindicating the right of the depressed classes to use a certain road in the town to which they were forbidden entry by caste Hindus. The Satyagraha went on for several months without any change of heart on the part of the caste Hindus, yet Ramaswami Naicker did not give up his agitation. Ultimately, his moral pressure and the fact that he was after all trying for a righteous cause started making the orthodox Hindus feel uneasy. All those who hated the Shudras regained their civic sense and sanity and threw open the road to the depressed classes.

In March, 1926, an Untouchable's bid to enter a Hindu temple in Madras caused a countrywide sensation. The culprit named Murugesan was discovered, arrested and convicted on a charge of defiling the Hindu temple. Ambedkar was aghast over this development. He realized that to secure their civic rights in the Hindu society, the depressed classes should get ready to lose their lives even. Unless they were prepared to face such tribulations, they could not get justice and would have to prepare themselves to live as Untouchables for ever. Not only their number in every village or hamlet was small, they were economically dependent on the caste Hindus for earning their bread and butter. Due to these handicaps, the depressed classes could not dare exercise even their civic rights for fear of being troubled and harassed by the caste Hindus. Ambedkar, however, exhorted the leaders of the depressed classes to educate their followers and get ready to fight for their lost rights and privileges.

The British government which had remained indifferent to the depressed classes earlier, gradually, following the arrival of Gandhi on the national scene, awoke to the changed situation. The government of Bombay and the municipalities all over the country started rendering financial aid to organisations of the depressed classes for running hostels for boys and girls studying in schools. By and by, the Governor of Bombay nominated Ambedkar to the Bombay legislative council. An organization of the Bombay depressed class teachers called a meeting on February 2, 1927, and decided to celebrate this event by presenting a purse to Ambedkar. Ambedkar thanked the depressed class teachers for their appreciation of whatever work he was doing but donated the purse to the Bahishkrit Hitakarini Sabha. Ambedkar's nomination to the legislative council served as a great morale booster for the depressed classes all over the state and they started looking up for a better tomorrow. No wonder, it was probably in the fitness of things that the municipality in Mahad, a picturesque town in Kolaba district (now re-named Raigad) of Maharashtra, decided to throw open the Chowdar Tank to the Untouchables in pursuance of the Bole resolution passed first in 1923 and reaffirmed with a slight change in 1926. However, the decision of the Mahad municipality remained a mere gesture, for the Untouchables had not exercised their right to draw water from the tank owing to the perceived hostility of the caste Hindus. But the situation changed with the decision of the Kolaba District depressed classes to hold a conference at Mahad on March 19 and 20, 1927. The leaders of the conference had informed Ambedkar about their decision. Seeing another opportunity to arouse his oppressed breathren against the caste system at the conference, Ambedkar readily agreed to attend it.

In July 1927 and again on October 5, 1927, when the Bombay University Act Amendment Bill was being discussed in the Bombay Legislative Council, Ambedkar, who was a member of the House, said: "When three-fourths of the population is drenched in ignorance and does not know its rights and responsibilities, there can be no hope of autonomy and our representative system will be a sham, and there would be a rule of wealth against poverty, of power against weakness. If we desire to have provincial autonomy we must ensure that every access must be given to every grade of modern education to the communities which are educationally backward, in order that they may realize their rights and liabilities of citizenship and that under the present circumstances special representation should be provided for them. The Backward Classes have come to realize that after all education is the greatest material benefit of civilization but we cannot forgo our right and opportunity to reap the benefit of the higher education to the fullest extent. That is the importance of the question from the point of view of the Backward Classes who have just realized that without education their existence is not safe."

Replying to allegations that he was always championing the cause of the Untouchables, Ambedkar burst out in the Legislative Council[2]: "I know that my position has not been understood properly in the country. It has often been misunderstood. Let me therefore take this opportunity to clarify my position. Sir, I say that whenever there has been a conflict between my personal interests and the interest of the country as a whole, I have always placed the claim of the country above my personal claims. I have never pursued the path of private gain. If I had played my cards well, as others do, I might have been in some other place. But I will leave no doubt in the minds of the people of this country that I have another loyalty to which I am bound and which I can never forsake. That loyalty is to the community of the Untouchables in which I was born, to which I belong, and which I shall never desert. So I have to assert that when there is a conflict of interests between the country and the Untouchables, the Untouchables' interest will take precedence over the interests of the country. So I conclude as between the country and myself, the country will take precedence, as between the country and the Depressed classes, the Depressed

Classes will take precedence. That is what I want to say with regard to my policy."

In order to bring about a new awakening amongst the depressed classes he went on a tour of near and far-flung villages in the whole of Bombay state. Ambedkar visited hamlets, villages and towns to rouse his people, calling upon them to start staging protests against the denial of civic rights to them. The new leader of the Untouchables sought to instill confidence in the people who had known no rights except to suffer and to remain at the beck and call of caste Hindus ever since they were born. Ambedkar knew he could not depend on Muslim or Christian leaders to get justice for the depressed classes for they could not be expected to array themselves against caste Hindus. He was not happy even with the British government as they were more concerned with the feelings of caste Hindus upon whom they depended for running their administration. But he noted that even amongst caste Hindus there were some people, though they were a very tiny minority, who were willing to support his struggle for a better deal for the depressed classes. Hindu leaders like S.K. Bole and Veer Savarker lent their whole-hearted support to Ambedkar in his movement for the uplift of the downtrodden.

Addressing a gathering of more than 10,000 half-clad men and women who had come from far and near in response to his call on March 19, 1927, in Mahad, Ambedkar dwelt at length on the plight of the Untouchables, recalled his own unhappy experiences since his childhood, and said: "There was a time when we, who are condemned as Untouchables, were much advanced, much ahead in education compared with communities other than the advanced classes. This part of our country was then pulsating with the action and authority of people. But all this ended with the decision of the British government to bar the entry of the Untouchables into the Army. It is nothing less than a betrayal and a treachery on the part of the British to have closed the doors of the Army to the Untouchables who had helped them establish the Indian empire while their home government was at grips with the French during the Napoleonic wars. No lasting progress can be achieved unless we put ourselves through a three-fold process of purification. We must improve the general tone of demeanour, re-tone our pronunciation and revitalize our thoughts. I, therefore, ask you now to take a vow from this moment to renounce eating carrion. It is high time that we rooted out from our mind the ideas of highness and lowness among ourselves. Make an unflinching resolve not to eat thrown out crumbs. We will attain self-elevation only if we learn self-help, regain our self-respect."

The conference adopted a resolution, calling upon the upper caste Hindus to help the Untouchables secure their civic rights, to employ them in service, offer food to untouchable students, and bury their dead animals themselves. The resolution appealed to the then British government ruling the country to ban eating of carrion by the Untouchables, enforce prohibition, provide them with free and compulsory primary education, assist the depressed classes in running hostels for their students in schools and colleges and make sincere efforts to implement the Bole resolution by enjoining upon the local bodies to proclaim Section 144 of the Indian Criminal Procedure Code for its enforcement. Probably reflecting the prevalent mood which made no scope for caste discrimination or hatred, a couple of caste Hindu spokesmen, local as well as outsiders, made speeches at the conference, justifying the rights of the depressed classes and promising their support in securing them. The Subject Committee of the Conference, taking the cue from the leaders of the caste Hindus who attended and participated in the deliberations of the conference, decided that the conference should go in a body to the forbidden Chowder Tank and help the depressed classes to establish their right to take water from it. In pursuance of the Mahad Municipality resolution throwing open the tank to the Untouchables, the delegates attending the conference led by Ambedkar himself began to march in a body to the Chowder Tank to establish their right of taking water from it.

Ambedkar, who represented the awakened spirit of the Untouchables, marched towards the tank from which the Muslims and Christians could take water along with the caste Hindus without any one raising even a little finger of protest. But the Untouchables, who worshipped Hindu gods and were claimed by even Arya Samajist leaders now as belonging to their own Hindu society, were not allowed to take even a drop of water from the tank, thanks to the dictates of Manusmriti. There was never such a bold and daring move in the whole history of the suppressed people when they had got together and marched in a procession to assert their civic rights. A virile and aggressive champion of social revolution, Ambedkar led an army of the Untouchables to attack the centuries-old norms. He was establishing new social levels, remaking and reshaping Hindustan, the sick Man of the World. Those 10,000 people who followed their messiah in a file of four represented the pent-up passions of the suppressed people with an intensity that could shake the entire Hindu social system. After all they had been suffering for ages and it was the first occasion when they had marched forward to register their protest against the iniquity of the Hindu society.

But the conference in Mahad had raised the level of communal tension to such an extent that it was becoming a serious problem for the local administration to deal with the situation. They could not stop the march. The custodians of law and order could not hold the irritated Hindus in check. Consequently, they appealed to Ambedkar to forestall trouble. A behind-the-scene understanding was reached with the police according to which Ambedkar would lead the procession of his followers peacefully to the Chowdar Tank and ensure nobody amongst them resorted to any provocative gesture or slogan which might invite violence from the other side. The police would keep the caste Hindus away. Thus Ambedkar became the first

Untouchable to take water from the tank and drink it. The long cavalcade of men and women behind him followed suit and all of them returned peacefully to the pandal where the conference was being held. But soon some evil-minded caste Hindus circulated a baseless rumour that the depressed classes were also planning to enter the local Hindu temple of Lord Veereshwar. In the surcharged atmosphere the rumour was enough to light the fuse of communal fire. A large crowd of caste Hindus armed with bamboos descended on the pandal and unleashed violence that spared neither women, nor men nor their children.

Since the conference had come to an end, some delegates had already left the pandal and were moving about in small groups in the town. They were spotted and beaten black and blue. The old and young Untouchables ran helter-skelter but no one could protect them from coming to harm. Ambedkar who was resting in the local traveller's bungalow rushed to the pandal and summoned the police. He tried to control his own followers for he feared retaliation on their part could result in more violence. Ambedkar was shocked to know that a baseless rumour was the real cause of the conflagration in which many of the delegates sustained serious injuries. While the rowdies were still being rounded up, about 100 lathi-wielding men belonging to the depressed classes appeared on the scene. As soon he got an inkling of what was about to happen, Ambedkar rushed and calmed them down to restore peace. Had he not intervened Mahad would have witnessed bloodshed on a bigger scale. Police reinforcements arrived on the scene from neighbouring areas. Nine caste Hindus were arrested and following a trial, were awarded four months's rigorous imprisonment each on June 6, 1927. Commenting on the judgement, Ambedkar said that under the Peshwa rule, the culprits would have been trampled to death by an elephant. But under the British raj, the miscreants could get away with such flimsy sentences.

Reading newspaper reports about the incident and hearing details of what had happened, Ambedkar's family in Bombay was worried about his safety. When he returned, they heaved a sigh of relief. His elder brother reprimanded Ambedkar for having caused so much anxiety to the family. He asked Ambedkar to keep himself aloof from activities which could invite the ire of caste Hindus. When he was gone, Ambedkar said he knew what was good for him and good for the Untouchables who had come to repose great faith in him. His wife who had been most worried said her prayers to God on seeing him safely back home. But whatever had happened at Mahad remained a topic of heated discussion for long not only among Ambedkar's family members but also among the people all over the country. In some places caste Hindus were blamed, while in others people spoke in their defence and said the provocation was far too serious and they could not take it lying down. The offended orthodox Hindus made the Untouchables the target of their venomous attack long after the incident. Public meetings were held in Bombay and other places to discuss the Mahad incident. At several places, the government was urged to take more stringent measures to implement the Bole resolution and see to it that the Untouchables were not barred from taking water from village wells and tanks.

But before the violence at Mahad could become a forgotten chapter, caste Hindus decided to rub salt into the wounds of the depressed classes by deciding to take steps for the purification of the Chowdar Tank which, they said, had been defiled by the touch of the Untouchables led by Ambedkar. Consequently, in accordance with the guidelines given in scriptures they made elaborate arrangements for the purification of the tank. A mixture of cow-dung, cow-urine, curd and cow-milk was the recipe for purification as mentioned in Manusmriti. One hundred earthen pots, as specified by priests summoned for performing the purification ceremony, were partially filled with water from the tank With the chanting of mantras, a mixture of cow-dung, cow-urine, curd and cow-milk was prepared in the earthen pots. Then all the pots were immersed in the tank. Thus the water of Chowder Tank was purified for use by caste Hindus.

But reports about the purification ceremony appearing in all widely circulated newspapers all over the country lacerated the hearts of the depressed classes. So deep was the wound caused by these reports on the mind of Ambedkar that he resolved to fight for the vindication of the rights of his people. Instead of remaining a silent spectators to such ceremonies performed wherever the Untouchables had dared to drink water from hitherto prohibited tanks, the depressed classes resolved to fight back. Indignant Ambedkar issued inflammatory statements, calling upon his followers all over the country to agitate and educate the illiterate people in their villages so that they could fight for their civic rights. He said: "Lost rights are never regained by begging and by appeals to the conscience of the usurpers but by relentless struggle. Goats are used for sacrificial offerings but not lions."

Ambedkar announced in his party organ on June 26, 1927, that those members of the depressed classes who wanted to wash out the stigma of pollution attached to them by caste Hindus following their participation in Mahad in drawing water from the Chowder Tank, should enlist themselves at the office of the Bahishkrit Hitakarini Sabha in Bombay. He declared: "The question whether we belong to the Hindu religion or not is to be decided by us once for all. The question is whether religion is meant for men or men for religion. The Depressed Classes would die for that religion which cares for them, but they would not care for the religion which did not care for them." In spite of the fact that the earlier Chowder Tank agitation had resulted in violence of which the victims were mostly members of the depressed classes, response to the appeal by Ambedkar for Satyagrahis for a fresh agitation at Chowder Tank was again overwhelming. In order to forestall the move for a fresh agitation, the Mahad Municipality, possibly under pressure from caste Hindus or the administration, revoked on August 4, 1927 its resolution allowing

Untouchables to draw water from the Chowder Tank. But the move infuriated the Untouchables as a result of which they gathered in Mahad in larger numbers on December 25, 1927 to participate in the proposed Satyagraha. To queer the pitch further, the caste Hindus claiming that the Chowder Tank was their ancestral property and not built with government funds, obtained a stay order on the right of the public to draw water from it.

Earlier, the depressed classes had held their conference in Mahad near the Veerashwar temple. But on the second occasion they had to change the venue for the caste Hindus did not allow them to set up their pandal near the temple. The conference was held on the other side of the Chowdar Tank with the consent of a Muslim landlord. As local grocers declined to sell provisions for the conference, the organizers of the conference had to make arrangements for bringing the provisions from outside Mahad. Addressing a gathering of more than 15,000 people, Ambedkar said: "At the outset let me tell those who oppose us that we did not perish because we could not drink water from the Chowdar Tank. We now want to go to the Tank only to prove that, like others, we are human beings. The conference had been called only to inaugurate an era of equality in this land. But obviously, all attempts are being made to frustrate us." Actually, the district magistrate of the town had called Ambedkar before the proceedings began to inform him about the court stay order obtained over the use of the Chowder Tank by caste Hindus. Consequently, Ambedkar agreed that in order not to violate the law, the participants in the conference would not draw water but just walk around the tank and return to the pandal where the conference was taking place.

Having invited the Satyagrahis in large numbers, the organizers of the conference did not allow the occasion to pass without making some progress in the fight of the Untouchables for a better deal from the caste Hindus. A number of resolutions aimed at the social, religious and political uplift of the depressed classes were moved and unanimously passed at the conference. One of the resolutions condemned Manusmriti, the most revered book of the caste Hindus, on the ground that it was the root cause of the sufferings of the Untouchables. Compiled over one thousand and five hundred years ago, it preaches caste-based inequality and directs that molten lead be poured into the ears of the Shudras if they dare hear or read the Vedas. The conference passed a resolution condemning the holy scripture outright for it hindered their growth, impaired their self-respect and literally sanctioned their social, economic, religious and political slavery. According to it the Shudras belonged to the lowest rung of society and therefore were condemned to do only menial jobs so that the upper castes could live in peace and comfort. The assembled participants decided to make a bonfire of copies of the Manusmriti.

At nine o'clock on the night of December 25, 1927, a pit was dug and a funeral pyre with a copy of Manusmriti on its top was lit by Ambedkar himself. But the burning of Manusmriti caused a strong reaction among the Hindus, pundits, the Acharyas and the Shankaracharya throughout the length and breadth of India. The following morning, the conference resumed proceedings with Ambedkar, making a stirring appeal for volunteers to offer Satyagraha. He said: "My heart leaps with joy to see that you are prepared for launching this attack in vindication of your rights and honour. I have no doubt about it. But, all the same, it would be proper on your part to accord approval to this proposed fight after giving a deep thought to the trials and tribulations you would be involved in its trail. Remember that nothing valuable in this world is achieved except by efforts. Mind you, do not leap into the fire because I tell you to do so. Do it if you are fully convinced of the justice of your cause. We want men who will annihilate untouchability even by immolating themselves. If your decision remains firm, you should not hesitate to launch the Satyagraha."

Within an hour over 4,000 delegates registered their names for the struggle. Meanwhile, two famous non-Brahmin leaders of Maharashtra, Jedhe and Javalkar, came to Mahad from Bombay. In their speeches, they exhorted the participants to fight fearlessly under the leadership of Ambedkar. But the Satyagraha, which was to take place on December 26, was abandoned following the pleadings of the district magistrate who said: "According to the resolution of the Bombay Legislative Council, public tanks, schools and roads are open to all. But 12 upper caste persons have filed a suit saying that the Chowdar Tank is a private property. You should therefore await the decision of the court. As a friend I advise you not to precipitate this issue till the decision of the court is out. "Ambedkar himself told the participants in the conference that violating the law would not serve any purpose and they had better wait for the Satyagraha until the court injunction on Chowder Tank was vacated.

Addressing the volunteers for the Satyagraha and the other delegates, Ambedkar said: "You are a brave people. The people who are prepared to lay down their lives for the vindication of their just rights are sure to prosper. But the moment now has come when you should think twice before you strike the blow. You know well that the Satyagrah movement started by Gandhi was backed up by the people as it was against foreign domination. Our struggle is against the mass of caste Hindus and naturally we have little support from outside. Taking these facts into consideration, I feel, we should not antagonize the government and put it on the side of our opposition. Do not suppose, that if you postpone the issue, humiliation will be its concomitant. As regards my person, I assure you I am prepared to face the three-fold danger – breaking of an order, being charged with a breach of rules governing the conduct of a lawyer, and the possibility of imprisonment. My brothers, you rest assured that a postponement of this struggle will not mean that we have given up the struggle. The fight will go on till we establish our claims to Chowder Tank".

Although the second conference of the depressed classes in Mahad ended on a peaceful note, the burning of Manusmriti raised the fury of the caste Hindus not only in Mahad but all over the country. Most of the widely circulated newspapers carried editorials, attacking Ambedkar. The incident made Ambedkar known throughout the length and breadth of India. Later, when asked about the burning of Manusmriti, Ambedkar said: "The bonfire of Manusmriti was quite intentional. It was a very cautious and drastic step, but was taken with a view to forcing the attention of caste Hindus. At intervals drastic measures are necessary. If you do not knock at the door none opens it. It is not that all the parts of the Manusmriti are condemnable, that it does not contain good principles and that Manu himself was not a sociologist, and was a mere fool. We made a bonfire of it because we view it as a symbol of injustice under which we have been crushed across the centuries. Because of the teachings of Manusmriti we have been ground down under despicable poverty and so we made the dash, staked all, took our lives in our hands and performed the deed. At the root of the Hindu social system lies Dharma as prescribed in the Manusmriti. Such being the case, I do not think that it is possible to abolish inequality in the Hindu society unless the existing foundation of the Smriti-religion is removed and a better one laid in its place. I, however, despair of the Hindu society being able to reconstruct itself on such a better foundation."

Ambedkar knew that the Chturvarnya system which had continued for almost 2000 years could not be abolished easily. On the contrary, burning of Manusmriti had caused such a violent reaction as to make Ambedkar very sad. The Untouchables were made the target of wrath of caste Hindus at many places all over India. But this did not deter the messiah of the downtrodden. He became more determined to get his followers justice and an honourable place in society.

The Chowdar Tank affair became a long-drawn fight in the court for three years and Ambedkar had to attend the proceedings to argue the case on behalf of the depressed classes. One day when he was returning from Mahad by car after the court proceedings, an otherwise dry river on the road was flooded by heavy rain as a result of which Ambedkar was stranded on the bank of the river for two days. He went without food and shelter because being Untouchable no caste Hindu came to his rescue. When he returned to Bombay he shut himself in a room in his house in great anguish. S.K. Bole and other friends and colleagues of Ambedkar prevailed upon him to calm down. In a perplexed state of mind he advised his people to renounce Hinduism and embrace any other religion where there was equality between man and man. Following this twelve of his followers embraced Islam in great haste. As the court verdict on the Chowdar Tank case, which was given later, was in favour of the Untouchables, Ambedkar's name and fame spread far and wide throughout the country.

References

1. The quotation is from page 13, Chapter 3 of the book, Legacy of Dr. Ambedkar by D.C. Ahir.
2. The quotation is from page 51 of the book, Legacy of Dr. Ambedkar by D.C. Ahir.

Volumes 2, 12 of Ambedkar's Writings and Speeches published by Maharashtra Government, Miscellaneous Writings of Ambedkar.

9

Clash of Titans

The Working Committee of the Congress Party at its meeting in Bardoli in February 1922 passed resolutions expressing party's concern with the plight of the depressed classes, suggesting measures to improve their lot and called upon Congress organizations all over the country to implement them. One of the resolutions urged the workers to organize the depressed classes to make a blow for their rights for a better life, to improve their social, mental and moral condition, induce them to send their children to schools and demand for them all such facilities which the other citizens enjoy. Following endorsement of these resolutions by other important organs of the Congress, a countrywide donation drive was launched for collecting funds for the uplift of the depressed classes. A huge sum was collected but most of it was utilized for activities from which the Untouchables could not benefit much.

Again, in May 1923, the Congress Working Committee at its meeting in Bombay passed the following resolution: " While some improvement has been effected in the treatment of the so-called Untouchables, this Committee is conscious that much work remains yet to be done in this respect and in as much as this question of untouchability concerns the Hindu community particularly, it requests the All India Hindu Mahasabha also to take up this matter and to make strenuous efforts to remove this evil from amidst the Hindu community." When Ambedkar saw this resolution, he was furious for he fully knew that there could not be a body more unsuited to take up the work for the uplift of the Untouchables than the Hindu Mahasabha, an organization of caste Hindus all of whom were wedded to uphold graded inequalities as ordained by the Manusmriti. He said: "If there is any body which is quite unfit for addressing itself to the problem of the Untouchables, it is the Hindu Mahasabha. It is a militant organization. Its aim and object is to conserve in ever way everything that is Hindu. It is not a social reform association. It is a purely political organization, formed to combat the influence of Muslims in Indian politics. Just to preserve its political strength, it wants to maintain its social solidarity, and its way to maintain social solidarity is not to talk about caste or untouchability. How could such a body have been selected by the Congress to work for the improvement of Untouchables passes my comprehension. This shows that the Congress wanted somehow to get rid of an inconvenient problem and wash its hands of it."[1]

Ambedkar could see that neither the Congress, nor the Hindu Mahasabha nor any other caste Hindu organization such as the Depressed Classes Mission or the Arya Samaj, the Brahmu Samaj or the Prarthana Samaj could be depended upon to initiate real and meaningful measures for the removal of untouchability. He wanted the Depressed Classes to organize themselves into big associations and begin to agitate for securing their legitimate rights in the country by taking the help of the well-meaning caste Hindu social reformers who were interested in their cause.

Judging from his writings and concern for the depressed classes, there is no doubt that Gandhi was as much appalled by the treatment meted out to Untouchables as Ambedkar. It would seem if they had joined hands, they could certainly bring about social change so that the Untouchables could gain self-respect and be liberated from the anathema which had dogged them for ages. But the very first meeting between these two titans of the 20th century foreshadowed the kind of relationship or misunderstanding they would have in future. During his visits to Bombay, Gandhi used to stay at Mani Bhawan. Having heard and read about Gandhi when he first launched a movement against the colonial oppressors in South Africa and later about his activities as a Congress leader upon his return to India, Ambedkar was keen to meet him. The opportunity came when Gandhi was on a visit to Bombay in the mid-twenties. Although Ambedkar had begun making waves by starting Bahishkrita Samaj, an organization dedicated to the liberation of Untouchables, he had not become so very well known at the all-India level as to make prominent leaders like Gandhi take notice of his presence even when they came face to face. Accompanied by a group of his followers, Ambedkar went to meet Gandhi at Mani Bhawan. Although the number of people he was talking to was not large when Ambedkar and party arrived on the scene, Gandhi did not take even notice of his presence in the small crowd sitting before him. The fact that Gandhi paid no heed to the presence of Ambedkar and his followers among his audience was taken as a snub by them. No wonder they resented Gandhi's attitude and got the impression that he was somewhat arrogant and conceited.

Gandhi started talking about social problems afflicting the society and drew attention to the Congress activities started under his leadership for the welfare of the people. During the discussion with people about social problems, Ambedkar stood up and intervened to say what he himself had been doing for the uplift of the Untouchables. He said he was addressing meetings to awaken in them the spirit to fight for a better deal from the caste Hindus, he had launched a paper to propagate his views and focus attention on the plight of Untouchables. Gandhi was surprised that someone should arrogantly try to claim credit for doing good to the Untouchables for he was of the view that nobody had been more active and dedicated in his concern for them than he was. After Ambedkar's intervention, Gandhi said: "What are you talking? You were not even born when I started working for the Untouchables. It is only due to me that welfare of these people is on the agenda of the Congress party. The Hindu-Muslim tension is also a cause for concern. But the suffering of the Untouchables is more important. Therefore Rs 20 lakh has been spent by the Congress on my initiative on programmes for their assistance and help. "

But Gandhi's reference to Rs 20 lakh spent for the welfare of Untouchables provoked Ambedkar to intervene and say: "There is no doubt that you had started movement for the welfare of the Untouchables even before I was born. But there is nothing unusual in that. It is common in our society for elderly people to think about problems confronting the weaker sections. You are older than me, I cannot deny. That the Congress started talking about the need for the welfare of Untouchables on your insistence is also a fact. But the truth is apart from doing lip service, the party has not really done anything practical for them. The Congress concern for the Untouchables smacks of hypocrisy. Since you claim that the Congress spent Rs 20 lakh for their welfare, I accept it. But I must tell you frankly that this money has gone down the drain and nobody has benefited from it. If I had been entrusted with such a huge sum as Rs 20 lakh for this purpose, I can say without exaggeration that I would have done a lot for them. Mr Gandhi we, the Untouchables, are self-reliant, self-confident and know what is good for us. We don't trust or believe in reformers. They have come and gone. Of course, by their voluble concern for Untouchables they cause a stir in society, raise a lot of dust by their activities, but actually they do little. History is a witness to this fact. Had the previous reformers succeeded in doing something, the plight of Untouchables, would not have remained so bad."

Gandhi had come to regard himself as a social reformer par excellence. He did not expect this kind of open and insulting intervention at a meeting which he had thought was being attended by all his unquestioning admirers. He was taken aback by what Ambedkar said. After making his point, Ambedkar walked out of the Mani Bhawan with his followers in a huff. Later, recalling this incident to his wife, Dr Savita Ambedkar, Ambedkar said first it seemed Gandhi had thought him to be a Brahmin who was active in social reforms and wanted to boast about what he had done for the Untouchables. That he was mistaken became clear to him only when Ambedkar and his followers had left the meeting after the outburst. Gandhi could not stand it for he thought he was emerging as a kind of lodestar for the Congress party those days.

Having been a victim of caste hatred since his childhood, Ambedkar knew that it was the worst evil plaguing the depressed classes. Whenever and wherever he got an opportunity to focus attention on the plight of Untouchables, he did it with a vehemence that compelled attention. He could not see eye to eye with Gandhi who said untouchability was due to the evils which had crept into the Hindu society and these could be removed with reforms; there was no need of abandoning the caste system. Ambedkar always stuck to his stand that Untouchables could not get justice in Hindu society until and unless the caste system was abolished.

Ambedkar was not satisfied with the indifferent attitude of the British government towards the Untouchables. He could see that being sensitive to the feelings of the caste Hindus on whom they depended for running the administration, the government perhaps could not help in not doing anything meaningful for the uplift of the downtrodden subjects. But at the same time he realized that antagonizing the British rulers would be inviting more trouble for his people. So he thought it wise and prudent to cooperate with the British government insofar as such cooperation would enable him to secure some relief for his people. Ambedkar's office from where he functioned as a lawyer was in a small room of a house belonging to a caste Hindu who was a member of the Social Equality League. The League was constituted in Bombay to secure equal rights for all in the Hindu society and its members were drawn both from the caste Hindu young men and from the Depressed Classes. Ambedkar was the President of the League. Although he had started having good practice, he remained unassuming, not boasting about the work he was doing for the welfare of the downtrodden, and fighting their cases in courts even without charging any fee. He soon acquired the reputation of being a poor man's barrister.

Just when he was engaged in intensifying struggle for the liberation of Untouchables the British Parliament constituted an Indian Statutory Commission headed by Sir John Simon, a leading constitutional lawyer, and sent it to India to study the question of constitutional reforms in the country and make suitable recommendations. The Commission visited the country in 1928. But this body which came to be known as the Simon Commission provoked a storm of protest. Wherever it went, the Commission was greeted by angry demonstrations. The Congress, the Muslim League and all other major parties boycotted it for they demanded some concrete measures which would pave the way for Independence of the country. Mere constitutional reforms could not satisfy them. But on behalf of the Bahiskrita Hitakarini Sabha (Depressed Classes League based in Bombay) of which he was the President, Ambedkar submitted to the Commission an exhaustive memorandum listing grievances and demands of the depressed classes in the Bombay Presidency.

He got even better opportunity to focus attention on the problems of the downtrodden all over the country when he was invited to attend the Round Table Conference held in London in 1931 for discussing with the British government proposals for the involvement of people's representatives in administration and legislative business in India. Grappling with the caste problem for long, he had come to the conclusion that until legislative enactments were made to safeguard the Untouchables, they would continue to suffer. He decided to make a strong case that the Untouchables were not part of Hindu society but a separate entity constantly discriminated and hated by the upper castes. If he could convince the British ruling class about his case, he thought, he would be able to counter all the arguments being advanced by Gandhi and his followers to keep the upper caste stranglehold on the depressed classes.

The Round Table Conference was a significant event. It meant that for the first time His Majesty's Government had recognized the right of people to be consulted in the matter of framing a constitution for India. For the untouchables, it was a landmark for it was the first occasion when they were allowed to be represented by their own leaders. Ambedkar and another leader of the Untouchables, Dewan Bahadur R. Srinivasan, were invited to the conference. It was clear the British government could see that the Untouchables were not merely a community separate from the Hindus but also of such importance as to have the right to be consulted in the framing of a constitution for India. But when invitations to various parties were extended to come to London for the Conference, the Congress was preoccupied with its civil disobedience campaign. Mahatma Gandhi was under detention. Therefore when the first session of the Round Table Conference began, the Congress was conspicuous by its absence.

The fact that Ambedkar instead of protesting against the Simon Commission, as almost all other parties in the country had done, had submitted a memorandum of demands of the Untouchables to it and the British government had chosen to invite him and another leader of the depressed classes had created the impression that Untouchables were the tools of the British. In order to clarify his stand, Ambedkar at the very first session of the Round Table Conference on November 12, 1931, stated: "The Untouchables are not opposed to freedom from British Imperialism. But they refuse to be content with mere freedom from the British Imperialism. What they insist upon is that free India is not enough. Free India should be made safe for democracy. Starting with this aim, they say that on account of the peculiar social formation in India there are minority communities pitted against a Hindu Communal Majority, that if no provisions are made in the constitution to cut the fangs of the Hindu Communal Majority, India will not be safe for democracy. The Untouchables therefore insist on devising a constitution which will take note of the special circumstances of India and contain safeguards which will prevent the Hindu Communal Majority in Indian society from getting the possession of political power to suppress and oppress the Untouchables and which will directly invest the Untouchables with at least a modicum of political power to prevent their suppression and exploitation, and to enable them at least to hold their own, in their struggle for existence against the Communal Majority. In short, what the Untouchables want are safeguards in the constitution itself which will prevent the tyranny of a Hindu Majority from coming into being".

Explaining his stand further, Ambedkar stated the Congress refused to accept the depressed classes as a separate and distinct element in India's national life and so refused separate electorates on the plea that "it is a vivisection of the nation." This plea is advanced to deny the safeguards to the depressed classes, because the Hindus stand to lose by them. Ambedkar's belief was that the Hindu majority was a religious and communal majority. Therefore it was not a passing phase but a permanent one, and a menace for ever. He therefore emphatically pointed out that in making a constitution for India the existence of a permanent Communal Majority cannot be ignored and the problem of devising safeguards so as to reconcile it with political democracy must be faced.

Lest the case of Untouchables should go by default, Ambedkar submitted a memorandum, listing measures for the protection of the depressed classes and arguing that unless all these measures were incorporated in the future constitution, Hindu society would never do justice to the depressed classes. The memorandum urged emancipation of the depressed classes from the curse of Untouchability. Otherwise, they could never become equal citizens under the Hindu majority rule in the country. The new constitution must make equal citizenship a fundamental right of all citizens and propose severe punishment for those who deny this right to the depressed classes. The memorandum drew attention of the British government to frequent occurrences of open violence against the Untouchables whenever they made a bid to enter temples or used public utilities such as wells for drawing drinking water. Their children were discriminated in schools, denied the right even to learn Sanskrit. And when they grew up, they were barred from jobs even though they were fully qualified for them.

The memorandum made a strong case for the depressed classes to be given sufficient political powers so that they could influence legislative and executive action for the purpose of securing their welfare. The electoral law should be amended so as to give the depressed classes right to adequate representation in the legislatures of the country; right to elect their own men as their representatives by adult suffrage and by separate electorates for the first ten years and thereafter by joint electorates and reserved seats. Joint electorates should be accompanied by adult suffrage for the Untouchables. The memorandum also drew attention to the enormity of suffering of the depressed classes at the hands of the high caste officers who had monopolized the Public Services by abusing the law or by misusing the discretion vested in them in administering it to the prejudice of the Untouchables and to the advantage of the caste Hindus without any regard to justice, equity or fair play.

The depressed classes should have seats in legislatures, so that they could have the opportunity to frame the general policy of the government. They can do this only if they are also accommodated in the Cabinet. The depressed classes therefore claimed that in common with other minorities, their moral right to be represented in the Cabinet should be recognized. With this purpose in view the memorandum proposed that in the Instrument of Instructions to the state governments, an obligation should be placed upon the Governor and the Governor-General to endeavour to secure the representation of the depressed classes in the Cabinet.

After examining the memorandum, the Minorities Committee of the Round Table Conference prepared a report embodying almost all the suggestions and demands made by Ambedkar for the uplift of the depressed classes. Just as was spelt out in the memorandum, the report stated that the number of seats reserved for a minority community should in no case be less than its proportion in the population. The methods by which this could be secured were mainly three : (1) nominations, (2) electorates and (3) separate electorates. Joint electorates were proposed with the proviso that a proportion of seats should be reserved. Thus a more democratic form would be given to the elections whilst the purpose of the electorate system would be secured.

Several other committees set up by the Round Table Conference also submitted their reports, all of which were passed. Although agreement on details was lacking, it was unanimously accepted that the Untouchables were entitled to recognition as a separate entity for political and constitutional purposes. The only political party whose attitude to this decision of the Round Table Conference was not known was the Congress. By the time the Second Session of the Round Table Conference became due, a compromise between His Majesty's Government and the Congress was reached in India as a result of which the Congress agreed to participate in the Conference. This paved the way for Gandhi to come to London. The first session of the Conference was marked by bonhomie and the spirit of give and take shown by the delegates. But the situation changed altogether in the second session thanks mainly to the presence of Gandhi as the Congress leader. Not only did he stubbornly oppose whatever was being demanded by Ambedkar, he went to the extent of raising doubts about Ambedkar's claim to be recognized as the leader of the Untouchables.

The British Prime Minister, J. Ramsay MacDonald, who was chairman of the Conference, had set up besides the Minorities Committee, the Federal Structure Committee so that the questions facing India could be discussed thoroughly by participants of these committees and their final recommendations could serve as guidelines for the Round Table Conference to arrive at well-considered decisions. But the Minorities Committee which was considering the most ticklish issue of communal relations and representation of various communities in the future constitution of India could not arrive at a unanimous decision. While Gandhi had no quarrel with Muslims and Sikhs, he had no patience for the arguments advanced by representatives of other minorities such as the depressed classes and the Christians. The Mahatma was proceeding on the assumption that the Congress represented the depressed classes for they were part of the Hindu society. But Ambedkar challenged this assumption. As a result of this the proceedings of the Minorities Committee were marked by heated exchanges between the two leaders.

To begin with Mahatma Gandhi stated that just as the Congress considered the Hindu-Muslim unity to be indispensable for the attainment of Swaraj, so also did the Congress consider the removal of the curse of untouchability as an indispensable condition for the attainment of full freedom. "So far as the Untouchables are concerned, I have not yet quite grasped what Dr Ambedkar has to say. But of course the Congress shares the honour with Dr Amedkar of representing the interest of the Untouchables. They are as clear to the Congress as the interests of any other body of any other individuals throughout the length and breadth of India. Therefore, I would most strongly resist any further special representation."

With this declaration by Gandhi in his very opening speech, it was clear to Ambedkar that the Congress would never agree to the demand for separate representation for Untouchables which he wanted the British government to concede. When Gandhi saw no hope of persuading Ambedkar to come round to his view, he began serious confabulations with Muslims and promised to support all their demands on the condition that they would oppose all that was being spelt out by Ambedkar. Despite adjournments and prolonged nightlong private sessions held by leaders of various parties and groups, proceedings of the Minorities Committee were marked by bitter wranglings. When a proposal was made to constitute a sub-committee to resolve the problem, Ambedkar interjected : "I do not know whether in the position in which I am today it would be of any use for me to work on the proposed committee. Unless I know that the depressed classes are going to be recognized as a community entitled to political recognition in the future constitution of India, I do not know whether it will serve any purpose for me to join the committee that is proposed by Mahatma Gandhi to be constituted to go into the matter. Unless, therefore, I have an assurance that this committee will start with the assumption that all those communities which were earlier recommended as fit for recognition in the future constitution of India will be included, I do not know that I can whole-heartedly cooperate with the committee that is going to be nominated."

Later, when the Prime Minister called upon Gandhi to explain why the Minorities Committee had failed to produce an agreed report, he said: "It is with deep sorrow and deeper humiliation that I have to announce utter failure on my part to secure an agreed solution of the communal question through informal conversations among and with the representatives of different groups. But to say that the conversations have to our utter shame failed is not to say the whole truth. Causes of failure were inherent in the composition of the Indian delegation. We are almost all not elected representatives of the parties or groups whom we are presumed to represent; we are here by nomination of the government. Nor are those whose presence was absolutely necessary for an agreed solution to be found here." Gandhi said many other things in the course of his speech, but all that he stated rubbed salt on Ambedkar's wounds.

Gandhi's veiled reference that some of those present were only nominees of the government provoked Ambedkar to retaliate later with these words: "What disturbs me after hearing Mr Gandhi is that instead of confining himself to his proposition, namely that the Minorities Committee should adjourn sine die, he started casting certain reflections upon the representatives of the different communities who are sitting round this table. He said that the delegates were nominees of the Government and that they did not represent the view of the respective communities for whom they stood. We cannot deny the allegation that we are nominees of the government, but speaking for myself, I have not the slightest doubt that even if the depressed classes of India were given the chance of electing their representatives to this conference, I would, all the same, find a place here. I say therefore that whether I am a nominee or not, I fully, represent the claims of my community. Let no man be under the mistaken impression that the Congress stands for the depressed classes, and that the Congress represents the depressed classes more than I or my colleague can do. To that claim, I can only say that it is one of the many false claims which irresponsible people keep on making, although the persons concerned with regard to those claims have been invariably denying them.

"Prime Minister, permit me to make one thing clear. The depressed classes are not anxious, they are not clamorous, they have not started any movement for claiming that there shall be an immediate transfer of power from the British to the Indian people. They have their particular grievances against the British and I think I have voiced them sufficiently. But, to be true to facts, the position is that the depressed classes are not clamouring for the transfer of political power. Their position, to put it plainly, is that we are not anxious for the transfer of power; but if the British government is unable to resist the forces that have been set up in the country which do clamour for transfer of political power, then our submission is that if you make that transfer, that transfer should be accompanied by such conditions and by such provisions that powers shall not fall into the hands of a clique, into the hands of an oligarchy, or into the hands of a group of people, whether Mahomedans or Hindus; but that solution shall be such that the power shall be shared by all communities in their respective proportions."

Not only the representatives of the depressed classes were agitated, representatives of all other communities were equally upset. Faced with such sharp division in the Indian delegation the Prime Minister had no choice but to call upon members of the Minorities Committee once again to ponder over the communal question in the country and make suggestions which could be incorporated in the proposed constitution. Following this various leaders again held discussion and produced a settlement and submitted it to the Prime Minister. The document was dubbed as the Minorities Pact.

But Mr Gandhi was furious over it and gave vent to his feelings by saying that the Congress would always accept any solution that may be acceptable to the Hindus, the Mahomedans and the Sikhs, but the Congress will not be a party to the special electorate for any other minorities. "I can understand the claims advanced by other minorities except the claims advanced on behalf of the Untouchables. I would not seal the vital interests of the Untouchables even for the sake of winning the freedom of India. I claim myself in my own person to represent the vast mass of the Untouchables. And I would work from one end of India to the other to tell the Untouchables that separate electorates and separate reservation is not the way to remove their bar-sinister, which is the shame, not of them, but of orthodox Hinduism.

"Let the whole world know that today there is a body of Hindu reformers who are pledged to remove this blot of untouchability. We do not want on our register and on our census Untouchables classified as a separate class. Sikhs may remain such in perpetuity, so may Mahomedans, so may Europeans. Will Untouchables remain Untouchables in perpetuity? I would go far rather that Hinduism died than that untouchability lived. Therefore, with all my regard for Ambedkar, and for his desire to see the Untouchables uplifted, with my regard for his ability, I must say in all humility that here the great wrong under which he has laboured and perhaps the bitter experiences that he has undergone have for the moment warped his judgment. It hurts me to have to say this, but I would be untrue to the cause of the untouchablity, which is as dear to me as life itself, if I did not say it. I would not bargain away their rights for the kingdom of the whole world. I am speaking with a due sense of responsibility, and I say that it is not a proper claim which is registered by Ambedkar when he seeks to speak for the whole of the Untouchables of India. It will create a division in Hinduism which I cannot possibly look forward to with any satisfaction whatsoever. I do not mind Untouchables, if they so desire, being converted to Islam or Christianity. I should tolerate that, but I cannot possibly tolerate what is in store for Hinduism if there are two divisions set forth in the villages. Those who speak of the political right of Untouchables do not know their India, do not know how society is today constructed, and therefore I want to say with all the emphasis that I can command that if I was the only person to resist this thing I would resist it with my life."

In the Minorities Committee, Mr Gandhi had said that if the Committee agreed to accept the claim of the Untouchables for separate recognition, it was free to do so, which meant that he would abide by the decision of the majority. But when he came to know that the other minorities had agreed to support the Untouchables, he did not hesitate to approach the Musalmans and turn them against the Untouchables by accepting their fourteen points which the Congress, the Hindu Mahasabha and even the Simon Commission had rejected. Even if Mr Gandhi was prepared to flout public opinion and public morality, this diabolical plot of Mr Gandhi fell through because the Musalmans refused to disgrace themselves by joining in it. When the second session of the Round Table Conference was dissolved the delegates to the Minorities Committee accepted the proposal of the Prime Minister to put in a signed requisition authorizing him to arbitrate and give his decision on the communal issue.

Describing what happened at the second session of the conference, Ambedkar in his inimitable style wrote: "Unfortunately, the Congress sent Mr Gandhi as its representative. A worse person could not have been chosen to guide India's destiny. As a unifying force he was a failure. Mr Gandhi presents himself as a man full of humility. But his behaviour at the Round Table Conference showed that Mr Gandhi can be very petty-minded. He treated the whole non-Congress delegation with contempt. He insulted them whenever an occasion furnished him with an excuse by openly telling them that they were nobodies and that he alone, as the delegate of the Congress, represented the country. Instead of unifying the Indian delegation, Mr Gandhi widened the breach. From the point of view of knowledge, Mr Gandhi proved himself to be a very ill-equipped person. On the many constitutional and communal questions with which the Conference was confronted, Mr Gandhi had many platitudes to utter but no views or suggestions of a constructive character to offer. He presented a curious complex of a man who in some cases would threaten to resist any compromise on what he regarded as a principle though others regarded it as a pure prejudice but in other cases would not mind making the worst compromises on issues which appeared to others as matters of fundamental principle on which no compromise should be made."

But when he came out of the Round Table Conference, Gandhi gave different reasons for the stand he had taken. He said: "The Untouchables are not well organized. There is very little political consciousness among them and they are so horribly treated that I want to save them against themselves. If they had separate electorates their lives would be miserable in villages which are the strongholds of Hindu orthodoxy. It is the superior class of Hindus who have to do penance for having neglected the Untouchables for ages.[2] The penance can be done by active social reform and by making the lot of the Untouchables more bearable by acts of services, but not by asking for separate electorates for them. By giving them separate electorates you will throw the apple of discord between the Untouchables and the orthodox. It would be a positive danger for the Untouchables. Separate electorates will ensure them bondage in perpetuity. Do you want the Untouchables to remain Untouchables for ever? Well, the separate electorates would perpetuate the stigma. What is needed is the destruction of untouchability.

"I have the highest regard for Ambedkar. He has every right to be bitter. That he does not break our heads is an act of self-restraint on his part. He is today so much saturated with suspicion that he cannot see anything else. He sees in every Hindu a determined opponent of the Untouchables and it is quite natural. But the separate electorates that he seeks will not give him social reform. He may himself mount to power and position but nothing good will accrue to the Untouchables. I can tell all this with authority, having lived with the Untouchables and having shared their joys and sorrows all these years. "

The Gaekwar of Baroda, who was among the princes attending the Round Table Conference, one day invited Ambedkar to dinner at the Hyde Park Hotel in London. The other guest at the dinner was Rai Bahadur Sir Annepu Patro. This was a unique event for never before a leader of the Untouchables had been known to break bread with a Prince and a Knight. But since Ambedkar had completed his education with scholarships granted to him by the Gaekwar and therefore was believed to be one of his favorites at the Conference, no Indian correspondent or the Society editors of London newspapers took any notice of it. But a dispatch on the event by its correspondent, Charles A. Selden, was given a very prominent display by the New York Times.[3] Taking note of the hatred and contempt for the Untouchables in India, the paper said that the dinner table set for three "was more a sign of an isolated miracle than a symptom of any material change as yet in India's 5,000-year-old social system." After describing the Gaekwar as a most unusual Maharaja who had been taking pains for imparting compulsory education, setting up village libraries and making provisions for free medical dispensaries throughout his principality, the paper focused attention on the fact that despite very humble beginnings Ambedkar had risen to be an outstanding scholar who had obtained doctoral degrees from the Columbia University in New York and the London School of Economics. Besides he had already written several important books.

The dispatch appeared under the headline," PRINCE AND OUTCAST AT DINNER IN LONDON END AGE-OLD BARRIER" with these subheads," Gaekwar of Baroda is Host to Untouchable and Knight of High Hindu Caste", "Scholar Wars on Stigma", " Dr Ambedkar Leads Fight to Free 43,000,000 in India From Ancient Fetters,", "Tells Own Sufferings", "He Braved Ostracism by Teachers and Pupils and Won Degrees at Two Universities". In an interview, which was part of the dispatch, Ambedkar said:" "Our programme now is to break down the barriers against intermarriage and inter-dining between caste and no caste. The matter is largely psychological. Prejudices of thousands of years' standing have assumed the fixity of principles pertaining to the deepest concerns of life. If we can get a decent Brahmin or other high caste Hindu to eat a meal with an Untouchable who is just as decent and well educated as he is, that is a great accomplishment in the way of reform.

"I have organized in Bombay the Social Equality League for the purpose of dining together monthly, alternating between the homes of untouchables and caste Hindus. So far we have about 200 members, nearly half of whom are men of caste. Our Untouchable members are all very poor men, many of them so poor they cannot afford to give dinners in their own homes. In such cases the guests pay for the food they eat. But the main point is to get them all round the same table and into each others' homes. The movement is growing very slowly, but it is growing. The Liberal Hindus who have joined us have got beyond the point of seeming self-conscious when accepting the hospitality of an Untouchable host, but they suffer estrangement from the orthodox members of their own caste. That is the chief obstacle to our progress.

"The plight of our 43,000,000 depressed people is not the problem of India alone. It should be international, for it affects the economic and social welfare of the entire world, and it is a case for the League of Nations just as slavery or the drug traffic is. Untouchability is far worse than slavery, for the latter may be abolished by statute. It will take more than a law to remove this stigma from the people of India. Nothing less than the aroused opinion of the world can do it. Our Untouchables are 95 per cent illiterate. Why? Because they are all desperately poor; and they are poor because practically all trades and industries are closed against them by their social status. They can't have shops, because none would buy from them. They can't enter industrial plants, because other employees would not work in the same room with them. They can own no land but must work as labourers in the fields of farmers who despise them. Except for occasional isolated jobs in which a man may work without coming in physical contact with other human beings, there is nothing for Untouchables but the most menial and humiliating tasks, with hopeless poverty and degradation.

"Just now, with the London round table conference in progress, there is some slight indication of a better attitude on the part of the Hindus. But we are afraid it may not be sincere or lasting. It may be only a temporary political expedient for the sake of proving to Great Britain that all Indians have a common cause and are unanimous in their demand for self-government. If they win, perhaps the Hindus will forget again that we Untouchables are human beings and will see no reason for removing caste slavery because they have gained political freedom. But we are trusting them and taking our chance by merging our cause with theirs in these London negotiations."

While returning from England Gandhi had given an interview to a newspaper correspondent in Rome where he had threatened to revive his campaign of civil disobedience. With a view to forestalling trouble by Gandhi's threat to revive this agitation, the government arrested him as soon he reached India. Fearing that the demand for separate electorates for the Untouchables might be accepted by the British government, Gandhi addressed a letter from Poona jail to Sir Samuel Hoare, the then Secretary of State for India, reminding him of his opposition to the claim of the Untouchables and also warning the government that in case provision for separate electorates was made he would go on a fast unto death as a protest against this move. He informed the government that he would resist with his life the grant of separate electorates to the Untouchables.

His letter stated:" You will have to appreciate my feelings in this matter by remembering that I have been interested in the condition of these classes from boyhood and have more than once staked my all for their sake. I say this not to pride myself in any way. For, I feel that no penance that the Hindus may do can in any way compensate for the calculated degradation to which they have consigned the depressed classes for centuries. But I know that separate electorate is neither a penance nor any remedy for the crushing degradation they have groaned under. I therefore, respectfully inform His Majesty's Government that in the event of their decision creating separate electorates for the depressed classes, I must fast unto death.

The Prime Minister announced his decision on the communal question on August 17, 1932. The announcement was a stunning blow to Mr Gandhi's prestige for the British government without paying any heed to his threat of fast unto death had accepted the demand for separate electorates for Untouchables. In a bid to undo what the government had decided after great deliberation, Gandhi addressed a letter to the Prime Minister, saying that his threat of fast unto death was not empty rhetoric but an expression of his feelings. Unless the communal award was revised, his proposed fast "will come into operation in the ordinary course from the noon of 20th September next." " I regret the decision I have taken. But as a man of religion that I hold myself to be, I have no other course left open to me. As I have said in my letter to the Secretary of State, even if His Majesty's government decided to release me in order to save themselves from embarrassment, my fast will have to continue. For I cannot now hope to resist the decision by any other means; and I have no desire whatsoever to compass my release by any means other than honorable."

The Prime Minister in his reply to Mr Gandhi stated:" "We have deliberately included all depressed class voters in the general or Hindu constituencies so that the higher caste candidates should have to solicit their votes or depressed class candidates should have to solicit the votes of the higher castes at election. We felt it was essential that the depressed classes whom you have yourself described in your letter to Sir Samuel Hoare as having been consigned by caste Hindus to calculated degradation for centuries, should return a certain number of members of their own choosing to legislatures of seven of the nine provinces to voice their grievances and their ideals and prevent decisions going against them without the legislature and the government listening to their case. In a word, we want to place them in a position to speak for themselves, which every fair-minded person must agree to be necessary.

Before going on fast unto death on 20th September 1932 in Yeravada Central Prison in Poona, Gandhi wrote another letter to the Prime Minister saying : "The mere fact of the depressed classes having double votes does not protect them or Hindu society in general from being disrupted. In the establishment of separate electorate for the depressed classes I sense the injection of poison that is calculated to destroy Hinduism and do no good whatever to the depressed classes. No matter how sympathetic you may be, you cannot come to a correct decision on a matter of such vital and religious importance to the parties concerned. I should not be against even over-representation of the depressed classes. What I am against is their statutory separation even in a limited form from the Hindu fold so long as they choose to belong to it. Do you realize that if your decision stands and the constitution comes into being, you arrest the marvellous growth of the work of Hindu reformers, who have dedicated themselves to the uplift of their suppressed brethren in every walk of life?"[4]

What raised Gandhi's hackles was not that some part of the nation of which he thought himself to be the undisputed leader was being denied social justice, but only because recognition of the Untouchables as a separate minority outside the Hindu fold would weaken the electoral strength of the Hindus. He was furious. No sooner did the British Prime Minister Ramsay Macdonald announce his decision about the communal electorates than he raised a storm of protest, saying many things which meant nothing more than what he wanted to push down the throat of all his Congress party followers: the British decision if accepted would weaken the Hindu majority in the country; this must be resisted at any cost.

Under instructions from Gandhi, the Congress Party formed an Emergency Committee to mobilize public opinion against the Communal Award announced by the British government. Some prominent Hindu leaders pleaded with Ambedkar to give up his demand for separate electorates for the Untouchables to save Gandhi's life who had embarked on a fast unto death as a protest against the Communal Award. Reports in newspapers focused attention on the worsening condition of Gandhi because of the fast. The Congress held meetings all over the country and denounced Ambedkar as monster[5], traitor and a British stooge out to take the life of the father of the nation because of his decision not to bend over the question of separate electorates for the Untouchables. The crisis created by Gandhi's fast made Ambedkar the subject of discussion in every political party, social circle and religious institution. He was flooded with telegrams and letters, some threatening his life, some appealing to his conscience and some supporting his stand. The Hindu leaders held a conference in Bombay to resolve the deadlock to save Gandhi's life. On the eve of the conference, Ambedkar issued a statement, saying:" So far as I am concerned, I am willing to consider everything, though I am not willing to allow the rights of the Depressed Classes to be curtailed in any way."

Ambedkar was astounded to read the correspondence between Mahatma Gandhi, Sir Slamuel Hoare and the Prime Minister, published in newspapers, and in which Gandhi had expressed his determination to starve himself unto death till the British government revised their opinion and withdraw their scheme of communal representation for the depressed classes. Explaining his stand Ambedkar issued a statement, saying[6] :" It passes my comprehension why Mr Gandhi should stake his life on an issue arising out of the communal question which he, at the Round Table Conference, said was one of a comparatively small importance. Indeed, to adopt the language of those of Mr Gandhi's way of thinking, the communal question was only an appendix to the book of India's constitution and not the main chapter. It would have been justifiable, if Mr Gandhi had resorted to this extreme step for obtaining independence for the country on which he was so insistent all through the R.T.C. debates. It is also a painful surprise that Mr Gandhi should single out special representation for the depressed classes in the Communal Award as an excuse for his self-immolation. Separate electorates are granted not only to the Depressed Classes, but to the Indian Christians, Anglo-Indians, Europeans, as well as to the Mahomedans and the Sikhs. Also separate electorates are granted to landlords, labourers and traders. Mr Gandhi has declared his opposition to the special representation of every other class and creed except the Mahomedans and the Sikhs. All the same, Mr Gandhi chooses to let everybody else except the depressed classes retain the special electorates given to them.

"The fears expressed by Mr Gandhi about the consequences of the arrangements for the representation of the depressed classes are, in my opinion, purely imaginary. If the nation is not going to split up by separate electorates to the Mahomedans and the Sikhs, the Hindu society cannot be said to be split up if the depressed classes are given separate electorates. His conscience is not aroused if the nation is split by the arrangements of special electorates for classes and communities other than the depressed classes. I am sure many have felt that if there was any class which deserved to be given special political rights in order to protect itself against the tyranny of the majority under the Swaraj constitution it was the depressed classes. Here is a class which is undoubtedly not in a position to sustain itself in the struggle for existence. The religion to which they are tied, instead of providing for them an honourable place, brands them as lepers, not fit for ordinary intercourse. Economically, it is a class entirely dependent upon the high caste Hindus for earning its daily bread with no independent way of living open to it. Nor are all ways closed by reason of social prejudices of the Hindus but there is definite attempt throughout the Hindu society to bolt every possible door so as not to allow the depressed classes any opportunity to rise in the scale of life. Indeed it would be an exaggeration to say that in every village the caste Hindus, however divided among themselves, are always in a standing conspiracy to put down in a merciless manner any attempt on the part of the depressed classes who form a small and scattered body of ordinary Indian citizens. In these circumstances, it would be granted by all fair-minded persons that as the only path for a community so handicapped to succeed in the struggle for life against organized tyranny, some share of political power in order that it may protect itself is a paramount necessity.

"I should have thought that a well-wisher of the depressed classes would have fought tooth and nail for securing to them as much political power as might be possible in the new constitution. But the Mahatma's ways of thinking are strange and are certainly beyond my comprehension. He not only does not endeavour to augment the scanty political power which the depressed classes have got under the Communal Award, but on the contrary he has staked his life in order to deprive them of little they have got. This is not the first attempt on the part of the Mahatma to completely ditch the depressed classes out of political existence.

"The Communal Award, in my opinion, satisfied both those who want separate electorates and those who want joint electorates. In this sense, it is already a compromise and should be accepted as it is. As to the Mahatma, I do not know what he wants. It is assumed that although Mahatma is opposed to the system of separate electorates, he is not opposed to the system of joint electorates and reserved seats. That is a gross error. Whatever his views are today, while in London he was totally opposed to any system of special representation for the depressed classes whether by joint electorates or by separate electorates. Beyond the right to vote in a general electorate based upon adult suffrage, he was not prepared to concede anything to the depressed classes by way of securing their representation in the legislatures. This was the position he had taken at first. Towards the end of the R.T.C., he suggested to me a scheme, which he said, he was prepared to consider. The scheme was purely convention without any constitutional sanction behind it and without any single seat being reserved for the depressed classes in the electoral law.

"The scheme was that the depressed class candidates might stand in the general electorate as against other high caste Hindu candidates. If any depressed class candidate was defeated in the election, he should file an election petition and obtain the verdict that he was defeated because he was Untouchable. If such a decision was obtained, the Mahatma said he would undertake to induce some Hindu members to resign and thus create a vacancy. There would be then another election in which the defeated depressed class candidate or any other depressed class candidate might again try his luck as against the Hindu candidate.

Should he be defeated again, he should get similar verdict that he was defeated because he was an Untouchable and so on ad infinitum. "I must, however, point out that I cannot accept the assurances of the Mahatma that he and his Congress will do the needful. I cannot leave so important a question as the protection of my people to convention and understandings. The Mahatma is not immortal person, and the Congress, assuming it is not a malevolent force, is not to have abiding existence. There have been many Mahatmas in India whose sole object was to remove Untouchability and to elevate and absorb the depressed classes, but every one of them has failed in his mission. Mahatmas have come and Mahatmas have gone. But the Untouchables have remained as Untouchables.

"I have enough experience of the pace of reform and the faith of Hindu reformers in the conflicts that have taken place at Mahad and Nasik, to say that no well-wisher of the depressed classes will ever consent to allow the uplift of the depressed classes to rest upon such treacherous shoulders. Reformers who in moments of crises prefer to sacrifice their principles rather than hurt the feelings of their kindred can be of no use to the depressed classes. I am therefore bound to insist upon a statutory guarantee for the protection of my people. If Mr Gandhi wishes to have the Communal Award altered, it is for him to put forth his proposals and to prove that they give a better guarantee than has been given to us under the Award.

"I hope that the Mahatma will desist from carrying out the extreme step contemplated by him. We mean no harm to the Hindu society when we demand separate electorates. If we choose separate electorates, we do so in order to avoid the total dependence on the sweet will of the caste Hindus in matters affecting our destiny. Like the Mahatma we also claim our right to err, and we expect him not to deprive us of that right. His determination to fast himself unto death is worthy of a far better cause. I could have understood the propriety of the Mahatma contemplating such extreme step for stopping riots between Hindus and Mahomedans or between the depressed classes and the Hindus or any other national cause. It certainly cannot improve the lot of the depressed classes. Whether he knows it or not, the Mahatma's act will result in nothing but terrorism by his followers against the depressed classes all over the country.

"Coercion of this sort will not win the depressed classes to the Hindu fold if they are determined to go out. And if the Mahatma chooses to ask the depressed classes to make a choice between Hindu faith and possession of political power, I am quite sure that the depressed classes will choose political power and save the Mahatma from self-immolation. If Mr Gandhi coolly reflects on the consequences of his act, I very much doubt whether he will find this victory worth having. It is still more important to note that the Mahatma is releasing reactionary and uncontrollable forces, and is fostering the spirit of hatred between the Hindu community and the depressed classes by resorting to this method and thereby widening the existing gulf between the two. When I opposed Mr Gandhi at the R.T.C, there was a hue and cry against me in the country and there was a conspiracy in the so-called nationalist press to represent me as a traitor to the nationalist cause, to suppress correspondents coming my side and to boost the propaganda against my party by publishing exaggerated reports of meetings and conferences, many of which were never held. "Silver bullets" were freely used for creating divisions in the ranks of the depressed classes. There have been also a few clashes ending in violence.

"If the Mahatma does not want all this to be repeated on a larger scale, let him, for God's sake, reconsider his decision and avert the disastrous consequences. I believe the Mahatma does not want this. But if he doe not desist, in spite of his wishes, these consequences are sure to follow as night follows the day. Before concluding this statement, I desire to assure the public that although I am entitled to say that I regard the matter as closed, I am prepared to consider the proposals of the Mahatma. I, however, trust the Mahatma will not drive to the necessity of making a choice between his life and the rights of my people. For I can never consent to deliver my people bound hand and foot to the caste Hindus for generations to come."

But all this did not make any change in Gandhi's resolve to go on fast unto death to force acceptance of his demand for the revision of the Communal Award. As acceptance of the demands for separate electorates for the depressed classes made by Ambedkar had aroused considerable interest throughout the country, Gandhi's protest fast against this move hit headlines in newspapers. Not only all important Congress leaders but also many religious leaders and intellectuals including the Nobel laureate, Rabindra Nath Tagore, reached Poona to express their sympathy and solidarity with Gandhi. All newspapers were full of critical commentaries against the leader of the depressed classes and held him mainly responsible for creating the political crisis which had made the Mahatma stake his life.

Commenting on the situation later Ambedkar said with wellsprings of sympathy for Mahatma overflowing all over the country and increasing danger of communal warfare to which he had already drawn attention in his statement, he had no alternative but to act to somehow defuse the situation. The only way out was alter the communal Award which Mr Gandhi said hurt his conscience. The Prime minister had made it quite clear that the British Cabinet would not withdraw it or alter it of its own, but that they were ready to substitute for it a formula that may be agreed upon by the caste Hindus and the Untouchables. As he had the privilege of representing the Untouchables at the Round Table Conference, it was assumed that the assent of the Untouchables would not be valid unless Ambedkar was a party to it. The surprising fact was that his position as the leader of the Untouchables of India was not questioned by Congressmen but it was accepted as a fact. All eyes naturally turned to Ambedkar as the man of the moment or rather as the villain of the piece.

No man was placed in a greater and graver dilemma than Ambedkar. It was a baffling situation. He had to make a choice between two different alternatives. There was before him the duty, which he owed as a part of common humanity, to save Gandhi from sure death. There was before him the problem of saving for the Untouchables the political rights which the Prime Minister had given them. He responded to the call of humanity, saved the life of Gandhi by agreeing to alter the Communal Award in a manner satisfactory to Gandhi. This agreement was known as the Poona Pact. Under this agreement seats reserved for the depressed classes out of the general electorate seats in the provincial legislatures were as follows: Madras 30; Bombay with Sind 15; Punjab 8; Bihar and Orissa 18; Central Provinces 20; Assam 67; Bengal 30; and United provinces 20. There were many other provisions which for the first time accorded recognition to the depressed classes as citizens with rights.

The Communal Award had given the Untouchables two benefits : (1) a fixed quota of seats to be elected by separate electorate of Untouchables and to be filled by persons belonging to the Untouchables; (2) double vote, one to be used through separate electorates and the other to be used in the general electorates. But the Poona Pact while increasing the fixed quota of seats for the Untouchables took away the right to the double vote. The increase in seats could never be deemed to be a compensation for the loss of the double vote. The second vote given by the Communal Award was a priceless privilege. Its value as a political weapon was beyond reckoning. The vote strength of the Untouchables in each constituency is one to ten. With this voting strength free to be used in the election of caste Hindu candidates, the Untouchables would have been in a position to determine, if not dictate, the issue of the general election. No caste Hindu candidate could have dared to neglect the Untouchables in his constituency or be hostile to their interest if he was made dependent upon the votes of the Untouchables. But all this advantage to the Untouchables was lost.

Soon after the Poona Pact was signed on 24th September 1932, a public meeting of prominent Hindus from all over the country was held under the chairmanship of Madan Mohan Malaviya in Bombay. A resolution was adopted here, saying among other things that "henceforth amongst Hindus, no one shall be regarded as an Untouchable by reason of his birth, and that those who have been so regarded hitherto will have the same right as other Hindus in regard to the use of the public wells, public schools, public roads and all other public institutions. This right shall have statutory recognition at the first opportunity and shall be one of the earliest Acts of the Swaraj Parliament, if it shall not have received such recognition before that time. It is further agreed that it shall be the duty of all Hindu leaders to secure, by every legitimate and peaceful means, an early removal of all social disabilities now imposed by custom upon the so-called Untouchable classes, including the bar in respect of admission to temples."

Following adoption of this resolution, the Hindus threw open temples to the Untouchables at some places. No week passed in which the Harijan, a weekly newspaper started by Gandhi, did not publish a long list of the temples thrown open, wells thrown open and schools thrown open to the Untouchables set out under special column headed "Week to Week" on the first page. But it is interesting to note how Gandhi changed his stance. Before 1932, he was opposed to allow Untouchables to enter Hindu temples, as mentioned in Gandhi Shikshan, Volume II, page 132: "How is it possible that the Antyajas (Untouchables) should have the right to enter all the existing temples? As long as the law of caste and ashram has the chief place in Hindu religion, to say that every Hindu can enter every temple is a thing that is not possible today." Why did Gandhi make this somersault is difficult to imagine. Was it an honest act of change of heart, due to a conviction that he was in error in opposing the entry of the Untouchables in Hindu temples? Or was it because Gandhi saw before him looming large a possibility of adding to his name and fame and rushed to make the most of it, as was his habit to do?

Later, Ambedkar wrote: "After a short spurt of activity in the direction of removing untouchability by throwing open temples and wells, the Hindu mind returned to its original state. The reports appearing in the "Week to Week" columns of the Harijan subsided, became few and far between and ultimately vanished. For myself I was surprised to find that the Hindu heart was so soon stricken with palsy. For I never believed that there was so much milk of human kindness locked up in the Hindu breast as the "Week to Week" column in the Harijan would have the world believe. As a matter of fact a large part of the news that appeared in the Harijan regarding temple entry was faked and was nothing but a lying propaganda engineered by Congressmen to deceive the world that the Hindus were determined to fight untouchability. Few temples if any were really opened and those that were reported to have been opened were dilapidated and deserted temples, which were used by none but dogs and donkeys. One of the evil effects of the Congress agitation was that it had made the political minded Hindus a lying squad which would not hesitate to tell any lie if it could help the party."

Neither the temple entry movement started by the Congress nor Bills introduced in legislatures for facilitating the entry of the Untouchables into places of worship made any headway, although for securing their entry into the Guruvayur temple in Kerala even Satyagrapha was launched. Gandhi asked Ambedkar to join the campaign for entry into the temples. But Ambedkar declined for he was deeply pained by the obduracy of the Hindus. Disgusted, he issued a long statement saying among other things: "Not very long ago there used to be boards on club doors and other social resorts maintained by Europeans in India, which said: "Dogs and Indians not allowed". The temples of Hindus carry similar boards today, the only difference is that boards on the Hindu temples practically say: All Hindus and all animals including dogs are admitted, only Untouchables not admitted: The situation in both cases is on a parity. But Hindus never begged for admission in those places from which the Europeans in their arrogance had excluded them. Why should an Untouchable beg for admission to a place from which he has been excluded by the arrogance of the Hindus? The depressed class man who is interested in his material welfare is prepared to say to the Hindus to open or not open your temples, for it is a question for you to consider and not for me to agitate. If you think, it is bad manners not to respect the sacredness of human personality, open your temples and be a gentleman. If you would rather be a Hindu than be gentleman, then shut the doors and damn yourself for I don't care to come."

"If Mahatma Gandhi and the reformers were to proclaim that the goal which they have set before themselves is for the advancement of the social status of the depressed classes, it would be easier for the depressed classes to define their attitude towards temple entry. What the depressed classes want is a religion, which will give them equality of social status. To prevent any misunderstanding, I would like to elaborate the point by drawing a distinction between social evils which are the results of secular causes and social evils which are founded upon the doctrine of religion. Social evils can have no justification whatsoever in a civilized society. But nothing can be more odious and vile than that admitted social evils should be sought to be justified on the ground of religion. The depressed classes may not be able to overthrow iniquities to which they are being subjected. But they have made up their mind not to tolerate a religion that will lend its support to the continuance of these iniquities.

"If the Hindu religion is to be their religion, then it must become a religion of social equality. The mere amendment of Hindu religious code by the mere inclusion in it of a provision to permit temple entry for all, cannot make it a religion of equality of social status. All that it can do is to recognize them as nationals and not aliens, if I may use in this connection terms which have become so familiar in politics. But that cannot mean that they would thereby reach a position where they would be free and equal, without being above or below any one else, for the simple reason that the Hindu religion does not recognize the principle of equality of social status; on the other hand it fosters inequality by insisting upon grading people as Brahmins, Kshatrias, Vaishyas and Shudras, which now stand towards one another in an ascending scale of hatred and descending scale of contempt. If the Hindu religion is to be a religion of social equality then an amendment of its code to provide temple-entry is not enough. What is required is to purify it of the doctrine of Chaturvarnya. That is the root cause of all inequality and also the parent of the caste system and untouchability, which are merely forms of inequality. Unless it is done not only will the depressed classes reject temple entry, they will also reject the Hindu faith.

"Chaturvarnya and the Caste system are incompatible with the self-respect of the depressed classes. So long as they stand to be its doctrine the depressed classes must continue to be looked upon as low. The depressed classes can say that they are Hindus only when the theory of Chaturvarnya and caste system is abandoned and expunged from the Hindu Shastras. Do the Mahatma and the Hindu reformers accept this as their goal and will they show the courage to work for it? I shall look forward to their pronouncements on this issue, before I decide upon my final attitude. But whether Mahatma Gandhi and the Hindus are prepared for this or not, let it be known once for all that nothing short of this will satisfy the depressed classes and make them accept templey entry. To accept temple entry and be content with it, is to temporize with evil and barter away the sacredness of human personality that dwells in them.

"There is, however, one argument which Mahatma Gandhi and the reforming Hindus may advance against the position I have taken. They may say acceptance by the depressed classes of temple entry now, will not prevent them from agitating hereafter for the abolition of Chaturvarnya and caste. If that is their view, I like to meet the argument right at this stage so as to clinch the issue and clear the road for future developments. My reply is that it is true that my right to agitate for the abolition of Chaturvarnya and the caste system will not be lost, if I accept temple entry now. But the question is on which side will Mahatma Gandhi be at the time when the question is put: if he will be in the camp of my opponents, I must tell him that I cannot be in his camp now; if he will be in my camp, he ought to be in it now."

Although the Poona Pact had raised hopes among the depressed classes that henceforth they would not only be able to gain entry into the temples but also get representation in legislatures and the Cabinet, yet they remained disappointed, cursing their lot. Not only the doors of temples remained barred to them, the elections to the provincial legislatures in February 1937 under the Government of India Act, 1935,did not improve their position in any way. The total number of seats allotted to the Untouchables as a result of the Poona Pact was 151. But thanks to the intriguing role played by the Congress only 73 seats could be won by them; all the remaining 78 seats going to the Untouchable candidates fielded by the Congress party. Most of the candidates loyal to Ambedkar could not win due to their failure to match the financial resources of candidates owing allegiance to the Congress. The Congress was bound by the terms of the Poona Pact to give representation to the Untouchables in the Cabinet. In fact under the Government of India Act 1935 the State governors had been empowered to ensure that after the elections ministries were constituted with due representation to minorities. But soon after the elections the Congress declared that they were not prepared to accept Governors' interference in the formation of the government. Following this the Governors surrendered their authority and allowed the Congress to ride roughshod as a result of which the Untouchables and the other minorities were deprived of their right to representation in the Cabinet.

It was clear that the Congress and Mr. Gandhi were determined on principle not to recognize the right of the Untouchables to be represented in the Cabinet. Mr Gandhi said a Cabinet minister should be a topmost man commanding universal confidence. A person after he has secured a seat in an elected body should depend upon his intrinsic merit and popularity to secure coveted position. Asked about the provisions of the Act under which the governments were to be constituted, Gandhi said he was not interested in the Act which is as good as dead. The Congress had selected candidates who came from high caste Hindus as Brahmins and the allied communities. In case there were no Brahmins, people with low qualifications were preferred to those with higher qualifications. And in the case of the Untouchables those with little or no qualifications were selected in preference to those who had. It was obvious that the party wanted legislatures to be packed with highly educated upper caste members so that members belonging to lower castes already suffering from inferiority complex never dared challenge what they were asked to do by the party.

Seeing the composition of provincial legislatures and the way Congress managed its affairs, Ambedkar commented Untouchable Congressmen were subjected to the rigours of party discipline. They were completely under the Congress Party Executive. They could not ask a question it did not like. They could not move a resolution it did not permit. They could not bring in legislation to which it objected. They could not vote as they chose and could not speak what they felt. They were there as dumb driven cattle. One of the objects of obtaining representation in the legislature for the Untouchables was to enable them to ventilate their grievances and to obtain redress for the wrongs. Under Gandhi's leadership, the Congress successfully and effectively prevented this from happening.

References

1. See page 23, Vol. 9.
2. See para three Vol. 9.
3. The New York Times clippings in the Columbia University folder on Ambedkar.
4. see page 87 Vol. 9 of Ambedkar's Writings and Speeches.
5. Microfilmed Ambedkar Papers in the Nehru Museum Library.
6. Ambedkar's statement on Gandhis fast page 311 Vol. 9 of Ambedkar's Writings and Speeches published by Maharashtra government in 1990.

10

An Enigma

Notwithstanding the fact that he was strongly opposed to the grant of any special concessions by way of separate electorates to the Untouchables by the British government, Mahatma Gandhi kept on stressing in his writings and speeches that they had been wronged in the Hindu society; the caste Hindus therefore should make amends for the grievous injury inflicted by their ancestors on them. Removal of untouchability is a penance that caste Hindus owe to Hinduism and to themselves. There is no vice that is special to the Untouchables, not even dirt and insanitation. It is our arrogance which blinds us, superior Hindus, to our own blemishes and which magnifies those of our downtrodden brethren whom we have suppressed and whom we keep under suppression. Gandhi was so much concerned with the problems of the Untouchabales that he attributed visitations like droughts, floods, earthquakes and other calamities to the sins of untouchability.

Writing in the Young India on April 27, 1921, Gandhi said: "I do not want Moksha. I do not want to be reborn. But if I have to be reborn, I should be reborn amongst Untouchables, so that I may share their sorrows, sufferings and the affronts, in order that I may endeavour to free myself and them from that miserable condition. I therefore pray that if I should be born again, I should do so not as a Brahmin, Kshatriya, Vaishya, or Shudra, but as an Atishudra. I love scavenging. In my Ashram, an eighteen years old Brahmin lad is doing the scavenger's work in order to teach the Ashram scavenger cleanliness. The lad is no reformer. He was born and bred in orthodoxy. But he felt that his accomplishments were incomplete until he had become also a perfect sweeper, and that, if he wanted the Ashram sweeper to do his work well, he must do it himself and set an example."

In an article in the Harijan on February 11, 1933, Gandhi wrote: "Untouchability as at present practiced is the greatest blot on Hinduism. It is (with apologies to Sanatanists) against the Shastras. It is against the fundamental principles of humanity; it is against the dictates of reason that a man, merely because of his birth, should be forever unapproachable and un-seeable. These adjectives do not convey the full meaning of the thing itself. It is a crime for certain men, women and their children to touch, or to approach within stated distances or to be seen by those who are called caste Hindus. The tragedy is that millions of Hindus believe in this institution as if it is enjoined by the Hindu religion.

"Happily, Hindu reformers have recoiled with horror from this practice. They have come to the conclusion that it has no support in the Hindu Shastras taken as a whole. Isolated texts torn from their contexts and considered by themselves can no doubt be produced in support of this practice, as of any evil known to mankind. But there is abundant authority in the Shastras to warrant the summary rejection, as being un-Hindu, of anything or any practice that is manifestly against the fundamental principles of humanity or morality, of Ahimsa or Satya. The Untouchable is, compared to us, really a Harijan, a man of God, and we are Durjan (men of evil). For while the Untouchable has toiled and moiled and dirtied his hands so that we may live in comfort and cleanliness,we have delighted in suppressing him. We are solely responsible for all the shortcomings and faults that we lay at the door of these Untouchables. It is still open to us to be Harijan ourselves, but we can only do so by heartily repenting of our sin against them."

For long Gandhi was a big enigma to Ambedkar. The man who day in and day out never tired of giving sermons to his followers to work for the improvement of the Untouchable wanted them to so do by means which could never deliver. Gandhi wanted the caste hierarchy governing the Hindu society to stay, Ambedkar wanted to end it for he was convinced so long as the caste system remained intact, the Untouchable would never be able to raise their status to gain equality in the Hindu society. Ambedkar was disenchanted with Gandhi. Apart from his opposition to the provision of separate electorates for the untouchables, Gandhi in the eyes of Ambedkar had come to be identified with several other things which stipulated that the untouchables must remain content with their lot for it was after all ordained by the caste system, which was nothing but the command of gods to Hindus. What Gandhi wanted was that caste Hindus should stop treating toilet cleaners as Untouchables and the untouchables engaged in this task must remain content with it for it was a divine dispensation. Even if they became educated, learned they should not give up their ancestral calling. What really annoyed Ambedkar was the fact that while calling upon the Untouchables to accept their position as ordained by the caste system, Gandhi's own life was not governed by such dictates.

Although it was not proper to make a personal reference in an argument which is general in its application, Ambedkar could not help doing so in the case of Gandhi because he had literally taken the untouchables for a ride by making promises which were never fulfilled. Nothing of what was promised to the untouchables in the Poona Pact had been done by the Congress Party of which Gandhi was the supreme leader. It could be that his failure to practice what he preached was due to the fact that the ideal, which Gandhi wanted the Untouchables to follow, was too high to be attained by them. Or it could be that his failure was due to his innate hypocrisy. Ambedkar argued that the Mahatma himself failed to live up to the ideal he held before the Untouchables to accept without question.

The Mahatma was a Bania by birth. His ancestors had abandoned trading in favour of ministership, a calling of the Brahmins. In his own life, before he became a Mahatma, when occasion came for him to choose his career, Gandhi preferred law to scales. On abandoning law he became half saint and half politician. He had never touched trading which was his ancestral profession. His youngest son – who was a faithful follower of his father – born a Vaishya had married a Brahmin's daughter and had chosen to serve a newspaper magnate. The Mahatma was not known to have condemned him for not following his ancestral calling. It may be wrong and uncharitable to judge an ideal by its worse specimens. But surely the Mahatma as a specimen was no better and if he failed to realize the ideal insofar as his family was concerned then the ideal must be quite opposed to the practical instincts of man. Ambedkar felt that Gandhi was given to speaking on a subject like caste stratifications in Hindu society without first thinking about it. Otherwise certain questions could not have escaped him. When a calling is deemed to have become an ancestral so as to make it binding on a man, must a man follow his ancestral calling even if it does not suit his capacities, even when it has ceased to be profitable? Must a man live by his ancestral calling even if he finds it to be immoral? If every one must pursue his ancestral calling, as Gandhi repeated again and again, then it must follow that a man must continue to be a pimp because his grandfather was a pimp and a woman must continue to be prostitute because her grandmother was a prostitute. Is the Mahatma prepared to accept the logical conclusion of his doctrine? His ideal of following one's ancestral calling is not only an impossible and impractical proposition, it is also morally indefensible.

The Mahatma saw great virtue in a Brahmin remaining a Brahmin all his life. Leaving aside the fact there are many Brahmins who do not like to remain Brahmins all their lives. What can we say about those Brahmins who have clung to their ancestral calling of priesthood? Do they do so from any faith in the virtue of the principle of ancestral calling or do they do so from motives of filthy lucre? The Mahatma does not seem to concern himself with such queries. He is satisfied that Brahmins living on alms freely given to them and giving freely what they have of spiritual treasures are real Brahmins. The Mahatma gives such examples only to justify his argument that the Savarna system is the bedrock of Hindu society and untouchables who are ordained by this system to remain devoted to their calling - removal of the society's filth so that upper castes can live and enjoy themselves - have no justification to protest.

According to Gandhi, caste system is better than class system on the ground that caste is the best possible adjustment of social stability. Everybody wants social stability and some adjustment must be made in the relationship between individuals and classes in order that stability may be achieved. . But there are two things, which nobody wants. One is static relationship, something that is unalterable, something that is fixed for all times. Stability is wanted but not at the cost of change when change is imperative. Second thing nobody wants is mere adjustment. Adjustment is wanted but not at the cost of social justice. But the Mahatma wanted the Untouchables to follow his advice and adjust themselves to whatever Savarna system ordained for them. Even after they are educated, become as competent as members of upper castes, they should continue to stick to their ancestral calling. No wonder, this kind of reasoning made Ambedkar mad. According to Gandhi's philosophy, despite his two doctorates, Ambedkar should have continued to do the work of Untouchable.

The essence of the Vedic conception of Savarna system is the pursuit of a calling which is appropriate to one's natural aptitude. But the essence of the Mahatma's concept of Savarna is the pursuit of ancestral calling irrespective of natural aptitude. What is the difference between caste and Varna as understood by the Mahatma? As defined by the Mahatma, Varna becomes merely a different name for caste for the simple reason that it is the same in essence – namely pursuit of ancestral calling. Far from making progress the Mahatma had suffered retrogression. Ambedkar thougt that by putting this interpretation upon the Vedic conception of Varna Gandhi had really made ridiculous what was sublime. The Mahatma's view of Varna not only made nonsense of the Vedic Varna but it made it also abominable. Varna and caste are two different concepts. Varna is based on the principle of each according to his worth while caste is based on the principle of each according to his birth. The two are as distinct as chalk is from cheese. If the Mahatmta believes as he does in every one following his or her ancestral calling, then he was advocating the caste system, in calling it the Varna system he was not only guilty of terminological inexactitude, but he was also causing confusion.

According to Ambedkar, Mahatma suffered from this confusion for two reasons. The first was his temperament. He had almost in everything the simplicity of the child with the child's capacity for self-deception. Like a child he could believe in anything he wanted to believe. The second source of confusion was the double role which the Mahatma wanted to play – of a Mahatma and a politician. As a Mahatma, he was trying to spiritualize politics. Whether he had succeeded in it or not politics had certainly commercialized him. A politician must know that society cannot bear the whole truth and that he must not speak the whole truth; if he is speaking the whole truth it is bad for his politics. The reason why the Mahatma was always supporting caste and Savarna was because he was afraid that if he opposed them he would lose his place in politics. Whatever might have been the source of this confusion the Mahatma was deceiving himself and also deceiving the people by preaching caste under the name of Varna.

Although Mahatma Gandhi was deeply concerned about the plight of Untouchables in Indian society, he could not see eye to eye with Ambedkar, who was destined to be their messiah. It was not a question of jealousy between two eminent leaders espousing the same cause. Their differences were deep-rooted. Ambedkar, who had made a bonfire of Manusmriti, which lays down the caste stratifications dear to all Hindus, was convinced that unless the caste system was abandoned, Untouchables could never get justice. Gandhi on the other hand propagated the view that Untouchables were at the receiving end of maltreatment, hatred and contempt only due to certain evil practices which had crept into the caste system over a long period. According to him, remedy lay not in giving up the Manusmriti but setting in motion the process of reforms in Hindu society.

Reacting to these observations, Ambedkar said: "Can there be a worse example of false propaganda than this attempt of Gandhism to perpetuate evils which have been deliberately imposed by one class over another? If Gandhism preached the rule of poverty for all and not merely for the Shudra the worst that could be said about it is that it is a mistaken idea. But why preach it as good for one class only? Why appeal to the worst of human failings, namely, pride and vanity in order to make him voluntarily accept what on a rational basis he would resent as a cruel discrimination against him? What is the use of telling the scavenger that even a Brahmin is prepared to do scavenging when it is clear that according to Hindu Shastras and Hindu notions that even if a Brahmin did scavenging he would never be subject to the disabilities of one who is a born scavenger? For in India a man is not a scavenger because of his work. He is a scavenger because of his birth irrespective of the question whether he does scavenging or not.

"If Gandhism preached that scavenging is a noble profession with the object of inducing those who refuse to engage in it, one could understand it. But why appeal to the scavenger's pride and vanity in order to induce him and him only to keep on scavenging by telling him that scavenging is a noble profession and that he need not be ashamed of it. To preach that poverty is good for the Shudra and for no one else, to preach that scavenging is good for the Untouchables and none else and to make them accept that onerous impositions as voluntary purposes of life, by appeal to their feelings is an outrage and a cruel joke on the helpless classes which none but Mr Gandhi can perpetuate with equanimity and impunity."

Ambedkar admitted it is true that Gandhism is prepared to remove the old ban placed by the Hindu Shastras on the right of Untouchables to education and permit them to acquire knowledge and learning. Under Gandhism the Untouchables may study law, they may study medicine, they may study engineering or anything else they may fancy. So far so good. But will the Untouchables be free to make use of their knowledge and learning? Will they have the right to choose their profession? Can they adopt the career of lawyer, doctor or engineer? To these questions the answer which Gandhism gives is an emphatic 'no'. The Untouchables must follow their hereditary professions. That those occupations became hereditary was the result of force and no volition does not matter to Gandhi..

The argument of Gandhism is that what is once settled is settled for every one even if it was wrongly settled. Under Gandhism the Untouchables are to be eternal scavengers. There is no doubt that the Untouchables would much prefer the orthodox system of Untouchability. A compulsory state of ignorance imposed upon the Untouchables by the Hindu Shastras made scavenging bearable. But Gandhism which compels an educated Untouchable to do scavenging because it is incumbent upon him according to the Shastras is nothing short of cruelty. The grace in Gandhism is a curse in its worst form. The virtue of the anti-Untouchability plan in Gandhism is quite illusory. There is no substance in it.

"What else is there in Gandhism which the Untouchables can accept as opening a way for their ultimate salvation? Barring this illusory campaign against Untouchability, Gandhism simply is another form of of Sanatanism which is the ancient name for militant orthodox Hinduism. What is there in Gandhism which is not to be found in orthodox Hinduism? There is caste in Hinduism, there is caste in Gandhism. Hinduism believes in the law of hereditary profession, so does Gandhism. Hindusim enjoins cow-worship. So does Gandhism. Hinduism upholds the law of karma, predestination of man's condition in this world, so does Gandhism. Hinduism accepts the authority of the Shastras. So does Gandhism. Hinduism believes in avatars or incarnation of God. So does Gandhism.

"All that Gandhism has done is to find philosophic justification for Hinduism and its dogmas. Hinduism is bald in the sense that it is just a set of rules which bear on their face the appearance of a crude and cruel system. Gandhism supplies the philosophy which smoothens its surface and gives it the appearance of decency and respectability and so alters it and embellishes it as to make it even attractive. This philosophy can be put in a nutshell. It is a philosophy which says that, 'All that is in Hinduism is well, all that is in Hinduism is necessary for public good.' Those who are familiar with Voltair's Candide will recognize that it is the philosophy of Master Pangloss and recall the mockery Voltair made of it. The Hindus are of course pleased with it. No doubt it suits them and accords with their interest."

Professor Radhakrishnan (who later become the President of India) - whether out of genuine feeling or out of sycophancy we need not stop to inquire — has gone to the length of describing Mr Gandhi as ' God on Earth'. What do the Untouchables understand this to mean? To them it means that:' This God by name Gandhi came to console an afflicted race; He saw India and changed it not saying all is well and will be, if the Hindus will only fulfill the law of caste. He told the afflicted race, "I have come to fuflil the law of caste." Not a tittle, not a jot shall I allow to abate from it.'

Ambedkar said notwithstanding the grand advocacy for Hinduism by Gandhi, the fact is "Hinduism is a veritable chamber of horrors for the Untouchables. The sanctity and infallibility of the Vedas, Smritis and Shastras, the iron law of caste, the heartless law of karma and the senseless law of status by birth are to the Untouchables veritable instruments of torture which Hinduism has forged against the Untouchables. These very instruments which have mutilated, blasted and blighted the life of Untouchables are to be found intact and untarnished in the bosom of Gandhism. How can the Untouchables say that Gandhism is a heaven and not a chamber of horrors as Hinduism has been. The only reaction and a very natural reaction of the Untouchables would be to run away from Gandhism."

"It would be a mistake to take refuge in Gandhi's more recent statement that caste is an anachronism. Reformers were gladdened by this declaration. And who would not be glad to see that a man like Mr Gandhi having such terrible influence over the Hindus, after having played the most mischievous part of a social reactionary, after having stood out as the protagonist of the caste system, after having beguiled and befooled the unthinking Hindus with arguments which made no distinction between what is fair and foul should have come out with this recantation? Those who are carried away by this recantation of Mr Gandhi, forget two things. In the first place all that Mr Gandhi has said is that caste is an anachronism. He does not say it is an evil. He does not say it is anathema. Mr Gandhi may be taken to be not in favour of caste. But Mr Gandhi does not say that he is against the Varna system. And what is Mr Ganhi's Varna system? It is simply a new name for the caste system and retains all the worst features of the caste system."

According to Ambedkar, Gandhi-led Congress promises to do wonders for the servile classes - the Congress speaks of masses, it ought really to speak of them as the servile classes held in bondage by the governing classes - when Swaraj comes. It says that it would like to make revolutionary changes but it has no power to make them and it must wait for Swaraj. It is nothing but glib talk which goes to deceive the gullibl foreigner. Leaving aside the boast of and bluster which are behind the statement, one may ask what really can happen if India does become a sovereign and an independent state. The fact is the governing class will not disappear by the magic wand of Swaraj. It will remain as it was, having been freed from the incubus of British Imperialism it will acquire greater strength and vigor. It will capture power as the governing classes in every country do. In short Swaraj will not be a government by the people but it will be a government run by the governing class and in the absence of government by the people, government for the people will be what the governing class will choose to make of it. "Personally, I have grave doubts about the governing class in India coming forward to carry out even such a modest programme of social amelioration as introduction of tenancy laws, enlargement of factory legislation, extension of primary education, introduce prohibition and train people to ply charkhas, construct roads and canals, improve currency, regulate weights and measures." How prophetic was Ambedkar in his writings!. All that he feared before the British quit India has come true. Of course the governing class has introduced reforms. But benefits from them have not percolated down to the lower rungs of society. Untouchables continue to suffer as before.

The Jat-Pat-Todak Mandal of Lahore had invited Ambedkar to preside over their annual conference in 1936. Since this organization was dedicated to bringing about an end to the caste system, Ambedkar prepared a scholarly address titled "Annihilation of Caste". It was an excellent exposition of the caste problem. But towards the end of his address Ambedkar indicated that this was his last speech as a Hindu for he had decided to renounce his faith and embrace some other religion. The organizers of the conference, while greatly appreciating the text of his address, wanted Ambedkar to drop from it any reference that he was going to renounce Hinduism. Since Ambedkar did not agree, the conference was cancelled. Ambedkar got his speech published and made his views about the caste system well-known. Gandhi strongly reacted to Ambedkar's observations about the Hindu religion and carried his views in the Harijan. Seeing critical references by Gandhi to the observations he had made, Ambedkar reacted strongly. The exchanges between the two leaders filled several editions of the Harijan.

Taking exception to observations made by Ambedkar on the caste system, Gandhi wrote : "Dr Ambedkar is a challenge to Hindusim. Brought up as a Hindu, educated by a Hindu potentate, he has become so disgusted with the so-called Savarna Hindus for the treatment he and his people have received at their hands that he proposes to leave not only them but the very religion that is his and their common heritage. Dr Ambedkar found that the vast majority of Savarna Hindus had not only conducted themselves inhumanly against their fellow religionists whom they classed as Untouchables, but they had based their conduct on the authority of their scriptures. The author of the address has quoted chapter and verse in proof of his three-fold indictment – inhuman conduct itself, the unabashed justification for it on the part of the perpetrators, and the subsequent discovery that the justification was warranted by their scriptures." Exchanges between the two leaders are all there in a publication entitled "Annihilation of Caste with a Reply to Mahatma Gandhi."

Gandhi wanted Untouchables whatever their plight or suffering to swear by caste, though almost every Brahmin had transgressed the caste rule. The number of Brahmins who sell shoes is far greater than those who practice priesthood. Not only have the Brahmins given up their ancestral calling of priesthood for trading but they have entered trades which are prohibited to them by the Shastras. Yet how many Brahmins who break caste every day will preach against caste and against the Shastras? For one honest Brahmin preaching against caste and Shastras due to the fact that his practical instinct and moral conscience cannot support a conviction in them, there are hundreds who break caste and trample upon the Shastras every day. Yet they are the most fanatic upholders of the theory of caste and the sanctity of the Shastras. Why this duplicity? Because they feel that if the masses are emancipated from the yoke of caste they would be a menace to the power and prestige of the Brahmins as a class. The dishonesty of this intellectual class who would deny the masses the fruits of their thinking is a most disgraceful phenomenon.

Ambedkar said the Hindus in the words of Mathew Arnold are "wandering between two worlds : one dead, the other powerless to be born." What are they to do? The Mahatma to whom they appeal for guidance does not believe in thinking and can therefore give no guidance which can be said to stand the test of experience. The intellectual classes to whom the masses look for guidance are either too dishonest or too indifferent to educate them in the right direction. We are indeed witnesses to a great tragedy. In the face of this tragedy all one can do is to lament and say – such be thy leaders, O ! Hindus.

Ambedkar saw no justification in Gandhi claiming to be the champion of the Untouchables better than those who were Untouchables themselves. Gandhi had refused without any regard to morality, justice and necessity, their claim to representation in legislatures which could be their only way to protection against social tyranny and social oppression while he was prepared to give to the Muslims, the Hindus and the Sikhs a goodly share of political power. Gandhi wanted the Untouchables to live under his providence and that of the Congress without any means of protection knowing full well that their lives were exposed to danger and humiliation every moment and when he came to know that the Untouchables were seeking outside aid in support of their claims Gandhi resorted to a terrible act of treachery, which was his so-called fast unto death after the British government had granted to the Untouchables separate electorates, which was nothing but an avenue for them to improve their lot.

As an organization which will devote itself exclusively to the problem of the Untouchables was necessary, the All-India Untouchability League was formed on September 28, 1932 following the signing of the Poona Pact according to which the Congress would strive to remove untouchability. The name, Gandhi thought, did not smell well. Therefore in December 1932, it was given a new name – The Servants of the Untouchables Society. That name again was not as sweet as Gandhi wished it to be. He changed and called it the Harijan Sevak Sangh. But Ambedkar and his vast number of followers detested being called Harijans. Since everybody knows that Harijans are none other than the Untouchables, the change of nomenclature does not provided them any guarantee against untouchability. With the new name they are damned as much as they were with the old. It is better for the patient to know what he is suffering from. It is better for the wrong doer that the wrong is there still to be redressed. Any concealment will give a false sense of both as to the existing facts. Also, Ambedkar felt that the name Harijan is indicative of pity. If the name meant "chosen people of God" as the Jews claimed themselves to be, it would have been different matter. But to call Untouchables "children of God" is to invite pity from their tyrants by pointing out their helplessness and their dependent condition. If only Harijans were the children of god, were the other castes children of monsters? This is how Ambedkar reacted to the new name coined by Gandhi for the Untouchables.

Although it was launced with much fanfare, the Harijan Sevak Sangh, failed to do anything in mitigating the sufferings of the people for whom it was created. By undertaking an All-India tour, Gandhi was able to collect Rs. 8 lakh by way of donations for the Sangh. But this sum was gradually exhausted. Whatever work it was doing would have been wound up for lack of resources had the Congress governments which were formed in the provinces not come to its rescue. The Congress governments handed over to the Sangh certain social welfare work projects which were earlier handled by different government departments. Initially Ambedkar was invited to join the Sangh, but he could not do so due to his preoccupation with other things. However, no other Untouchable was extended this courtesy. When the Untouchables made a grievance of the fact that although it was intended for their welfare, they had no say in its administration, Gandhi dismissed their protest. He said : "The welfare work of the Untouchables is penance which the caste-Hindus have to do for the sin of untouchability. The money that has been collected has been contributed by the Hindus. From both points of view the Hindus alone must run the Sangh. Neither ethics nor right would justify Untouchables in claiming a seat on the Board of the Sangh."

Gandhi had threatened fast unto death against separate electorates for the Untouchables on the ground that it would cause a split in the Hindu community. He argued that Untouchables were part and parcel of it. But now concerning the affairs of the Harijan Sangh he debarred them from any say in the affairs of the Sangh because it was funded only by Hindus and not Untouchables in any way. That the move amounted to creating a barrier between Untouchables and caste Hindus did not bother Gandhi. The Sangh openly advocated separate schools, separate hostels, separate dispensaries, and separate wells for the Untouchables, as if they were not part of the Hindu community. What the Untouchables wanted was not education, but the right to be admitted to common schools. The Untouchables did not want medical aid; what they wanted was the right to be admitted to the general dispensary on equal footing. The Untouchables did not want water, but the right to draw water from the same well from which they had been barred for ages on account of their caste. They wanted equality with other castes. But the Sangh in its actual functioning and management was not bothered about these issues.

Ambedkar could see that Gandhi did not want to do anything that might offend the caste Hindus. If the Harijan Sevak Sangh or Gandhi himself did anything which was not to the liking of the caste-Hindus, they would leave the Congress, contingency which Gandhi never wanted to happen for the sake of his own ambition to be the undisputed leader of the country. Ambedkar said: "I wonder if life would be worthwhile to Gandhi if for some reason he ceased to be at the head of the nation. He is, I think, the most ambitious politician. I know, he regards as his rivals those whom he calls as friends. To be at the head of the nation means that he must preserve the integrity of the Congress. The Congress is ninety nine per cent composed of Hindus. How can Gandhi succeed in maintaining the integrity of the Congress if he were to direct the Sangh to carry on Satyagrah against the Hindus for the sake of Untouchables? The Hindus would leave the Congress and the party would disrupt. That is why Gandhi and the Sangh adopted peaceful persuasion as the only means of removing untouchability. Not only in big matters but even in small things Gandhi and the Sangh were careful to see that the caste-Hindus were not hurt or annoyed."

Assessing Gandhi's role vis-à-vis the depressed classes, Ambedkar frankly stated that Gandhi did not want the Untouchables to organize and be strong. For he feared that they might thereby become independent of Hindus and thus weaken the Hindu majority. This was best illustrated by the activities of the Harijan Sevak Sangh. The whole object of the Sang was to create a slave mentality among the Untouchables towards their Hindu masters. Examine the Sangh from any angle and one could see that the creation of slave mentality appeared to be its dominant purpose. That Sangh was to the Untouchables what Putana, the wet nurse who wanted to kill, was to Krishna. The Sangh under the pretence of service was out to kill the spirit of independence amongst the Untouchables. Of course it is true that the Untouchables in the early stages of their agitation had taken the support of some well-meaning Hindus and had accepted their leadership. By the time of the Round Table Conference, the Untouchables had become completely self-reliant and independent. They were no longer satisfied with charity from the Hindus. They demanded what they thought was their right.

Ambedkar felt that it was only to kill this spirit of independence among the Untouchables that Mr Gandhi started the Harijan Sevak Sangh. The Harijan Sevak Sangh by its petty services had collected a swarm of grateful Untouchables who were employed to preach that Mr Gandhi and the Hindus were the saviours of the Untouchables. Daniel O'Connel, the Irish leader, once said that no man can be grateful at the cost of his honour, no woman can be grateful at the cost of her chastity and no country can be grateful at the cost of liberty. The Untouchables are too simple minded to know that the cost of the service which the Harijan Sevak Sangh offered to render was loss of their independence. This is exactly what Gandhi wanted.

Even as a sympathizer of the Untouchables Gandhi's concern for them was limited by two factors: his social aims and his politics. In 1938, when there was a ministerial crisis in the Central Provinces, the then Prime Minister Dr Khare fell out with his colleagues and asked all of them to resign. He reconstituted his ministry by including an Untouchable as a minister. Normally this should have been a cause of satisfaction for Gandhi. But on the contrary what happened was really the opposite. Dr Khare was indicted for dissolving the old ministry and constituting a new one including a Harijan as a minister. The Congress Working Committee guided by Gandhi found Khare guilty of breach off party discipline and he was deposed from his premiership. One of the charges levelled against Khare by Gandh was that he included an Untouchable in his new Cabinet. Khare, who had done so on the presumption that Gandhi would be happy, was aghast at what the Mahatma said. Khare confided to Ambedkar: "Mahatmaji took me to task for including a Harijan in my second cabinet. I retorted by saying that it was a Congress programme of uplift of Harijans for which he had fasted unto death and that I did what I could in furtherance of that programme when opportunity offered itself. Thereupon Mahatmaji charged me with doing this from selfish ambition. Mahatmaji said that by my action I have thrown open an apple of discord among the members of that simple community and have rendered disservice to the Congress by throwing this temptation in their way."

A crowd of Untouchables went to Shegaon to meet Gandhi and ask for an explanation about what he had done. Anticipating this Gandhi started observing silence – Maun Barat – so that nobody would ask him to open his mouth. Angry Untouchables launched Satyagraha against Gandhi for not including an Untouchable in the Congress Cabinet of the government in Central Provinces. Obviously, to escape this embarrassment Gandhi left Shegaon and went on a tour to the North Western Frontier Provinces purportedly for teaching non-violence to the Pathans. Gandhi's silence on this occasion was not to commune with God. He resorted to this stratagem so that he could escape being driven under the fire of cross examination to disclose his inner-most thoughts about the Untouchables. There was no answer from Gandhi for what he was doing. But it was obvious that even if Gandhi had opened his mouth he could give no better reply. Gandhi had his own ideas about Untouchables although he never tired of swearing by concern for their well-being. He did not have any high opinion about them. Gandhi's sympathies for the Untouchables were limited by his politics.

That there was a trace of hypocrisy in his love for the Untouchables was demonstrated by another incident involving the rape of Bachuma, a 14-year old girl belonging to an Untouchable family living in Wardha. One evening she was decoyed into the house of a Mahomedan who was the police sub-inspector. She was kept in his house and during the night she was raped by three Mahomedans; one was the Superintendent of Police himself, second a Sub-Inspector of Education Department and third a lawyer. The rapists were prosecuted and two of them were sentenced to two years rigorous imprisonment. The lawyer was acquitted as the victim was not able to identify him. The two who were convicted appealed to the High Court but the High Court rejected their appeals and confirmed their convictions and sentences. From gaol they sent to the Governor-in-Council petitions for mercy. But the petitions were also rejected. This happened before the Congress came into office. After the Congress came to power, they submitted fresh applications for mercy to the government. The minister-in-charge, who was also a Mahomedan, thought there was nothing wrong in a Mohmedan commiting rape on an untouchable girl and decided to set the culprits free. The Inspector of Education was released first.

But before the other could be set free, the untouchables of the area launched an agitation against the minister. Following the uproar over what he had done, the minister had to resign his office. Everybody expressed resentment against the shameless act of the minister. But Gandhi kept mum. He did not utter even a word of condemnation against the minister. On the contrary he initiated moves for the reinstatement of the dismissed minister. Ambedkar was horrified over what Gandhi was doing. Writing about the incident, Amedkar raised a hypothetical question: one likes to ask if Gandhi would have remained so silent and unmoved if Bachuma who was raped by the three Mahomedans instead of being the daughter of an Untouchable had been Mr Gandhi's own daughter? Why was Gandhi not able to make Bachuma's case his daughter's case. There were two answers. One was that Mr Ganhi was not an Untouchable. Secondly, Mr Gandhi obviously felt that by condemning the Muslim minister for the sake of Bachuma he might destroy Hindu –Muslim unity the maintenance of which was a fundamental creed of the politics of the Congress, the party he was leading. "Does this not show that Mr Gandhi's sympathies for the Untouchables are limited by his politics?" Ambedkar asked.

In an outburst of anger over what had happened, Ambedkar shot a letter to the Times of India, which appeared on March 19, 1938, protesting against the release of the culprit who had been sentenced to three years' imprisonment in 1936. He said: " I think this act of the Congress minister is a most shameless act, for which one can find no parallel. What does the Hindu public which is so blindly supporting the Congress think of these acts? I would not have troubled you with this letter if the matter concerned the caste Hindus – not that it would not have been a grave thing if the girl was a caste Hindu girl, because the Hindus have cultivated a religious faith no party other than Congress and no man other than the Mahatma can bring them salvation! They have placed their destiny in the hands of one party and have refused to examine the acts of those in whom they trust. If they come to grief it is their fault. But the girl belongs to the depressed classes. She is Chamar by caste. It is because of that I feel deeply concerned.

"What hope have the depressed classes of fair play and justice if such acts as those of the home minister who ordered the release of the convict are tolerated by the Hindu public, are endorsed by the Prime Minister and overlooked by the Mahatma? In any other country such a minister would have been dismissed. But this is not to be expected in India. The Mahatma owes the depressed classes an explanation as to how he and his Prime Minister can justify this reprehensible act of their minister."

Ambedkar was puzzled about the motive behind the drive to accord Untouchables entry into temples. If it was the final goal of their advancement in social status as part of the Hindu society, the Depressed Classes would never accept it. However, if it is only to be a first step in that direction, they may be inclined to support it. If Mahatma Gandhi and reformers were to proclaim that the goal which they set before themselves is for the advancement of the social status of the Depressed Classes in the Hindu fold, it would be easier for the Depressed Classes to define their attitude towards temple entry. The Depressed Classes want a religion, which will give them equality of social status. But Gandhi wanted Untouchables to accept their vocation as the will of gods and stop agitating against the Hindus.

Under Gandhi's leadership the Congress had strictly forbidden the Untouchables who had joined the party to do anything to focus attention on their plight without the approval by the Congress High Command. The result was that even in those provinces where the Untouchables had joined the Congress the movement of the Untouchables was almost dead. When a bill was introduced to secure the entry of the Untouchables into Hindus temple in the Madras Presidency, the Congress government had promised to support it at first. But subsequently, the government changed its stand and opposed the measure. It was a dilemma for the Untouchable members of the Madras legislature. But they had no choice. The whip was applied and they in a body voted against the measure. The representatives of the Untouchables instead of being watchdogs of their rights were nothing but a pack of muzzled dogs. Far from biting they were even not able to bark.

Ambedkar could see that the Untouchables were being told constantly that preaching of reforms for ending untouchability was bound to bring about a moral transformation of the Hindus and the quickening of their conscience. This type of propaganda sought to impress upon the Untouchables that they therefore should rely on the goodwill and sense of duty of the Hindus. No Untouchable believed in this facile proposition. If there were any who did, they were hypocrites willing to agree to whatever Gandhi had to say so that by their grace they might be put in places reserved for the Untouchables. They were a predatory band of Untouchables who were out to feather their own nests by any means open to them. All this made Ambedkar impress upon his followers that they should bear in mind two things. First, that it is futile to expect the Hindu religion to perform the mission of bringing about social justice. Such a task may be performed by Islam, Christianity or Buddhism. The Hindu religion is itself the embodiment of inequity and injustice to the Untouchables. For it, to teach the gospel of justice is to go against its own being. To hope for this is to hope for a miracle. Secondly, assuming that this was a task which Hinduism was fitted to perform, it would be impossible for it to perform. The social barrier between them and the Hindus is much greater than the barrier between the Hindus and their men. Religion, however efficacious it may be within a community or a nation, is quite powerless to break these barriers and make them one whole.

Gandhi's anxiety to keep untouchables within the Hindu fold made him take on even Christian missionaries. He said: "The social work of the missions is undertaken not for its own sake, but as an aid to the salvation of those who receive social service. While you give medical help, you expect the reward in the shape of your patients becoming Christians. The masses of Harijans and for that matter of Indian humanity cannot understand the presentation of Christianity, and that, generally speaking conversion, wherever it has taken place, has not been a spiritual act in any sense of the term. They are conversions of convenience. They (the Harijans) can no more distinguish between the relative merits than can a cow. Harijans have no independence, no intelligence, no sense of difference between God and no-God. If Christian missions will sincerely play the game, they must withdraw from the indecent competition to cover the Harijans. Forget that you have come to a country of heathens and (to) think that they are as much in search of God as you are; just feel that you are not going there to give your spiritual goods to them, but that you will share worldly goods of which you have a good stock. You will then do your work without mental reservation and thereby you will share your spiritual treasures. The knowledge that you have this mental reservation, i.e. you are expecting a man to be a convert in return for service, creates a barrier between you and me."

The Untouchables of Bombay Presidency had launched Satyagraha at Mahad for establishing their right to take water from the public tank and at Nasik for establishing their right to enter Hindu temple. But Gandhi instead of supporting the Satyagraha condemned it without any justification. The Untouchables argued if Civil Disobedience was the weapon which, according to Mr Gandhi, the Hindus could legitimately use against the British for securing their freedom, why were the Untouchables not justified in using the same weapon against the caste Hindus for securing their emancipation? But Gandhi had no patience for this type of argument. He tried to meet their logic by his logic. He argued that Untouchability was the sin of the Hindus. It is the Hindus who must therefore do penance. It is they who must offer Satyagraha for the removal of untouchability. Satyagraha was not the business of Untouchables because they were not sinners, far from being sinners, they were sinned against. This was of course not Aristotalian logic. It was a Mahatmian logic which was another name for casuistry. The Untouchables replied that if that was the view of Mr Gandhi - namely that Satyagraha is penance which is for the sinner to offer - then why should he call upon the Hindus to offer Satyagraha against the British? British imperialism was the sin of the British and therefore according to Gandhi's logic the Satyagraha must be offered by the British and not by the caste Hindus.

Mr Gandhi was a politician wedded to uphold the Congress whatever the consequences or significance of his moves. While he was opposed to Satyagrah at Mahad and Nasik, where Untouchables had been barred from temple entry, he was in favour of the Satyagrah for temple entry by the Untouchables at Vaikom in the South. In fact, he blessed and encouraged it. Was there any difference between the two? Yes, the Vaikom Satyagrah was carried by the Untouchables under the auspices of the Congress. The other two were launched by the Untouchables independent of the Congress. Had the opposition of Mr Gandhi something to do with this difference? Obviously Mr Gandhi was not prepared to protect the lambs who would not accept him as their shepherd. When Mr Gandhi refused to give his blessings to the Satyagrah by the Untouchables it was a foregone conclusion that no Congressman would or could come and help the Untouchables in their struggle against the orthodox Hindus. This was not the only mischief Mr Gandhi did by his most illogical if not perverse attitude. He came out openly against all non-Hindus and prohibited them from helping the Untouchables in their Satyagraha struggle against the caste Hindus.

Although he had strong reservations about Gandhi, Amebdka was sorry over Gandhi's assassination on 30th January, 1948. He visited Birla House where his body lay after the outrage and even accompanied the mourning procession when Gandhi was being taken for cremation to the Raj Ghat. In a letter to Dr Savita Kabir whom he married later, Ambedkar said: "I was very much moved on seeing his dead body. I went with the funeral procession for a short distance as I was unable to walk and then returned home. Again, I went to the Raj Ghat on the Yamuna bank but could not get to the burning place being unable to break the ring formed by the crowd. My own view is that great men are of great service to their country but they are also at certain times a great hindrance to the progress of their country. There is one incident in Roman History which comes to my mind on this occasion. When Caesar was done to death and the matter was reported to Cicero, Cicero said to the messengers, "Tell the Romans your hour of liberty has come." While one regrets the assassination of Mr Gandhi, one can't help finding in his heart the echo of the sentiment expressed by Cicero on the assassination of Caesar. Mr Gandhi had become a positive danger to his country. He had choked all free-thought. He was holding together the Congress, which is a combination of all the bad and self-seeking elements in society who agreed on no social or moral principle governing the life of society except the one of praising and flattering Mr Gandhi. Such a body is unfit to govern a country. As the Bible says 'that good cometh out of evil', so also I think that good will come out of the death of Mr Gandhi. It will release people from bondage to a superman, it will make them think for themselves and it will compel them to stand on their own merits."

References

- What Congress and Gandhi have done to the untouchables.
- Mr. Gandhi and the Emancipation of the untouchables. See Vol. 9 of Ambedkar's writings and speeches.

11

Joins Viceroy's Executive Council

The freedom struggle led by Mahatma Gandhi continued to gather momentum. It was becoming increasingly clear to the British that they would have to go beyond offering mere sops to the agitating masses. Their attempts to unleash a reign of terror against rebellious elements were not proving effective. The whole country was in turmoil. It was against this background that the Government of India Act, 1935, which incorporated provisions giving some sort of provincial autonomy to different regions, was passed by the British Parliament. An announcement was made that elections would be held in the country to constitute legislatures comprising elected representatives of the people. Since the Congress was the largest party with a well organised setup in every province, it was clear that after the elections the Congress would be in a position to form its own ministries in almost all the provinces.

Although several provinces had Muslim majorities, the Muslim League leader, Mohammed Ali Jinnah, was not enthused by the prospect of elections. This was possibly because he had come to realize that the Muslim members of the Congress whose number was by no means small were bound to dent the Muslim League majority in every province. Not only that, what really worried Jinnah was the fact that the Muslims constituted a majority in the population in a small number of provinces. Although Gandhi and Jinnah had seldom seen eye to eye, prospects of coming to power and virtually becoming potentates following the British withdrawal from the subcontinent only made their angularities come into sharper focus. Commenting on the two leaders, Ambedkar wrote that it would be difficult to find two persons who could rival them for their colossal egotism, to whom personal ascendancy is everything and the cause of the country a mere counter on the table. They had made Indian politics a matter of personal feud. Consequences could not deter them; indeed they were not bothered at all about them, until they happened. In all eventualities they preferred to stand on a pedestal in isolation.

Both the leaders opened themselves only to their inferiors. They were very unhappy at and impatient of criticism, but were very happy to be fawned upon by flunkeys. Both had developed a wonderful stagecraft and arranged things in such a way that they were always in the limelight. Each of course claimed to be supreme. If supremacy was their only claim, it would have been a small wonder.

In addition to supremacy each claimed infallibility for himself. Pope Pius IX, during whose sacred regime the issue of infallibility was raging, said: "Before I was Pope I believed in Papal infallibility, now I feel it." This feeling of supremacy and infallibility was strengthened by the Press, a section of newspapers always highlighting whatever Gandhi did and the other equally staunchly supporting Jinnah. Entrenched behind the plaudits of the Press, the spirit of domination exhibited by these two great men transgressed all limits. By their domination they demoralized their followers and depraved politics.

Politics in the hands of these two great men became a rivalry in extravaganza. If Gandhi was known as Mahatma, Jinnah was known as Quaid-e-Azim. If Gandhi had the Congress, Jinnah must have the Muslim League. If the Congress had a Working Committee, the Muslim League must have its own Working Committee and its Council. The session of the Congress must be followed by a session of the League. If the Congress issued a statement the League must also follow suit. If the Congress passed a resolution of 17,000 words, the Muslim League's resolution must necessarily exceed it by at least a thousand words. If the Congress President held a Press Conference, the Muslim League President must do this. If the Congress addressed an appeal to the United Nations, the Muslim League must not allow itself to be outfoxed.

When was all this to end? When was there to be a settlement? But would they meet, except on preposterous conditions? With Jinnah insisting that Gandhi should admit that he is a Hindu, and Gandhi insisting that Jinnah should admit that he is a leader of the Muslims. Never had there been such a deplorable state of bankruptcy of statesmanship as one saw in these two leaders of India. They were making long and interminable speeches like lawyers whose job it is to contest everything, concede nothing and talk by the hour. Suggest anything by way of solution for the deadlock to either of them, and it would be met by a categorical "Nay." Neither would consider a solution of the problem which was not eternal. Between them Indian politics had become "frozen," to use a well-known phrase, and no political action was possible.

But instead of being bothered about what these two great leaders were planning to do to solve India's problems, Ambedkar floated his own organization, the Independent Labour Party, in 1936, to contest elections. Although the Scheduled Castes were spread all over the country he decided to concentrate only on the Bombay province for winning the elections. The election manifesto announced by Ambedkar held out promises of a better tomorrow for all the depressed classes. According to this manifesto, unless industrial development was given a new impetus there would never be enough jobs in the country for all those in the farming sector whose plight was becoming worse day by day due to the fragmentation of holdings and the pressure of increasing population. For raising the productive capacity of the people, the party declared itself in favour of an extensive programme of technical education and the principle of state management and state ownership of industries wherever necessary. The manifesto stated that the party would undertake legislation to protect agricultural tenants from the exactions and evictions by the landlords and extend the same benefits to them as would be provided for industrial workers.

The party would endeavour to introduce legislation to control the employment, dismissal and promotion of employees in factories, to fix maximum hours of work, would make provisions for adequate wages and leave with pay, and provide cheap and sanitary dwellings for the workers. New projects would be launched to offer employment to the jobless, and steps would be taken for the protection of the lower middle class in matters concerning house rents in industrial centres and big towns. The party would penalize all forms of orthodoxy and use surplus from charity funds for such secular purposes as education. Halls for weddings and such other functions besides libraries and cinema halls would be built in villages. No doubt, the party manifesto became the topic of discussion in market squares, shops and offices. Even newspapers lauded it in their editorial comments.

The Independent Labour Party was pitted mainly against the Congress, the party which had no dearth of resources to fight elections. Ambedkar toured all the districts in the Bombay Presidency, made short speeches at Nasik, Ahmednagar, Sholapur, Satara and Belgaum. He placed a wreath on the Samadhi of his mother when he was touring Satara. Memories of the days gone by when his mother was alive overwhelmed him and he broke down with tears in his eyes. Some of the candidates he had fielded were not well-qualified and the voters seemed to have reservations about them. But he told the electorate not to worry about the merits of his candidates for he himself possessed the strength of hundreds of graduates and would be there to guide the party. But Ambedkar decided to support even some upper caste candidates fielded by other parties on the ground that he knew them well and they had stood by him through thick and thin.

The Congress had fielded candidates in all the provinces and tried its level best to turn the tables against Ambedkar in a Bombay constituency from where he himself was contesting the election. The party also tried to put in all its might and resources in ensuring the defeat of a Brahmin candidate, Bhopatkar, the leader of the Democratic Swaraj Party, who was being supported by Ambedkar and who was contesting the election from a constituency in Poona. The election was held on February 17, 1937, and when the result was declared the Congress, though a winner in most of the provinces, was disappointed because Ambedkar had been elected. It was cold comfort to the party that the other candidate supported by Ambedkar in Poona had been defeated. Of the

17 candidates fielded by Ambedkar fifteen had won. No doubt this was a moment of great rejoicing for the leader of the depressed classes and his supporters. The new Congress government was installed in office on July 19, 1937.

Although he had emerged only as a leader of the Opposition in the Bombay Legislative Assembly after the elections, Ambedkar was widely applauded for his performance in the polls. No wonder this acted as a tonic for him and he redoubled his efforts to arouse his followers not to suffer from any inferiority complex and always make a bold bid for their rights. Addressing a big meeting organized by his party at the Kamgar Maidan in Bombay, Ambedkar reiterated his view to work wholeheartedly for the success of the new Constitution under which the elections had been held, although the Congress had reservations about it.

He criticized Congress leaders like Jawaharlal Nehru for putting up even menials as candidates to contest the seats with chosen men from the depressed classes. He specially mentioned Nehru's servant Hari who had been fielded in the elections. He pointed out how Brahminism was asserting itself in India through ministries installed by the Congress. All the Congress governments in provinces were led by Brahmins and there was not even a single depressed class minister although some lackeys belonging to the Scheduled Castes had been fielded and had also got elected.

Presiding over the Sholapur district conference of the depressed classes on December 30, 1937, Ambedkar said there were three problems before them. Whether they would ever be given an equal status in Hindu society is the first problem. The second was whether they would get a proper share of the national wealth; and the third was what would be their plight if they failed to get self-respect in society. As long as the caste system existed, they would never get an equal status with the caste Hindus. As the Congress was in the hands of the capitalists, they could not rely on the present government to do anything for the betterment of their economic conditions. They must form a united front against the capitalists who were out to exploit them. He said the time had come for them to win their economic independence. They had nothing to lose, but everything to gain by opposing their oppressors.

Speaking at another meeting of the depressed classes held in Sholapur on January 4, 1938, Ambedkar used very strong words: "In the political situation that has developed in the country, there has grown the habit among the people of paying homage to only one political party, the Congress. I am no believer in democracy as an ideal to be pursued in all circumstances; and having regard to the present-day conditions in India, democracy is a most unsuitable system of government. At any rate, for the time being India needs to be ruled by a strong and an enlightened autocrat. In this country we have democracy, but it is a democracy which has ceased to exercise its intelligence. It has bound itself hand and foot to one organization. It is not prepared to sit in judgment over the doings or thinking of this organization. I consider it the greatest malaise, a disease and a sickness.

"Unfortunately, the Indian people are by tradition men who have more faith and less wit. Anyone who does anything out of the ordinary, does something so eccentric as to be called in other countries an insane person, acquires in this country the status of a Mahatma or Yogi. And people follow him as the sheep follow the shepherd. Democracy must learn to give a respectful hearing to all who are worth listening to. I am glad that the Sholapur Municipality has set an example in voting an address to me who does not belong to an organization which claims to be the only organization in the country and which all people are in a mood to uphold at present."

Addressing a meeting of the Christians under the presidentship of the Rev. Gangadhar Jadhav, Ambedkar said that since the day he had declared his intention to abjure Hindu religion, he had become a commodity for bargain or a source of comedy. Whatever people might think, he was firm in his resolve. From his study of comparative religions he could say that two personalities could captivate him. They were the Buddha and the Christ. He wanted a religion which instructed people how they should behave with one another and prescribed for man his duty to another and relation with God in the light of equality, fraternity and liberty. He told the Christians that their co-religionists in southern India observed caste system in churches. Besides they lagged behind politically. If the Mahar boys became Christians they would lose their scholarships. Thus there was no economic gain in their being Christians. The Indian Christians as community never fought for the removal of social injustice.

Ambedkar was the first legislator in India to think of agrarian reforms. In the Bombay Legislative Assembly he introduced a bill for the abolition of the serfdom of agricultural tenants. He desired the abolition of the Khoti tenure and substitution of the ryotwari system to make provisions for payment of reasonable compensations to the Khots for the loss of their rights and to give those inferior holders, who were in actual possession of the land, the status of occupants within the meaning of the Land Revenue Code, 1879. But as the legislation was likely to hurt landlords many of whom were financial supporters of the Congress, the Congress government saw to it that the Bill could not be moved for lack of adequate support in the House. This provoked Ambedkar to organize a massive march of the peasants to the Council Hall in Bombay. Peasants from Thana, Kolaba, Ratnagiri, Satara and Nasik assembled in large numbers in Bombay to participate in the protest demonstration. Wearing torn clothes and carrying blankets and bundles on their shoulders and staffs in their hands, they came to Bombay to voice their grievances.

They marched on to the Council Hall from three directions; one from Parel, the other from Alexandra Docks and the third from Chowpatty. They carried posters bearing slogans such as, "Down with the Khot System," "Support Dr Ambedkar's Bill." They reached the Esplanade Maidan near the Victoria Terminus from where they were not allowed by the police to proceed further. Twenty leaders of the peasants led by Ambedkar presented a memorandum to the Chief Minister demanding enforcement of the minimum standard of wages for agricultural labourers. They urged that immediate legislation should be made to provide, with or without compensation, for the abolition of the Khoti System and the Inamdar System. Also, the memorandum demanded an end to landlordism, which was economically wasteful and socially tyrannous. The last demand was for the reduction of 50 per cent of irrigation rates payable by the small holders.

Later, addressing the mammoth gathering of peasants, Ambedkar said that there were two classes of people in the world – the haves and the have-nots; the rich and the poor; the exploiters and the exploited. The third category of people were the middle class. He called upon the peasants and workers to think over the causes of their poverty and told them that only the exploiters were responsible for their poverty. The way out for them was to organize a labour front without any regard to caste or creed and elect to the legislatures those who were their real representatives. If they did so, they would have shelter and clothing and they, who produced the food and wealth of the nation, would not die from want and hunger. The force, logic and sharpness of Ambedkar's speech made a profound impression on the peasants. No wonder, some of his opponents, who were watching the scene from the sidelines, felt that Ambedkar would develop into a dangerous leader of the peasants, workers and the landless. Ambedkar's growing popularity as a political leader, as a spokesman of the mill workers in Bombay and as a formidable leader of the depressed classes to whichever profession or walk of life they belonged, began to cause concern to his political foes, especially upper caste Congress leaders who always regarded him as a thorn in their side.

Ambedkar addressed a big meeting of peasants at Mahad on January 6, 1939. Without making any bones about it, he said that the Congress ministry had utterly failed in mitigating the suffering and woes of peasants in the State. Premier Kher, who was heading the government, was simply a figurehead. He described the other ministers of the provincial government as dogs at the door of Sardar Patel. Drawing attention to the boastful statement of Sardar Patel, which he had made at a reception given to Kher in Gujarat, saying that they welcome Kher as a devotee of Gandhi and not as Premier Kher, Ambedkar said nothing could be more disgraceful than the treatment meted out to Premier Kher, he would wreak vengeance on Patel for the insult inflicted upon a Maharashtrian. If Patel had dared insult him in this manner, Ambedkar said, he would have thrashed him. This was not a soliloquy; this was a public speech. It was outburst of anger which had erupted out of a strong mind, consistent with its contempt for the Congress leader's rude mentality and arrogance.

It was about this time that the World War II broke out in Europe. With a view to safeguarding their interests in England and the colonies they ruled, the British Government sought to maintain peace by winning over parties agitating for liberation of their country from the colonial clutches. Lord Lilinthgow, the then Viceroy of India, invited 52 Indian leaders for talks the main purpose of which was to assure opinion makers in the country that the British Government was not opposed to Indian Independence and would certainly take further steps to achieve this goal after the war. For the time being the Viceroy sought to impress upon his interlocutors that they should suspend their agitations and instead cooperate with the government in fighting Hitler, who was becoming a big menace all over Europe. The leaders who had been invited by the Viceroy for talks included Gandhi, Jinnah, Nehru, Savarkar, Patel, Rajendra Prasad, Subhash Bose, Ambedkar and others. After these talks, the Viceroy issued a statement explaining the position of the British Government on India keeping in view the growing restlessness against its continuing presence in the country. The Viceroy said that after the war, the Government of India Act would be revised in consultation with all the leading parties in India and no substantial political advance would be made without the consent of the minorities. A consultative committee on which all parties were duly represented would be formed during the war.

But barring a few exceptions, reaction to the Viceroy's statement was hostile. Leaders argued that it was nothing but a clever British move to ensure peace in the country so that the imperial power could pursue its objective without any let or hindrance from any quarter. If the British government was serious about relinquishing power, it should have made an announcement now. No wonder, the Working Committee of the Congress issued a rejoinder, saying the Viceroy's statement was wholly unsatisfactory and any help to Britain at this juncture would amount to endorsement of its polices. The Working Committee called upon all the Provincial Ministries to submit their resignations and in view of the British obduracy to continue to stick to power in India announced its resolve to intensify the freedom struggle. The Congress ministries resigned in the first week of November, 1939. But before relinquishing office, the Congress ministries introduced a war resolution in all Provincial Assemblies. The resolution declared that the British government had made India a participant in the war between Britain and Germany without the consent of the people of India, and "have further in complete disregard of the Indian opinion passed laws and adopted measures curtailing the powers and activities of the Provincial Governments." Since the Congress was the most well-organized party with its network of supporters and active members all over the country, the Congress decision was a big setback for the British government, especially when it was looking for allies to fight the growing Nazi threat all over the world.

In the political turmoil caused by the Congress decision, only Ambedkar stood by the British. It was not a question of being unpatriotic but exploiting the situation to advantage so that something concrete and solid could be gained from the colonial rulers for the depressed classes. Ambedkar knew that the caste leaders and capitalists dominating the Congress party would never allow justice for the Untouchables because of their unshaken belief in the Savarna system governing the Hindu society. Whatever hope was there could be realized only if the British made some provision for the depressed classes before they quit India. Ambedkar issued a statement saying that the minorities' problem would never be solved unless Gandhi and the Congress gave up their egoistic and insolent attitude towards persons and parties outside the Congress. Patriotism was not a monopoly of the Congress, Ambedkar said, and added that persons having views divergent from the Congress had a perfectly legitimate right to exist and be recognized.

Speaking on the war resolution in the Bombay Provincial Assembly, Ambedkar said: "I know my position has not been understood properly in the country. It has often been misunderstood. Let me, therefore, take this opportunity to clarify my position. Whenever there has been a conflict between my personal interests and the interests of the country as a whole, I have always placed the claims of the country above my personal claims. I have never pursued the path of private gain. If I had played my cards well, as others do, I might have been in some other place. I do not want to say about it, but I did not do it. There were colleagues with me at the Round Table Conference who, I am sure, would support what I say – that so far as the demands of the country are concerned, I have never lagged behind. Many European members who were at the conference rather felt embarrassed that I was the enfant terrible of the conference."

"But I will also," he thundered, "leave no doubt in the minds of the people of this country that I have another loyalty to which I am bound and which I can never forsake. That loyalty is to the community of Untouchables, in which I was born, to which I belong, and which I hope I shall never desert. And I say this to this House as strongly as I possibly can, that whenever there is any conflict of interests between the country and the Untouchables, so far as I am concerned, the Untouchables' interest will take precedence over the interests of the country. I am not going to support a tyrannizing majority simply because it happens to speak in the name of the country. I am not going to support a party because it happens to speak in the name of the country. I shall not do that. Let everybody here and everywhere understand that is my position. As between the country and myself, the country will have precedence: as between the country and depressed classes, the depressed classes will have precedence–the country will have no precedence. That is all that I wanted to say." After the Congress ministries had resigned from Provincial Assemblies, both Ambedkar and the Muslim League leader, Jinnah, were happy and called it a "Day of Deliverance." If Jinnah was pleased it was only because the Congress was no longer in a dominant position to dictate terms to the British or the other minorities in the country. A large number of Parsees, who were hit by the prohibition policy of the Congress, also heaved a sigh of relief over this development, for they could now buy their liquor from the market as they had been doing in the past.

As Nazis went on the rampage over most of Europe, the war took a serious turn for Britain and her allies. The situation was hardly any better for the British in their largest colony, India. Reports of sustained struggle for freedom and the repressive measures being used by the British to quell rebellions made the allies like America mount pressure on the British government to expedite the process for handing over power to Indians and prepare for leaving the country. In October 1940, Gandhi launched the civil disobedience movement based on the principle of non-violence, preaching non-participation in the war. Thousands of Congress members offered satyagraha and willingly courted arrest. Almost all Congress leaders were thrown behind bars. Subhash Bose, who was elected as the Congress President but was subsequently removed thanks to politicking in the party, tried to rally Indian forces against the British power. Although he was put under house arrest in Calcutta, he managed to escape and started mobilising public opinion for Indian independence abroad.

A meeting with Savarkar changed Subhash's mind and he began to ponder over the possibility of fighting a war of Independence against the British from outside. The colonial rulers of India became panicky when they got such intelligence reports. Ambedkar criticised Gandhi for launching the civil disobedience movement. He said: "By calling upon people to abjure the use of force, the pacifist is only helping those who will insist on using force after victory. That the Congress is fighting for the cause of the country is humbug. The Congress is fighting to obtain the keys of power in its hands. Why did Gandhi not start civil disobedience immediately after the Defence of India Act was passed a year ago?"

Faced with heavy losses in their war against Germany, the British Government had launched a fresh recruitment drive in India also to replenish their depleting ranks. Ambedkar seized the opportunity to mount pressure on the government to recruit the Untouchables, especially Mahars who were famous for their fighting qualities. He met the Governor of Bombay and voiced his grievances against the militarization policy of the government which discouraged Mahars on the basis of the senseless distinction between martial and non-martial classes. He recalled the role played by the Mahars under the East India Company in helping establish British dominance in India. Lord Linlithgow, the Viceroy, who was in Bombay happened to read the protest lodged by Ambedkar against denial of recruitment to Mahars in a local newspaper. He reprimanded the Governor of Bombay for having alienated the depressed classes at a critical juncture.

Soon after this the Bombay government revoked the unjust orders against the recruitment of non-martial races into the Army and thus allowed the Mahars to line up and get themselves recruited in the Indian Army which was already engaged in sending troops to help fight the Germans in the war. Later addressing public meetings Ambedkar again targeted the Congress leaders who felt that the government should not be helped in fighting the war. He said these leaders had lost the sense of proportion and the relative value of things. Every Indian must help the British for if the Nazis overran the country, there would not be much left. He said he was not prepared for a change of rulers and starting the struggle once again for self-government right from the beginning. He called upon the Mahar youths to suspend their studies and try for military commissions to preserve their high martial traditions.

The fiftieth birthday of Ambedkar, which fell on April 14,1942, was celebrated with great pomp and show by his followers. The Independent Labour Party and 45 other institutions in Bombay and its suburbs organized a nine-day celebration which included flag salutations, processions and public meetings. In Poona, his followers took out processions through the main streets and the Cantonment. Ambedkar was highly praised for his selfless services to the cause of the Untouchables. The President of the District Local Board, Poona, unveiled a portrait of Ambedkar and said that Ambedkar was not only an outstanding leader of the depressed classes, he was also one of the great leaders of India. By his dedication and selfless service to the cause of the Untouchables, he had carved a niche in the heart of the nation. Addressing a meeting of the women's branch of Rohidas Tarun Sudharak Sangh in a local cinema hall in Kalyan, Ambedkar called upon the youth to emulate the spirit of Kacha, a mythological hero, in not deviating from the purpose of life. Whenever Ambedkar spoke at public meetings organized by his followers he cited inspiring anecdotes from the Mahabharata such as the love of self-respect of Dronacharya, the story of Yayati and the devotion of Kacha.

The main function of the golden jubilee celebrations was held at Chowpatty in Bombay on April 19, presided over by Dr M.R. Jayakar. Paying glowing tributes to Ambedkar, Dr Jayakar said that his independent line of thinking and action had brought about a phenomenal change in the status of the depressed classes. It had infused confidence in them and awakened the caste Hindus to the iniquity of the Savarna system which was responsible for the inhuman treatment meted out to the Untouchables. He recalled how Ambedkar had outshone all other participants in the Round Table Conferences held in London. M.R.A. Baig, Sheriff of Bombay, extolled Ambedkar's contribution to ushering a dawn of hope for the depressed classes who had been suffering cruel treatment and contempt of the caste Hindus for ages.

On April 21, almost all leading newspapers paid rich tributes to Ambedkar. The *Times of India*, Bombay, observed: "Without political and economic power, the Harijans will find it hard to attain social equality, and Dr Ambedkar has done well in realizing this fact. He brings to his difficult task considerable acumen and a gift for pungent, often barbed utterance. Since the removal of untouchability must strengthen the Hindu social structure and also make for the general advancement of Indian people, Dr Ambedkar's efforts on behalf of the Harijans deserve wide support."

The Bombay Chronicle commented that Ambedkar brooded day in and day out over the unending inhumanity to his community, and it was no wonder, therefore, that his devotion to the Harijans was equalled, if not exceeded, by his bitterness against their tormentors. B.G. Horniman, the editor of the *Bombay Sentinel*, said Ambedkar's real intellectual qualities and his service to the country and his community had put him in the front rank of the great men of India. He added that his work would command the respect and gratitude of all those concerned for the achievement of human freedom throughout the world generally and in India particularly

The Maharashtra, a newspaper published from Nagpur, said Ambedkar was one of the few Maharashtrian leaders who came to the forefront in Indian politics by the sheer force of their personality, struggle, sacrifices and scholarship. The depressed classes owed their present political status to his ceaseless campaign for a better deal for them. *The Prabhat*, a Marathi daily of Bombay, hailed Ambedkar as a revolutionary leader of modern India and added that without meaning any disrespect to Dayanand, Gandhi and Savarkar, Ambedkar's services to the Untouchables ranked higher. Replying to felicitations at the last meeting organized by the jubilee committee at Kamgar Maidan, Parel, Bombay, Ambedkar said that the practice of celebrating his birthday should be discontinued for, according to him, a society which idolized and raised a mere man to the level of God was set well on the path of destruction. No one, he stressed, was endowed with superhuman and divine attributes; and one rose and fell through one's own efforts.

Because of the emergency created by the war, the Viceroy expanded his Executive Council by including eight prominent Indians and established a Defence Advisory Committee. Ambedkar was included in the Defence Advisory Committee along with Jamnadas Mehta, Ramrao Deshmukh, M.C. Rajah and some other well-known leaders and Indian Princes. But Ambedkar protested why he had not been included in the Executive Council. Certainly, he expected to be rewarded by the government in keeping with his importance as the undisputed leader of the depressed classes. Not only that, he had been going out of the way, all of course for his own reasons, to attack the Congress leaders for not supporting the government in this hour of crisis when the British government was engaged in a serious struggle against the Nazis. That Ambedkar should not have been ignored when the Executive Council was expanded was also pointed out in a confidential communication Sir R. Lumlley, Governor of Bombay, sent to the Viceroy, the Marques of Linlithgow. In his communication dated April 24, 1942, the Bombay Governor referred to the financial difficulties being faced by Ambedkar and said: "I would very much like to see something done for him, and I hope that, if a further expansion of your council is now possible, he will be included – not on personal grounds alone, but for the reason so that we may retain the interest of the depressed classes. He has been unhelpful about recruitment of Mahars, and does not put his weight behind it overmuch, in spite of the fact that he has long clamoured for Mahars being taken into combatant units. Nevertheless, the recruitment of Mahars continues, but not as well as it would be if he were keen to help."

The Viceroy again expanded his Executive Council in June 1942, raising the number of Indians in it to 14 as against 5 European members. Ambedkar was made member of the Council and given the charge of the Labour portfolio. There was no dearth of Ambedkar's opponents in the country who were always looking for an opportunity to hit or denounce him. But his appointment did not provoke any harsh criticism in any quarter. Although some Congress papers criticized it, yet they did not hesitate in saying that Ambedkar's appointment might bring in some good for the labour. *The Sunday Standard* of Bombay said that if the independent Dr Ambedkar had not become a thorn in the side of the government, he would not become a rubberstamp either. The fact that he had been given the labour portfolio must be a matter of great satisfaction for a man who had spent his lifetime championing the cause of the underdog and fighting for labour's rights. *The Times of India* observed that it was the first time in the history of the country that an Untouchable Hindu was appointed a Member in the Executive Council of the Government of India. Indeed, it was an unprecedented event.

Never before in history a member of the depressed classes had held such a high office in the governance of the country. Ambedkar was the first mass leader to be appointed to the Viceroy's Executive Council. The depressed classes had clamoured for the appointment and even brought pressure on the government to do so. However, it is also a fact that he was so well equipped as few Indians of that rank were in the past. His study of the world labour movement and the problems and legislation about them in India, in Europe and in America, was profound. Ambedkar was the first social rebel to be appointed member of the Chief Executive Council of India. *The Kal*, a Marathi daily of Poona, said that Ambedkar was a representative leader of Maharashtra, and, like other great Maharashtrian leaders, he was not only a leader of great ability and intelligence but also a man of letters, of selfless heart and sterling integrity.

Later, when there was a debate on the situation in India in the wake of Gandhi's call for civil disobedience in the Central Assembly, Ambedkar said: "The critics of the government have said there was no justification in arresting the members of the Congress for the Congress is a body which believes in non-violence. If the Congress had been allowed to be free, they certainly would have controlled the situation in such a manner that they would have prevented violence. But it seems to me that members who take this line have not correctly read what has happened to the Congress during the last two years. I have read the proceedings of the Congress and the impression that has been left upon my mind is that there has been a terrible landslide in the principle of non-violence as has been proclaimed by the Congress. The non-violence has been deeply buried – I have no hesitation on that point at all."[1]

Ambedkar made out a case on the basis of irrefutable evidence that the Congress Working Committee was split on the question of non-violence. A section of the party felt that there would be nothing wrong if violent means were adopted to harass the British government already feeling panicky because of the Nazi might and aggression. He said that there was enough body of evidence to indicate that inside the Congress there was an attempt being made for a planned campaign of violence whatever Gandhi and his admirers might claim. There is no doubt that a section of the Congress party comprising Jayaprakash Narayan, Aruna Asaf Ali and many other leaders had come to realize that India's Independence could not be won by non-violent means alone. Subhash Bose, former Congress President, had gone to the extent of forming an Indian National Army outside the country for fighting the British.

The losses being suffered by the British troops in fighting the Nazis in various theatres of war created a panicky situation for the British government. With the loss of Singapore to Japan, it seemed the sun on the British empire was fast setting. Under pressure from the USA, the British government decided to end the Indian political deadlock, which had resulted in imprisonment of a large number of freedom fighters and provoked many Congressmen and members of other parties to resort to violence to bend the British to hasten India's Independence. Consequently, the British Government sent to India Sir Stafford Cripps to hold talks with various leaders and suggest what could be done to ensure that there was no back-stabbing of the British in India when they were engaged in a do-or-die struggle with the Nazis. Following his meetings with the leaders of the Congress party, the Muslim League, the Hindu Mahasabha, the Sikhs' organizations, the Princes' Chamber, besides Ambedkar and several other leaders, Cripps submitted his recommendations to the British government. According to Cripps' proposal, a constituent assembly was to be convened after the cessation of hostilities to draft the Constitution in cooperation with the Indian States.

Gandhi termed the Cripps proposals for resolving the political deadlock in India a "post-dated cheque." The Hindu Mahasabha rejected the proposals in toto, saying they were nothing but a scheme to balkanize India. The liberals termed the proposals as a travesty of self-determination. Since there was no unequivocal announcement about the formation of Pakistan, the Muslim League also rejected them despite the fact that by allowing the provinces to boycott the Constituent Assembly if they so desired the Cripps' recommendation had indirectly conceded the Muslim leaders' demand for Pakistan. Ambedkar also rejected the scheme for it was calculated to do the greatest harm to the depressed classes as it did not make any separate provision for them and instead bound them hand and foot to Hindu rule that would lead them again to the doldrums where there would be no hope of escape from the Savarna system governing the Hindu society. Ambedkar and other leaders of the depressed classes asked Sir Cripps to convey to the British Government that the depressed classes would look upon the proposals as a breach of faith, if the British government decided to force upon them a Constitution to which they did not give their consent. Ambedkar said the attitude of the British Government to the depressed classes reflected a Munich mentality, the essence of which was to save oneself by sacrificing others. He said one could not help saying that the Cripps' formula for ending the Indian deadlock was the result of a loss of nerve by the British due to reverses being suffered by them in the combat against the Germans.

Speaking at the All-India Depressed Classes Conference, held in Nagpur on July 18 and 19, 1942, Ambedkar said that it was a matter of immense satisfaction that the Untouchables had made great strides along all sides. They had acquired a great degree of political consciousness. They had made considerable progress in education, secured a foothold in the institutions of public service in the country. They should all be proud of this fact. It was an achievement which was entirely the result of their own labour. The basis of his politics lay in the proposition that the Untouchables were not a sub-section of the Hindus, but a distinct element in the national life of India, as separate and distinct as the Muslims. Therefore, he wanted separate political rights as against the Hindus. A seat for the depressed classes in the Executive Council, he said, was a death blow to Brahminism. "My final words," he declared, "of advice to you is educate, agitate, and organize; have faith in yourself. With justice on our side, I do not see how we can lose our battle. The battle to me is a matter of joy. The battle in the fullest sense is spiritual. There is nothing material or social in it. For ours is a battle for the reclamation of human personality."

An announcement regarding the formation of the All-India Scheduled Castes Federation was made at this conference. Before the conference concluded, Ambedkar made a moving speech protesting against the charges levelled against him that he was indifferent to society and lived among books. He replied that he had no ill-feeling against anybody. He had to achieve the maximum progress in the minimum time. "Many Hindus regard me as their enemy. But I have personal friends from even the Brahmin community. Situated as I am, it has fallen to my lot to lash out at the anti-social actions of the Brahmins who treat my people worse than dogs and cats and impede their progress." Speaking at a reception given to him by the All-India Depressed Classes Conference on July 20, 1942, Ambedkar said: "Ours is a battle not for wealth or power. It is a battle for freedom. It is a battle for the reclamation of human personality which has been suppressed and mutilated by the Hindu social system and will continue to be suppressed and mutilated if in the political struggle the Hindus win and we lose. My final words of advice to you is to educate, agitate and organize, have faith in yourselves and never lose hope. I shall always be with you as I know you will be with me."

Later, addressing the Depressed Classes Women's Conference at the same venue, he said: "There cannot be an occasion for greater happiness to anyone interested in the advancement of the depressed classes than to witness this gathering of women. I know what you all can do to improve the condition of society if you are convinced about the eradication of social evils. Ever since I began to work among the depressed classes I made it a point to carry women along with men. I measure the progress of a community by the degree of progress which women have achieved, and when I see this assembly, I feel both convinced and happy that we have progressed. I shall tell you a few things which I think you should bear in mind. Learn to be clean. Keep free from all vices. Give education to your children. Instill ambition into them. Inculcate in their minds that they are destined to be great. Remove from them all inferiority complex. Do not be in a hurry to marry. Marriage is a liability. You should not impose it upon your children unless they are financially able to meet the liability arising from marriage. Those who marry will have to keep in mind that to have too many children is a crime. The paternal duty lies in giving each child a better start than its parents had. Above all, let every girl who marries stand by her husband, claim to be her husband's friend and equal, and refuse to be his slave. If you follow this advice, you will bring honour and glory to yourselves and to the depressed classes."

With the farsightedness of a great man, Ambedkar founded the People's Education Society in Bombay on July 8, 1945, to promote higher education in society, especially among the poor middle classes in general and the Scheduled Castes in particular. This organization derived its inspiration from the teachings of Lord Buddha, which had made a deep impression on Ambedkar. Lord Buddha believed in the principle of social equality and justice. The Society founded by Ambedkar was intended to promote higher education among the poorer people in general and the Scheduled Castes, Scheduled Tribes and other backward classes in particular. Its motto was "Knowledge and Love," for knowledge is power and love governs the whole universe. Ambedkar had come to realize that education was the only effective lever for the uplift of the down-trodden. He was not only an educationist but also a social revolutionary, a thinker, a philosopher, a statesman, a politician, and above all, the apostle of social equality in the Hindu society where graded inequality was the governing principle ordained by the Manusmriti.

Ambedkar was dismayed to see that the backward classes were for all practical purposes treated like subject people. They had no authority in any place. They had no place in Administration. They had no place in the Executive. The Executive and the Administration were monopolised by the higher classes. They were monopolizing it by reason of the fact that they had been able to get good education. The son and daughter of every Secretary in the Government was to be found in Cambridge or Oxford. Twice and thrice they made journeys in order to lodge their children there because they had the amplest means. The backward class man's son could not get even primary education. This sort of anomalous position in the two different classes had been on for centuries. The surest way for the salvation of the Untouchables lies in higher education, higher employment and better ways of earning a living. Once they become well-placed in the scale of social life, they would become respectable, and once they become respectable the religious outlook of the orthodox Hindus towards them is sure to undergo a change. Even if it does not happen, education can do no injury to the material interest of the downtrodden."

With the financial assistance of Rs 3 lakh from the Government of India and a loan of an equal sum, he started the Siddharth College of Arts, Science and Commerce, which paved the way for educational advancement of the downtrodden. The college was started in the old military barracks at Marine Lines, Bombay, which he obtained from the government on a temporary lease. These hutments were remodelled to meet the requirement of the college until 1949 when two spacious buildings – Anand Bhavan and Buddha Bhavan— were acquired for the college. The launching of the Siddharth College was a turning point in the social life of the Untouchables. It was also an epoch-making event in the reconstruction of the Indian Society. This was the only centre of higher learning free from the taint of untouchability. It threw open the doors of higher education for youngsters from the working classes and from amongst the Untouchables who wanted to change their lot.

After starting the Siddharth College at Bombay, Ambedkar turned his attention towards the Marathawada region, which had a very rich cultural heritage as evidenced by the world famous caves of Ajanta and Ellora but which was the most backward area then. He devoted all his attention now in starting a prestigious educational complex in Aurangabad which is part of the Marathwada region. Thus the People's Education Society set up the Milind Mahavidyalya there in 1950. This was the first educational institution in Marathawada offering facilities for higher education. Milind Mahavidyalaya was named after the renowned Greek king Minander who embraced Buddhism at the hands of the Buddhist scholar and philosopher, Nagasen. The sprawling campus, spread over 210 acres and surrounded by hillocks with Buddhist caves, was named Nagasen Vana. When plans were ready for starting the construction of a magnificent building for the Milind College, Dr Rajendra Prasad, the President of India, laid its foundation stone on September 1, 1951. Speaking on the occasion, Dr Prasad paid glowing tributes to Ambedkar for his erudition and for his zeal in spreading education among the poor classes.

Ambedkar said: "Coming as I do from the lowest order of the Hindu society, I know what is the value of education. The objective of raising the lower order is deemed to be economic. This is a great mistake. The objective of raising the status of the lower order in India is not to make them better off so that they can feed themselves properly, clothe themselves well and thus be ready to serve the higher classes as they had been doing for ages. The lower classes need to be raised so that they can overcome the inferiority complex which has stunted their growth and made them slaves to others. The problem is to create in them the consciousness of the significance of their lives for themselves and for the country, of which they have been cruelly robbed by the existing social order. Nothing can achieve this purpose except the spread of higher education. This is in my opinion the panacea for our social troubles."

Ambedkar had also the ambition of establishing a Buddhist University in Aurangabad, but his dream remained unfulfilled largely on account of his failing health in the last phase of his life. However, Ambedkar succeeded in establishing the Marathwada University in Aurangabad. Ambedkar was not only instrumental in establishing the university but also raising its educational standards through his efforts. Throughout his life Ambedkar worked hard to promote the interests of the institutions set up by him. He often said: "I will not forsake my pet child, which needs looking after in its teething troubles." His concern for the educational institutions he had started made him visit Bombay and Aurangabad more frequently. Thousands of students in Maharashtra are studying in colleges he had started. He was of the view that education is contributing grace to the young, consolidation to the old, wealth to the poor and ornaments to the rich.

References

1. See first paragraph page 22 Vol. 10 of Ambedkar's Writings and Speeches.

   D. Keer's Ambedkar's Life and Mission published in 1962, Gandhi Ambedkar Dispute by A.K. Vakil published in 1991 by Ashish Publishing House, Punjabi Bagh, New Delhi.

12
Women's Role

Often it is said that there is a woman behind every successful man. But in the case of Bhimrao Ramji Ambedkar, who was easily one of the most outstanding Indians of the 20th century, no single woman had played any great role in his formative years when he was young or later in life when he was engaged in a struggle for survival in a hostile world. He had risen from the poverty to Olympian heights to the great astonishment of caste Hindus. But he had accomplished all this without the solace, care of a mother, a sister, a girl friend or a wife. Of course, women were there in his life but they came like passing birds to charm him. They did not remain with him for long and flew away when he needed them most.

When he was born as the fourteenth child to Bhimabai, some astrologers had predicted that his birth would have a baleful influence on her life. But defying all predictions, he soon became the darling of the family, loved by his parents and siblings alike. His childhood pranks were so fascinating that his mother grew increasingly fond of him. But just when he was about six years old, Bhimabai passed away. His paternal aunt, Mirabai, a hunchbacked woman, took charge of his upbringing. She loved him but because of her physical deformity, she was quite unlike his mother. However, Mirabai's indulgences to the youngest child in the family and her painstaking efforts to keep him happy so that he could stop grieving for his mother made him readjust to the changed situation. When his father went in for a second marriage, Ambedkar was very unhappy. But he was helpless. Although he couldn't bear the sight of his step-mother wearing the ornaments which once adorned his mother, he could not do anything except to resign to his fate.

Just when he was 14 and studying in the fifth standard, his father, in accordance with the prevalent custom of child marriages then, fixed his marriage with Ramabai, a nine-year-old daughter of a Mahar labourer, Bhiku Dhutre, who was already dead. The poor family could not afford a lavish celebration to mark this important event in Ambedkar's life. The marriage ceremony took place in what was a fish market in Bombay. Just when it was closed for the night and all the fish mongers had pulled down their shutters, both parties, Ambedkar's family members and Ramabai's relations, gathered in the open enclosure of the fish market and performed the ceremony. Thus Ambedkar and Ramabai became husband and wife. Although she was totally untutored to play the role of a wife, Ramabai was fully conscious of her duties and started taking great interest in the welfare and well-being of her husband. By her sheer simplicity and innocence, she made a deep impression on Ambedkar. Living as the family was in a tenement, having intimate relations was not easy for the newly-wedded couple. In any case, doing well in studies was Ambedkar's obsession those days and he was day and night absorbed in his books. Ramabai could see the devotion and dedication of her husband to study and did whatever was possible for her to make him succeed. Although he could not do anything for her, like taking her out once in a while just as young couples do, Ambedkar became aware of the pains she used to take to ensure that he could remain happy and study in peace and comfort to attain whatever he had set his sights on.

In fact, following the death of Ambedkar's father in 1913, and due to his elder brother's drinking habits, there was nobody except Ramabai in the house whom Ambedkar could treat with love and affection. Although his step-mother who had been widowed now was also there, she could not endear herself to Ambedkar. Of course, he treated her with respect but there was little love lost between them. If he cared for anybody in the family it was only his devoted and dedicated wife, Ramabai. Unlike other young girls of her age, Ramabai being acutely aware of the financial difficulties facing the family never made any demands on her husband to buy her fancy dresses or jewellery. Day and night, she prayed that her husband should succeed in achieving his academic goals. Her main concern was that Ambedkar should have no problem on account of her and pursue his studies just as he wanted. He had no means to support his family and was really feeling miserable. It was one of the most critical periods of his life. The only solace to Ambedkar was his devoted wife now. When he was selected by the Baroda State for studies at the Columbia University in New York, Ramabai's joy knew no bounds. Before he embarked for the U.S.A., she gave birth to a son. Ambedkar was very happy and before leaving specifically asked her to take good care of the child.

But taking good care of the child, named Yashwant, was by no means easy. Ambedkar's elder brother given to drinking was not able to take care of himself and so could not be expected to do anything for the family. Ambedkar started sending remittances to his wife from America. These remittances were whatever little he could save from his monthly scholarship for studies. But his remittances were in fact so small that Ramabai could hardly feed her son. While her husband was starving in America, she started starving in India only to save whatever little she could, so that their child could grow well. For poor Ramabai life was becoming a nightmare. But despite all these hardships Ramabai would find time almost every day to pray for the well-being and success of her husband in his studies abroad. Even when Ambedkar returned with a Ph.D degree from the Columbia University, there was no end to the sufferings of the family. Ambedkar was refused jobs wherever he tried because he was an Untouchable Mahar. Ramabai really did not know how to console or comfort her husband. At last there was some respite when he landed a lecturer's job at Sydenham College in Bombay. The couple had two more children. Financially also they were now better off. Ambedkar had interrupted his studies at the London School of Economics because the period for which his scholarship had been granted had run out. Now he thought of returning to London again. When Ambedkar told his wife he wanted to go back to England to complete his doctoral work, Ramabai did not protest. On the contrary, she urged him to do so quickly so that he could return to her soon after that.

Following Ambedkar's return to India with a D.Sc. Degree from the London School of Economics and a barrister-at-law degree from the Gray's Inn in 1923, the couple had two more children. In all they had four sons and a daughter. But Ambedkar remained preoccupied with his own work for the welfare of the Untouchables and his unending search for employment. They did not have enough money even to provide good medical care for their children. As a result, four children died. But the death of the last child who was a boy really gave Ambedkar a great shock. While he was lost in gloom over this tragedy, his wife, a healthy young woman, became a weakling. The death of their last child was like a bolt from the blue. So stunned was Ambedkar by this tragedy that he was unwilling even to cremate the body of his son, lying dead on the ground. He wondered over the injustice done to him by gods despite the fact that he had been a sincerely devoted, dedicated, god-fearing and upright man all his life. The plight of Ramabai was even worse when she saw her husband day after day plunged in gloom.

Writing about his grief in a letter to Dattoba Santram Pawar, a leader of the Chambhar community, who was his well-wisher, Ambedkar stated: "There is no use pretending that my wife and I have recovered from the shock of my son's death and I do not think that we ever shall. We have in all buried four precious children - 3 sons and a daughter - all sprightly and handsome. The thought of this tragedy is sufficiently crushing. We are living no doubt in the sense that days are passing over us as does the cloud. With the loss of our kins the salt of our life is gone and as the Bible says, 'Ye are the salt of the earth, if it leaveth the earth wherewith shall it be salted?' I feel the truth of this every moment in my almost vacant and empty life. My last boy was a wonder boy the like of whom I had seldom seen. With his passing away life to me is a garden full of weeds. But enough of this. I am too overcome to write any more."

Looking at the devotion and dedication of his wife to his welfare and the welfare of his surviving son, Yashwant, Ambedkar regained some composure to fight the travails of life with determination, just as he had been doing earlier.

Thanks to Ramabai's prayers and his determination, he resumed his legal practice and started making some money to keep the wolf from the door. Ramabai who had been facing hardships ever since she was married, started coming to terms with life not only because she did not want to be a source of continuing worry to her husband but also because she wanted her husband to pursue whatever goals he had set his sights on without any let or hindrance. But Ramabai's suffering did not end. Because of his low caste nobody was willing to have any truck with Ambedkar. While struggling for survival in a hostile world, he also intensified his determination to end untouchability to liberate his community from the curse from which they had been suffering for ages.

Instead of spending much time at home, Ambedkar started addressing meetings of the depressed classes to awaken in them a desire for a better tomorrow and not remain resigned to their fate which had consigned them to the lowest position in Hindu society. As a lecturer in the Sydenham College in 1918, he had made a profound impression on the students who came in contact with him. He was offered teaching jobs again on his return from England, but instead he started practicing at the Bombay bar. His outstanding ability in preparing his briefs began making a favourable impression both on the bench and the bar. He started getting briefs and came to have a somewhat steady and regular income. This gave great relief to Ramabai, but she remained worried about him because of the hostility he provoked amongst the caste Hindus by championing the cause of the Untouchables. Although she was deeply devoted to Ambedkar, she could not understand why time and again he was courting dangers and controversies and thus risking his life. Ambedkar's involvement in the Mahad Satyagraha had provoked his elder brother to strongly criticise him. But she could not say anything to him. When Ambedkar returned safe from there, she only heaved a sigh of relief.

She was a constant companion willing to do anything for her husband, but not being educated, she could not share his thoughts. So long as his father was alive, he kept on encouraging Ambedkar in doing whatever he wanted to do. Ramabai could only say her prayers to gods to keep her husband happy. Although Ramabai could not discus anything with him on an intellectual level, her very presence in the house was a comfort to Ambedkar.

Ultimately, after having been married to Ambedkar for 27 years, weak and emaciated Ramabai became very ill and died in 1935. She had been Ambedkar's companion during the worst days of his life. She bore all the hardships without a murmur. When he was abroad, Ambedkar would write to her, informing her about the progress of his work. Although Ambedkar had not been able to look after his wife well because of his pre-occupations with the service of his community, her death was a stunning blow. Ambedkar was so much grieved that he put on a hermit's dress hardly talking to anyone. All those close to him became very worried. They feared he might do something desperate or renounce the world in sorrow for his departed wife. However, he recovered after three to four weeks and again started to piece his life together. After some time, he was back in the struggle for getting the Untouchables their rightful place under the sun with all the rights they were entitled to as human beings.

During his stay in London between 1920 and 1923, the period when he was engaged in completing his doctoral thesis at the London School of Economics, Ambedkar had chanced to meet a young Irish widow who was working in the Secretariat of the House of Commons in the British Parliament. It was because of her help that he could observe and study the parliamentary proceedings. Although no recorded evidence has come to light, it is obvious from the letters she wrote to Ambedkar that they had a very close relationship. After 1923, Ambedkar visited England thrice, for attending the Round Table Conferences as a representative of the Untouchables in India. Presumably, he must have remained in regular touch with her. This seems obvious from the letters she wrote to Ambedkar. One of her letters to Ambedkar dated 15th May 1924 ran as follows:

My darling Bhim,

You have not written to me again this week, so I feel very neglected[1]. I often wonder if someone else has supplanted me in your affections. But I try to console[2] myself with the thought that it cannot possibly be, you are different from other men.

I thought of you on Monday and Tuesday, 10 and 11th. How did you get on? I do hope that you will write to me and I get a letter this next mail. If not I shall think that something has really happened.

No more news this time and just going to the "House." I had been out for lunch.

With fondest love,

May God bless you dear,

Ever your little,

Pal

Another letter dated March 11, 1925, stated:

My dear Bhim,

I was glad to get a few lines from you this week, although I was very sorry to hear your loss. I had no idea that you had a little pet deer. They are so lovely. I do not think any animal has such beautiful eyes as the deer. Where did you use to keep him?

So you are overworking yourself again. I do wish you would not. How are you going to work if you are ill? It is much better to go slowly. It is not as if you had a wife and family depending on you. You have only yourself to consider.

Do please take care of yourself for my sake.

With fondest love

Yours,

F.X

A letter dated 15th January 1937 from her to Ambedkar was as follows:

1. Primrose 5997

Primrose Hill

10, King Henry's Road

15 - 1 - 37

I noticed in *The Telegraph* this morning that your boat had reached Bombay. I do hope, dear, that the journey was pleasant and that you feel better for the change. Now you have to start work, don't overdo it, keep well until I come. I am marking off each day. I am glad to say that all enquires concerning you seem to have faded away. I have heard nothing more since I wrote you. Thank you for your letter posted at Port Said. It reached me on Wednesday evening, so I went off on Thursday morning to see about the books. They will be out by the next mail. I find the work at the India Office very interesting and it gives me so much pleasure to do it for you.

I have been to the market today and I have bought a beautiful pair of silver candlebars. You will like them. I can picture them on your table. I am ever so sorry you did not get my card at Xmas and my farewell letter. You won't get it now. It must have gone astray in the rush although I well-packed it and wrote Xmas Card on the outside. I am thinking of you all the day and longing to be with you.

God bless you, my darling.

With fondest love,

Ever yours

F. X.

It may be recalled here that the *Vividhavritta* of Bombay on the 7th of January 1937 carried a news item, saying that Ambedkar had secretly married an English widow. As F.X., the old friend of Ambedkar, was an Irish widow, the news seemed baseless. Not only this insinuation, but also the marriage per se was refuted by Ambedkar. The refutation appeared in *The Times of India* on 15th January 1937. It is a coincidence that on the same day F.X. wrote the above letter which is self-explanatory and is in no way from a newly-wedded to a lover turned husband. Apparently, the report about Ambedkar's wedding had been planted in the paper and was aimed at character assassination of a man who was becoming prominent despite his low caste. The Hindu leaders resorted to such derogatory tactics owing to Ambedkar's declaration in 1936 that although he had been born a Hindu he would not die a Hindu.

A letter dated May 13, 1937, went as follows:

Primrose 5997

10, King Henry's Road

Primrose Hill

N.W. 3

My darling Bhim,

I am sorry not to have written you last week. I remember I have not had the heart to do anything. I am trying to recover from the great disappointment. I am not blaming you dear, you could not have done otherwise.

I do hope you are keeping well. You must be busy watching your college grow. What about our Cottage, is that also in the making? Do write and give me some idea as to when you will be ready for me.

Have you been able to fix up a holiday? I hope so. Have you any more cases on hand? It is still very cold here and we have had such a lot of rain.

God bless you, my darling,

My love and prayers are with you,

Ever Yours,

F.X.

If these letters reflect a deep attachment between Ambedkar and the Irish widow, it must be due to mutual admiration and love. Ambedkar had gone to the extent of dedicating one of the books he wrote to F.X. Unfortunately, there is no trace of letters Ambedkar wrote to F.X. It is obvious that the messiah of the Untouchables in India could not afford to openly acknowledge his love for the Irish widow for his enemies in the Congress would only have exploited this fact to propagate that Ambedkar was not sincere and had been cheating his wife, Ramabai. Already they were branding him as a British stooge who tried to oppose the Congress at every stage. The Congress leaders had made much of Ambedkar's opposition to the 'Quit India' call given by Gandhi.

As a matter of fact, the chief concern of Ambedkar in his lifetime was the betterment of the Untouchables. He opposed the Congress because he felt the party's avowed concern for the Untouchables was nothing but hypocrisy. Unless the Chaturvarnya system was abolished, there could be no justice for the Untouchables in Hindu society. But what to talk of the upper caste Hindus, even Gandhi, a Bania by caste which ranks lower than the Brahmins and the Kshatriyas, would not accept this.

The Irish widow who began doting on him was educated, could understand the meaning and purpose of his life, but he could not own her for his enemies would have used his attachment to a foreign lady to discredit and defame him. However, it cannot be denied that they were quite close to each other and had a very warm relationship until her death in 1944. That Ambedkar could not forget her is more than obvious from the dedication of his book, 'What Congress and Gandhi Have Done to the Untouchables,' to her published in 1945. The dedication to the book starts with the biblical reference to Ruth.

DEDICATION

"And Naomi said, Turn again, my daughter; why will ye go with me? Go your way. And they lifted up their voice, and wept again, and Orpah kissed her mother-in-law; but Ruth clave unto her. And she said, Behold thy sister-in-law is gone back unto her people, and unto her gods; return thou after thy sister-in-law. And Ruth said, Entreat me not to leave thee; or to return from following after thee; for whither thou goest, I will go; and where thou lodgest, I will lodge; thy people shall be my people, and thy God my God. Where thou diest, will I die, and there will be buried; the LORD do so to me, and more also, if aught but death part thee and me,"

"I know how, when we used to read the Bible together, you would be affected by the sweetness and pathos of this passage; while you will be glad to read it again, you will, I am sure, ask me what made me recall it in this connection. I wonder if you remember the occasion when we fell into discussion about the value of Ruth's statement: 'Thy people shall be my people, and thy God my God.' I have a clear memory of it and can well recall our difference of opinion. You maintained that its value lay in giving expression to the true sentiments appropriate to a perfect wife. I put forth the view that the passage had a sociological value and its true interpretation was the one given by Prof. Smith, namely, that it helped to distinguish modern society from ancient society; Ruth's statement 'Thy people shall be my people and thy God my God' defined ancient society by its most dominant characteristic, namely, that it was a society of man plus God while modern society is a society of men only (pray remember that in men I include women also).

"My view was not then acceptable to you. But you were interested enough to urge me to write a book on this theme. I promised to do so. For as an oriental I belong to a society which is still ancient and in which God is a much more important member than man. What is the part of the conversation which is important to me at this stage is the promise I then made to dedicate the book to you if I succeeded in writing one. Prof. Smith's interpretation had opened a new vista before me and I had every hope of carrying out my intention. The chances of developing the theme in a book form are now very remote. As you know I am drawn in the vortex of politics which leaves no time for literary pursuits. I do not know when I shall be out of it. The feeling of failure to fulfil my promise has haunted me ever since the war started. Equally distressing was the fear that you might pass away as a war casualty and not be there to receive it if I were to have time to complete it. But the unexpected has happened. There you are, out of the throes of death. Here is a book ready awaiting dedication. This happy conjunction of two such events has suggested to me the idea that rather than postpone it indefinitely I might redeem my word, by dedicating this book which I have succeeded in bringing to completion. Though different in theme it is not an unworthy substitute. Will you accept it?

B.R.A.

To,

F.

In thy Presence is the Fullness of Joy.

Following the death of his wife in 1935, perhaps Ambedkar could have made his relationship with the Irish widow public after some time. But obviously preoccupied as he was in his struggle for the uplift of the Untouchables, he could not seriously consider this possibility. However, with the passage of time, and the increasing hostility of caste leaders against him, Ambedkar did start feeling weak and lonely. Perhaps a wife at home could have been some comfort to him. But even before he could have toyed with the idea of inviting to India his Irish friend, she was already dead in the bombardment on London during the Second World War. The ailments which afflicted him began to cause him great pain and anxiety. Although he had tried all sorts of drugs and treatment his well-wishers had recommended him, he could not get rid of his arthritis, gout and blood pressure. He needed the constant attention of some nurse at home to help him take medicines on time and take all other precautions doctors had advised him. But keeping a nurse at home would only have invited accusations of moral turpitude. No wonder, Ambedkar did not opt for this course. He frankly told his well-wishers that he would certainly like to go in for a second marriage provided he could find some suitable educated woman as life partner.

It was against this background that he chanced to meet Dr Savita Kabir at the house of his old friend, Prof Rau, in Bombay. Since Rau's daughters were friends of Savita, she used to call on them now and then. One day when both Dr Kabir and Ambedkar were at his home, Prof. Rau introduced them to each other.

Ambedkar was already a famous man with an enormous reputation as the leader of the Untouchables. Dr Kabir was overwhelmed by meeting him. The fascination for him was not because he was the most eminent leader of his community. His outstanding ability to rise above all his peers despite the crippling tag of his caste was what made him adorable.

Whenever Ambedkar was visiting Bombay, a meeting with Prof. Rau was a must on his agenda. Because of this both Ambedkar and Savita started seeing each other. When Ambedkar touched upon his failing health problems with his new young friend, Savita, who was herself a doctor, she asked him to come for consultation to Dr Madhav G. Malvankar, a physio-therapist, who ran a clinic where she was also employed. Ambedkar met Dr Malvankar and started his treatment. As a result of this Ambedkar could meet Savita whenever he went for consultation to Dr Malvankar, besides meeting her at his friend Prof. Rau's house where they had come in contact for the first time.

They were meeting each other whenever Ambedkar was on a visit to Bombay. One day Savita asked him to avail himself of the services of some nurse so that he could be given medicines at proper time. She volunteered to be a nurse for him, saying she won't mind spending two to three months in his house in Delhi so that he could be given medicines regularly. She said since he lived in a large house in Delhi, a room could be spared for her as long as she stayed with him to take care of his failing health. But Ambedkar turned down the suggestion, saying he would not like to give rise to a scandal by keeping her in his house. However, Ambedkar was surprised when even Dr Malvankar suggested to take Savita along with him for some time to take care of his health.

Ambedkar reacted to Dr Malvankar's suggestion rather strongly. He felt that Savita must have put it in his head to make this suggestion. Upon this development, he did not hesitate in expressing his inner feelings even if they were likely to hurt Savita. Expressing his resentment he said: "Why did you ask Dr Malvankar to broach the subject with me? It is a most thoughtless act and hysterical in the extreme. Your idea of having a woman as a companion to look after me, I am sorry to say, was not quite welcome to me. I have been brought up in a terribly moral and religious atmosphere. I could never entertain such a thought, much less a proposal which would give rise to unsavoury public comment. My wife died fourteen years ago. Since then I have remained unmarried and have resolved to remain so. My friends who think I must live as long as it is possible have not been very happy about my resolution. They want me to remarry. It is very difficult to say what sort of wife the woman I marry in the circumstances would turn out to be. Intelligence is not the only qualification that is to be sought in selecting a woman nor beauty. Moral virtue is the chief criterion.[3]

"I am a difficult man. Ordinarily I am quiet as water and humble as grass. But when I get into temper I am ungovernable and unmanageable. I am a man of silence. There is a charge against me that I don't speak to women. But I don't even speak to men unless they are my intimates. I am a man of moods. At times I can talk endlessly, at other times, I do not utter a word. At times I am very serious. Sometimes I am full of humour. I am no gay person; pleasures of life do not attract me. My companions have to bear the burden of my austerity and asceticism. My books have been my companions. They are dearer to me than wife and children

"I am very fond of literature and particularly biography. Every man and woman's life is short and the channel in which it runs is always very narrow.

Consequently, the experience of every individual is always very limited. A limited experience gives a narrow range of sympathies. Such a person is a misfit in life. For in one's life one is bound to meet persons who have led a different sort of life and have different experiences to recount and unless one is aware of such experiences undergone by other people, there is no enjoyment and enrichment in the value of life. Tolstoy is not my hero. In fact, no author is my hero. I am very selective. I choose what is worth choosing from any author worthy of perusal and assimilate into my self and build my own personality which, if you will allow me to say, is not an imitation of anybody, however high. It is my own original self.

"You were perhaps disappointed when I declined to accept your services as a nurse to accompany me to Delhi and stay there for a month. But you don't know my whole position in public life is built upon my reputation as a man of character and unsullied morals. If my enemies are afraid of me and respect me, it is because of this. I can never be a party to damage it in any way. If it was damaged the whole purpose of my life would not only vanish but my people for whom I have lived and sacrificed and who rightly or wrongly think that I am their god would be destroyed. The long and short of it is that if circumstances compel me to depart from my resolution I may marry but will not agree to keep a nurse or companion especially when there is no other woman in the house. It may be a long search for a woman who could be satisfactory wife to me."

He said he would prefer a doctor to live with him. Savita responded by saying in that case he should be on the lookout for some such person. Following this long discussion in Bombay, Savita was pleasantly surprised to receive a big packet sent to her by Ambedkar himself from Delhi. She opened it and was stunned to find in it a letter from Ambedkar proposing to marry her provided she was willing to do so. The packet also contained an ornamental gift he had sent her. But Ambedkar plainly told her he would be the last man to force her to marry him. The marriage could take place only if she was interested in the proposal. Otherwise, she should just forget whatever had transpired between them.[4]

This was a marriage proposal from a Central Minister for Savita who belonged to an ordinary middle class family. She really did not know how to respond. She thought of consulting Dr Malvankar who had also become chummy with Ambedkar because of his frequent visits for treatment. Dr Malvankar plainly told her to make up her mind and then respond to Ambedkar's offer in whatever way she liked. When Savita broached the subject with her brothers at home, they were overjoyed. Obviously impressed by Ambedkar's enormous reputation as a leader of the Untouchables and as Minister in the Nehru's Cabinet, everybody thought that it was a great opportunity for her to become a Central Minister's wife.

After pondering over the proposal for sometime, she replied to him giving a nod. Lonely Ambedkar's happiness knew no bounds when he read that Savita was willing to marry him. Overjoyed by the fact that they would be marrying shortly now, they started calling each other by lovable names. He addressed her as Sharu and she called him Raja. Ambedkar was surprised over the choice of the name she had chosen for him. When he was a student in Elphinstone School in Bombay, his friends also used to call him Raja. This is what Ambedkar wrote to Savita after receiving her acceptance of his proposal

Dear Sharu,

I received your letter of the 16th February this afternoon. The joy with[5] which I read it was indeed boundless, infinite as they say. I said that you were first to be a casualty. But you were quite right in saying that I had concealed my feelings though more successfully. For I too was a casualty from the very beginning. I wonder if there is a similar case of love at first sight from both sides. I am sure we shall be two bodies animated by one soul. Nothing but death shall put us asunder. I am sorry my letter made you weep. Tears are good. They wash off all impurities and make the heart clean. If you have wept believe me, I too, have wept probably for a different reason – namely the realization of a dream, of finding a woman possessed of both virtue and intellect to be my wife and the joy that has come in its wake. Let us make a determination to make each other happy. I am glad Guruji (Dr Malvankar) has blessed our decision.

How strange and mysterious are the ways of destiny! Who could have thought that I and you would be husband and wife. Born in different strata, lived in different circles, treaded different paths, here we are meeting as patient and nurse and then lead to the altar. Destiny has been kind to me in establishing this contact.

One must learn to control even love. I am afraid, you have become a victim of it.[6] I know you can't bear separation any longer. I too, am tired of the loneliness. I long to have you near me. But pray give me some little time. I assure you, I will not tire out your patience. Please do not be disgruntled when we have to live together for the rest of our lives, a little time lost before we join cannot be a matter of grievance.

But I was very much grieved to learn that you had not taken food for three days. What on earth you did that for? I thought Sharu was a wise girl. I hope you will not do this again. You are my treasure. I do not want you to suffer either in body or in mind.

Another mysterious thing is the pet name you have given me. It was the very name by which I was called by my fellow students when I was studying in the Elphinstone High School. I am wondering what suggested it to you? You are welcome to use it.

With fondest and dearest love

from - Raja

In another letter written later[7], he made it plain the kind of life she could expect with him. He was 54. He stated: "At this age I cannot be as active as a man of 20/25. My disease has made me more inactive than I would otherwise be. Since you seem to abhor sex, my condition is an advantage to you. I cannot, however, say that I am altogether devoid of sexual urge. However, you can rest assured I will not force a woman against whom I have rights of a husband, I can practice self-control and continence which I have been used to for the last 15 years. But having given my word to take you as my wife I will not paw, sniff and snot as an angry cat does if it is annoyed. I am determined to make you happy no matter what that is.

"I gave you in my letter some idea of my habits and ways of life. My purpose was to let you know in advance what sort of a man you would have to deal with. I painted the dark shades deliberately because I know how facts which come to light afterwards cause ill-will between husband and wife and are interpreted as a deliberate concealment. I have no desire to conceal anything from you. Indeed I want to disclose anything and everything especially as our acquaintance is so short and so fitful. Instead of appreciating the spirit behind this concession you go to say it would be all right so long I did not pick up a stick and start beating you. Why on earth you thought that I would be capable of doing such a brutish thing, I am quite unable to follow. You did not even stop to think that I was an educated person and that my contacts with the best minds must have at least introduced me to civilized modes of behaviour with the weaker sex.

"You wish that the idea of your marrying me should not be communicated to your relations before the marriage takes place. There are cases of boys and girls running away from their homes and marrying secretly. Surely the reasons why you propose to follow the course are different from which actuate such couples. The reason I believe that your relations would object to your marrying me on account of my low origin. My origin will remain what it is. I cannot change it nor any body else can. What guarantee is there that your relations will be reconciled after your marriage? If they are not reconciled then they will be lost to you and you will be lost to them permanently. If this happens what will be your feelings towards me. I am afraid you will say that I have been the cause which has brought about the loss of love and affection of your parents. I should not like to be placed in this miserable position. I have always been of opinion that marriage between members belonging to two communities which are unequal in their status is bad and is hurtful to the one which comes from the low status. This is my experience. I don't want a wife who will despise me because of my birth and feel ashamed to walk with me in the public because somebody is likely to point his finger at him as being of low origin. I am however prepared to make a departure from these rules. You have however added a new complication by raising the question of secrecy. I am afraid I am not very happy about it.

"There are two other matters to which I would like to make reference. One is about our respective ages. I should have given you some particulars about my age in my first letter. Unfortunately, I forgot to do so. Officially my age is 54. Actually I am 52. You have given your age as 37. There is a difference of about 15 years. Your mode of address (Babasaheb) could not be questioned if one takes into account this difference. It is quite possible that on knowing this you may consider this disparity in our ages too big to be overcome. I mention this fact particularly because my looks are deceptive and many people even in my sickly condition say that I do not even appear to be forty. I had a letter from Dr Malvankar about you. It describes your career and your qualifications and status in the medical profession. One not knowing you might feel that it was loaded with praise. But knowing you as I do what he has said are mere facts, if there is any praise you richly deserve it. There is however one statement in his letter which has disturbed me. He says your monthly earnings easily come to Rs 1,500. I have no doubt that it is a correct statement. Question is whether it is worthwhile to lose so much money. In your letter you do say you want economic independence for yourself even after marriage and join a poor middle class man like me who has to struggle hard to maintain himself at a decent standard of life.

"In my mind there is some doubt about the real feelings by which you were actuated in saying yes. I have been wondering what course to adopt to have my fears removed. You have of course added and even underlined that notwithstanding these statements your decision stands. On a mature consideration of the matter I have come to the conclusion that it would be wrong on my part to take advantage of your decision and forget or ignore your statements. The proper thing is to give you a further opportunity to reconsider your decision. You must take into account all the factors set out about me and find out if you have a longing to belong to me. Search your heart, look around, take your time and come to a definite conclusion which is cold and calculated. Do not be afraid to revise your opinion if you think you should. I shall not take it amiss. At this stage of my life my aim is to reach the end of my existence, how it is I can't say — in peace and with honour. It would be better if happiness was added to it. A loving wife can do that if there is none. The loss would be loss of happiness only. I would at least have peace and honour. By your adverse decision you would be doing me neither wrong nor loss. I shall be where I was. Therefore avoid all sentiments."

Until Savita came in his life, the only emotional attachment Ambedkar had was with his son Yashwant and nephew Mukund, the son of his elder brother who died in 1927, leaving Mukund in his charge. Before his marriage, he was naturally worried that Savita's arrival on the scene might not impair his relationship with the two wards he had been looking after. He thought of taking into confidence his future wife about this relationship and wrote her a letter, frankly telling her that both of them were dear to him and he would like his relationship to continue on the same plane even after his marriage. But Savita could not appreciate his sentiments and raised the question that if he cared so much for them, how could he love her? Following this he wrote back. "I have no doubt you are more generous than you have shown yourself in your letter I have just received. You ask me if I love my children so much, have I any love for you? I have no doubt what the answer is. There is no contradiction in my loving my children and loving you. If love was such an exclusive thing then the conclusion will be that to love one must hate all others. Because you love your father, brothers and sisters, can I say that you don't love me? How stupid that would be. One can love all and indeed must love all. The only thing is that loving all does not mean that one has the same interest or equal interest in all these in whom he is interested.

"In India people have more interest in their children than they have in their wives and wives have more interest in their parents and relatives than in their husbands. I have always held this view to be wrong. The wife must have her proper place in the affection of her husband and that is why I don't believe in joint family which is always detrimental to woman.

"There is no spirit of revenge in me. I have done more good to the people than any one else can boast of. There are many who turned enemies. But I have never sought to take revenge. I always forgive even where I am not able to forgive. So you need have no fear regarding my attitude to your relations. They are always welcome as guest.

"I wrote to you about my children because I know that the relationship between step children and step-mothers are not always happy. These unhappy relations start with prejudice and end up in complete antagonism which destroys the happiness of all. I do not wish this to happen. That is why I wanted to induce goodwill, understanding from the beginning between the two sides. I regret you did not show enough response. I hope that this one is due to shyness and not to any prejudice. My second reason in writing on this point was that my son who is in business and who has a great business head might be of help to your brother if you were friendly to him. Evidently you did not realize this.

"You are averse to writing and I have no desire to force you myself. I am too busy to write often. The telephone is no use. It causes exasperation. We can only depend upon such intermittent correspondence as we have."

Fondest love from

Raja

But Ambedkar was surprised on hearing reports from his own friends that one of his lieutenants in the All India Federation for the Scheduled Castes had been poisoning Yashwant's ears against Dr Savita. In the circumstances, he could do nothing except to take into confidence another trusted lieutenant of his, Kamlakant Chitre. Chitre had earlier contacted him, underlining the need for early marriage. He had drawn Ambedkar's attention to the gossip and a sort of vilification campaign already launched by his critics who had been completely taken by surprise by the decision of Dr Kabir, a Saraswat Brahmin lady, agreeing to marry an Untouchable much older than her. On 3rd April 1948, Ambedkar wrote the following letter to Kamlakant.

My dear Kamalakant,

One of my close colleagues is sowing seeds of ill feeling between Yashwant and Dr Kabir. It is very strange. All my well-wishers wanted me to marry some one in the interest of my health. Now that I have found a suitable girl, all kinds of malicious things are being said.

I agree that there should be no postponement of the event. It is irrevocably fixed on the 15th April. Postponement will open a field for wider publicity and greater opportunity for evil tongues to wag. I feel no moral turpitude in what I am doing. Nobody can have any ground for complaint, not even Yashwant. To the latter I have given about Rs 30,000 and in addition a house which is today worth at least Rs 80,000. I am sure no father can do more for his son than I have done for him. Yashwant's disaffection comes to me as a surprise for I remember his writing to me of his own free will that in the interest of my health I should marry.

I am sending a cheque for Rs 100 to cover the cost of your journey and the cost of Dr Kabir's luggage. Please don't forget to bring the following things from Rajgrah with you when you come.

1. Photo of Buddha

2. Chest expander which is in the inner room along with the books.

With kind regards,

Yours sincerely,

B.R. Ambedkar

Now that Ambedkar and Savita had decided to get married on 15th April, they started making preparations for the wedding. Ambedkar sent her a remittance of Rs 1,700 so that she could buy for herself dresses for the wedding. Lest she should be labouring under the impression that being a Central Government Minister he was a very rich man, Ambedkar frankly told her not to entertain any such hopes. Nor should her marriage raise the expectations of her relations for any pecuniary advantage from him. Naturally, Savita did not like him to say such things and angrily replied to his insinuations, addressing him as May It Please Your Honour, the language of the courts, instead of just calling him Raja, as she had been doing earlier in her letters to him. When he got her letter, Ambedkar could sense her resentment over his tight-fisted attitude and other things he had told her about her relations. In somewhat retaliatory tone, Ambedkar in his reply to her dated April 9, addressed her as may it please your excellency, instead of Sharu, which he had been doing in his earlier letters, and went on to explain in detail the reason for using the expressions which had offended her in his communication.

Without making any bones about it, Ambedkar wrote to her he deeply regretted the tone of her letter. "Who would not regret on receiving a communication couched in a painful language which you have sent? It seems you are by nature intolerant. I wanted that there should be motherly love between you and my son, Yashwant. My idea was that you should be able to see each other before the marriage. But you did not like it. I had not raised any objection on the money you spend on bridal dresses. But you say that whatever the expenditure you incur with my money would be a kind of loan to you which would be returned later. I cannot understand what you have in your mind. All that I had said was that whatever money we have we should spend it carefully, and not extravagantly. What is wrong in it? You have gone to the extent of saying that your relations would rather beg than come to me for help if at any time they were in need of help. I never said that I would not do anything for your relations. Your relations would always be welcome in my house.

"You have said if at any time I am in distress or fallen on bad days, you would earn and help me out. Honestly, I tell you my desire is to live only on my own income whatever hardship it may entail. I would never look to anybody else for help. The day I am not able to provide for you and myself, I would rather commit suicide than do anything ignoble or unworthy. This is my firm determination. You don't worry on this score. It seems from your letter that you think I am tight-fisted, miserly, illiberal and ignoramus fellow. I may be tight-fisted, in fact I have been like this since my birth, because I am not a man with resources to flaunt money. I may be miserly, but I am not lacking in the milk of human kindness. Yet I am proud to say that it will not be easy to find a person who is more benevolent, more helpful than I am. I have never been given to caste considerations while helping people. If ever any of your relations need my help I would go out of the way to do so.

"You are worried about your freedom following our marriage. I hope you are not under the impression that you are marrying an uncivilized, immoral brute, drunkard, gambler or licentious person. I have no idea what kind of freedom you are talking about. All my life I have been shouldering responsibilities. I could not afford to live in freedom without any thought or consideration for anyone else. Don't think marrying me would undermine your freedom. You will have as much freedom, even more, than your mother has in her house. Perish the thought that you would not be happy with me after the marriage. I have been the greatest champion of the elevation and emancipation of women and in my own community, I have done my best to raise the status of women and I am proud of it."

Why was the marriage fixed for April 15 and not April 14, which was Ambedkar's birthday and therefore would have been more auspicious? Answering this question raised by Savita, Ambedkar said there was no certainty that he was actually born on April 14 or some other day. According to the school records, his date of birth was April 14. But astrologers had given different dates of his birth. Some said it was April 15, some were of the view that it was April 17. Another eminent astrologer had opined that he was born on May 17. In any case there was no sanctity about April 14. He had deliberately decided April 15 for the wedding because on April 14, a large number of people visited his house to wish him happy birthday. But he wanted a quiet wedding and therefore fixed April 15 as the date for it. Another reason for him to opt for April 15 was because it would be a Thursday and Thursday had always been an auspicious day for him in life.

Consequently, as arranged by Ambedkar, Savita arrived from Bombay on the morning of April 15. She was received at the Safdarjung airport and escorted to Ambedkar's residence—1, Hardinge Avenue, New Delhi – where the Deputy Commissioner was already waiting for completing the formalities of Ambedkar's civil marriage with Savita. A daughter-in-law of one of Ambedkar's trusted lieutenants was there to receive her as she reached the bungalow and then took her to the first floor of the house for the bridal make-up. As soon as Savita came down, the civil marriage ceremony was gone through and a small number of people, whom Ambedkar had invited, congratulated them. Soon after this ceremony, Ambedkar took his bride to the bungalow of Sardar Vallabbhai Patel, who was the Central Home Minister then and who had arranged a reception for the newly wedded couple. Sardar Patel, who was not well on that day, was lying on a bed in the inner lawn of his house. As soon as he saw the newly wedded couple, he got up and congratulated them. While chatting with the couple, Patel remarked, had Bapu (Mahatma Gandhi) been alive today, he would have been overjoyed to see his dream fulfilled: an upper caste Brahmin woman marrying an Untouchable.

But the news of their marriage caused a big splash in social circles for it was very rare in Hindu society that an upper caste woman would opt to marry an Untouchable. Savita had done this. Their wedding was reported widely not only in India but also abroad. A special dispatch on their wedding appeared in the *New York Times* under the following heading:

HINDU BRAHMIN WEDS UNTOUCHABLE LEADER
FORFEITING HER CASTE RIGHT TO ENTER HEAVEN

NEW DELHI, APRIL 15: To millions of orthodox Hindus, one of the most significant news in free India is the marriage today of Dr B.R. Ambedkar, an Untouchable, to Dr Savita Kabir, a member of the supreme Brahmin caste. Only a few years ago, such a union could hardly have happened in caste-bound India, and it still is rare enough for a front page display in Indian newspapers.

Dr Ambedkar, Minister of Law in the Indian Cabinet and President of the All India Scheduled Castes (Untouchables) Federation, is best known as a champion of equal rights for those 60,00,000 Indians, who in the social system are the lowest of the low – a people without caste, doomed to be reincarnated as Untouchable throughout eternity. Partly through his efforts over many years, the Untouchables are now admitted to many Hindu temples as a legal right.

By her marriage to Untouchable, Miss Kabir, according to orthodox Hindu doctrine, forever forfeited her right to enter heaven. She has violated the strict bars of caste and thereby, according to a belief still held in the thousands of Indian villages, has placed herself and her descendants beyond the pale for the end of time.

That a Brahmin girl could thus defy one of the strongest religious conventions in the world is taken here as a milestone on the road of new age in Hindu India. It is far more significant than the wedding of royalty to a commoner.

Dr Ambedkar, who was 55 yesterday, studied at Columbia and European Universities under the patronage of Maharaja Gaekwar of Baroda. He has had a distinguished career in Indian politics, becoming famous for his bitter differences with Mohandas K.Gandhi on the issue of a Separate Electorate for Untouchables, which Dr Ambedkar favoured.

In a dispatch from New Delhi, the API, a well-known news agency of those days, reported:

LAW MINISTER WEDS

Dr B.R. Ambedkar, the Law Minister, Government of India, was married to Dr (Miss) Savita Kabir on Thursday morning at his residence at 1, Hardinge Avenue. The bride is a Medical Practitioner in Bombay. The marriage was solemnized under the Civil Marriages Act by the Deputy Commissioner of Delhi in the presence of a few personal friends of Dr Ambedkar, who entertained them to lunch.

A large number of Ambedkar's followers wanted to celebrate his wedding with public receptions attended by one and all but the messiah of the Untouchables was against this. In view of the generally chastened mood and atmosphere in the country following Mahatma Gandhi's assassination by a Maharashtrian on 30th January, 1948, Ambedkar wanted his marriage to be a quiet affair. Because Mahatma Gandhi was no ordinary man, his assassination had given rise to strong anti-Maharashtrian feeling in the country. Ambedkar feared that in the prevailing situation her family members could be made the target of attack in Maharashtra not only because of Gandhi's assassination, but also because she herself had committed a kind of blasphemy by marrying an Untouchable, an action which no upper caste Maharashtrian would ever condone. But his close friends and admirers were very happy over his wedding. They felt that with a doctor wife at home, she will be able to take good care of his failing health, which had been causing great anxiety to all of them.

Ambedkar himself was overjoyed and soon after the ceremony he took his bride to Simla for the honeymoon. According to an account of their short stay in Simla by his wife, Savita Ambedkar, they were very happy. She was surprised to find him as a jovial man who would charm the heart of anybody. Recalling little anecdotes from his life, he would send her and other guests, who were staying with them in the government guest house, into peals of laughter. Although he had been quite happy even with his first wife, Ramabai, with Dr Savita Kabir it was altogether different. His joy really knew no bounds because Savita was not only young and attractive, but in her he had also found a good doctor and nurse to take care of him, which was what he needed most at this stage in his life.

Describing in a book about her life with Ambedkar, Savita says that his meetings with her in Bombay before the marriage would have been perhaps more frequent had he not been obsessed with his responsibility to complete the drafting of free India's new Constitution within the allotted time, the last date for which was February 28, 1948. While he was piloting the Hindu Code Bill in Parliament, their house had literally become a repository of ancient texts and latest modern books on women which Ambedkar consulted every day to marshal his facts so that he could not be faulted by anyone in Parliament. He even consulted Savita on many occasions on various clauses in the Bill. Although he himself was quite depressed over his failure to push through the Bill for which he had worked hard, Ambedkar's wife tried to console and comfort him as best she could in the circumstances. When he resigned as law minister, Savita became more active in order to ensure his re-election to the Rajya Sabha. She wrote letters to leaders of various parties to extend him their full support in re-entering Parliament.

Whenever he was to speak in Parliament on some important issue, Ambedkar would like his wife to be present in the VIP gallery. Later, Savita recalled that perhaps Ambedkar, like Winston Churchill in the British Parliament, wanted to have his wife watching him from the VIP gallery. Churchill also always had his wife in the VIP gallery when he spoke on important issues. But Ambedkar was not only particular about her presence in Parliament, he was also keen that she was very well dressed. In fact, before going to Parliament he would often suggest to Savita the sari she should wear. Once it so happened that Savita took out from her wardrobe a heavily embroidered sari to wear for her visit to Parliament. But since Ambedkar did not like it he was irritated and before leaving asked her not to follow him to Parliament that day. But before he left, she sneaked up to their driver and secretly asked him to come back after dropping Ambedkar in Parliament. When Ambedkar rose to speak and nonchalantly looked towards the VIP gallery he was surprised to find his wife seated on her usual favourite seat. But seeing that she was not wearing the sari he had rejected and instead was clad in the sari he liked, he was pleasantly surprised and gave her a smile. As the House adjourned, he happily escorted her home.

According to his wife, Ambedkar not only had a good dress sense, he was also a great connoisseur of food and quite an expert in cooking. Once, when his old friend Varle had come from Bombay on a visit to Delhi, the family decided to have a picnic in Okhla. But soon after reaching there, he asked his wife to leave the cooking arrangements to his care. The cooks did as he ordered them to boil, roast, fry chicken, mutton, fish and onions and ultimately had a lavish table laid for all to eat. Not only the biryani but everything before the guests was so tasty that they went on licking their plates and thoroughly enjoyed the treat.

In 1953, Ambedkar had taken his wife to Aurangabad where the Milind College building was under construction. At various functions held in his honour he was presented with donations for the college building. The well-known film actor of those days, Dilip Kumar, was also staying in the same hotel where accommodation had been reserved for the Ambedkars. One day Savita's younger brother chanced to meet Dilip Kumar in the hotel lobby and when he learnt that Ambedkar those days was trying to raise funds for the college building, Dilip Kumar expressed his desire to meet him. Savita's brother brought him along to the suite where his brother-in-law was staying and introduced him to Ambedkar. But when Ambedkar was told that the actor wanted to make some contribution to the building fund, he bluntly refused to accept anything from him. He said he did not want to taint the college with the contribution of a man who made his money by disreputable means. Dilip Kumar politely asked him not to be rash in his judgement for all film stars were not alike. But Ambedkar would not listen to any such argument. Following this the actor quietly moved out.

Ambedkar's failing health was always a serious cause of concern to his wife. She was very strict insofar as administration of drugs to Ambedkar was concerned, because she feared he could suffer a relapse without the regular intake of medicines. But surprisingly, while they were in Aurangabad, Savita herself was taken ill. Ambedkar got worried and immediately sought the best medical help for her treatment. It was found that the formation of a tumour on her chest could be the possible cause of her illness. He was advised to consult experts for the treatment of his wife's ailment. Following this he took her to the Tata Hospital in Bombay. After thorough investigations the doctors said that cancer could be the cause of her tumour. In any event it would require surgery for treatment. For pathological examination of her turmour, doctors took samples and told the couple that although they were not certain yet, cancer could not be ruled out. They were advised to sleep separately for the time being.

Ambedkar was very worried. He could not even imagine that his young wife whom he adored so much could contract such malignancy as the doctors suspected. Savita was surprised to see him weeping loudly with his head buried in pillows when they retired to their bedroom that day. She tried to comfort him asking him not to take it so seriously even before doctors had given their final opinion. "But what will I do, Sharu, without you? If something happened to you it will be the worst misfortune for me," cried Ambedkar. However, luckily for the couple, a complete and thorough evaluation of the tests ruled out cancer. She was prescribed some drugs and soon the tumour subsided, leaving the couple happy.

In her book on life with Dr Ambedkar, Savita said that every morning after she had given him a hot water bath like a child and helped him dress up by handing him over whatever suit, shirt or tie he wanted, he would look at the mirror repeatedly to satisfy himself about his apparel and looks. He would start his breakfast with porridge, follow it up with some cornflakes and then eggs to his taste. He would like everything to be served hot and oven-fresh. She had specially got a hot plate placed near the dining table so that whatever he wanted was served hot. After the breakfast she would almost daily accompany him up to the porch of their bungalow, open the door of the car for him to be seated comfortably and drive out, waving back to her until the car had reached the outer gate. Despite his heavy work schedule, he was always concerned about the welfare of his staff, and sometimes when he was free, relaxing in the verandah of his bungalow or on the lawn, he would make enquiries about them.

Savita stated that with his reputation as the architect of the Indian Constitution, a leader of the Untouchables, an outstanding scholar who had two doctorate degrees from two world famous universities, he was like an ocean and she was only a bubble in his life. She said Ambedkar was like the proverbial philosopher's stone which had the unique quality of turning into gold whatever it came in contact with. She was insignificant compared with Ambedkar. But following her marriage she remained with him like a shadow.

References

1. The letter is on page 30 in the book Letters of Ambedkar by Dr. Surendra Ajnat. Ambedkar's Miscellaneous Writings.

   Dr. Savita Kabir's book on her life with Ambedkar published in Marathi.

2. See 60, 61 pages of the book, Reminiscenes and Remebrances of Dr. B.R. Ambedkar by Nanak Channd Rattu, published by Falcon Books, Delhi, 1995.

3. *Ibid.*

4. For all these references. See Dr. Savita Ambedkar's book, my Years With Ambedkar, she wrote after his death. The book is in Marathi. Some of these letters also figures in Rattu's book on reminiscences and remembrances of Dr. Ambedkar.

5. *Ibid.*

6. *Ibid.*

7. *Ibid.*

13

The Partition of India

Often the greatest achievement of the British rule in India is described as the unity of the subcontinent. From Khyber Pass in the North-West to Kanyakumari in the South, the entire territory was under one government. No doubt it was a great feat. Before the British started laying the foundation of their largest empire in the world, India was a congeries of States ruled by the Mughals and several other royal dynasties. Gradually, the British writ had started running all over India. And it continued for over 150 years. But when the imperial power was planning to quit India, fissiparous tendencies were again very strong. In fact, the entire country seemed to be splitting on communal lines. The Scheduled Castes led by Ambedkar wanted to part company with the Hindu society. The most important and worrying problem was the claim of the Muslims to have their own separate nation by parting company with the Hindu majority even if it led to the partition of the subcontinent.

The desire of the Scheduled Castes to be a separate entity so that there could be no Hindu domination had been nourished for long by Ambedkar. But their movement to get out of the clutches of caste Hindus was still not very strong. Whatever case they had for a separate existence from the caste Hindus was often overshadowed by the writings and speeches of Mahatma Gandhi who did not want the Untouchables to go out of the Hindu fold and always argued that step-motherly treatment meted out to them was the result of the evil practices which had crept into the Hindu society. Their salvation lay not in separation but in the reformation of the caste-based Hindu social order. The upper caste Hindus, Gandhi stressed, must change their attitude towards the Untouchables so that they could have no grudge. But Ambedkar wanted Gandhi to change his views and instead do something concrete and substantial for their uplift. The father of the nation, however, wielded so much influence and enjoyed so much prestige being the supreme leader of the Congress that he was not much bothered about whatever Ambedkar said or thought. In any case, the Congress party was packed with caste Hindus and Gandhi would rather not like to do anything which might rub them on the wrong side. So he contented himself by preaching that the Untouchables were part and parcel of the Hindu society and should be accorded better treatment.

The recurrence of the Hindu-Muslim clashes all over the country, the growing impatience of the Muslim leaders not to live with Hindus as their brethren as they would be dominated by the Hindu majority, and their increasing desire to have their separate homeland even if it meant the division of the subcontinent made Ambedkar go deeper into the demand for Pakistan for which the Muslims were agitating. After studying the problem for several years he wrote a book, *Pakistan or the Partition of India*. Keeping in view the communal situation in the country, Ambedkar justified the demand for Pakistan. The publication of this book in December 1940 came as a bombshell in the political and intellectual circles, for without making any bones about it, Ambedkar had exposed all that had gone behind into the making of the demand for a separate Muslim nation as a powerful movement. Gandhi and other Congress leaders were worried over this development because the creation of Pakistan would divide India and in any case would not be a matter of credit or satisfaction to them.

Although the book was not entirely flattering to Muslims, the fact that it supported the division of the subcontinent into two nations was like a boon to the hardliners in the Muslim League. Ambedkar had argued that the Hindus need have no fear that the creation of Pakistan would deprive India of a nationally safe frontier because geographical conditions are not decisive in the modern world. As the resources of Hindustan are far greater than those of Pakistan, the formation of Pakistan would not make India weak. It is better for the Hindus not to live with Muslims whose loyalty to India is always suspect. A safe army without the Muslim preponderance would be better than a safe border. Ambedkar suggested measures for securing peace and homogeneity by arranging a total exchange of population, Hindus from Pakistan and Muslims from Hindustan, as did Turkey, Greece and Bulgaria to solve their internecine problems. Tracing history, Ambedkar concluded that Islam can never allow a true Muslim to adopt India as his Motherland and regard a Hindu as his kith and kin. The spirit of aggression is Muslim's natural endowment. He takes advantage of the weakness of the Hindus.

Ambedkar's thesis on Pakistan sold like hot cakes and within a few years, publishers of the book had to come out with its third edition to meet the growing demand. What Ambedkar wrote was indeed the ground for the partition of India. In those days, youngsters enquiring of their elders or teachers as to why should there be a Pakistan as demanded by the Muslim League were often told to read Ambedkar's book though the Congress and the Muslim League politicians and even the British colonial rulers dismissed it as trash. The reason for their attitude was not that Ambedkar's book was based on lies or conjectures; their grouse was because he had exposed everybody : the Hindu leaders, the Muslim leaders and the British masters, all of whom had contributed to the creation of an atmosphere in which the division of the subcontinent seemed inevitable. True to Ambedkar's prognosis, India was divided into two nations on August 15, 1947. The Muslim majority provinces in the north and the eastern wing of the country became Pakistan and the rest of the subcontinent, which had a Hindu majority remained India. Bharat Mata was never so short and shrunk as the overreaching ambitions of politicians had made it for the first time in recorded history.

Ambedkar blew the lid off the discreditable role of all those who had sought to bring this about. He wrote:[1] "I do not think the demand for Pakistan is the result of mere political distemper, which will pass away with the afflux of time. It seems to me that it is a characteristic in the biological sense of the term, which the Muslim body politic has developed in the same manner as an organism develops a characteristic. Whether it will survive or not, the process of natural selection, must depend upon the forces that may become operative in the struggle for existence between Hindus and Musalmans. I am not staggered by Pakistan; I am not indignant about it; nor do I believe that it can be smashed by shooting into it similes and metaphors. Those who believe in shooting it by similes should remember that nonsense does not cease to be nonsense because it is put in rhyme, and that a metaphor is no argument though it be sometimes the gunpowder to drive one home and imbibe it in memory. It would be neither wise nor possible to reject summarily a scheme if it has behind it the sentiment, if not the passionate support of 90 per cent Muslims of India.

"The essence of Pakistan is the opposition to the establishment of one Central Government (dominated by Hindus) having supremacy over the whole of India. Protagonists for Pakistan want two Central Governments, one for Pakistan and the other for whatever is left of India after the division of the country. It will be the greatest folly to suppose that if Pakistan is buried for the moment, it will never raise its head again. Burying Pakistan is not the same thing as burying the ghost of Pakistan. So long as there is hostility to one Central Government for India, which is the ideology underlying Pakistan, the ghost of Pakistan will be there, casting its ominous shadow upon the political future of the country. Neither will it be prudent to make some kind of a make-shift arrangement for the time being, leaving the permanent solution to some future date. To do so would be something like curing the symptoms without removing the disease. But, as often happens in such cases, the disease is driven in, thereby making certain its recurrence, perhaps in a more virulent form."

The Muslims, who had been masters of India for nearly 600 years before the British rule began, were the worst sufferers. Their decline and fall became evident in every walk of life. Every change—executive, administrative, or legal - introduced by the alien rulers inflicted a series of blows upon the Muslim community. The Muslim rulers of India had allowed the Hindus to retain their law in civil matters. But the British first abrogated the Hindu Criminal Law and made the Muslim Criminal Law the law of the State and then even replaced it with Macaulay's Penal Code. This was a big blow to the prestige and position of the Muslim community. The British went further and restricted the application of the Shariat or the Muslim Civil Law to matters concerning personal relations, such as marriage and inheritance, and then only to the extent permitted by them. In 1837, the British abolished Persian as the official language of the Court and the general administration and substituted it by English and the vernaculars. In place of Qazi, who during the Muslim rule, administered Shariat, there were appointments of law officers and judges, who might be of any religion but who were invested with the authority to interpret the Muslim Law and whatever their decisions, they were made binding on the erstwhile ruling community of India.

According to the Muslim Canon Law, the world is divided into two camps, Dar-ul-Islam (abode of Islam) and Dar-ul-Harb (abode of war).[2] A country is Dar-ul-Islam when it is ruled by Muslims and is Dar-ul-Harb when Muslims only reside in it but are not rulers of it. The 1857 mutiny had made India into Dar-ul-Harb for the Muslims. They were reduced to the lowest depths of broken pride, black despair and general penury. Without prestige, without education and without resources, the Muslims were left to face the Hindus. The British conquest of India brought about a complete political revolution in the relative position of the two communities. The Muslims had been brought down to the level of the Hindus and they had no hope or alternative except to accept the new reality. No wonder, eminent Muslim leaders like Sir Sayed Ahmed, founder of the Aligarh movement, started saying that the Muslims should not regard living under the British rule as Dar-ul-Harb because they were perfectly free to exercise all the essential rites and ceremonies of their religion. Such teachings started discouraging the movement of Muslims for Hijrat (migration to other Muslim countries so that they could live under Dar-ul-Islam).

Since they were former conquerors of the Indian sub-continent, Muslims although humbled after the failure of the mutiny, continued to receive special treatment from the new rulers of the country. The British saw to it that they were not given any chance or scope for reorganizing themselves and start posing challenge to their authority. Therefore, attempts were always made to ensure that they should have no grievance or grudge against the government and as far as possible should not associate with the Hindus. With a view to weaning away the Mussalmans from the Congress, Lord Dufferin, the Viceroy, went to the extent of giving the Muslims special representation in legislatures in India under the Indian Councils Act, 1892, passed by the British Parliament. Under the Act, special representation was to be made not through election but nomination. However, to be eligible for nomination a person must be a member of an important public body such as municipalities, district boards, universities and associations of merchants. But neither the Act nor the Regulations conferred any right of selection upon the Muslim community, nor did the Act give the Muslim community a right to claim a fixed number of seats. But Lord Dufferin did not bother about these limitations and liberally chose Muslims for benefits under the Act.

The Indian National Congress was founded in 1885. It began with a demand for good government as distinguished from self-government. But the British rulers were not happy over this development. Consequently, behind the scenes moves were made to ensure that the Muslims were not attracted to this organization. It was against this background that Sir Sayed Ahmed, who was also the founder of the Aligarh Muslim University, was said to be the originator of the process which began to cause Hindu-Muslim divergence in the subcontinent. He started propagating that Muslims should keep away from this organization. In his speeches, one delivered at Lucknow on December 28, 1887, and the other at Meerut on March 16, 1988, he urged the Mussalmans not to join the Congress for it was a Hindu organization.

Initially, the formation of the Congress party was not such a serious development as to cause concern to the British, for after having quelled the forces behind 1857 mutiny, they felt quite confident to remain in power for long in India. They had already initiated moves to favour the Muslims and thus make the community toe their line rather than respond to the appeals of the Congress leaders. However, with the increasing popularity and membership of the Congress, the British government became somewhat cautious about its activities and the resolutions it passed. The swelling number of people coming from far and near to attend Congress sessions started becoming a cause for real concern to them. It was feared that if this organization went on gathering strength with the participation of more and more people, it could pose a threat to the British power.

The colonial rulers were already favouring the Muslims in order to keep them away from the Congress. They started paying greater attention to the need to keep the two communities apart. With inspiration and support coming from the then British government, a deputation of the Muslim community was organized to present an address to the new Viceroy and Governor-General of India, Lord Minto at the Viceregal Lodge in Simla on October 1, 1906. The deputation included top-notch Muslim nobles, jagirdars, taluqdars, lawyers, zamindars, merchants and others from the influential sections of society. That the address was a command performance, meaning thereby that it was all arranged by the British government itself, was confirmed by none other than Maulana Mohammad Ali in his presidential address at the Congress session held later. The address has a historical importance because it marked a decisive change in the British government's policy towards Muslims, even if it constituted nothing but flagrant favouritism. The address was a kind of petition to the Viceroy drawing his attention to the grievances of the Muslim community and the Viceroy in his reply made it clear that his government would not mind even going out of the way to keep the Muslim subjects of the British empire happy and satisfied.

Plainly, it marked the beginning of the British Government's policy of giving Muslims more jobs and seats in legislatures even if they did not deserve such concessions, for after all they were a numerical minority in the country's population[3]. The whole purpose of this policy, which was first initiated by Lord Dufferin, was to ensure that the Muslims did not join hands with the Congress. The policy was intended to create a breach and disunity between the Hindus and Muslims. It was a reflection of the 'divide and rule' policy, which the British government had adopted to remain in power in India. In his dispatch on the function in which the address was presented to the new Viceroy the correspondent of the *Indian Daily Telegraph*, a paper then published from Lucknow wrote: "The representatives of the Mohamedan community who were to present the address to His Excellency the Viceroy this morning at the Viceregal Lodge collected in the Ballroom at 11 a.m. They numbered thirty-five and were seated around a horse-shoe table facing His Excellency's chair. Precisely at 11 a.m. Lord Minto, preceded by his staff, entered the room, all standing to receive him. His Excellency was taken round and personally introduced to each member by the Aga Khan. The Khalifa from Patiala then asked permission for the presentation of the address and the Aga Khan then advanced and facing His Excellency read the petition, all the representatives standing."

Among other things, the petition said: "The Mohamedans of India number, according to the census taken in the year 1901, over sixty-two millions or between one-fifth and one-fourth of the total population of His Majesty's Indian dominion, and if a reduction be made for the uncivilized portion of the community enumerated under the heads of animist and other minor religions, as well as for those classes who are ordinarily classified as Hindus but properly speaking are not Hindus at all, the proportion of Mohamedans to the Hindu majority becomes much larger. We therefore desire to submit that under any system of representation extended or limited to any community, it must be kept in view that Muslim community in itself is more numerous than the entire population of any first class European power except Russia and therefore may justly lay claim to adequate recognition as an important factor in the State.

"We venture, indeed, with Your Excellency's permission to go a step further, and urge that the position accorded to the Mohamedan community in any kind of representation, direct or indirect, and in all other ways affecting their status and influence should be commensurate, not merely with their numerical strength, but also with their political importance and the value of the contribution which they make to the defence of the empire and we also hope that Your Excellency will in this connection be pleased to give due consideration to the position which they occupied in India a little more than hundred years ago and of which the traditions have naturally not faded from their minds. The Mohamedans of India have always placed implicit reliance on the sense of justice and love of fair dealing that have characterized their rulers, and have in consequence abstained from pressing their claims by methods that might prove embarrassing, but earnestly as we desire that the

Mohamedans of India should not in the future depart from that excellence and time-honoured tradition. Recent events have stirred up feelings, especially among the younger generation of Mohamedans, which might, in certain circumstances and under certain contingencies, easily pass beyond the control of temperate counsel and sober guidance.

"We Mohamedans are a distinct community with additional interests of our own which are not shared by other communities, and these have hitherto suffered from the fact that they have not been adequately represented. Even in the provinces in which the Mohamedans constitute a distinct majority of the population, they have too often been treated as though they were inappreciably small political factors that might without unfairness be neglected. This has been the case, to some extent, in the Punjab, but in a more marked degree in Sind and in Eastern Bengal. Before formulating their views with regard to the election of representatives, we beg to observe that the political importance of a community to a considerable extent gains strength or suffers detriment according to the position that the members of that community occupy in the service of the State. If, as is unfortunately the case with the Mohamedans, they are not adequately represented in this manner, they lose in the prestige and influence which are justly their due.

"Although the number of qualified Mohamedans has increased, a tendency is unfortunately perceptible to reject them on the ground of relatively superior qualifications having to be given precedence. This introduces something like the competitive element in its worst form, and we may be permitted to draw Your Excellency's attention to the political significance of the monopoly of all official influence by one class. We venture to submit that the generality of the Mohamedans in all parts of India feel aggrieved that Mohamedan Judges are not more frequently appointed to the High Courts and Chief Courts of Judicature. Qualified Mohamedan lawyers eligible for these appointments can always be found, if not in one province then in another. We beg permission further to submit that the presence on the Bench of these Courts of a Judge learned in the Mohomedan Law will be a source of considerable strength to the administration of justice."

Further the petition demanded greater representation for Muslims in Municipal and District Boards, Senates and Syndicates of Indian Universities, in Legislative Chambers of the country, in the Viceroy's Imperial Legislative Council and the Viceroy's Executive Council. The proportion of Mohamedan representatives in various bodies should not be determined on the basis of the numerical strength of the community. For representation in various bodies Mohamedan members should be chosen from among Mohamedan landowners, lawyers, merchants and representatives of other important interests of a status to be subsequently determined by the government. Mohamedan members of the Provincial Councils and Mohamedan Fellows of Universities should be invested with electoral powers to be exercised in accordance with such procedure as may be prescribed by the government keeping in view the interests of the Muslim community.

After the address, Lord Minto delivered a most sympathetic reply, which was frequently punctuated with cheers and cries of "Hear, hear" from the members of the deputation. Dealing with all the points raised in the long petition, Lord Minto observed: "All you have said emanates from a representative body basing its opinions on a matured consideration of existing political conditions in India, totally apart from the small localities, and I am grateful to you for the opportunity you are affording me of expressing my appreciation of the just aims of the followers of Islam and their determination to share in the political history of our Empire. I can only say to you that the Mohamedan community may rest assured that their political rights and interests as a community will be safeguarded in any administrative reorganization with which I am concerned and that you and the people of India may rely upon the British Raj to respect, as it has been its pride to do, the religious beliefs and the national traditions of the myriads composing the population of His Majesty's Indian Empire."

Following the submission of their petition to the Viceroy, no doubt the Muslim community started receiving greater attention of the colonial rulers especially when official favours were to be distributed. The British were doing it only to divide Hindus and Muslims and knowingly or unknowingly sowing seeds which sprouted and grew into the demand by Muslims for a separate nation. Of course many other things also happened between then and 1947 when the sub-continent was partitioned. But the divisive tendencies were the intent of the British policy from day one. The British policy after presentation of the address to the Viceroy set in motion a process which started polluting the communal atmosphere in the country as a result of which communal clashes all over India started happening as they had never happened before. The majority Hindu community by and large was feeling much better than was their plight when they were under the Muslim rule before the advent of the British. But having been at the receiving end for over 600 years of Muslim rule, the Hindus, by and large, and possibly because of their religious beliefs which discouraged violence and encouraged fatalism, were always worsted by the Muslims in communal clashes, wherever they occurred. For instance the number of Hindus murdered and looted, their women assaulted in communal clashes all over the country was always more than that of the Muslims despite the fact that the Hindus were a majority community in the country.

Dominated by caste Hindus and led by Gandhi, the Congress was the largest political organization in India. But the British encouragement and support to the Muslim minority had also given birth to the Muslim League and several other parties which had started demanding separate electorates for themselves so that the Muslims could escape Hindu domination. Not only that, they had started even raising the demand for a separate State for Muslims even if it resulted in the division of India into two nations, Hindus on one side and Muslims on the other. Gandhi and the other Congress leaders were worried over this prospect and instead of taking the Muslim fanatics head on started making compromises with them even when there was serious provocation from the other side, calling for a tougher retort and reaction. This made Gandhi start overlooking Muslim aberrations and creating a false impression amongst the Muslims that they could get away with whatever they wanted because Hindus were afraid of them. However, all this did not altogether blind the entire Muslim intelligentsia to what was happening in Hindustan and some of them started ringing alarm bells to alert the people against British designs in creating walls of suspicion and jealousy among different communities in India.

There were separate electorates for the Muslims and many other unjustified concessions were given to the community by the British. But the leader who raised a voice of protest against this practice was none other than Mohammed Ali Jinnah, who later became the Quaid-e-Azam of Pakistan. How it happened is another story. For the time being let us see the reactions of Jinnah to separate electorates for the Muslims introduced by the colonial rulers only to ensure that they don't hobnob with Hindus. Giving evidence before the Joint Select Committee appointed by the British Parliament on the Government of India Reform Bill, professedly appearing on behalf of the Muslim League, Jinnah said : "I really hope and expect that the day is not very far when separate electorates for the Muslims will disappear. Of course, it is a fact that at its Agra session in 1913, the Muslim League was in favour of separate electorates for Muslims. However, since then I have had many opportunities of discussing this matter with various Mussalman leaders, and they are changing their angle of vision with regard to this matter."[4]

Although Jinnah appeared as a witness on behalf of the Muslim League, he did not allow his membership of the League to come in the way of his loyalty to the other political organizations of the country. As he said in his evidence before the Joint Parliamentary Committee, he was a member of the Muslim League, the Home Rule League and also of the Congress. That he was an independent but a nationalist was obvious from his relationship with the Khilafat Conference, which virtually became the voice of Muslims from 1919 to 1924 in India. Jinnah refused to join the Khilafat movement. He was opposed to the Indian Musalmans engaging themselves in extra-territorial affairs relating to Muslims outside India, although the Gandhi-led Congress, seeing in the Khilafat movement an opportunity to win over Muslims, was supporting the Khilafat agitation.

The Muslim League became active again in Indian politics after the Khilalfat storm had blown over. At the session of the League held in Bombay on December 30, 1924, under the presidentship of Raza Ali, a resolution was moved which called for the desirability of representatives of various Muslim organizations meeting in a conference in Delhi or at some other central place to "develop a united, sound practical activity" to supply the needs of the Muslim community. While explaining the resolution, Jinnah said: "The object is to organize the Muslim community, not with a view to quarrelling with the Hindu community, but with a view to uniting and cooperating with it for their motherland. He was sure once they had organized themselves they would join hands with the Hindu Mahasabha and declare to the world that Hindus and Mohamedans are brothers." The Muslim League also passed a resolution in the same session for appointing a committee of 33 prominent Musalmans to formulate the political demands of the Muslim community.

Moved by Jinnah, the resolution, among other things, stated:[5] "The charge that I am standing on the platform of the League as a communalist is baseless. I am a nationalist. I want the best and the fittest men to represent the Muslims in Legislatures of the land (Hear, hear and applause). But unfortunately my Muslim compatriots are not prepared to go as far as I am willing to do. I cannot be blind to the situation. The fact is that there is a large number of Muslims who want representation separately in Legislatures and in the country's Services. They are talking of communal unity. But where is unity? It has to be achieved by arriving at some suitable settlement. My fellow religionists are ready and prepared to fight for Swaraj, but want some safeguards. As a practical politician I have to take stock of the situation. The real block to unity is not the communities themselves, but a few mischief makers on both sides."

And Jinnah did not hesitate to arraign mischief makers in the sternest possible language that could only come from an earnest nationalist. In his capacity as the President of the session of the Muslim League held in Lahore on May 24, 1924, Jinnah said: "If we wish to be free people, let us unite; but if we wish to continue as salves of bureaucracy, let us keep fighting among ourselves and gratify petty vanity over petty matters, Englishmen being our arbiters. In the two All Parties Conferences, one held in 1925 and the other in 1928, Jinnah was prepared to settle the Hindu-Muslim question on the basis of joint electorates. In 1927 he openly said from the League platform: "I am not wedded to separate electorates, although I must say that the overwhelming majority of the Musalmans firmly and honestly believe that it is the only method by which they can be sure and safeguard their future."

In 1928, the Congress boycotted the Simon Commission and surprisingly Jinnah joined in the protest.[6] He did so even though the Hindus and Muslims had failed to come to a settlement and when many office-bearers of the Muslim League he headed were opposed to this course. The U.P. Muslim League Conference was held in Allahabad on August 8, 1931 with Jinnah as the chief guest. In his observations at this conference he said: "It is now absolutely essential and vital that Muslims should stand united. For heaven's sake close all your ranks and files and stop this internecine war. I urge this most vehemently and I plead to the best of my ability before Dr Ansari, Mr T.A.K.

Sherwani, Maulana Abdul Kalam Azad and Dr Syed Mahmud. I hope that before I leave the shores of India to attend the Round Table Conference in London, I shall hear the good news that whatever may be our differences, whatever may be our convictions, this is not the moment to quarrel between ourselves.

"There is a certain section of the Press, there is a certain section of the Hindus, who constantly misrepresent me in various ways. I was only reading the speech of Mr Gandhi this morning and Mr Gandhi said that he loves Hindus and Muslims alike. I again say standing here on this platform, although I may not put forward that claim but I do put forward this honestly and sincerely that I want fair play between the two communities. As the most important question which to my mind is the question of Hindu-Muslim settlement, all I can say to you is that I honestly believe that the Hindus should concede to the Muslims a majority in the Punjab and Bengal (and agree to the formation of governments headed by Muslims in these two provinces) and if that is conceded, I think a settlement can be arrived at in a very short time.

"The next question that arises is one of separate vs. joint electorates. If majority is conceded in the Punjab and Bengal, I would personally prefer a settlement on the basis of joint electorate (applause). But I also know that there is a large body of Muslims – and I believe a majority of Muslims – who are holding on to separate electorate. I would rather have a settlement even on the footing of separate electorate, hoping and trusting that when we work our new Constitution and when both Hindus and Muslim get rid of distrust, suspicions and fears, and when they get their freedom, we would rise to the occasion and probably separate electorate will go sooner than most of us think.

"I am for a settlement and peace among the Muslims first; I am for a settlement and peace between the Hindus and Mohamedans. This is not a time for argument, not a time for propaganda work and not a time for embittering feelings between the two communities, because the enemy is at the door of both of us and I say without hesitation that if the Hindu-Muslim question is not settled, I have no doubt that the British will have to arbitrate and that he who arbitrates will keep to himself the substance of power and authority. Therefore, I hope they will not vilify me. After all, Mr Gandhi himself says that he is willing to give the Muslims whatever they want, and my only sin is that I say to the Hindus give to the Muslims only 14 points, which is much less than the 'blank cheque' which Mr Gandhi is willing to give."

The 14 points which Jinnah mentioned were the following demands. The Congress should withdraw all opposition to the Communal Award and should not describe it as a negation of nationalism. The share of the Muslims in the State services should be fixed in the Constitution by statutory enactment. Muslim personal law and culture should be guaranteed by statute. The Congress should take in hand the agitation in connection with the Sahidganj Mosque and use its moral pressure to enable the Muslim to gain possession of the mosque. The Muslims' right to call Azan and perform their religious ceremonies should not be fettered in any way. Muslims should have freedom to perform cow slaughter. Muslim majorities in the provinces, where such majorities exist at present, must be effected by territorial redistribution or adjustments. The "Bande Mataram" song should be given up. Muslims want Urdu to be the national language of India and they desire to have statutory guarantees that the use of Urdu shall not be curtailed or damaged. Muslim representation in the local bodies should be governed by principles underlying the Communal Award, that is, separate electorates and population strength. The tricolour flag should be changed or alternatively the flag of the Muslim League should be given equal importance. Recognition of the Muslim League as one authoritative and representative organization of Indian Muslims should be accepted. Coalition ministries should be formed.

"I say to Hindus, do not misrepresent everybody. I hope and trust that we shall be yet in a position to settle the question which will bring peace and happiness to the millions in our country. One thing more I want to tell you. During the Round Table Conference, it is now an open book and anybody who cares to read it can learn for himself. I observed the one and the only principle was that when I left the shores of Bombay I said to the people that I would hold the interests of India sacred, and believe me – if you care to read the proceedings of the Conference, I am not bragging that I have done my duty – that I have loyally and faithfully fulfilled my promise to the fullest extent and I venture to say that if the Congress or Mr Gandhi can get anything more than I fought for, I would congratulate them."

Not only Mr Jinnah but several other important Muslim leaders also seemed keen on some kind of settlement with the Congress so that both Hindus and Muslims could live together and remain united to work for the liberation of India from the British.[7] Malik Barkat Ali, who was the chairman of the reception committee of the Punjab Nationalist Muslim Conference held in Lahore in 1931, said: "We believe first and foremost in the full freedom and honour of India. India, the country of our birth and the place with which all our most valued and dearly cherished associations are knit, must claim its first place in our affection and in our desires. We refuse to be parties to that sinister type of propaganda which would try to appeal to ignorant sentiment by professing to be Muslim first and Indian afterwards. To us a slogan of this kind is not only bare, meaningless cant, but downright mischievous.

"We cannot conceive of Islam in its best and last interests as in any way inimical to or in conflict with the best and permanent interests of India. India and Islam in India are identical, and whatever is to the detriment of India must, from the nature of it, be detrimental to Islam whether economically, politically, socially or even morally. Those politicians, therefore, are a class of false prophets and at bottom the foes of Islam, who talk of any inherent conflict between Islam and the welfare of India. Further, howsoever much our sympathy with our Muslim brethren outside India, i.e., the Turks and the Egyptians or the Arabs – and it is a sentiment which is at once noble and healthy – we can never allow that sympathy to work to the detriment of the essential interests of India.

"We not only believe in a free India but we also believe in a united India – not the India of the Muslims, not the India of the Hindus or of the Sikhs, not the India of this community or of that community but the India of all. India was one in the days of Ashoka and Chandragupta and India remained one even when the scepter and rod of Imperial sway passed from Hindus into Mughal or Muslim hands. And India shall remain one when we shall have attained the object of our desires and reached those uplands of freedom, where all the light illuminating us shall not be reflected glory but shall be light proceeding direct as it were from our very faces. The conception of a divided India, which Sir Mohammad Iqbal put forward while presiding over the Muslim League session in Lucknow in 1930, could not be justified. I am glad to be able to say that Sir Mohammad Iqbal has since recanted it. It must not therefore delude anybody into thinking that it is Islam's conception of the India to be.

"Even if Dr Iqbal had not recanted it as something which could not be put forward by any sane person, I should have emphatically and unhesitatingly repudiated it as something foreign to the genius and the spirit of the rising generation of Islam, and I really deem it as a proud duty to affirm today that not only must there be no division of India into communal provinces but that both Islam and Hinduism must run co-terminously with the boundaries of India and must not be cribbed, cabined and confined with any shorter bounds. To the same category as Dr Iqbal's conception of a Muslim India and a Hindu India, belongs the sinister proposals of some Sikh communalists to partition and divide the Punjab.

"Whatever may have been the value or utility of separate electorates at a time when an artificially manipulated high-propertied franchise had the effect of converting a majority of the people in the population of a province into a minority in the electoral roll, and when communal passions and feelings ran particularly high, universal distrust poisoning the whole atmosphere like a general and all-pervading miasma, – we feel that in the circumstances of today and in the India of the future, separate electorates should have no place whatever."

But expressions of such noble thoughts by nationalist leaders were just a cry in the wilderness. All efforts for Hindu-Muslim unity failed and within a couple of years Muslim ideology underwent a complete change. During the Round Table Conferences in London, a Muslim group was very active in propagating the idea of Pakistan. The members of this group circulated pamphlets and other type of literature, making a special case for the division of India. Sir Mohammad Iqbal, who was the first to talk of Pakistan was also present in London. But participants in the Round Table Conferences, although they had picked up the literature distributed by some Muslims in support of the Pakistan demand, did not attach much importance to it. But the communal award announced by the British Government after these conferences conceded the Muslim demand for separate electorates.

Normally, concessions given to Muslims in the communal award announced by the British government ought to have satisfied the Muslim League. But what to talk of hardliners, Mr Jinnah himself had changed his stand. It was clear from the 14-point charter of demands he had submitted to the Congress earlier that there could be no settlement between the Congress and the Muslim League. Jinnah supplemented his list by demanding 50 per cent share in everything. By raising the demand for 50 per cent share in everything, the Muslims were not only seeking to reduce the Hindu majority to a minority but they were also cutting into the political rights of other communities. The Muslim were speaking the language of Hitler and claiming a place in the sun as Hitler had been doing for Germany. Their claim for the recognition of Urdu as the national language was extravagant for Urdu was not only not spoken all over India, it was not even the language of all the Musalmans of India. Of the 68 millions of Muslims (according to the 1921 census) only 28 millions spoke Urdu. The proposal of making Urdu the national language meant that the language of 28 millions of Muslims was to be imposed particularly upon 40 millions of Musalmans or generally upon 322 millions of Indians. No wonder the spectre of the division of India began to loom large on the horizon.

But the talk of the possible division of India to create a separate homeland for Muslims queered the communal pitch so much that Hindus and Muslims started regarding each other as enemies. The way the two communities started projecting their demands, it seemed there was absolutely no love lost between them. If the Hindus had the Benares University, the Musalmans raised the communal flag on the Aligarh University campus. If the Hindus had the Rashtriya Swayamsevak Sangh, the Muslims raised the militant organization called the Khaksars. The Muslims started fearing that Hindus were making plans to subjugate them. The Hindus felt that the Muslims were engaged in reconquering them after the British withdrawal from the subcontinent. The two communities seemed to be at war with each other, although hostilities had not broken out on a large scale and were still confined to communal clashes and stabbings, here and there. The Muslim endeavour to increase their forces provoked the Hindus to do the same. There seemed little possibility of mutual adjustment. The number of communal clashes and stabbings increased sharply.

Commenting on the developments, Ambedkar said:[8] "The policy of divide and rule cannot succeed unless there are elements which make division possible, and further if the policy succeeds for such a long time, it means that the elements which divide are more or less permanent and irreconcilable and are not transitory or superficial. Mr Jinnah can never be suspected of being a tool in the hands of the British even by his worst enemies. He may be too self-opinionated, an egotist without the mask and has perhaps a degree of arrogance which is not compensated by an extraordinary intellect or equipment. It may be that he is unable to reconcile himself to a second place and work with others in that capacity. He may not be overflowing with ideas although he is not, as his critics make him out to be, an empty-headed dandy living upon the ideas of others. But it is doubtful if there is a politician in India to whom the adjective incorruptible can be more fittingly applied. Anyone who knows what his relations with the British Government have been, will admit that he has always been their critic, if indeed he has not been their adversary. No one can buy him. For it must be said to his credit that he has never been a soldier of fortune.

"The real explanation of this failure of Hindu-Muslim unity lies in the failure to realize that what stands between the Hindus and Muslims is not a mere matter of difference, and that this antagonism is not to be attributed to material causes. It is formed by causes which take their origin in historical, religious, cultural and social antipathy, of which political antipathy is only a reflection. These form one deep river of discontent which, being regularly fed by these sources, keeps on mounting to a head and overflowing its ordinary channels. Any current of water flowing from another source however pure, when it joins, instead of altering the colour or diluting its strength becomes lost in the main stream. The silt of this antagonism which this current has deposited, has become permanent and deep. So long as this silt keeps on accumulating and so long as this antagonism lasts, it is unnatural to expect this antipathy between Hindus and Muslims to give place to unity."[9]

"If there is ideological transformation of the Muslim leaders it cannot be attributed to any dishonest drift in their opinion. All this is probably due to the dawn of a new vision pointing to a new destiny symbolized by a new name, Pakistan. The Muslims appear to have started a new worship of a new destiny for the first time. This is really not so. The worship is new because the sun of their new destiny which was so far hidden in the clouds has only now its appearance in full glow. The magnetism of this new destiny cannot but draw the Muslims towards it. The pull is so great that even men like Jinnah have been violently shaken and have not been able to resist its force. No one who looks at the map, can miss it. It lies there as though it is deliberately planned by Providence as a separate Nation State for Muslims. Not only is this new destiny capable of being worked out and put in shape but is also catching because it opens up the possibilities of realizing the Muslim idea of linking up all the Muslim kindred in one Islamic State and thus avert the danger of Muslims in different countries adopting the nationality of the country to which they belong and thereby bring about the disintegration of the Islamic brotherhood. With the separation of Pakistan from Hindustan, Iran, Iraq, Arabia, Turkey and Egypt are forming a federation of Muslim countries constituting one Islamic state extending from Constantinople down to Lahore, as is clear from talk in Muslim circles. A Musalman must be really stupid if he is not attracted by the glamour of this new destiny and completely transformed in his view of the place of Muslims in the Indian cosmos."

Because of the preponderant Hindu majority all over the country, the Congress won most of the seats in the provincial assemblies elections for which were held in 1937 under the Government of India Act, 1935. Results of the elections were a warning to the Muslim League that in the undivided sub-continent after the British quit India, it would be Hindu Raj. Fanatics amongst Muslim leaders started propagating that no matter what Gandhi or other Congress leaders say, Hinduism is a menace to liberty, equality and fraternity. It is incompatible with democracy and therefore it must be prevented at any cost. It was against this background that the erstwhile national leader, Mr Jinnah, made his entry into Muslim politics in 1937. Because of the respect he commanded, the Muslim League hailed his return to active politics with demonstrations, processions and slogan-shouting all over the country. Overnight, he regenerated Muslim League, which was dying and decaying and only a few years earlier, the nationalist Jinnah would have been glad to see its demise. But the non-Muslims also heaved a sigh of relief that with Jinnah heading the League now, it would not become a merely communal organization.

At the annual session of the Muslim League held at Lucknow in October 1937, 15 resolutions were passed. These included the following two resolutions which made clear what the Muslim League under Jinnah was going to do.
The first of the two important resolutions stated:[10] "This meeting of the All India Muslim League deprecates and protests against the formation of ministries in certain Provinces by the Congress parties in flagrant violation of the letter and spirit of the Government of India Act, 1935, and the Instrument of Instructions and condemns the Governors for their failure to enforce the special powers entrusted to them for the safeguards of the interest of the Musalmans and other important minorities." And the second resolution was: "Resolved that the object of the All India Muslim League shall be the establishment in India of Full Independence in the form of federation of free democratic States in which the rights and interests of the Musalmans and other minorities are adequately and effectively safeguarded in the Constitution."

At the next session of the Muslim League held at Patna in December 1938, another noteworthy resolution was passed. It stated: "The All India Muslim League reiterates its view that the scheme of Federation embodied in the Government of India Act, 1935, is not acceptable, but in view of the further developments that have taken place from time to time it hereby authorizes the President of the All India Muslim League to adopt such course as may be necessary with a view to exploring the possibility of a suitable alternative which will safeguard the interests of the Musalmans and other minorities in India." A determined Jinnah went a step ahead in 1939 by getting a resolution passed demanding in unequivocal terms nothing but only Pakistan.

Commenting on these developments which made clear that the Muslim League led by Jinnah now would not rest until and unless the Indian subcontinent was divided into two nations, Ambedkar wrote: "What is the reason for isolation? Nothing but the change of view that the Musalmans are a nation or community. But one finds it extremely difficult to understand how the mere fact that the Muslims are a nation makes political isolation a safe and sound policy. Unfortunately Muslims do not realize what disservice Mr Jinnah has done to them by this policy. But let Muslims consider what Mr Jinnah has achieved by making the Muslim League the only organization for the Musalmans. It may be that it has helped him to avoid the possibility of having to play the second fiddle (in undivided India Jinnah could not become the Prime Minister and could only have second position in the government hierarchy). Now inside the Muslim camp he can always be sure of the first place for himself. But does the League hope to save by this plan of isolation the Muslims from Hindu Raj? Will Pakistan obviate the establishment of Hindu Raj in provinces in which the Musalmans are in a minority. Obviously, it cannot. Take an All India view. Can Pakistan prevent the establishment of Hindu Raj at the Centre over Muslim minorities that will remain in Hindustan. It is plain that it cannot." It was clear that for the sake of becoming the Quaid-e-Azam of Pakistan, Jinnah had not be bothered about Muslims who will be left in India and whose number will be more than that of Muslims in the Pakistan that he was demanding.

Under the leadership of Mr Jinnah, the Muslim League at its session held in Lahore on March 26, 1940, passed a resolution which made Gandhi and the other senior Congress leaders sit up and ponder over what they could do to prevent the division of India. The resolution said: "This session of the All India Muslim League emphatically reiterates that the scheme of federation embodied in the Government of India Act, 1935, is totally unsuited, and unworkable in the peculiar conditions of this country and is altogether unacceptable to Muslim India.

"It further records its emphatic view that while the declaration dated October 18, 1939 made by the Viceroy on behalf of His Majesty's Government is reassuring in as far as it declares that the policy and plan on which the Government of India Act, 1935, is based will be reconsidered in consultation with the various parties, interests and communities in India, Muslim India will not be satisfied unless the whole constitutional plan is reconsidered de novo and that no revised plan would be acceptable to the Muslims, unless it is framed with their approval and consent;

"Resolved that it is the considered view of this session of the All India Muslim League that the constitutional plan would not be workable in this country or acceptable to the Muslims unless it is designated on the following basic principle, viz. that geographically contiguous units are demarcated into regions which should be so constituted with such territorial readjustments as may be necessary, that the areas in which Muslims are numerically in a majority as in the North-Western and Eastern zones of India should be grouped to constitute "Independent States" in which the Constituent Units shall be autonomous and sovereign.

"The adequate, effective and mandatory safeguards should be specifically provided in the Constitution for minorities in these units and in the regions for the protection of their religious, cultural, economic, political, administrative and other rights, and interests in consultation with them; and in other parts of India where the Musalmans are in a minority, adequate, effective and mandatory safeguards shall be specifically provided in the Constitution for them and other minorities for the protection of their religious, cultural, economic, political, administrative and other rights, and interests in consultation with them. This session further authorizes the Working Committee to frame a Scheme of Constitution in accordance with these basic principles, providing for assumption finally by the respective regions of all powers such as defence, external affairs, communication, customs, and such other matters as may be necessary."

In his reaction to the demand for Pakistan made in the resolution passed by the Muslim League, Gandhi said: "To partition India is a moral wrong and a sin to which he will never be a party." Then he started protesting that the Muslim League did not represent the Muslims and that Pakistan was only a fancy of Jinnah. Obviously, Gandhi was not aware of Jinnah's influence over the Muslim masses which had been growing day by day and how he had engaged himself in mobilizing all his forces for battle. Never before was Jinnah a man of the masses. Earlier, he distrusted them to such an extent that, according to Pandit Jawaharlal Nehru, Jinnah wanted the Congress to restrict its membership to matriculates. To exclude the masses from political power, he was always for a high franchise.

Of course, Jinnah was not known to be a very devout, pious or a professing Muslim. Except kissing the holy Quran as and when he was sworn in as an M.L.A, he did not appear to have bothered much about its contents or special tenets. In the past, he was rarely found in the midst of Muslim mass congregations, religious or political. But he was altogether a changed man now. Now that the Muslim League members had raised him above themselves and called him their Qaid-e-Azam, Jinnah had not only become a believer in Islam, but was prepared to die for Islam. Now he knew more of Islam than the mere 'Kalama.' He had started going to the mosque to hear 'Khutba' and taking delight in joining the Id congregational prayers.

Although he did not openly say anything, Gandhi could see the hand of the imperial power behind the demand for the division of the sub-continent.

So instead of negotiating with Mr Jinnah and the Muslim League for some settlement to defuse the crisis, Gandhi got the Congress to pass the famous Quit India Resolution on August 8, 1942. The resolution was a challenge to the British Government. It was also an attempt to do away with the intervention of the British Government in the discussion of the minority question and thereby securing for the Congress a free hand to settle it on its own terms and according to its own perceptions. It was in effect, if not in intention, an attempt to win Independence by bypassing the Muslims and the other minorities.

In view of these developments, Gandhi decided to talk it out with Jinnah himself and therefore wrote him a letter on July 17, 1944, expressing his desire to meet him to discuss the communal question.[11] Following this Jinnah invited Gandhi to his house in Bombay on September 9, 1944. The talks centred round the offer for settlement of the communal problem made by Mr Rajagopalachariar to Mr Jinnah in April 1944. The detailed terms of this were: (1) The Muslim League should endorse the Indian demand for Independence and cooperate with the Congress in the formation of a provisional interim government which shall function until the British quit India. (2) After the termination of the War, a commission shall be appointed for demarcating contiguous districts in the north-west and east of India, wherein the Muslim population is in absolute majority. In the areas thus demarcated, plebiscite of all the inhabitants held on the basis of adult suffrage or other practicable franchise shall ultimately decide the issue of separation from Hindustan. If the majority decide in favour of forming a sovereign state separate from the Hindus, such decision shall be given effect to, without prejudice to the right of districts on the border to choose either state. (3) It will be open to all the parties to advocate their points of view before the plebiscite is held. (4) In the event of separation, mutual agreements shall be entered into for safeguarding defence, and commerce and communications and for other essential purposes. (5) Any transfer of population shall only be on an absolutely voluntary basis. (6) These terms shall be binding only in the case of transfer by Britain of full power and responsibility for the Government of India.

The Gandhi-Jinnah discussions for the settlement of communal question on the basis of these terms continued for 18 days till September 27, but they could not reach any settlement.[12] Why Jinnah rejected these terms was mainly due to the fact that he was being asked to endorse the Congress demand for Indian Independence outright whereas the Muslim League demand for Pakistan had to wait until the war was over and was to be accepted by the Provisional Government only on the basis of plebiscite in the Muslim majority districts in the north-west and eastern Bengal. The promise of the Congress to agree to the formation of Pakistan was to be fulfilled by the Provisional Government. But being a sovereign body, the Provisional Government was not subject to any superior authority and for the Muslim League there was no guarantee that it would agree to accept the plebiscite verdict in Muslim majority areas.

There was no clear-cut indication as to what would be the boundaries of Pakistan. Whether the boundaries would be the present administrative boundaries of the Punjab and Bengal or whether they would be decided on the basis of ethnological considerations was not clear. Mr Jinnah thought it was a snare and not a solution to his demand for Pakistan. Gandhi tied up the communal question with the political settlement and made clear that if there was no political settlement, there would be no communal settlement. It invited Mr Jinnah to enter into a deal which was: "If you help us in getting Independence, we shall be glad to consider your proposal for Pakistan." But since there was no guarantee for the formation of Pakistan, the talks failed.

Ultimately, as future events proved, Jinnah got for Pakistan whatever portion of Indian territory he wanted and India won Independence. But since negotiations had been brokered by the British, not much attention was paid to the political upheaval which would result from the division of India. Several million lives were lost in the communal bloodbath triggered by these events. Ambedkar had correctly anticipated in his book that there would be no alternative to Pakistan. Apart from political factors and the question of personal ambitions, the 600 years old Hindu-Muslim animosity, which began with the first Indian invasion by Mohammed Bin Qasim and which continued even after the end of the Muslim rule in the subcontinent, could not be dissolved by any political settlement. The cementing force of a common religion was not there to keep the two communities together. From a spiritual point of view Hindus and Musalmans are not merely two classes or two sects such as Protestants and Catholics or Shaivas and Vaishnavas, they are two distinct ethnic communities. Neither the Hindus nor the Muslims can be expected to recognize that humanity is an essential quality present in them both, and that they are not many but one and that the differences between them are no more than accidents. For them their divinity is divided and with the division of divinity their humanity, too, is divided and with the division of humanity they must remain divided.

References

1. See the third para of introduction on page 7 to Ambedkar's book, Pakistan or the Partition of India, which has been published in Vol. 8.
2. See the first para, p. 294, Vol. 8.
3. See the starred footnote on p. 430, Vol. 8.
4. See question 3892 on p. 317, Vol. 8.
5. See the resolution Mr. Jinnah moved on p. 319, Vol. 8.
6. See p. 320, Vol. 8.
7. See p. 323, Vol. 8.
8. See the commentary beginning from p. 328, Vol. 8.
9. *Ibid.*
10. See starred resolutions on p. 360, Vol. 8.
11. See the closing lines of the first para on p. 409, Vol. 8.
12. See the last para on p. 410, Vol. 8.

14

Taken for a Ride

Although Ambedkar rose to be a Titan among his contemporaries, disappointments and frustrations in one form or the other continued to dog him throughout his life. That he was treated like a pariah in childhood, denied even the right to sit along with his classmates, barred from touching the water tap in school lest he should pollute it, and several other incidents relating to the treatment meted out to him, all because he was a Mahar, an Untouchable community in Maharashtra, haunted him all his life. The irony was that even when he got what he wanted, he succumbed to social pulls and pressures and landed himself again in the doldrums.

At the Round Table Conferences in London which were held in 1931—1932, he had made a strong case for the grant of separate electorates to the Untouchables. The British government conceded this demand. But just as he had won a major victory, he was prevailed upon by the Congress leaders to drop the demand and instead accept their assurances for better representation of the Untouchables in legislatures. No one expected Ambedkar to bend over the issue, but he gave up to save Gandhi's life, who had gone on an indefinite fast as a protest against the grant of separate electorates to the Untouchables and whose condition was becoming critical.

Of course, Ambedkar agreed to all this under assurances that henceforth removal of untouchability would be an article of faith with the Congress Party. The Poona Pact signed by Ambedkar and the Congress took away from the Untouchables not only separate electorates but also the concession of dual voting rights specially given by the British government to enable them to exercise their franchise not only from reserve constituencies but also from the general constituencies. The Congress promised to launch a campaign that all public wells, dharamshalas, roads, schools, crematoriums, burning ghats and temples should be thrown open to the Untouchables. But no sooner did the ink dry on the Poona Pact than the Congress party stopped bothering about any of the assurances given to Ambedkar for the uplift of the Untouchables. On the contrary, the Congress leaders became anxious to nullify the provisions of the Pact.

The net result of all that happened after Gandhi's fast against the grant of separate electorates to Untouchables and the signing of the Poona Pact between Hindu leaders and Ambedkar was that the plight of the Untouchables remained unchanged. No wonder, Ambedkar was greatly disappointed and rightly concluded that he and his followers had only been taken for a ride. The Congress leaders were more concerned in dashing Ambedkar's hopes in elections than honouring the provisions of the Poona Pact under which they were committed to accord greater representation to Harijans. All this made Ambedkar aware of the malicious game being played by the Congress only to embarrass him and demonstrate to the world that he was merely a British stooge who lacked any following in India.

Ambedkar could see that with the intensification of the freedom movement by the Congress the days of the British rule were numbered. And if the British before quitting India handed over power to Congress leaders there would never be an end to the suffering of the Untouchables. In these circumstances he sought to distance himself from the party which was struggling against the British for its own reasons. Ambedkar had come to realize that if the British quit India without providing any constitutional safeguards for the Untouchables, their position in society would never change. But their reluctance to join hands with the Congress gave rise to baseless stories that the Untouchables are the tools of British imperialism and that is why they refrain from joining the "fight for freedom." However, all those who knew the reality of the Indian situation could see that it was a false accusation.

Ambedkar was pained to note that even some foreigners could believe the Congress propaganda that Untouchables were the mere tools of the British. This made Ambedkar proclaim that if the Untouchables have not joined the "fight for freedom" it is not because they are the tools of British imperialism but because they fear that freedom of India would establish Hindu domination which is sure to foreclose for them any prospects of a life of equality, liberty and the pursuit of happiness and they would continue to suffer as they had been for centuries. The reason which had led the Untouchables to non-cooperation with the Congress was openly stated by them when they said that they did not wish to be placed under a Hindu Raj in which the governing class would be the Bania and the Brahmin with low class Hindus as their policemen, all of whom have been the hereditary enemies of the Untouchables. Such language could sound offensive but what could the Untouchables do when whatever hope there was for them under the British rule was about to be dashed under the imminent Congress Raj. Precisely for these reasons Ambedkar and many of his followers remained indifferent to the Quit India movement.

Explaining the stand he had taken, Ambedkar wrote : "Translated in the language of political science, what does their stand indicate? The Untouchables are not opposed to freedom from British imperialism. The fact is they refuse to be content with mere freedom from British imperialism. What they insist upon is that free India is not enough. Free India should be made safe for democracy. Starting with this aim, they say that on account of the peculiar social formation in India there are minority communities pitted against a Hindu Communal Majority, and if no provisions are made in the constitution to cut the fangs of the Hindu Communal Majority, India will not be safe for democracy. The Untouchables therefore insist on devising a constitution which will take note of the special circumstances of India and contain safeguards which will prevent this Hindu Communal Majority from getting possession of political power to suppress and oppress the Untouchables. They want a constitution which will directly enable Untouchables to have at least a modicum of political power to prevent their suppression and exploitation, and to hold their own, in their struggle for existence against the Hindu majority. In short, what the Untouchables want are safeguards in the constitution itself which will prevent the tyranny of a Hindu communal majority from coming into being.

"The Congress on the other hand regards the freedom of India from British Imperialism to be the be-all and end-all of Indian nationalism. Nothing more, it thinks, is necessary for the welfare of the Indian people in a free India. As to the question of a constitution for a free India, the Congress simply does not look upon it as a problem. Asked what about the constitution of a free India? The Congress says, it will be a democracy. What sort of democracy would it be? The Congress answer is that it will be based on adult franchise. Will there be any other safeguard, besides adult suffrage for preventing the tyranny of a Hindu communal majority? The Congress reply is emphatically in the negative. Asked why this opposition to safeguards, the Congress says that it is a vivisection of the nation – an argument the picturesqueness of which is intended to cover its stupidity and which has its origin in the genius of Mr Gandhi, and for which the high class Hindus, who stand to lose by these safeguards, feel so grateful to him."

With the outbreak of World War-II, the British Government came under greater pressure from the world opinion to expedite Indian Independence. But the problem was which party should be entrusted with power when the British quit India. Explaining the situation the Secretary of State, Mr Amery, said in the House of Commons on August 14,1940: "Congress leaders have built up a remarkable organization. If the Congress could, in fact speak, as it professes to speak, for all the main elements in Indian national life, then however advanced their demands our problem would have been in many respects far easier than it is today. It is true that they are numerically the largest single party in British India, but their claim by virtue of the fact to speak for India is utterly denied by very important elements in India's complex national life. These others assert their right to be regarded not as mere numerical minorities but as separate constituent factors in any future Indian policy.

"The foremost among these elements stands the great Muslim community. They will have nothing to do with a constitution framed by a Constituent

Assembly elected by a majority vote in geographical constituencies. They claim the right in any constitutional discussion to be regarded as an entity and are determined only to accept a constitution whose actual structure will secure their position as an entity against the operations of a mere numerical majority. The same applies to the great body of what are known as the Scheduled Castes who feel that in spite of Mr Gandhi's earnest endeavours on their behalf that, as a community, they stand outside the main body of the Hindu community which is represented by the Congress."

The British government clarified that it could not contemplate the transfer of their present responsibilities for the peace and welfare of India to any system of government whose authority is directly denied by large and powerful elements in India's national life. Nor could they be a party to coercion of such elements into submission to such a government. India's future constitution should be essentially an Indian constitution, framed in accordance with the Indian conception of Indian conditions and Indian needs. The only essential condition is that the constitution itself and the body which is to frame it must be the outcome of agreement between the principal elements in India's national life.

In its pronouncements made right from the time Montague-Chelmsford reforms were announced in 1917 till the cessation of hostilities after the end of the Second World War in 1945, the British had taken a definite stand that the they would under no circumstances transfer power to Indian hands until they were satisfied that position of the Scheduled Castes was safeguarded by adequate constitutional provisions. When the transfer of power was being discussed again, clarifying its position the British government had stated: "The Hindu religion by its dogma of untouchability has separated the Scheduled Castes from the main body of the Hindus in a manner which made the separation far more real and far wider than the separation which exists either between Hindus and Muslims or Hindus and Sikhs or Hindus and Christians. It is difficult to conceive of a more effective method of separation and segregation than the principle of untouchability and it is only those who are actuated by malicious spirit of finding excuses to deny the Scheduled Castes their claim to political rights would indulge in this type of jugglery." In view of the latest declaration which was nothing but endorsement of the stand the British government had taken from 1917 to 1941, Ambedkar felt confident and assured that the Scheduled Castes would not be ignored in the transfer of power from the British to the representatives of the people of India. But all his hopes were dashed to the ground in the developments which took place after the British War Cabinet accepted the Cripps proposals for the transfer of power. Under these proposals a Constituent Assembly for drafting the constitution would be formed after the war without any special provision for the Scheduled Castes.

In the post-war general elections held in Britain in 1945, the Tories led by Winston Churchill lost to the Labour party which had fought the elections under the leadership of Clement Attlee, who was the Deputy Prime Minister in the National Government headed by Churchill during the war. The new British Prime Minister had been sympathetic to the cause of Indian Independence for long. Now with the mounting pressure from the U.S.A and his own conscience rather uneasy because of the freedom movement launched by Mahatma Gandhi in India and the widespread response it was generating among all sections of opinion in the country, Attlee felt like doing something significant for India. But obviously he could make moves only after ascertaining the latest situation in the country. So after becoming the British Prime Minister one of the important things he did was to send in January 1946 a 10-member Parliamentary delegation to India. The delegation held talks with the leading politicians including Ambedkar, and soon after its return to England in February, 1946, recommended early transfer of power. Following this, the British Government sent a three-member delegation called the Cabinet Mission to India.

On March 16, 1946, after holding talks with the Governor-General of India and the leaders of the Indian freedom movement, the Cabinet Mission announced its proposals, suggesting among other things the formation of a Constituent Assembly to frame a Constitution for the future governance of India. But Ambedkar strongly protested against these proposals. He said the most galling and astounding feature of these proposals is that they do not treat the Untouchables as a separate and distinct element in the national life of the country. The Untouchables have not been given the right to nominate their representatives to the Central Executive as has been done in the case of Sikhs and Muslims. They have not been given the right to separate representation in the Constituent Assembly. The Cabinet Mission's proposal not to give separate representation to the Untouchables is not the result of their individual judgment arrived at on an honest examination of the relevant facts. What the Mission has done is to pander to the prejudices of Mr Gandhi who is vehemently opposed to the recognition of Untouchables as a separate element in the national life of India. Anxious to make a success of their proposals, the Cabinet Mission gave Mr Gandhi whatever he demanded as his price which was the sacrifice of the separate political existence of the Untouchables.

Disgusted, Ambedkar circulated a pamphlet in which he argued that the Untouchables would not like to suffer the fate of the American Negroes, who valiantly fought in the civil war, died in large numbers, but when hostilities ended, were denied equality with other Americans. It was to prevent such treachery that the Untouchables had taken such an attitude with regard to this 'fight for freedom.' Are they doing anything more than following the advice of Burke who said it is better to be accused of timidity than to be ruined by over-confident victory. The pamphlet said : "The British Government admits the right of Indians to frame their own constitution. There can be no greater proof of this new angle of vision than the Cripps Proposals. The conditional precedent laid down by the British Government for India's freedom is that

Indians must produce a constitution which has the concurrence of the important elements in the national life of the country. Such is the stage we have reached. The Untouchables cannot therefore understand why the Congress, instead of trying to achieve agreement among Indians, should keep on talking in terms of a "Fight for Freedom" and maligning the Untouchables for not joining in it.

"The Untouchables are quite prepared to submit themselves to the rule of the Hindu majority, notwithstanding the unsocial and the undemocratic character of its ethics, provided the constitution gives them reasonable safeguards. To say that the Untouchables will exercise a veto on India's freedom by raising impossible demands is thus a gross libel, for which there is not the slightest justification. Assuming the fear is well-founded, the Congress is not altogether without a remedy. For it is still open to the Congress to say that if there is no agreement between the Hindus and the Untouchables the dispute should be referred to an International Board of Arbitration. If the Congress took this stand, I am sure, neither the British Government nor the Untouchables will have the slightest objection to it. But when, instead of making an honest and sincere attempt to bring about an agreed constitution, the Congress goes on launching its campaigns for achieving freedom – not without occasional rests and retreats – the only conclusion, which the Untouchables can draw, is that the Congress wants to coerce the British Government to transfer power or to use Mr Gandhi's phrase, 'hand over the keys to the Congress,' without being obliged to agree to the safeguards demanded by the Untouchables. In short, what the Congress wants is a free India with full, unrestricted freedom to the Hindus to dispose of the Untouchables in any way they like. No wonder the Untouchables have refused to take part in such a dishonest agitation, elevated though it may be by such high sounding name as "Fight for Freedom".

In a secret meeting with the Cabinet Mission delegation and Lord Wavell, the Viceroy of India, Ambedkar made it clear that the Scheduled Castes Federation would never accept any constitution which did not give its members adequate representation in the government and the public services. Ambedkar also made it clear that the formation of a Constituent Assembly would not solve the problems he was faced with as leader of the Untouchables. The Assembly would be dominated by the caste Hindus and the Scheduled Caste members would be no more than a small minority which would always be outvoted if three-quarters or a two-thirds majority were required for the Assembly's decisions. All the assurances of protection which His Majesty's Government had given to the minorities would go by the board. Moreover there would be an immense amount of corruption in the Assembly – members would be bought over to vote against the interests of their communities. Among other things he said, owing to the preponderance of caste Hindus in the Subordinate Police and Revenue Services, the Government was already, from the point of view of the Untouchables, not a British but a Hindu one. Ambedkar said that in self-governing India the strings of political power will be in the hands of the ambitious members of the upper strata of Indian society drawn from the high-placed, well-educated and affluent castes, i.e. in the hands of the aristocracy of wealth, education and social standing. In politics as in other walks of life the victory is always to the stronger. The aristocracy will have the resources derived from wealth and education. But this will not be the only advantage in favour of the aristocracy against which members of the minor and weaker communities will have to struggle for their share of political power. There is another advantage which though subtle in its operation is yet real. It consists in its social determinism. In this kind of social determinism there is no place for merit or ability. The only thing that counts is kinship which prompts the Indian to discriminate against persons who are not his kindred. The effect of this determinism operating in the minds of the members of the majority community is bound to put members of the smaller communities at a formidable disadvantage and may indeed for ever shut them out from political power. The working out of this social determinism is bound to be most pernicious for the depressed classes. The gradation of castes in India, founded as it is in theology, forms an ascending scale of reverence and a descending scale of contempt.

He asserted that aristocracy cannot escape the charge that its members have in them a class bias, a definite clannishness, a tendency to favour their own kindred, which makes them quite unworthy of being entrusted with power to decide the destiny of the masses. Indeed one might go to the length of saying that due to the great social gap that separates it from the masses and the superior isolation in which it lives, it cannot be said to be charged with the wants, the carvings and the desires of the masses, or it may even be said that it is quite inimical to their aspirations. "What makes me so emphatic in my assertion that the aristocracy cannot be trusted with political power is because the root notions of democracy on the operation of which alone self-governing India can be safe for the masses run counter to all the ideas which for thousands of years have formed and do form even today the common stock of their beliefs."

"The fundamental principle of the modern democratic state is the recognition of the value of the individual, and the belief that as each individual has but one life, full opportunity should be accorded to each to attain his maximum development in that life. Neither of these propositions can be said to form part of the accepted philosophy of the aristocracy of India. They rather hold that the present life is for each only one of a series of existences, that the position of each individual in this life has been determined for him by his merits or demerits in his previous births, and that therefore no character howsoever high, no ability howsoever great, which a man may have to his credit can alter his place in the social strata in which he is born. With the aristocracy the notion that a man born a Brahmin cannot be other than a Brahmin and a man born a pariah cannot be other than a pariah is not idle talk, it is a living and operative faith. To give unrestricted power in the hands of the people of this sort is to arm the hangman with a knife."

Equality of opportunity and its negation by untouchability roused Ambedkar to moral political rage. He warned: "But one cannot pass over certain very shameful things for the continuance of which the aristocracy of this country must be held responsible. In this country there are between 50 and 60 millions of people who are suffering from the curse of untouchability – a curse and a calamity unknown in any other part of the world. They are denied the elementary rights due to every human being and refused the benefits of civilization and culture. Without equality of opportunity theirs is the most degraded condition. Besides the Untouchables, there is still in this country an equally huge population of aboriginal and hill tribes who are left to roam about in a nomadic and barbarous state without any attempt to bring them within the pale of civilization and culture. These things bear an eloquent testimony to the spirit of service and the sense of responsibility which the aristocracy has shown in the past. We are asked to believe that the conduct of the aristocracy will be entirely different in the future. I am not sufficiently credulous to accept this. For, I know of no instance of the Satans of today to have been transformed overnight into angels of the morrow."

Ambedkar issued a printed leaflet, saying the Cabinet Mission's proposal not to give separate representation to the Untouchables is not the result of their individual judgment arrived at on an honest examination of the relevant facts. On the contrary, what the Mission has done is what Gandhi wanted. Gandhi is vehemently opposed to the recognition of the Untouchables as a separate element in the national life of India. He opposed their recognition at the Round Table Conference. When he found that notwithstanding his opposition they were recognized as a separate element by the Communal Award of Ramsay Macdonald, he threatened to go on fast unto death if the separate recognition of the Untouchables was not withdrawn. Again in 1945 at the First Shimla Conference, Gandhi raised his opposition when he found that His Majesty's Government had given separate recognition to the Untouchables by inviting their leaders for discussion.

But Ambedkar was unwilling to take all this lying down. Apart from writing letters of protest to Prime Minister Atlee and several other important members of the British Government, he wrote a long letter to A.V. Alexander, Member of the Cabinet Mission, whom he believed to be sympathetic to the struggle of the Untouchables in India. Ambedkar said[1]: "I cannot help saying the Cabinet Mission's effort to settle reminds me of an old Baniya who being without a son to inherit his wealth married a young girl with the hope of begetting a heir. The bride conceived but the bridegroom was stricken with a fell disease. He, however, refused to die without having a look at the baby and would not wait for delivery which was far off. He was so impatient that he called the doctor, asked him to open the stomach of his wife and let him see whether it was a boy or a girl. The result of the operation was that both the baby and the mother died. If I may say so, the Mission wanted to do very much what the Baniya did. You may not be aware but there are many who, like me, feel that the Mission was engaged in bringing about a forced delivery earlier than the natural period of gestation."

Ambedkar made it clear to Alexander that the problem of the Untouchables was a formidable one for the Untouchables to face. The Untouchables are surrounded by a vast mass of Hindu population which is hostile to them and which is not ashamed of committing any iniquity or atrocity against them. For a redress of these wrongs which are matters of daily occurrence, the Untouchables have to depend on the aid of the administration. What is the character and composition of this administration? To be brief, the administration in India is completely in the hands of the Hindus. It is their monopoly. From top to bottom it is controlled by them[2]. There is no department which is not dominated by them. They dominate the Police, the Magistracy and the Revenue Services, indeed any and every branch of the administration. The next point to remember is that the Hindus in the administration are not merely non-social, they are positively anti-social and inimical to the Untouchables. Their one aim is to discriminate against the Untouchables and to deny and deprive them not only of the benefits of law, but also of the protection of the law against tyranny and oppression. The result is that the Untouchables are placed between the Hindu population and the Hindu-ridden administration, the one committing wrongs against them and the other protecting the wrong-doer instead of the victims.

Ambedkar said the Congress is clamouring for Swaraj, but it will not do any good to the Untouchables. It only means one thing, namely, that while today it is only the administration which is in the hands of the Hindus, under Swaraj, the legislature and executive will also be filled with Hindus. It goes without saying that Swaraj would aggravate the sufferings of the Untouchables. For, in addition to their having to face a hostile administration, the Untouchables will have to face an hostile or indifferent legislature, a callous executive and an administration uncontrolled and unbridled in venom and in harshness in its iniquitous attitude towards the Untouchables. To put it differently, under a Swaraj of the Congress variety, the Untouchables will have no way of escape from the destiny of degradation which the Hindus and Hinduism have fixed for them.[3] The only way by which the Untouchables can prevent this Swaraj from becoming a calamity to them is to have their representatives in the legislature so that they may keep on protesting against wrongs and injustices done to them by the Hindus, to have their representatives in the Executive so that they may make plans for their betterment and to have representatives in the services so that the administration may not be wholly hostile to them. If you accept the justice of the demand of the Untouchables for constitutional safeguards, you will have no difficulty in understanding why the Untouchables want separate electorates. The Untouchables will be a minority in the legislature. They are destined to remain a minority. They cannot overcome the majority which being communal in its making is, so to say, fixed and pre-ordained. But if they are in the legislatures and the majority refuses to work with them and declines to redress their wrongs, they would at least be free to utter their protest against the majority on the floor of the legislature. No safeguards are going to be of any value to the Untouchables unless the Untouchables get a separate electorate.

Calling upon the Cabinet Mission to reconsider its recommendations, Ambedkar conveyed to Alexander that every other party except the Congress accepts that the demand for separate electorates by the Scheduled Castes is very justified. "Otherwise, the Untouchables will never be free from the political yoke of the Hindus. What has the Cabinet Mission done for the Untouchables? Are they going to throw them to the wolves by favouring the system of joint electorates in order to make friends with the Congress and the Hindu majority whom it represents? The Scheduled Castes are entitled to ask His Majesty's Government that before the British abdicate, His Majesty's Government shall make sure that Swaraj does not become a stranglehold for the Untouchables. The British have a moral responsibility towards the Scheduled Castes. It is a pity how few Britishers are aware of it and how fewer are prepared to discharge it. British Rule in India owes its very existence to the help rendered by the Untouchables.[4] Many Britishers think that India was conquered by the Clives, Hastings, Cootes and so on. Nothing can be a greater mistake. India was conquered by an army of Indians and the Indians who formed the army were all Untouchables. British Rule in India would have been impossible if the Untouchables had not helped the British to conquer India. Take the Battle of Plassey which laid the beginning of British Rule or the battle of Kirkee which completed the conquest of India. In both these fateful battles the soldiers who fought for the British were all Untouchables.

"What have the British done to these Untouchables who fought for them? It is a shameful story," stated Ambedkar and went on, "The first thing they did was to stop their recruitment in the army. A more unkind, more ungrateful and more cruel act can hardly be found in history. In shutting out the Untouchables from the Army the British took no note that the Untouchables had helped them to establish their rule and had defended it when it was menaced by a powerful combination of native forces in the Mutiny of 1857. Without any consideration as to its effects upon the Untouchables the British by one stroke of the pen deprived them of their source of livelihood and let them fall to their original depth of degradation. Did the British help them in any way to overcome their social disabilities? The answer again must be in the negative.

"The schools, wells and public places were closed to the Untouchables. It was the duty of the British to see the Untouchables, as citizens, were entitled to be admitted to all institutions maintained out of public funds. But the British did nothing of the kind and what is worse, they justified their inaction by saying that untouchability was not the creation of the British. But for the government of the day, surely the removal of untouchability was its responsibility. No government with any sense of functions and duties could have avoided it. What did the British Government do? They refused to touch any question which involved any kind of reform of Hindu society. So far as social reform was concerned, the Untouchables found themselves under a government distinguished in no vital respect from those native governments under which they had toiled and suffered, lived and died, through all their weary and forgotten history. From a political standpoint the change was nominal. The despotism of Hindus continued as ever before."

Further, Ambedkar stated in his letter to Alexander[5]: "You have come here to announce that the British are abdicating. It cannot be wrong for the Untouchables to ask 'to whom are you leaving this legacy of authority and power?' To the protagonist of Brahmanism, which means to the tyrants and oppressors of the Untouchables. Such a method of liquidating the British Empire in India need not raise any qualms of conscience among members of other parties. But what about the British Labour Party? The Labour Party claims to stand for the unprivileged and the downtrodden. If it is true to its salt, I have no doubt that it will stand by the sixty million Untouchables of India and do everything necessary to safeguard their position and not allow power to pass into the hands of those who by their religion and their philosophy of life are unfit to govern and are in fact the enemies of the Untouchables. It will be no more than bare act of atonement on the part of the British for the neglect of the Scheduled Castes whose trustees they always claimed to be."

But Ambedkar's lament on behalf of the people who had come to regard him as their Messiah was like a cry in the wilderness. The British Government was in a hurry to quit India. In desperation, he paid a visit to London to personally meet the Prime Minister and his old friends who always had a very high opinion about him despite the fact that he was a born Untouchable. But all this was in vain. Disappointed, he returned to India. When it became clear that he could do nothing to get any concessions for the Untouchables, disgusted and despondent Ambedkar, along with the other members of the Viceroy's Executive Committee, resigned. He was more miserable than ever before because all his life he had been trying to liberate the Untouchables from the clutches of the caste system. Now again, in free India they will have to accept their subordination to caste Hindus without any hope in hell.

But it was not only the British colonial rulers who let Ambedkar down when he needed their help to safeguard the interests of the Untouchables for whom he had been fighting all his life. Even many of those educated Untouchables who had come to occupy important positions in government service mainly with the help of Ambedkar did not stand by him when he was faced with a difficult situation and needed their help. One such situation arose when the house he had started building with all his life's saving at Dadar in Bombay was completed. The final bill was Rs 40,000 in excess of the quotations the building contractor had submitted first before starting work on the project. Ambedkar was very upset to see the inflated bill presented to him. Even if he had wanted to settle the bill, he could not do so because he had no money. He had calculated the entire cost in accordance with the original quotations and felt confident that he would be able to clear the bill for the construction with whatever bank balance he had. But the additional demand for Rs 40,000 by the building contractor upset all his plans. He did not have enough cash to pay this inflated bill and plainly told the contractor that he would not pay the additional sum added to the original estimate submitted by him.

But the contractor filed a suit for the recovery of the excess amount in a Bombay court. Ambedkar hoped that the verdict would not be against him because he was on a firmer ground, based as his refusal to pay the excess amount was on the original quotations submitted for the purpose. But it so happened that the judge hearing the petition was a caste Hindu, who in his private conversations with his friends and colleagues had been very critical of Ambedkar's move to embrace Buddhism. Regarding the case filed against Ambedkar, the judge had been telling his friends outside the court that if Ambedkar could afford to fly in great style to go to Nagpur to change his religion he could certainly find money to pay the contractor who had built his house. But often remaining preoccupied with reading and writing books, and sometimes worried about his failing health, Ambedkar was not much bothered about the case, which he felt, could not in any case go against him. But when he was served with a court notice in Delhi to deposit Rs 40,000 in the treasury in Bombay by a certain date, he was really taken aback. He did not have money to make the payment.

What to do in the circumstances, where to go for help and such other thoughts began to prey on his mind. The court notice was a bolt from the blue for both Ambedkar and his wife, Savita. They were completely at a loss over this development. Ambedkar did not want to go begging for money to people. He was not prepared even to ask anybody for a loan. Mulling over possibilities which could happen if the court notice was not obeyed, they at last thought of one Puran Chand who was a Superintending Engineer in the Central Public Works Department. Some years ago, unemployed Puran Chand had knocked on Ambedkar's door to seek his help in getting some suitable government job. Recalling his experience as civil engineer earlier, Puran Chand had said that he was responsible for plugging a breach in the Taj in Agra. But senior engineers in the CPWD had closed his file containing his application for a job in the Department. Ambedkar felt sorry for him and agreed to escort him to the Governor-General to plead his case for employment. Following Ambedkar's intervention it was at the highest level Puran Chand was appointed in the CPWD and by dint of his merit was occupying a senior position now. Ambedkar's wife persuaded him to seek Puran Chand's help in the crisis they were facing. Ambedkar agreed to do so reluctantly.

The following morning they set out for Puran Chand without asking the driver of their car to go with them. Savita herself drove the car. They had not called the driver deliberately lest anybody should get wind of what they were about to do.. Savita took Ambedkar to Puran Chand's bungalow. As Ambedkar refused to come out of the car, Savita went inside and brought Puran Chand out to meet Ambedkar. Mentioning the court notice he had received Ambedkar asked Puran Chand if he could help him tide over the crisis. But Puran Chand took the facetious plea that he had no money and so could not help them. However, he added, he would talk to his daughter about the problem and if she could spare the amount, he would send her to their house tomorrow with the cash. Ambedkar did not expect this kind of attitude on the part of a man whose career he had made with his intervention at the highest level. But he could not do anything now. Disappointed the couple returned home. The following morning, Puran Chand's daughter called on the Ambedkars and said all that she could manage was Rs 20,000. She handed over the amount and returned. But this did not solve their problem. They needed Rs 20,000 more to pay the court or face the consequences.

Quite some time before this event Ambedkar had launched the Peoples' Education Society for looking after the educational institutions like colleges and schools he had started for the Untouchables and entrusted the job of running its affairs to Kamlakant Chitre. Chitre was sincerely attached to the work and had great affection and respect for Ambedkar. When he was sounded about help to tide over the problem created by the court notice, Chitre immediately agreed. He said the society he was managing could start functioning from the ground floor of the new building which Ambedkar had built and give him Rs 20,000 by way of rent immediately. Following this assurance, the Ambedkars felt relieved. But the problem now was Ambedkar in his failing health could not undertake the journey to Bombay. Consequently, the couple decided that only Mrs Ambedkar would fly to Bombay for the purpose. Accordingly, Mrs Ambedkar flew by the afternoon flight and was received in Bombay by Chitre and her own younger brother. On the following day, she made the payment as desired in court and returned to Delhi.

But when she got back home, she was astounded to find that Ambedkar had remained seated in the very same chair in the verandah of their bungalow since she had left for Bombay. What to talk of moving to his bedroom at night, he had not even eaten anything in his wife's absence. Obviously, having sent her alone on a mission which involved the kind of work she had not done ever before in her life, Ambedkar was worried. No wonder, his eyes were filled with tears of joy seeing his wife return home.

This incident happened in November 1956, three to four weeks before Ambedkar died in sleep. But it had an even more embarrassing fallout for the family. Soon after Ambedkar's death Puran Chand started pestering Savita for the return of the Rs 20,000 he had loaned them. Since she could not pay the amount, Puran Chand dragged her to court. But luckily for her and for Ambedkar's reputation, the judge ruled that Mrs Ambedkar could not be asked for return of the amount which had been given to her husband. Since Ambedkar was not alive the case was dismissed.

References

1. See p. 492, Vol. 10. Ambedkar was not happy with the Cabinet Mission's proposal regarding the transfer of power. To his great chagrin, the Scheduled Castes had been lumped together with the Hindus. They were not given any representation in the proposed Constituent Assembly. A leaflet containing his views finds mention in the starred footnote on p. 492, p. 523, Vol. 10.
2. See from the very first line on 494, Vol. 10.
3. See second para, p. 494, Vol. 10.
4. See second para, p. 496, Vol. 10.
5. See the para marked 10, p. 497, Vol. 10.

15

Architect of India's Constitution

There was jubilation all over the country over the announcement of the Cabinet Mission's proposals for the formation of an Interim Government in India by the elected representatives of the people after the Second World War. They also clearly stated that on the basis of elections to be held in provincial assemblies, a Constituent Assembly would be formed which would formulate proposals for the type of government people of India want. It was clear now that the British Government was ready to hand over power for governing the country to Indians. The formation of the Constituent Assembly for framing the Constitution was a significant step in this direction.

But in the elections held for the formation of provincial assemblies, the Scheduled Caste members fielded by Ambedkar were defeated. Only Congress nominees from amongst the Untouchables were elected in most of the provinces. It demonstrated that a big chunk of Scheduled Castes were Congress supporters. In the light of these results, the British government ignored Ambedkar's claim that he was the undisputed leader of the Scheduled Castes. Ambedkar protested that candidates fielded by him could not win because of the patriotic fervour created by the Congress due to the trial of the Indian National Army leaders in the Red Fort, New Delhi. Also, he said, he had been ignored by the electorate because of his criticism of the 'Quit India' movement launched by Gandhi. But the British Government having decided to quit India paid no heed to Ambedkar.

The defeat of his nominees in the elections was not the only blow Ambedkar suffered. When the newly formed provincial legislatures elected their representatives for the formation of the Constituent Assembly, Ambedkar failed to get elected from the Bombay legislature. The Congress bosses saw to it that he was humiliated. Ambedkar was heart-broken. However, with the support of the Scheduled Caste members from Bengal he managed to enter the Constituent Assembly. But he did not figure in the Interim Government formed by Jawaharlal Nehru. To give representation to the depressed classes in the government, Nehru ignored Ambedkar and opted for Jagjivan Ram, who was elected from Bihar and who was a loyal supporter of Gandhi and Nehru.

Jagjivan Ram's inclusion in the government was the result of Congress manoeuvres to sidetrack and ignore Ambedkar altogether. Although he had been fighting for the liberation of the depressed classes from the stranglehold of caste Hindus for over 30 years, Ambedkar could see no ray of hope now. It was clear that the transfer of power from the British to the Congress party, which was the largest political organization in the country, would mean no change in the lot of the depressed classes, for the Congress was dominated by caste Hindus wedded to the Chaturvarna system, which ordained for the Shudras the lowest position in Hindu society. .

Following the election of its members from provincial legislatures, the Constituent Assembly embarked on its arduous task of framing free India's Constitution on December 9, 1946. In all 296 members were entitled to take part in the inaugural session. But the Muslim League led by Mohammed Ali Jinnah saw to it that all the elected Muslim members, especially from Muslim majority areas in the country, boycotted the Constituent Assembly. The League was pressing for the partition of the Indian subcontinent and obviously could not be a party to the formation of a Constitution when its main demand for a separate homeland to be called Pakistan was being ignored. As such, only 207 members were present at the inaugural session of the Constituent Assembly. But since there was no clear indication that the British rulers of the subcontinent would partition it into two countries, to be known as India and Pakistan, many of the elected members of the Constituent Assembly present at its inaugural session were wondering whether they should go ahead with the task for which they had been elected or wait until the departing colonial rulers made their decision known about the Muslim League demand for a separate nation for Muslims.

Without taking any notice of the prevailing uncertainty over the future of the subcontinent, and in accordance with the Congress strategy to go ahead with the move to gain Independence from the British, Jawaharlal Nehru, on December 13, 1946, moved a resolution regarding the aims and objects of the Constituent Assembly. Among other things he stated that the Constitution to be prepared by the Assembly would be for all the territories, which now comprise British India. There could be no doubt that the Constituent Assembly would prepare a Constitution for what was until then British India. But the resolution did not reflect the prevailing situation which was that certain areas of what then formed part of British India could become a separate nation comprising Muslim majority areas as the Muslim League was demanding. As such, the resolution did not reflect the reality.

An eminent constitutional expert, Dr M.R. Jayakar, who had been elected from Bombay, moved an amendment to Nehru's resolution which caused a flutter in the Congress camp where no one seemed willing to believe that Nehru could have faulted in his resolution and that it did need some change. Dr Jayakar's amendment was: "The Assembly declares its firm and solemn resolve that the Constitution to be prepared by this Assembly for the future governance of India shall be for a free and democratic Sovereign State; but with a view to securing, in the shaping of such a Constitution, the cooperation of the Muslim League and the India States, and thereby intensifying the firmness of this resolve, this assembly postpones further consideration of this question to a later date, to enable the representatives of these two bodies to participate, if they so choose, in the deliberations of this Assembly." Dr Jayakar spoke at length for acceptance of this amendment but since the Congress bosses could not tolerate anything which questioned the wisdom of Jawaharlal Nehru, it was apparent that the amendment would not be carried.

However, in order to give the whole discussion over the issue a semblance of fair play, Dr Rajendra Prasad, who was presiding over the Constituent Assembly, called upon Ambedkar to express his views. Since there was no love lost between the Congress leaders and the leader of the depressed classes, Dr Prasad's naming of Ambedkar to speak on the issue under discussion caused whispers of protest in the Congress benches. Everybody felt that poor Ambedkar would be stirring a hornets' nest by speaking on the amendment. But Ambedkar remained unperturbed and to the utter astonishment of the Congress benches spoke so candidly and convincingly that he was greeted with tremendous applause when he finished his speech. In the lobby Congressmen congratulated him over his exposition of the problem. The amendment was accepted by the whole House and the discussion on Nehru's resolution was postponed until the next session of the Assembly in January 1947.

The resolution on the aims and objects of the Constituent Assembly moved by Nehru was as follows:

(1) This Constituent Assembly declares its firm and solemn resolve to proclaim India as an Independent Sovereign Republic and to draw up for her future governance a Constitution;

(2) Wherein the territories that now comprise British India, the territories that now form the Indian States, and such other parts of India as are outside British India and the States as well as such other territories as are willing to be constituted into the Independent Sovereign India, shall be a Union of them all; and

(3) Wherein the said territories, whether with their present boundaries or with such others as may be determined by the Constituent Assembly and thereafter according to the Law of the Constitution, shall possess and retain the status of autonomous units, together with residuary powers, and exercise all powers and functions of government and administration save and except such powers and functions as vested in or assigned to the Union, or as are inherent or implied in the Union or resulting therefrom; and

(4) Wherein all power and authority of the Sovereign Independent India, its constituent parts and organs of government, are derived from the people; and

(5) Wherein shall be guaranteed and secured to all the people of India justice: social, economic and political; equality of status, of opportunity and before the law; freedom of thought, expression, belief, faith, worship, vocation, association and action, subject to law and public morality; and

(6) Wherein adequate safeguards shall be provided for minorities, backward and tribal areas, and depressed and other backward classes; and

(7) Whereby shall be maintained the integrity of the territory of the Republic and its sovereign rights on land, sea and air, according to justice and the law of civilized nations; and

(8) This ancient land attains its rightful and honoured place in the world and makes its full and willing contribution to the promotion of world peace and the welfare of mankind.

Ambedkar pointed out that although the mover of the resolution, Jawaharlal Nehru, is reputed to be a great socialist, he has made no provision for the State to make economic, social and political justice a reality.[1] "I should have expected the Resolution to state in most explicit terms that there would be nationalization of industry and nationalization of land. I do not understand how it could be possible for any future government which believes in doing justice socially, economically and politically, unless its economy is a socialist economy. Therefore the resolution to my mind is somewhat disappointing. I have not the slightest doubt in my mind as to the future evolution and the ultimate shape of the social, political and economic structure of this great country. I know today we are divided politically, socially and economically. We are a group of warring camps and I may go even to the extent of confessing that I am probably one of the leaders of such a camp. But, Sir, with all this I am quite convinced that given time and circumstances nothing in the world will prevent this country from becoming one (Applause). With all our castes and creeds, I have not the slightest hesitation that we shall in some form be a united people (Cheers). I have no hesitation in saying that notwithstanding the agitation of the Muslim League for the partition of India, some day enough light would dawn upon the Muslims themselves and they too will begin to think that a United India is better even for them (Loud cheers and applause).

"So far as the ultimate goal is concerned, I think none of us need have any apprehensions. Our difficulty is not about the ultimate future. Our difficulty is how to make the heterogeneous mass that we have today take a decision in common and march on the way which leads us to unity. Mr Chairman, therefore, I should have thought that in order to make us willing friends, in order to induce every party, every section in this country to take on to the road it would be an act of greatest statesmanship for the majority party even to make a concession to the prejudices of people who are not prepared to march together and it's for that, that I propose to make this appeal. Let us leave aside slogans, let us leave aside words which frighten people. Let us even make a concession to the prejudices of our opponents, bring them in, so that they may willingly join with us on marching upon that road, which as I said, if we walk long enough, must necessarily lead us to unity. If I, therefore, from this place support Dr Jayakar's amendment, it is because I want all of us to realize that whether we are right or wrong, whether the position that we take is in consonance with our legal rights, leave all that aside. This is too big a question to be treated as a matter of legal rights. It is not a legal question at all. We should leave aside all legal considerations and make some attempt, whereby those who are not prepared to come, will come. Let us make it possible for them to come, that is my appeal.

"Paragraph 3 envisages the future constitution of India. I do not know what is the intention of the mover of the resolution. But I take it that after this Resolution is passed, it will act as a sort of a directive to the Constituent. Assembly to frame a constitution in terms of paragraph 3 of the Resolution. What does paragraph 3 say? Paragraph 3 says that in this country there shall be two different sets of polity, one at the bottom, autonomous Provinces or the States or such other areas as care to join a United India. These autonomous units will have full power. They will have also residuary powers. At the top, over the Provincial units, there will be a Union Government, having certain subjects for legislation, for execution and for administration. As I read this part of the resolution, I do not find reference to the idea of grouping, an intermediate structure between the Union on the one hand and the provinces on the other. Reading this paragraph in the light of the Cabinet Mission's statement or reading it even in the light of the resolution passed by the Congress at its Wardha session, I must confess that I am a great deal surprised at the absence of any reference to the idea of grouping of the provinces. So far as I am personally concerned, I do not like the idea of grouping (hear, hear). I like a strong united Centre, (hear, hear) much stronger than the Centre we had created under the Government of India Act of 1935.

"The Congress Party, for reasons best known to itself, consented, if I may use that expression, to the dismantling of a strong Centre which had been created in this country as a result of 150 years of administration and which I must say, was to me a matter of great admiration and respect and refuge. But having given up that position, having said that we do not want a strong Centre, and having accepted that there must or should be an intermediate polity, a sub-federation between the Union government and the Provinces, I would like to know why there is no reference in paragraph 3 to the idea of grouping. I always thought that if the provinces which are placed within different groups consent to form a Union or Sub-federation, the Congress would have no objection to that proposal. The question I ask is this: Why did not the mover of the resolution make a reference to the Union of Provinces or grouping of provinces on the terms on which he and his party was prepared to accept it? Why is the idea of Union completely effaced from this resolution? I find no answer. None whatever . I, therefore, say that the Muslim League is bound to take advantage of paragraph 3 and justify its continued absence.

"Sir, my friend, Dr Jayakar, in arguing his case for postponing a decision on this issue put his case, if I may say so, without offence to him, somewhat in a legalistic manner. The basis of his argument was : have you the right to do so? He read out certain portions from the statement of the Cabinet Mission which related to the procedural part of the Constituent Assembly and his contention was that the procedure that the Constituent Assembly was adopting in deciding upon this resolution straightaway was inconsistent with the procedure that was laid down in that Paper. Sir, I like to put the matter in a somewhat different way. I am not asking you to consider whether you have the right to pass this resolution straightaway or not. It may be that you have the right to do so. The question I am asking is this: Is it prudent for you to do so? Is it wise for you to do so? Power is one thing; wisdom is quite a different thing, and I want this House to consider this matter from the point of view, namely, whether it would be wise, whether it would be statesman-like, whether it would be prudent to do so at this stage. The answer that I give is that it would not be prudent, it would not be wise.

"I suggest that another attempt may be made to bring about a solution of the dispute between the Congress and the Muslim League. The subject is so vital, so important that I am sure it could never be decided on the mere basis of dignity of one party or the dignity of another party. When deciding the destinies of nations, dignities of people, dignities of leaders and dignities of parties ought to count for nothing. The destiny of the country ought to count for everything. It is because I feel that it would be in the interest not only of this Constituent Assembly so that it may function as one whole, so that it may have the reaction of the Muslim League before it proceeds to the decision that I support Dr Jayakar's amendment – we must also consider what is going to happen with regard to the future, if we act precipitately. I do not know what plans the Congress party, which holds this House in its possession, has in its mind? I have no power of divination to know what they are thinking about. What are their tactics, what is their strategy, I do not know.

"Applying my mind to the issue that has arisen, it seems to me that there are only three ways by which the future will be decided. Either there shall have to be surrender by one party to the wishes of the other – that is one way. The other way would be what I call a negotiated peace and the third way would be open war. I must confess that I am appalled at the idea that anybody in this country should think of solving the political problems of this country by the method of war. I have no hesitation and I do want to place before this House in the clearest terms possible that if war comes in this country and if that war has any relation to the issue with which we are confronted today, it will not be a war on the British. It will be a war on the Muslims or, what is probably worse, it will be a war on a combination of the British and the Muslims."

Then Ambedkar quoted from a speech by Burke on a conciliation with the Americans which, he had made in the British Parliament when the issue being discussed was the question of war against the rebellious colonies of the United States to bring them under their subjection contrary to their wishes. In repelling the idea of conquering these colonies, Burke had said that the use of force alone was but a temporary remedy.[2] "It may subdue for a moment; but it does not remove the necessity of subduing again. Terror is not always the effect of force and an armament is not a victory. If you do not succeed, you are without resources for conciliation. Power and authority are sometimes bought by kindness; but they can never be begged as alms by an impoverished and defeated violence. By using force you impair the object by your very endeavour to preserve it. The thing that you fought for is not the thing which you recover; but depreciated, sunk, wasted and consumed in the contest." Ambedkar clearly stated that if there was anybody who had in his mind the project of solving the Hindu-Muslim problem by force in order that the Muslims may be subjugated and made to surrender to the Constitution that might be prepared without their consent, this country would be involved in perpetually conquering them. "Let us prove that if this Assembly has arrogated to itself sovereign powers, it is prepared to exercise them with wisdom. This is the only way by which we can carry with us all sections of the country. There is no other way that can lead us to unity."

After Ambedkar's speech, which was packed with irrefutable reasoning and remarkable logic, the Constituent Assembly postponed the consideration of the resolution moved by Nehru till the next session. The Constituent Assembly met on January 20, 1947. By that time it had become clear that the Muslim League was not interested in the Constituent Assembly and therefore the question of waiting for it to participate in the deliberations did not arise. Dr Jayakar withdrew his amendment. The resolution on aims and objects, as moved by Nehru, was unanimously passed. Although there was little love lost between the Congress leaders and Ambedkar earlier, their relations had undergone a change now. Ambedkar's speech on the Jayakar amendment had convinced even his worst critics that he was an erudite scholar who could make a useful contribution in framing free India's Constitution for which the Constituent Assembly was now starting its deliberations.

In accordance with the recommendations of the Cabinet Mission, the Constituent Assembly formed on January 24, 1947, an Advisory Committee on

Fundamental Rights with Sardar Patel as its chairman. Ambedkar was among the 50 members of this committee. With a view to facilitating its work, the Advisory Committee appointed four sub-committees, which were: Fundamental Rights Sub-Committee; Minorities Sub-Committee; North East Frontier Tribal Areas and Assam Excluded and Partially Excluded Areas Sub-Committee; Excluded and Partially Excluded Areas (other than those in Assam) Sub-Committee. Ambedkar was member of both the Sub-Committees on Fundamental Rights and the Minorities. Ambedkar was also made member of the Union Constitution Committee.

The report of the Union Constitution Committee was submitted to the President of the Assembly by its Chairman, Jawaharlal Nehru, on July 4, 1947. The work done by Ambedkar in the various sub-committees of the Assembly was highly praised and convinced the Congress bosses that the legislation and solidification of freedom would not be easy without Ambedkar's services. Following the partition of Bengal, Dr Ambedkar ceased to be a member of the Constituent Assembly. The Congress Party which had earlier opposed tooth and nail his entry into the Constituent Assembly came forward and sponsored his candidature. The President of the Constituent Assembly, Dr Rajendra Prasad, requested Mr B.G. Kher, the then Prime Minister of Bombay, to elect Dr Ambedkar immediately. He wrote: "We have found Dr Ambedkar's work both in the Constituent Assembly and the various committees to which he was appointed to be of such an order as to require that we should not be deprived of his services. As you know, he was elected from Bengal and after the division of the Province he has ceased to be a member of the Constituent Assembly. I am anxious that he should attend the next session of the Constituent Assembly commencing from July 14 and it is therefore necessary that he should be elected immediately."

Accordingly Ambedkar was re-elected in July 1947 from Bombay as a member of the Constituent Assembly. Soon after, Prime Minister Nehru invited him to join the Cabinet he formed on August 15, 1947 on the eve of Independence. Ambedkar accepted the invitation and became India's first Law Minister. When a deputation of the Delhi Scheduled Castes Welfare Association met him to draw his attention to the plight of the Scheduled Castes left in Pakistan, Ambedkar said: "I am unable to do anything for them. All I can do is invite them to come to Hindustan. But the condition of the Scheduled Castes in India is no better than those in Pakistan. In Hindustan, they are being tyrannized by caste Hindus. In Pakistan they are subjected to forcible religious conversion, in Hindustan they are subjected to forcible political conversion. They are compelled to join the Congress party and if they refuse, they are boycotted and their lives made miserable."

Following a massive demonstration by the Scheduled Castes outside his bungalow, Ambedkar, who was a law minister in the interim government formed by Jawaharlal Nehru, sent a communication to the Prime Minister on

December 18, 1947, drawing his attention to alarming reports about the plight of the Scheduled Castes left in Pakistan. He urged the Prime Minister to take up with the Pakistan government the question of rehabilitation of the Scheduled Castes. Ambedkar asked the Prime Minister to depute special officers to provinces of Pakistan, such as North Western Frontier Punjab, Sind and Bahawalpur to see that the Scheduled Castes from these provinces were not prevented by the Pakistan Government from coming over to India. He also drew the Prime Minister's attention to the discriminatory treatment being meted out to the Scheduled Castes from Pakistan in the refugee camps on this side of the border.

"The Sikhs and Jats," wrote Ambedkar, "who occupy prominent positions in East Punjab were trying to evacuate the Scheduled Castes from their original houses in Hamirpur Tehsil and several other places to misappropriate their lands." A week later, Nehru replied to Ambedkar saying: "We have been trying our utmost to help in the evacuation of the Scheduled Castes from Pakistan, notably Sind, where they have been prevented from coming away. Our High Commissioner in Pakistan is seized of the problem and taking steps to deal with it in whatever way it is possible in the circumstances. Instructions have also been sent to the East Punjab government to ensure that there was no forcible evacuation of the Scheduled Castes from anywhere in the province."

He issued an appeal to the Scheduled Castes who were impounded in Pakistan and those living in Hyderabad state to emigrate to the Indian Union by such means as may be available to them. It would be fatal for the Scheduled Castes, whether in Pakistan or in Hyderabad, to put their faith in the Muslim League. He urged the Scheduled Castes not to regard Muslims as their friends, they simply dislike Hindus. This is a mistaken view. "The Muslims," he said, "wanted the support of the Scheduled Castes but they never gave their support to them. Mr Jinnah was all the time playing a double game. He was very insistent that the Scheduled Castes were a separate entity when it suited him, but when it did not suit him he insisted with equal emphasis that they were Hindus. The Muslims and the Muslim League, charged as they are with passion to make the Muslims a governing class as quickly as possible, will never give consideration to the claims of the Scheduled Castes. As for reports of increasing conversion to Islam, I ask all the Scheduled Castes not to succumb to it as an easy way of escape. I cannot say that they should die rather than being converted. They should look upon conversion as a last resort forced upon them by violence. Fortunately, for us, we are not hampered by the rules of the Hindu Shastras, according to which once a convert always a convert. To those who are forcibly converted, I pledge my word that if they wish to come back I shall see that they are received back into the fold and treated as brethren."

However, with the partition of the subcontinent what worried Ambedkar most was the plight of the Scheduled Castes. They were either converted to Islam or forced to stay back in Pakistan to do their menial jobs and serve as landless labourers for the feudal lords of Pakistan. They wanted the sweepers to remain with them and consequently declared them belonging to Essential Services, making migration to India impossible for them. They were forcibly converted to Islam in Hyderabad also to increase the strength of Muslim population there. The Ittehad-ul- Muslemeen, a fundamentalist organization, started burning the houses of Untouchables in order to strike terror in their hearts and thus prevent them from joining the agitation for responsible government in the state.

Although the Congress got Ambedkar back into the Constituent Assembly and even went to the extent of making him Law Minister, the caste Hindu-dominated party could not stomach that he should be entrusted with a more responsible position which might bring him into the limelight. He was the most highly qualified and competent person in the country, yet the party bosses could not accept the idea of making him the Chairman of the Drafting Committee of the Constitution. They started toying with the idea of inviting some foreign constitutional expert for the job. Nehru and Sardar Patel wanted to invite Sir Ivor Jennings, an internationally acknowledged constitutional expert, who had drafted the Constitutions of many Asian countries. While names of various scholars were being mentioned, Nehru, Sarojini Naidu and Sardar Patel sought Gandhiji's advice to select the Chairman.

Meanwhile, the then Governor-General of India, Lord Mountbatten, for whatever reason, got interested in lobbying support for Ambedkar for the post of Chairman. Mountbatten had a meeting with Gandhi but whether he had broached the subject of making Ambedkar Chairman of the Drafting Committee is not known. There is no historical record of what had transpired between the two. However, Gandhi, who had been at the receiving end of many a barb of criticism fired by Ambedkar in the past, told Nehru to drop the idea of inviting any foreigner for the post and instead choose Ambedkar for it. Although Gandhi and Ambedkar were deeply committed to the uplift of Untouchables, they had seldom seen eye to eye. But on this occasion Gandhi is believed to have strongly recommended Ambedkar for the post. Thus Ambedkar, who was a strong opponent of the Congress, had now become their friend, philosopher and guide in Constitutional matters.

The Drafting Committee first met on August 30, 1947, and elected Ambedkar as its Chairman unanimously. The Committee sat from October 27, 1947, day to day, discussing and revising articles of the draft prepared by the office of the constitutional adviser. The Committee in which Dr Ambedkar himself conducted all the business met in all on 44 days till February 13, 1948. A fresh draft of the Constitution, as settled by the Drafting Committee, was submitted to the President of the Assembly on February 21, 1948. The Committee continued to function and dealt with suggestions for amendments made from time to time. The Draft Constitution had been before the public for eight months and came up before the Constituent Assembly for discussion on

November 4, 1948. The discussion on the Articles of the Draft Constitution commenced on November 15, 1948 and barring short adjournments continued for long. The third Reading of the Draft Constitution commenced on November 17, 1949 and continued till November 26, 1949 when the motion for the adoption of the Constitution was moved by Ambedkar and it was unanimously adopted amidst prolonged cheers.

Paying a tribute to Ambedkar for drafting the Constitution, T.T. Krishanamachari,[3] an important Congress member from the South, said: "The House is perhaps aware that of the seven members nominated by you, one had resigned from the House and was replaced. One died and was not replaced. One was away in America and his place was not filled up and another person was engaged in State affairs and there was void to that extent. One or two people were far away from Delhi and perhaps reasons of health did not permit them to attend. So it happened ultimately that the burden of drafting the Constitution fell on Dr Ambedkar and I have no doubt that we are grateful to him for having achieved this task in a manner which is undoubtedly commendable." The picture will be complete when it is noted that only Dr Ambedkar and his secretary were present at some of the meetings of the Drafting Committee.

Frank Anthony, a Christian leader, said: "I do not believe that any one of us can really gauge the involvement of word and the intensity of concentration that must have been involved in the production of the voluminous and by no means easy document. And while, on occasions, I may not have agreed with him, it always gave me the greatest pleasure to listen to his tremendous grasp not only of fundamentals but of details, of the clarity with which he invariably presented his case." Tajamul Hussain stated: "The credit for framing this Constitution goes to the Law Minister. He is a genius. He knows every thing about all the Laws and Constitutions of the world. What he does not know is not worth knowing. He has worked very hard from the beginning to end in spite of his indifferent health. Due to his ceaseless labour, this remarkable Constitution has been framed."

H.J. Khandekar, a Maharashtrian Congress member, said: "I call this Constitution the Mahar law because Dr Ambedkar is a Mahar and now when we inaugurate this Constitution on the 26th of January, 1950, we shall have the law of Manu replaced by the law of Mahar and I hope that unlike the law of Manu under which there was never a prosperity in the country, the Mahar law will make India virtually a paradise. Well, Sir, even the social, political and religious reformers in the country like Gautama Buddha, Ramanuja, Kabir, Sant Tukaram, Raja Ram Mohan Roy, Swami Dayanand Saraswati, Ramkrishna Paramahamsa, Mahatma Jyoti Rao Phuley, Vithal Ramji Shinde, Thakkar Bapa and, last but not the least, Mahatma Gandhi, found it very difficult to get rid of the ghost of untouchability. They agitated in the country but they did not succeed. Now, Sir, we have embodied an Article No 17 in this Constitution to remove untouchability and I am sure that untouchability will be removed."

Referring to the criticism that the Assembly had taken too long a time to finish its work on account of the fact that it was going on leisurely and wasting public money, Ambedkar said there was no justification for this complaint when compared with the time taken by Constituent Assemblies in other countries. The American Convention met on March 25, 1787, and completed its work within four months on September 17, 1787. The Constitution convention of Canada met on October 10, 1864 and completed its work by March 1867 involving a period of two years and five months. The Australian Constitutional Convention assembled in March 1891 and completed its task on July 9, 1900, after a period of 9 years. The South African Convention met in October 1908 and the Constitution became law in the country on September 20, 1909.

Dr Ambedkar said:[4] "It is true that we have taken more time than what the American or South African Conventions did. But time taken in India was not more than in Canada and much less than was taken in Australia. In making comparisons on the basis of time consumed, two things must be remembered. One is that the Constitution of America, Canada, South Africa and Australia are much smaller than ours. Our Constitution contains 395 Articles while the American has just seven articles, the four of which are divided into sections which total up to 21; the Canadian has 147, Australian 128 and South African 153 sections. The makers of the Constitutions of America, Canada, Australia and South Africa did not have to face the problems of amendments. Having regard to these facts the charge of dilatoriness seems to me quite unfounded and this Assembly may well congratulate itself for having accomplished so formidable a task in so short a time. Referring to the charge that the Drafting Committee was not drafting but drifting, Ambedkar said if it was drifting it was never without mastery over the situation. It was not merely angling with the off chance of catching a fish. It was searching in known waters to find the fish it was after. To be in search of something better is not the same as drifting. The Drafting Committee would have been guilty of gross dereliction of duty and of a false sense of dignity if it had not shown the honesty and the courage to withdraw amendments which it thought faulty and substitute what it thought was better.

"As to the compliments that have been showered upon me both by the members of the Assembly as well as by my colleagues of the Drafting Committee, I feel so overwhelmed that I cannot find adequate words to express fully my gratitude to them. I came into the Constituent Assembly with no greater aspiration than to safeguard the interests of the Scheduled Castes. I had not the remotest idea that I would be called upon to undertake more responsible functions. I was therefore greatly surprised when the Assembly elected me to the Drafting Committee. I was more than surprised when the Drafting

Committee elected me to be its Chairman. There were in the Drafting Committee men bigger, better and more competent than myself such as my friend Sir Alladi Krishnaswami Ayyar. I am grateful to the Constituent Assembly and to the Drafting Committee for reposing in me so much trust and confidence and to have chosen me as their instrument and given me this opportunity of serving the country (cheers). The credit that is given to me does not really belong to me. It belongs partly to Sir B.N. Rau, the Constitutional Adviser to the Constituent Assembly, who prepared a rough draft of the Constitution for consideration of the Drafting Committee. A part of the credit must go to the members of the Drafting Committee who, as I have said, have sat for 141 days and without whose ingenuity to devise new formulae and capacity to tolerate and accommodate different points of view, the task of framing the Constitution could not have come to so successful a conclusion. Much greater share of the credit must go to Mr S.N. Mukherjee, the Chief Draftsman of the Constitution.

"The task of the Drafting Committee would have been a very difficult one if this Constituent Assembly had been merely a motley crowd, a tasseled pavement without cement, a black stone here and white stone there in which each member of each group was a law unto itself. There would have been nothing but chaos. This possibility of chaos was reduced to nil by the existence of the Congress Party inside the Assembly which brought into its proceedings a sense of order and discipline. It is because of the discipline of the Congress Party that the Drafting Committee was able to pilot the Constitution in the Assembly with the sure knowledge as to the fate of each article and each amendment. The Congress Party is, therefore, entitled to all the credit for the smooth sailing of the Draft Constitution in the Assembly. However, the proceedings of this Constituent Assembly would have been very dull if all members had yielded to the rule of party discipline. Party discipline, in all its rigidity, would have converted this Assembly into a gathering of "yes" men. Fortunately, there were rebels. They were Mr Kamath, Dr P.S. Deshmukh, Mr Sidhva, Prof. Saxena and Pandit Thakur Das Bhargava. Along with them I must mention Prof. K.T. Shah and Pandit Hirday Nath Kunzru. The points they raised were mostly ideological. That I was prepared to accept their suggestions does not diminish the value of their suggestions nor lessen the service they have rendered to the Assembly in enlivening its proceedings. I am grateful to them. But for them, I would not have had the opportunity which I got for expounding the principles underlying the Constitution which was more important than the mere mechanical work of passing the Constitution.

"However good a Constitution may be, it is sure to turn out bad because those who are called to work it, happen to be a bad lot. However bad a Constitution may be, it may turn out to be good if those who are called to work it, happen to be a good lot. The working of a Constitution does not depend wholly upon the nature of the Constitution. The Constitution can provide only the organs of State such as the Legislature, the Executive and the Judiciary.

The factors on which the working of those organs of the State depend are the people and the political parties they will set up as their instruments to carry out their wishes and their politics. Who can say how the people of India and their parties will behave? Will they uphold constitutional methods of achieving their purposes or will they prefer revolutionary methods of achieving them? If they adopt revolutionary methods, however good the Constitution may be, it requires no prophet to say that it will fail. It is therefore futile to pass any judgment upon the Constitution without reference to the part which the people and their parties are likely to play.

"The condemnation of the Constitution comes from two quarters, the Communist Party and the Socialist Party. Why do they condemn the Constitution? The Communist Party wants a Constitution based upon the principle of Dictatorship of the Proletariat. They condemn the Constitution because it is based upon parliamentary democracy. The Socialists want two things. The first thing they want is that if they come to power, the Constitution must give them the freedom to nationalize or socialize all private property without payment of compensation. The second thing that the Socialists want is that the Fundamental Rights mentioned in the Constitution must be absolute and without any limitations so that if their party fails to come into power, they would have the unfettered freedom not merely to criticize, but also to overthrow the State. These are the main grounds on which the Constitution is being condemned. I do not say that the principle of parliamentary democracy is the only ideal form of political democracy. I do not say that the principle of no acquisition of private property without compensation is so sacrosanct that there can be no departure from it. I do not say that Fundamental Rights can never be absolute and the limitations set upon them can never be lifted. What I do say is that the principles embodied in the Constitution are the views of the present generation or if you think this to be an overstatement, I say they are the views of the members of the Constituent Assembly. Why blame the Drafting Committee for embodying them in the Constitution? I say why blame even the Members of the Constituent Assembly? Jefferson, the great American statesman who played so great a part in the making of the American Constitution, had expressed some very weighty views which makers of Constitution can never afford to ignore.

In one place, he has said: "We may consider each generation as a distinct nation, with a right, by the will of the majority, to bind themselves, but none to bind the succeeding generation, more than the inhabitants of another country." In another place he has said: "The idea that institutions established for the use of the nation cannot be touched or modified, even to make them answer their end, because of rights gratuitously supposed in those employed to manage them in the trust for the public, may perhaps be a salutary provision against the abuses of a monarch, but is most absurd against the nation itself. Yet our lawyers and priests generally inculcate this doctrine, and suppose that preceding generations held the earth more freely than we do; had a right to impose laws on us, unalterable by ourselves, and that we, in the like manner, can make laws and impose burdens on future generations, which they will have no right to alter; in fine, that the earth belongs to the dead and not the living."

"What Jefferson has said is not merely true, but is absolutely true. There can be no question about it. Had the Constituent Assembly departed from this principle laid down by Jefferson, it would certainly be liable to blame, even to condemnation. But I ask, has it? Quite the contrary. One has only to examine the provision relating to the amendment of the Constitution. The Assembly has not only refrained from putting a seal of finality and infallibility upon this Constitution by denying to the people the right to amend the Constitution as in Canada or by making the amendment of the Constitution subject to the fulfillment of extraordinary terms and conditions as in America or Australia, but has provided a most facile procedure for amending the Constitution. I challenge any of the critics of the Constitution to prove that any Constituent Assembly anywhere in the world has, in the circumstances in which this country finds itself, provided such a facile procedure for the amendment of the Constitution. If those who are dissatisfied with the Constitution have only to obtain 2/3 majority and if they cannot get two-third majority in Parliament elected on adult franchise in their favour, their dissatisfaction with the Constitution cannot be deemed to be shared by the general public."

Referring to the criticism that there is too much centralization and the States have been reduced to municipalities in the Constitution, Ambedkar said this view was not only an exaggeration but was founded on a misunderstanding of what exactly the Constitution contrived to do. As to the relation between the Centre and the States, it is necessary to bear in mind the fundamental principle on which it rests. The basic principle of federation is that the Legislative and Executive authority is partitioned between the Centre and the States not by any law to be made by the Centre but by the Constitution itself. This is what Constitution does. The States under our Constitution are in no way dependent upon the Centre for their legislative or executive authority. The Centre and the States are co-equal in this matter.

"It is difficult to see how such a Constitution can be called centralism. It may be that the Constitution assigns to the Centre too large a field for the operation of its legislative and executive authority than is to be found in any other federal Constitution. It may be that the residuary powers are given to the Centre and not to the States. But these features do not form the essence of federalism. The chief mark of federalism lies in the partition of the legislative and executive authority between the Centre and the Units by the Constitution. This is the principle embodied in our Constitution. There can be no mistake about it. It is therefore wrong to say that the States have been placed under the Centre. The Centre cannot by its own will alter the boundary of that partition. Nor can the Judiciary.

"Of course the Centre has been given the power to override the States. But before condemning the Constitution for containing such overriding powers, certain considerations must be borne in mind. The first is that these overriding powers do not form the normal feature of the Constitution. Their use and operations are expressly confined to emergencies only. The second consideration is: Could we avoid giving overriding powers to the Centre when emergency has arisen? Those who do not admit the justification for such overriding powers to the Centre even in emergency, do not seem to have a clear idea of the problem which lies at the root of the matter. The problem is so clearly set out by a writer that I offer no apology for quoting the following extract from what he has said in his article published in a magazine. 'Political systems are a complex of rights and duties resting ultimately on the question, to whom, or to what authority, does the citizen owe allegiance. In normal affairs the question is not present, for the law works smoothly, and a man goes about his business obeying one authority in this set of matters and another authority in that. But in a moment of crisis, a conflict of claim may arise, and it is then apparent that ultimate allegiance cannot be divided. The issue of allegiance cannot be determined in the last resort by a juristic interpretation of statutes. The law must conform to the facts or so much the worse for the law. When all formation is stripped away, the bare question is, what authority commands the residual loyalty of the citizen. Is it the Centre or the Constituent State?' There can be no doubt that in the opinion of the vast majority of the people, the residual loyalty of the citizen in an emergency must be to the Centre and not the Constituent States. For it is only the Centre which can work for a common end and for the general interest of the country as a whole. Herein lies the justification for giving to the Centre certain overriding powers to be used in an emergency."

Ambedkar said India would be an Independent country from January 26, 1950, but what worried him was the thought: will she maintain her Independence or will she lose it again? Not that India was never an Independent country. The point is she once lost the Independence she had. Will she lose it a second time? "What perturbs me greatly is the fact that not only India has once before lost her Independence, but she lost it by the infidelity and treachery of some of her own people. In the invasion of Sind by Mahommed-Bin-Kasim, the military commanders of King Dahar accepted bribes from the agents of Mahommed Bin Kasim and refused to fight on the side of their King. It was Jaichand who invited Mahommed Ghori to invade India and fight against Prithvi Raj and promised him the help of himself and the Solanki kings. When Shivaji was fighting for the liberation of Hindus, the other Maratha noblemen and the Rajput kings were fighting the battle on the side of Moghul emperors. When the British were trying to destroy the Sikh rulers, Gulab Singh, their principal commander, sat silent and did not help to save the Sikh kingdom. Will history repeat itself? It is this thought which fills me with anxiety. The anxiety is deepened by the realization that in addition to our old enemies in the form of castes and creeds we are going to have many political parties with diverse and opposing political creeds. Will Indians place the country above their creed or will they place creed above country? I do not know. But if the parties place creed above country, our Independence will be put in jeopardy a second time and probably be lost for ever. This eventuality we must all resolutely guard against. We must be determined to defend our Independence with the last drop of our blood (cheers).

"On the January 26, 1950, India would be a democratic country in the sense that India from that day would have a government of the people, by the people and for the people. But the thought that comes to my mind is: what would happen to her democratic Constitution? Will she be able to maintain or will she lose it again? It is not that India did not know what is Democracy. There was a time when India was studded with republics, and even where there were monarchies, they were either elected or limited. They were never absolute. It is not that India did not know Parliaments or Parliamentary Procedure. It is clear from the Buddhist Bhikshu Sanghas that not only there were Parliaments – for the Sanghas were nothing but Parliaments – but Sanghas knew and observed all the rules of Parliamentary procedure known to modern times. They had rules regarding seating arrangements, rules regarding motions, resolutions, quorum, whip, counting of votes, voting by ballot, censure motion, regularization, etc. Although these rules were applied by the Buddha to the meetings of the Sanghas, he must have borrowed them from the rules of the political assemblies functioning in the country in his time. This democratic system India lost. Will she lose it a second time? In a country like India, where democracy from its long disuse must be regarded as something quite new, there is danger of democracy giving place to dictatorship. It is quite possible for this new born democracy to retain its form but give place to dictatorship in fact.

"If we wish to maintain democracy not merely in form, but also in fact, what must we do? The first thing in my judgment we must do is to hold fast to constitutional methods for achieving our social and economic objectives. It means we must abandon the bloody methods of revolution. It means that we must abandon the method of civil disobedience, non-cooperation and satyagraha. When there was no way left for constitutional methods for achieving economic and social objectives, there was a great deal of justification for unconstitutional methods. But where constitutional methods are open, there can be no justification for those unconstitutional methods. These methods are nothing but the Grammar of Anarchy and the sooner they are abandoned, the better for us. The second thing we must do is to observe the caution which John Stuart Mill has given to all who are interested in the maintenance of democracy, namely, not 'to lay their liberties at the feet of even a great man, or to trust him with powers which enable him to subvert their institutions.' There is nothing wrong in being grateful to great men who have rendered life-long services to the country. But there are limits to gratefulness. As has been well said by the Irish Patriot Daniel O'Connel, 'no man can be grateful at the cost of his honour, no woman can be grateful at the cost of her chastity and no nation can be grateful at the cost of its liberty.' This caution is far more necessary in the case of India than in the case of any other country, for in India, Bhakti or what may be called the path of devotion or hero-worship, plays a part in its politics unequalled in magnitude by the part it plays in the politics of any other country in the world.

"On the January 26, 1950, we are going to enter into a life of contradictions. In politics we will have equality and in social and economic life we will have inequality. In politics we will be recognizing the principles of one man one vote and one vote one value. In our social and economic life, we shall, by reason of our social and economic structure, continue to deny the principle of one man one value. How long shall we continue to live this life of contradictions? How long shall we continue to deny equality in our social economic life? If we continue to deny it for long, we will do so only by putting our political democracy in peril. Political democracy cannot last unless there lies at the base of it social democracy. What does social democracy mean? It means a way of life which recognizes liberty, equality and fraternity as the principles of life. These principles of liberty, equality and fraternity are not to be treated as separate items in a trinity. They form a union of trinity in the sense that to divorce one from the other is to defeat the very purpose of democracy. Liberty cannot be divorced from equality, equality cannot be divorced from liberty. Nor can liberty and equality be divorced from fraternity. Without equality, liberty would produce the supremacy of the few over the many. Equality without liberty would kill individual initiative. Without fraternity, liberty and equality could not become a natural course of things. We must begin by acknowledging the fact that there is complete absence of two things in Indian society. One of these is equality. On the social plane, we have in India a society based on the principle of graded inequality which means elevation for some and degradation for others."

Without making any bones about it, Ambedkar said: "It must be realized and appreciated by all that the people divided into several thousands of castes could not be a nation. The sooner we realize that we are not as yet a nation in the social and psychological sense of the word, the better for us. For then only we shall realize the necessity of becoming a nation and seriously think of ways and means of realizing the goal. The realization of this goal is going to be very difficult – far more difficult than it has been even in the United States. In India there are castes. The castes are anti-national. In the first place because they bring about separation in social life. They are anti-national also because they generate jealousy and antipathy between caste and caste. But we must overcome all these difficulties if we wish to become a nation in reality. For fraternity, accorded the pride of place in our Constitution, can be a fact only when there is a nation. Fraternity means a sense of common brotherhood of all Indians. Without fraternity, equality and liberty will be no deeper than coats of paint."

Drawing attention to the problems facing the nation which was to become Independent shortly, Ambedkar said: "The political power in this country has too long been the monopoly of a few and the many are not only beasts of burden, but also beasts of prey. This monopoly has not merely deprived them of their chance of betterment, it has sapped them of what may be called the significance of life. These downtrodden classes are tired of being governed, they are impatient to govern themselves. This urge for self-realization in the downtrodden classes must not be allowed to develop into a class struggle or class war. It would lead to a division of the House. That would indeed by a day of disaster. For as has been well said by Abraham Lincoln, a house divided against itself cannot stand very long. Therefore the sooner room is made for the realization of their aspiration, the better for the few, the better for the country, the better for the maintenance for its independence and the better for the continuance of its democratic structure. This can only be done by the establishment of equality and fraternity in all spheres of life.

"Independence is no doubt a matter of joy. But let us not forget that this Independence has thrown on us great responsibilities. By Independence, we have lost the excuse of blaming the British for anything going wrong. If hereafter things go wrong, we will have nobody to blame except ourselves. There is great danger of things going wrong. Times are fast changing. People including our own are being moved by new ideologies. They are getting tired of government by the people. They are prepared to have Government for the people and are indifferent whether it is government of the people and by the people. If we wish to preserve the Constitution in which we have sought to enshrine the principle of Government of the people, for the people and by the people, let us resolve not to be tardy in the recognition of evils that lie across our path and which induce people to prefer Government for the people to Government by the people, nor to be weak in our initiative to remove them. That is the only way to serve the country. I know of no better."

Notwithstanding the fact that some members had criticized Ambedkar, after his speech he received a thunderous applause in the House. He was overwhelmed, acknowledging the praise showered on him. Ambedkar beautifully summed up the situation by saying among other things[5]: "The Hindus wanted the Vedas, and they sent for Vyasa who was not a caste Hindu. The Hindus wanted an epic, and they sent for Valmiki who was an Untouchable. The Hindus wanted a Constitution and they sent for me." By these words he brought the whole House down. Finally, the chairman of the Constituent Assembly, Dr Rajendra Prasad, said: "Ambedkar has not only justified his selection but has added lustre to the work which he has done."

After his historic triumph in presenting the Constitution, which was hailed by one and all in the Constitutent Assembly, Ambedkar accompanied by his wife, Savita, flew to Bombay in a jubilant mood on January 2, 1950. He was lustily cheered by his lieutenants as he came out of the plane at the Santa Cruz

Airport. The Bombay Scheduled Castes Federation, at a meeting in Parel on January 11, presented him a copy of India's Constitution he had drafted in a golden casket. Speaking on the occasion, Ambedkar said he had been branded as a British stooge and a pro-Muslim in the past. But now the Hindus would understand on account of his much-applauded role in framing free India's Constitution that all their accusations against him were not justified. Ambedkar asked his followers to shed their narrow outlook and start thinking in terms of the welfare of the nation as a whole for the new Constitution accorded them full equality as citizens. Not only that, untouchability had been totally banned under Article 17 of the Constitution.

References

1. See from sixth line on p. 9, Vol. 13.
2. See footnote on p. 13, Vol. 13.
3. See p. 72 for T.T. Krisnamachari's tribute, Vol. 13.
4. See from 7th line on p. 2007, Vol. 13.
5. See first para on p. 174 in the book Reminiscences of Dr. B.R. Ambedkar by Nanak Chand Rattu.

16

Hindu Code Bill

Notwithstanding the fact that he was unhappy with the caste-based inequalities in Hindu society, Ambedkar was a devoted patriot and wanted to make India great. He was not only worried about the miserable condition of the Untouchables, but also about the appalling customs and traditions in Hindu society. Women were not accorded equal treatment with men. Hindu laws governing the society were heavily biased in favour of the man not only with regard to marriage and divorce but also in relation to the question of inheritance. The colonial British rulers were also not happy with the treatment meted out to women, the laws of inheritance and adoption in the country. But they did not do anything to set things right lest it should provoke opposition.

However, the Viceroy's Executive Council, which used to take important decisions regarding administrative matters, set up a Committee of Hindu Law Reforms. The Committee studied the problems and submitted its report, which remained unimplemented because by the time the then colonial government could consider its recommendations, the British had decided to quit India. Following his appointment as Law Minister in the government formed by Jawaharlal Nehru, Ambedkar examined the report and improved upon the recommendations of the committee. Guided by the committee's recommendations and his own observations, he drafted a legislation, called the Hindu Code Bill, for reforming Hindu society.

But the introduction of the Bill on April 11,1947, in the Constituent Assembly, which continued to function as the country's Parliament until general elections were held for the first time in free India in 1952, raised a political storm. Revolutionary changes in the Hindu society proposed in the Bill were unacceptable to many. So vociferous was the condemnation of the Bill that the man in the street without even understanding the reforms proposed in it, came to regard the Bill as a major assault on Hinduism. Although the Bill was a part of social engineering through law, it was by the social norms of those days, a revolutionary measure. There were heated debates in the Constituent Assembly on it.

Educated women and the liberal intelligentsia hailed Ambedkar as a modern Manu out to correct the ages-old inequalities which were a part and parcel of the Hindu society. If Ambedkar was praised sky high by many, he was also described as the annihilator of Hinduism by an equally large, perhaps even larger, number of people, all over the country. The issue caused a nationwide debate, the Hindu Code Bill becoming the topic of discussion in every household. Acharya Kriplani, a prominent Congress leader of those days, frankly admitted that reluctance on his part to support the Bill provoked his wife to give him curtain lectures. In fact women individually, and organizations devoted to their welfare collectively, mounted heavy pressure on the politicians to support the Bill.

The debate on the Bill in the Constituent Assembly continued for more than four years. This was probably the longest discussion on any single Bill in free India's Parliament. In view of the fierce controversy it had caused, the government decided to refer the Bill to a Select Committee consisting of top-level judges, politicians, religious leaders, academicians and bureaucrats. It was hoped that the Select Committee, after examining whatever criticism of the Bill was being made, would make suitable recommendations so that the revised Bill could be passed without any problem. Moving a motion for referring it to the Select Committee in the Constituent Assembly, Ambedkar said the Bill seeks to codify the rules of Hindu law which are scattered in innumerable decisions of the High Courts and the Privy Council and which form a bewildering motley for the common man giving rise to litigation. It sought to codify the law relating to seven different matters. Firstly, the law relating to the rights of property of a deceased Hindu, male or female, who has died intestate. Secondly, it prescribed a somewhat altered form of the order of succession among the different heirs to the property of a deceased dying without making a will. It also dealt with the law of maintenance, marriage, divorce, adoption, minority and guardianship.

The Bill sought to give the widow, the daughter, the widow of a pre-deceased son the same right and status as the son in the matter of inheritance. In addition to that the daughter also was given a share in her father's property; her share prescribed as half of that of the son. The second change which the Bill made, so far as the female heirs were concerned, was that the number of female heirs recognized now was much larger than under either in the Mitakshara or the Dayabhag systems. Earlier, under the old law, a discrimination was made among female heirs as to whether a particular female was rich or poor in circumstances at the death of the testator, whether she was married or unmarried, or whether she was with issue or without issue. All these considerations, which led to discrimination were abolished. A woman who had a right to inherit got it due to the fact that she was declared to be the heir irrespective of any other consideration.

What is given as dowry to the girl on the occasion of her marriage shall be treated as a trust property, the use of which will be restricted to her and she would be entitled to claim that property when she came of age at 18, so that neither her husband nor the relations of her husband would have any interest in that property; nor would they have any opportunity to waste that property and make her helpless for the rest of her life. The dependants of a deceased would be entitled to claim maintenance from those who inherit his property either under the rules of intestate succession or those who inherit his property under his will. Even a concubine was included in the category of dependants. The liability to maintenance was cast upon those who took the estate of the deceased. Generally under the provisions of the Hindu law, a wife is not entitled to claim maintenance from her husband if she does not live with him in his house. The Hindu Code Bill, however, recognized that there were undoubtedly circumstances where if the wife had lived away from the husband, it must be for causes beyond her control, and it would be wrong not to recognize the causes and not to give her a separate maintenance.

Although the existing Hindu law recognized only what was called sacramental marriage performed according to the prescribed religious ceremonies, the Hindu Code Bill recognized civil marriages also. There were five conditions for a sacramental marriage. The bridegroom must be 18 and the bride must be 14 years old. Neither party must have a spouse living at the time of marriage. Under the old law, polygamy was permissible. But the Bill prescribed only monogamy.

The sacramental marriage was indissoluble. But any party which married under the new code had three remedies to get out of the contract of marriage. One was to have the marriage declared null and void; secondly, to have the marriage declared invalid; and thirdly, to have it dissolved. The grounds for the invalidation of marriage were four: first, impotency; second, parties being sapindas; third, parties being either idiotic or lunatic; and fourth, guardians' consent obtained by force or fraud. Not to keep the sword of dissolution hanging on the head, the Bill provided that a suit for the invalidation of marriage must be filed within three years from the date of the marriage; otherwise, the suit would be barred and the marriage would continue as though there was no ground of invalidity. The invalidation of marriage would not affect the legitimacy of the children born and they would continue to be legitimate just the same. The Bill gave seven grounds on which divorce could be obtained: (1) desertion (2) conversion to another religion (3) keeping a concubine or becoming a concubine (4) incurably unsound mind (5) virulent and incurable form of leprosy (6) veneral disease in communicable form and (7) cruelty.

Under the Hindu Code, it was necessary for the husband, if he wanted to make an adoption, to obtain the consent of his wife, and if there were more than one, at least the consent of one of them. Secondly, it also laid down that if the widow wanted to adopt, she could only adopt if there were positive instructions left by the husband authorizing her to adopt, and in order to prevent litigation as to whether the husband had, as a matter of fact, left instructions to his wife, the Code provided that the evidence of such instructions should be either by registered deed or by a provision in the will. No oral evidence would be admissible, so that chances of litigation were considerably reduced. The Code also provided that the adoption would be registered. One of the most fruitful sources of litigation in this country was the question of adoption. All sorts of oral evidence was manufactured, concocted; witnesses were suborned; widows were fooled; they one day declared that they had made an adoption and subsequently they made an avowal that they had not adopted. The Code made a salutary provision that there must be a registration of adoption by a Hindu. All this was intended to reduce litigation.

Many members of the Constituent Assembly hailed the Bill and said this was a piece of legislation for which the country had been waiting for long. Having been ruled by foreigners for nearly a thousand years, India had not been able to effect that social progress which was incidental to changes in society in the world, and which took place imperceptibly by force of ever changing custom. So long as the Muslims were ruling India, they copied our customs and we copied their customs; there was an inter-mixture and inter-currency of customs and therefore, some measures of social progress. But when the British came, they were afraid of any social interference with the socio-religious structure, which was a delicate structure almost like a chemical balance and bore the repercussions of the smallest changes coming from abroad. The British feared that such repercussions would be ruinous to the stability of their empire and therefore they adopted the plausible and seemingly reasonable attitude of not interfering with the religion or the custom of the land. Thus custom became petrified and as a result, progress was impeded altogether. Even missionaries drew attention to social evils in a spirit of carping criticism rather than in a spirit of progressive helpfulness.

The Hindu Code Bill was a progressive measure of reform, comprehensive in outlook, far-reaching in its results, medical in its nature insofar as it dealt with the rights of women in regard to inheritance, marriage, property, divorce and personal freedom. According to the Shastras, a woman is like the bonded slave of her father when she is young, of her husband when she is middle aged and of her son when she is an old mother. Of course, all epigrams, aphorisms, proverbs, platitudes and truisms are half-truths. Under the old Hindu laws, women rotted in their own homes because they lacked rights of inheritance and remarriage in the event of divorce or widowhood. Ambedkar sought to correct this injustice. A woman must have her own right and means to do whatever she prefers. The doctrine of self-effacement on the part of the woman had been carried on in Hindu society for ages, yet the fact remains that in the modern day the conception of self-respect has completely altered the position. If a man feels free and has the right to stay abroad and to do whatever he wants to do, if he can marry a second time when the first wife is alive, then of course it must be equally open for the wife also to marry a second husband while the first one is alive. All this was provided in the Hindu Code Bill.

But Ambedkar's Bill was like a bolt from the blue for the Hindu orthodoxy. The predominant feeling among this section of society was that the Hindu law inspired by the Vedic literature and the post-Vedic literature known as the Shrutis and the Smritis had a divine origin. But the Bill goes against the very religious basis and the very religious structure of the Hindu society. In one fell stroke, it seeks to demolish Hinduism in the very land of Rishis and Munis. The cherished belief that marriages are made in heaven would become a thing of the past if women are given the right to divorce and contract another matrimonial alliance. If daughter is given her share of property in an agricultural family, there would be fragmentation of land. Instead of treating their sisters as their protégé, brothers would look upon them as rivals out to take a part of the property which earlier belonged to them. In such a situation, customs like Raksha Bandhan would cease to have any importance. The majority of members in the Constituent Assembly hoped that the Select Committee would seriously ponder over the implications of changes proposed in the Bill and make suitable amendments. But even after the Select Committee had seriously pondered over the implications of changes in the Hindu law introduced in the Bill and made many amendments, the Bill remained the subject of fierce controversy.

Members opposing the Bill in the Constituent Assembly made no bones about their anger. They said, if in the name of reform, you uproot the Hindus from their safe and ancient moorings which have protected them from the stress and storm of centuries, it will be a great tragedy for India. All those who find fault with our Shastras, the fountainhead of Hindu law, must remember that they have always had a very salutary effect as a stabilizing force in our society. If we ignore them and make a fetish of conditions we will cast Hindu Law into a mould absolutely inflexible and rigid; we will be unnecessarily foisting upon it a character which never belonged to it. We will be transforming it into something which will never be able to adjust itself to the needs of the times, as it has been in the past. The Bill seeks to bring radical changes in the concept of marriage, in the scheme of Hindu laws, including the law of inheritance and succession. It will create endless and needless complications including such things as Civil Marriage Register, Sacramental Marriage Register, Marriage Notice Book, Director General of Marriages, Registrar of Marriages, and so on and so forth.

A member commented: "Are we going to enact a Code which will facilitate the break-up of our households? Will the summum bonum of social life be reached when every single family is broken up and domestic peace driven away? These changes are bound to happen if we pass the Hindu Code Bill. Anybody who is false to his nation's traditions, to his glorious heritage and culture is a traitor, and is a person who should be given capital punishment. I do not understand the patriotism of those, the nationalism of those, who have nothing but contempt and jeer for anything that is their ancient culture and heritage. Champions of changes in the Hindu law had better remember that Greece, Rome, Assyria, Babylonia were great civilizations but they all crumbled with the passage of time. Hindu culture and community alone, which cannot date its origin, still continues to function with all the vigour and vitality. Providence will allow it to function because its laws, its social structure, its principles are good. We must resist reckless and light-hearted ways that are being adopted to force the passage of Ambedkar's Hindu Code Bill.

"There will be practical difficulties in implementing the provisions of the Bill. Just imagine how long it will take government to educate the people that they should go to law court for getting their marriages registered. Just imagine what complications and confusion will the provision for void and voidable marriages create. What havoc will the provision for the dissolution of marriages and divorce play in the domestic life of the people whose conception of society has so far been quite different from the one on which these provisions are based. Many interested persons will come into the picture to disrupt the domestic life of their neighbours, relatives, etc. for their selfish ends. The provisions regarding successions will make the management of property difficult and become a prolific source of intrigue by designing persons in society. Lawyers and law courts may prosper but families will be broken up and domestic peace will decay."

Following country-wide uproar against the Bill and daily protest demonstrations outside Parliament organized by parties which regarded the Bill as a major assault on Hinduism, the government decided to confine its scope to marriage and divorce. But still there was no let-up in the opposition blast against it. It was argued that the Hindu society rests upon the foundation of marriage. By making provisions for easy divorce, the Bill sought to make a mockery of marriage. In Hindu society, just as is the case in any other society, there is a class of people to whom the real zest of life, the real zest of existence lies in their ability to do whatever they like with regard to marriage. It is for them that today's marriage and divorce laws have been framed, so that they can do whatever they like. A man can today discard a marriage relation and take up another partner almost in the twinkling of an eye. Such people will have to wait for months, they will have to go through law courts, they will have to go through the entire gamut of procedures before they can do the same under the provisions of the new Bill. No doubt the Bill is intended to safeguard the interests of women. But in practical terms, this will lead to murders in villages. If men find new impediments put in their way, impediments to which they have not been used, to which they are not accustomed, and they find themselves thwarted in a tiresome manner, they may not have in themselves that much of restraint, they may not have that much of control to wait for the law and respect it. Society may be faced with an upheaval which is probably not even imaginable today. The Bill may have been prepared innocently, but it has within it the potentialities for untold and immeasurable mischief.

An agitated opponent of the Bill said : "In Hindu society, from time immemorial, laws have prevailed without the authority of the State, without the authority of the police, without the authority of any legislature as such. There has been no government sanction behind the laws which were promulgated by men who had attained perfection as nearly as man could, who were held in universal respect, who worked for the good of the people. The laws which were promulgated have always been followed. In the whole of this country, throughout its length and breadth, Hindu laws have been observed not because anyone found them to be comfortable or otherwise, found them to be pleasant or irksome, but because people in this country have been steeped in the conviction and belief that what they are doing today will have repercussions hereafter, what they go through now will bring its own reward. They have been all bred up to believe that it is not 'Preya' alone which matters in life, but it is the 'Shreya' of things which must be assiduously inculcated. Let not the government make a hasty mistake in demolishing that fabric upon which the respect for and adherence to the law has prevailed. If one set of legislators, one set of wise men or wiseacres today legislate in one particular manner as they think fit, people will cease to worry about 'Apoorva,' the unseen. People will know that it is possible for them the next day to get a law made to suit their pleasure and their convenience. The moral fabric of Hindu society will disappear and man might go back to the old age where there was no method or system of marriages, where a state of things prevailed which probably, in decent society, would not be considered worth mentioning.

"There should be a fundamental agreement with regard to the need for introducing reforms in our great country, which will make our civilization more progressive and more advanced. Those who are following the existing practices, those who are abiding by the provisions of the existing laws are not retrograde. The tragedy is that many of the supporters of the Bill, who have been carried away by their notions of the so-called progress and advance, in their exuberance think that what they think is the last word on the subject, that only they represent progress and all others are retrograde. That is very unfortunate.

We should see the other man's point of view, the point of view of man who believes in the existing ideology, unless it can be pointed out that something is happening in society which is absolutely rotten, immoral, backward. When you introduce social reforms in such a vast country as India, where opinions differ, where attitudes differ and where ideologies differ, then the only way in which you can do it is to go at a slow pace. First, go and convince the people, the Hindu people, who still claim to live under canons and codes which are in no way inferior to those existing in any other part of the world. Matters concerning social reform can be discussed in a spirit of give and take. There should be no police standing outside this Parliament to help ensure the smooth passage of a Bill dealing with social reform. Any Bill whose object is to introduce social reform must have the support of the vast majority of the people of this country.

"If you believe monogamy as a social system is the best that India should have, then, do not try to look at it through the Hindu door; look at it through the human door, and make it applicable to all. Behave like a secular State at least in this instance. Take courage in both hands and say that monogamy will be made applicable to all citizens of India. If you cannot do it, do not do it for one section alone. We are living in days of statistics. We swear by statistics, either real or manufactured. The number of people marrying second time is extremely small. It is really no problem. Already, on account of advanced views, society has adjusted itself, and on account of economic conditions, general public censure etc., this system has gone out. Why make a parade of this that you are introducing a great reform and legislating for this? If you accept it as a principle, apply it to the whole of India. Of course, the Law Minister, Dr Ambedkar, and those who are associated with him, have done a marvellous piece of work in drafting the Hindu Code Bill. But don't push it down the throat of millions of Hindus who are opposed to it."

Half a dozen or so women members of the Constituent Assembly and many others marshalled facts and figures to demolish the argument that Hindu Code Bill was an assault on Hindu religion. They argued that the Bill does not seek to disturb the Hindu religion but to amend and modify the Hindu civil law. There is no rigidity about the law, which has changed from time to time. The authors of the Dharma Shastras changed the law according to the consciousness of the community at the time. The right to make changes was recognized by the Dharma Shastra. The Hindu law became rigid and static only after the advent of the British. Unless the Hindu society is to remain static and dead, the law must change to fit in with the changing circumstances. The Hindu religion is very catholic and so the argument that religion is in danger does not behove us. Some of the measures embodied in this Bill such as Succession Bill and Marriage Bill were introduced in the House in 1943. The Hindu Law Committee was appointed in 1944 and its report was published in 1945 or 1946. Many of the recommendations of the Hindu Law Committee have been incorporated in the Bill. Why then this hue and cry?

Several women members said: "When under the new Constitution we are pledged to do away with all sex discrimination, give women equal status in society, usher in an era where people of all castes will be equal, there is absolutely no justification in opposing the Bill. Unless women get their full share of property you cannot expect them to fulfill their obligations to the State. Of course, whenever there are any changes, established custom and established rules are disturbed. It causes a certain amount of dislocation and inconvenience, but we have to tolerate them. Dr Ambedkar and several other members have told us that the Smritis recognized the right of property of women. What law gave us, practice denied us. In practice the right was abrogated. The provisions of the Bill are not going against the fundamentals of Hindu religion or Hindu custom or Hindu law. Whatever was granted to us by the Hindu law was arbitrarily withdrawn in the past and is now being restored. By the Act of 1937 the government gave property right to the wife, to the daughter-in-law, to the grandson's wife and so on and so forth. The only person left out was the poor daughter. It is in the fitness of things that she should be included here. If woman can inherit from the husband's side, let the daughter inherit from the father's side, which is very natural and justified. There is no justification in saying that innate affection and natural love between brother and sister will cease to exist if daughter is also given a share. Loves are of different kinds, but the love that a sister has for her brother is so unassuming and pure that no other kind of love can stand up to it. The glory of our religion lies in natural affection, mutual love and in being on good terms with others."

A former judge said: "It is being argued that the Bill would lead to the break-up of the joint family. The fact is, most of the people already want to get out of the joint family. The sons do not like to stay with the father. Most of the families are already distributed all over the country. Joint family is a very rapidly crumbling institution. Even the legal position of the joint family is very faulty as pointed out by Dr Ambedkar. Much was said about the protection given to the unprotected women in the joint family. No doubt unprotected women did get protection. Even now some of them are protected. But at the same time the fact cannot be ignored that hundreds of women who, failing to get shelter in the joint family, have no economic resources of their own, and are hounded to a life of degradation and shame. Not only is it right, not only is it just to give the woman her portion, but it is absolutely essential to give her the share if you want to safeguard the Hindu society. The sacramental and civil marriages as proposed in the Bill are such that they can be put into practice by the poorest and the most backward classes. There is some objection to the registration of sacramental marriages. But it is purely sentimental because registration is only permissive. If you do not want to avail of the registration you are free not to do it.

"The criticism of inter-caste and Sagotra marriages is unjustified. A very large number of such marriages are already taking place in society. When it is there, why shy away from the fact? When it is a practice, why not recognize it and give it legality. When polygamy is being looked down upon, what is wrong in accepting monogamy as is provided in the Bill? It is unjustified to find fault with provision of divorce in the Bill. Divorce did exist in ancient scriptures. Of course, divorce should not be made very cheap and easy. Incompatibility of temperament should be one of the grounds for it. The grounds of divorce are extremely reasonable and just as provided in the Bill. Unlike the practice in the western world, divorce has not been permitted on frivolous grounds. Hindu social tradition is such that we will not on flimsy grounds rush to the court and break up a marriage. Those who think that the right of divorce may amount to disruption of the family life of the Hindus are absolutely unjustified. Actually, the system of divorce is already there in the country. Divorce is permitted without any question in Baroda, Travancore, Cochin and Malabar. Heavens will not fall if the practice is extended all over the country.

"The cry has been raised that Hindu society is in danger because of the Hindu Code Bill, which is nothing but a mild, halting measure of reform. If the Hindu society is in danger, the danger is from those who would bind and fetter it; the danger is from those who would not allow out-worn customs to be changed but would allow them to choke up the life-blood of the society. If those who today appear to be so concerned about Hindus society would give a little thought, they would agree with what Dr Ambedkar said, namely, that you must repair if you want to survive.' Who has given the prerogative to some people to stand up for Hindu society? These people are those who wish to bind and fetter the Hindu law which has been changing with changing times throughout the centuries. They have no right to be the exponents of Hindu society and Hindu law, for all they want is to bring it back once again to the culture and heritage of our forefathers. If Hindu society is to regain all that it has lost during the many years and the many centuries of decadence when Hindus were slaves, it has to come in line with the atmosphere of freedom that prevails in this country today. Men and women have to come forward equally to work for the country and there cannot be equality if there is no equality in the social laws of this country.

A former Congress President said much is being made of the fact that the Bill is mainly aimed at improving the lot of women. What is wrong with this approach? After all the plight of women in our society is pitiable. Throughout history they have played a distinguished role in our life and in our culture. In ancient times many of them were great writers, philosophers and poets. In mediaeval times when we were down and out, when wave after wave of foreign invasions came, our women confined themselves and protected our culture. And when wounded and disappointed we went home they soothed our wounds and kept the home fire burning. Not only that, they kept our religion, traditions and culture alive. All those who are opposed to the Bill should first see the condition of widows not only in Bengal but in other States also. Even when women get what they deserve to have, their traditional devotion to home, their menfolk will not diminish. It is said that, if women are given inheritance, the love between brother and sister will diminish. Love of our sisters is not made of such flimsy stuff. It has centuries of tradition behind. Times have changed. If foreign rule had not been here, our Shastras would have changed; our laws would have changed. Foreign rule made Hindu laws very rigid, and it is time that we brought in some new life and new light into them.

Sharp division in the Constituent Assembly over the Hindu Code Bill made the Prime Minister Jawaharlal Nehru intervene in the debate to assure agitated members that the government had no intention of pushing through the Bill merely by virtue of a majority when there was a considerable variety of opinion with regard to it. The position of the government, so far as this Bill was concerned, was this. "We stand committed to the broad approach of the Bill as a whole. We are prepared, however, to consider every clause in a spirit of accommodation. Naturally, the government has put forward this measure as it is because they believe in it. But in such matters they desire to have as large a measure of support as possible. The government is sincerely interested to carry the Bill through this House and through the country with the largest measure of support. That does not mean that in any matter over which we may disagree violently, we give up our opinions or surrender to anyone else's judgment. No one expects any member of this House to do that if he believes in something. But it is the essence of democratic procedure for us to debate and consider and try to convince each other and try to meet each other's points, by sometimes giving up something so as to arrive at a decision which can be enforced with the largest measure of consent.

"I do not wish the House to think in the slightest degree that we consider this Hindu Code Bill as not of any importance, because we do attach the greatest importance to it, as I said, not because of any particular clause or anything, but because of the basic approach to this vast problem, economic and social. We have achieved political freedom in this country, political independence. That is a stage in the journey, and there are other stages, economic, social and several others. If society is to advance, there must be this integrated advance on all fronts. It is for this House to accept a measure, but if a government takes an important measure and the House rejects it, the House rejects that Government and the Government goes and another Government comes in its place. It should be clearly understood that this is one of the important measures to which the government attaches importance and on which it will stand or fall."

Notwithstanding the fact that the Prime Minister had himself supported the Bill, there was no end to its criticism even by Congress members in the Constituent Assembly. Outside Parliament many influential people including the then President of India, Dr Rajendra Prasad, had reservations about it. Dr Prasad had gone to the extent of saying that even if the Bill was passed he would not allow it to be made a law in India by declining to give his assent. Another factor provoking criticism both in and outside the House was Ambedkar himself. While replying to the debate, he had sought to make light of the Hindu Shastras by observing that they had little value when they could not save Sita from being banished by lord Rama. His remarks about Sita caused a turmoil in the House and made many learned Pandits and politicians issue statements condemning him. The government came under intense pressure to drop or postpone the Bill.

But Ambedkar could see clearly that Nehru did not see eye to eye with him despite the fact that all that he wanted to do was the reformation of the Hindu society. Frustrated Ambedkar started giving vent to his feelings whenever he got an opportunity to do so. While laying the foundation stone of Ambedkar Bhavan in New Delhi in the middle of April 1951, Ambedkar made no bones about the fact that the government was not bothered about the rights of the depressed classes. Since the government had been attacked by a Cabinet Minister, no wonder almost all the newspapers went to town with the story. This raised hackles of caste Hindus in the Congress party. Some of the party members were so exercised over the issue that they started demanding Ambedkar's expulsion from the government. Some of the newspapers commented in their editorials whether the Cabinet observed the principle of joint or individual responsibility. Nehru who had never liked Ambedkar and who had been prevailed upon to accommodate him in the Cabinet by Gandhi was really very upset.

Undaunted by the bitter reaction in the Congress party to his criticism of the government for its failure to take care of the Scheduled Castes, Ambedkar delivered another broadside against his tormentors on the occasion of the Buddha Jayanti Celebrations in May 1951 in New Delhi. This hurt the sentiments of caste Hindus and Congress leaders more since this was delivered in the presence of the diplomatic fraternity who were there in large numbers. While speaking on the occasion, Ambedkar dwelt at length on all the vices of Hindu society such as violence, immorality and corruption in government offices and said all this was happening because of deterioration in Hinduism. He argued that Buddhism came on the scene in India just when ethical and moral values and a sense of justice had been relegated to the background. Since the situation was similar now, there was urgent need for the revival of Buddhism in India to save society from descending into the doldrums of anarchy and chaos. The then Ambassador of France who had been specially invited was presiding over the function. The caste Hindus saw in Ambedkar's utterances veiled attempts to belittle them before the international community. They could not bear this insult and started redoubling their efforts to secure Ambedkar's ouster from the government. Newspapers, as was to be expected, joined in the chorus of attack on the leader of the Untouchables.

Angry Congress MPs made Ambedkar the main target of their attack when two days later he introduced in Parliament the Representation of the People (Amendment) Bill. Heated arguments between the Law Minister and his critics marked the proceedings. As a result of increasing bitterness, stories were planted in several newspapers that Nehru was about to submit his resignation to the President in order to permit himself to reorganize his Cabinet. Some reports hinted that Ambedkar had been asked to tender his resignation in view of the criticism he had made of the government while inaugurating the Ambedkar Bhavan. If all this did not result in the parting of ways between Ambedkar and the government, it was mainly on account of the fact that Nehru himself, although he did not say so openly, supported some of the provisions of the Hindu Code Bill which was being piloted by Ambedkar, and wanted it to be passed.

However, on September 26, 1951, the Prime Minister announced the government's change of stand on the Hindu Code Bill. He said: "It is not necessary for me to assure the House of the desire of the government to proceed with this measure insofar as we can proceed with it within possibilities, and so far as we are concerned we consider this matter as adjourned till such time as the next opportunity – I hope it will be in this Parliament – offers itself. With the best will in the world, we cannot brush aside the opposition to the Bill and get things done quickly." But since the President of the country, Dr Rajendra Prasad, Home Minister Sardar Patel and several other important politicians had strong reservations about the Bill, Nehru ultimately chose to go along with the critics of the Bill. Strategically it suited him also because the rejection of the Bill was likely to cause embarrassment to Ambedkar for whom he had no love or sympathy.

But the Prime Minister's announcement broke Ambedkar's heart. Throughout the debate in the Constituent Assembly, he had been painstakingly listening to speeches by members, many criticizing him and many lauding him. In fact, in his mind he had prepared a formidable defence for the Hindu Code Bill and felt sure that when he would draw the attention of the House to the Shastras containing most of the provision he had incorporated in the Bill, whatever opposition was there to the Bill would dissolve. Personally, he had nothing to gain or lose whether the Bill was passed or shelved. But he could not understand why Nehru had changed his mind when every development concerning the Bill was discussed at the highest level. In any case, the Prime Minister ought to have taken Ambedkar into confidence before announcing his decision. Ambedkar could not put up with the government's decision to postpone consideration of the Bill over which he had worked so hard and therefore decided to resign.

Replying to Ambedkar's letter in which he had offered his resignation over the issue, the Prime Minister said: "I can quite understand your great disappointment at the fact that the Hindu Code Bill could not be passed in this session, that even the Marriage and Divorce part of it had ultimately to be postponed. I know very well how hard you have laboured at it and how keenly you have felt about it. Although I have not been intimately connected with this Bill, I have been convinced of its necessity and I was anxious that it should be passed. I tried my utmost, but the fates and the rules of Parliament were against us. It seemed clear to me that nothing that we could do could get it through during this session. Personally, I shall not give up this fight because I think it is intimately connected with any progress on any front that we desire to make."

Since he was not allowed to make a statement about his resignation in the House, Ambedkar issued a statement to the Press and the following day when newspapers all over the country carried his statement, he was hailed by the intelligentsia and the vast number of organizations devoted to women's welfare as a great leader who had to bow out before the Hindu orthodoxy. Of course, in his Press statement, Ambedkar listed many reasons for parting company with the Nehru government. Regarding the immediate provocation for it, he said:[1] "It is the treatment that was accorded to the Hindu Code. The Bill was introduced in the Constituent Assembly on April 11,1947. After a life of four years, it was killed and died unwept and unsung. While it was before the House, it lived by fits and starts. For full one year the government did not feel it necessary to refer it to a Select Committee. It was referred to the Select Committee on April 9,1948. The motion for consideration of the report of the Select Committee on the Bill was moved on August 31, 1948. It was merely for moving the motion that the Bill was kept on the agenda. The discussion of the motion was not allowed to take place until the February Session of the year 1949. Even then it was not allowed to have a continuous discussion. It was distributed over 10 months, 4 days in February, 1 day in March and 2 days in April 1949. After this, one day was given to the Bill in December 1949, namely the 19th December on which day the House adopted my motion that the Bill as reported by the Select Committee be taken into consideration. No time was given to he Bill in the year 1950. Next time the Bill came before the House was on February 5, 1951 when the clause by clause consideration of the Bill was taken. Only three days, 5th, 6th and 7th of February were given to the Bill and after that it was left there to rot.

"This being the last session of the present Parliament, the Cabinet had to consider whether the Hindu Code Bill should be got through before this Parliament ended or whether it should be left over to the new Parliament. The Cabinet unanimously decided that it should be put forth in this Parliament. So the Bill was put on the agenda and was taken up on September 17, 1951, for further clause by clause consideration. As the discussion was going on the Prime Minister put forth a new proposal, namely, that the Bill as a whole may not be got through within the time available and that it was desirable to get a part of it enacted into law rather than the whole of it to go waste. It was a great wrench to me. But I agreed, for, as the proverb says 'it is better to save a part when the whole is likely to be lost.' The Prime Minister suggested that we should select the Marriage and Divorce part. The Bill in its truncated form went on for discussion. After two or three days the Prime Minister came up with another proposal. This time his proposal was to drop the Bill, even the Marriage and Divorce portion. This came to me as a great shock – a bolt from the blue. I was stunned and could not say anything. I am not prepared to accept that this dropping of the Bill was due to want of time.

"I am sure that the truncated Bill was dropped because other and more powerful members of the Cabinet wanted precedence for their Bills. I am unable to understand how the Benaras and Aligarh University Bills, how the Press Bill could have been given precedence over the Hindu Code even in its attenuated form? It is not that there was no law on the Statute book to govern the Aligarh University or the Benaras University. It is not that these universities would have gone to wrack and ruin if the Bills had not been passed in this session. It is not that the Press Bill was urgent. There is already law on the Statute book and the Bill could have waited. I got the impression that the Prime Minister although sincere, had not the earnestness and determination required to get the Hindu Code Bill through."

The statement added: "In regard to this Bill I have been made to go through the greatest mental torture. The aid of party machinery was denied to me. The Prime Minister gave freedom of vote, an unusual thing in the history of the party. I did not mind it but I expected two things. I expected a party whip as to time limit on speeches and instruction to the Chief Whip to move closure motion when sufficient debate had taken place. A whip on time limit on speeches would have got the Bill through. When freedom of voting was given there could have been no objection to have given a whip for time limit on speeches. The conduct of the Minister for Parliamentary Affairs, who is also the Chief Whip of the party in connection with the Hindu Code, to say the least, has been most extraordinary. He has been the deadliest opponent of the Code and has never been present to aid me by moving a closure motion. For days and hours filibustering has gone on a single clause. But the Chief Whip, whose duty it is to economise government time and push on government business, has been systematically absent when the Hindu Code was under consideration in the House. I have never seen a case of a Chief Whip so disloyal to the Prime Minister and a Prime Minister so loyal to a disloyal Whip. Notwithstanding this unconstitutional behaviour, the Chief Whip is really a darling of the Prime Minister. For notwithstanding his disloyalty he got a promotion in the party organization. It is impossible to carry on in such circumstances.

"Now they say that the Bill had to be dropped because the opposition was strong. How strong was the opposition? This Bill has been discussed several times in the party and was carried to division by the opponents. Every time the opponents were routed. The last time when the Bill was taken up in the party meeting, out of 120 only 20 were found to be against it. When the Bill was taken in the party for discussion, 44 clauses were passed in about 3½ hours. This shows how much opposition there was to the Bill within the party. In the House itself there have been divisions on three clauses of the Bill – 2, 3 and 4. Every time there has been an overwhelming majority in favour even on clause 4 which is the soul of the Hindu Code. I was, therefore, quite unable to accept the Prime Minister's decision to abandon the Bill on the ground of time. I have been obliged to give this elaborate explanation for my resignation because some people have suggested that I am going because of illness. I wish to repudiate any such suggestion. I am the last man to abandon my duty because of illness.

"Although I was not satisfied with the government's foreign policy and the treatment meted out to Backward Classes and the Scheduled Castes, I was continuing in the government because of the Hindu Code Bill, which was the greatest social reform measure ever undertaken by the Legislature in the country. No law passed by the Indian Legislature in the past or likely to be passed in the future can be compared to it in point of its significance. To leave inequality between class and class, between sex and sex, which is the soul of Hindu Society untouched, and to go on passing legislation relating to economic problems is to make a farce of our Constitution and to build a palace on a dung heap. This is the significance I attached to the Hindu Code. It is for its sake that I stayed on notwithstanding my differences. So if I have committed a wrong it is in the hope of doing some good. My exit from the Cabinet may not be a matter of much concern to anybody in this country. But I must be true to myself and that I can be only by going out."

The Press statement issued by Ambedkar also explained how he had joined the Nehru Cabinet although earlier he had been condemned by Congress leaders as unworthy of association. "I was called by the Prime Minister to join his government and accept the office of Law Minister in his Cabinet. The offer was a great surprise to me for I was in the opposite camp. I was left to speculate as to what could have happened to bring about this change in the attitude of the Prime Minister. I did not know how I could carry on with those who had never been my friends. I had doubts as to whether I could, as a Law Minister, maintain the standard of legal knowledge and acumen which had been maintained by those who had preceded me as Law Ministers of the Government of India. But I kept my doubts at rest and accepted the offer on the ground that I should not deny my cooperation when it was asked for in the building up of our nation. As a result of my being a member of the Viceroy's Executive Council, I knew the Law Ministry to be administratively of no importance. It gave no opportunity for shaping the policy of the government. We used to call it an empty soap box only good for old lawyers to play with. When the Prime Minister made the offer, I told him besides being a lawyer, I was competent to run any administrative department and that in the old Viceroy's Executive Council I held two administrative portfolios, that of Labour and C.P.W.D., where a great deal of planning projects were dealt with by me and would like to have some administrative portfolio. The Prime Minister agreed and said he would give me in addition to Law the Planning Department which, he said, he was intending to create.

"Unfortunately the Planning Department came very late in the day and when it did come I was left out. During my time, there have been many transfers of portfolios from one minister to another. I thought I might be considered for any one of them. But I have always been left out of consideration. Many ministers have been given two or three portfolios. Others like me have been wanting more work. I have not even been considered for holding a portfolio temporarily when a minister in charge has gone abroad for a few days. It is difficult to understand what is the principle underlying the distribution of government work among ministers which the Prime Minister follows. Is it capacity? Is it trust? Is it friendship? Is it pliability? I was not even appointed to be a member of main committees of the Cabinet such as the Foreign Affairs Committee or the Defence Committee. When the Economic Affairs Committee was formed, I expected, in view of the fact that I was primarily a student of Economics and Finance, to be appointed to this Committee. But I was left out. I was appointed to it by the Cabinet, when the Prime Minister had gone to England. But when he returned, in one of his many essays in the reconstruction of the Cabinet, he left me out. In a subsequent reconstruction my name was added to the Committee, but that was as a result of my protest. I have never been a party to the game of power politics inside the Cabinet or the game of snatching portfolios which goes on when there is a vacancy. I believe in service, service in the post which the Prime Minister, who as the head of the Cabinet, thought fit to assign to me. It would have, however, been quite inhuman for me not to have felt that a wrong was being done to me.

"Another matter that made me dissatisfied with the government relates to the treatment accorded to the Backward Classes and the Scheduled Castes. I was very sorry that the Constitution did not embody any safeguards for the Backward Classes. It was left to be done by the Executive Government on the basis of the recommendations of a Commission to be appointed by the President. More than a year has elapsed since we passed the Constitution. But the government has not even thought of appointing the Commission. The year 1946 during which I was out of office, was a year of great anxiety to me and to the leading members of the Scheduled Castes. The British had resiled from the commitments they had made in the matter of constitutional safeguards for the Scheduled Castes and the Scheduled Castes had no knowledge as to what the Constituent Assembly would do in that behalf. In this period of anxiety I had prepared a report on the condition of the Scheduled Castes for submission to the United Nations. But I did not submit it. I felt that it would be better to wait until the Constituent Assembly and the future Parliament was given a chance to deal with the matter. The provisions made in the Constitution for safeguarding the position of the Scheduled Castes were not to my satisfaction. However, I accepted them for what they were worth, hoping that the government will show some determination to make them effective. What is the position of the Scheduled Castes today? So far as I see, it is the same as before. The same old tyranny, the same old oppression, the same old discrimination which existed before, exists now, and perhaps in a worst form. I have been wondering whether there is any other parallel in the world to the condition of the Scheduled Castes in India. I cannot find any.

"Why is no relief granted to the Scheduled Castes? Compare the concern the government shows over safeguarding the Muslims. The Prime Minister's whole time and attention is devoted for the protection of the Muslims. I yield to none, not even to the Prime Minister, in my desire to give the Muslims of India the utmost protection wherever and whenever they stand in need of it. But what I want to know is, are the Muslims the only people who need protection? Are the Scheduled Castes, the Scheduled Tribes and the Indian Christians not in need of protection? What concern has been shown for these communities? I could not contain within myself the indignation I have felt over the neglect of the Scheduled Castes by the government and on one occasion I gave vent to my feelings at a public meetings of the Scheduled Castes. A question was asked from the Home Minister, whether my charge that the Scheduled Castes had not benefited by the rule which guaranteed to them 12½ per cent representation was true. The Home Minister was pleased to say that my charge was baseless. Subsequently for some reason – it may be for satisfying the qualms of his conscience – he, I am informed, sent round a circular to the various departments of the Government of India asking them to report how many Scheduled Caste candidates had been recently recruited in government service. I am informed that most departments said in reply "NIL" or nearly nil. If my information is correct, I need make no commentary on the answer given by the Home Minister.

"From my early childhood I have dedicated myself to the upliftment of the Scheduled Castes among whom I was born. It is not that there were no temptations in my way. If I had considered my own interests, I could have been anything I wanted to be and if I had joined the Congress I would have reached the highest place in that organization. But as I said, I had dedicated myself to the upliftment of the Scheduled Castes and I have followed the adage which says that it is better to be narrow-minded if you wish to be enthusiastic about a cause which you wish to accomplish. You can, therefore, well imagine what pain it has caused me to see that the cause of the Scheduled Castes has been relegated to the limbo of nothing."

Commenting on his resignation, the Times of India wrote: "Bereft of the crown of Manu, Dr Ambedkar nonetheless leaves the government with a considerable record of achievement behind him. The Cabinet is not overburdened with talent, and the departure of this discerning scholar and industrious student of public affairs cannot but dim its limited lustre. Political memories, it is true, are short but in shedding old prejudices Dr Ambedkar showed himself capable of rising to the height of new responsibilities and occasions. India can ill afford to lose the service of this able politician and it would be little short of tragedy, personal and national, if Dr Ambedkar were to relinquish the national stage and relapse into communal politics. A formidable ally, Dr Ambedkar is also a foreman worthy of one's steel. The last few years have seen him harnessing his outstanding abilities to constructive purposes and both the country and his community stand to gain if he continues in that path."

Denial of the trappings of office of a Central government minister, whatever the provocation or justification for it, would make any one sad. But after tendering his resignation from the Nehru government mainly on the ground that the government no longer seemed interested in the passage of the Hindu Code Bill he had drafted, and had been piloting with great enthusiasm in Parliament, the messiah of the Untouchables was not a sadder man. On the contrary he felt himself considerably relieved of pressure for conformity that was upon him as a member of the Nehru's Cabinet. Now he was free to choose any occasion to exhort his followers to gird up their loins and get ready for fighting for their rights. The first opportunity that presented itself for Ambedkar to unburden his mind was a meeting of the Scheduled Castes at Jalandhar in Punjab in the last week of October 1951. Without any let or hindrance he thundered that there was no place for the socially downtrodden in the Congress party dominated by caste Hindus. He clearly stated that Nehru suffered from Muslim mania and there was no place in his heart for the Scheduled Castes.

Free from any official obligation to remain in Delhi for attending Cabinet meetings or discharge other official functions, Ambedkar was now a free bird, travelling up and down the country. A couple of days later, he was in Lucknow, addressing a meeting of the Lucknow University students. Speaking on the occasion he warned the country against the neglect of the downtrodden and plainly said if they were frustrated in their attempts to gain social equality due to the presence of Manuwadis in Indian society, the Scheduled Caste Federation might prefer to go with Communists. This would be a significant development, he said, because of their vast number that would tilt the political balance in the country in favour of Karl Marx's followers.

Reference

1. See second para on p. 1323, Vol. 14, Part II, of Speeches and Writings of Ambedkar Published by Maharashtra Government.

17

Embraces Buddhism

All his life having been at the receiving end of hatred, contempt and discrimination in the Hindu society in which he was born, Ambedkar was greatly frustrated and disgusted. He was so highly educated, well-read and intelligent that he would compel attention of many of the eminent caste Hindus he knew. Yet he could always perceive an underlying reservation about him on the part of all those he came in contact with. His brushes with ill-treatment meted out to him ever since he was a small child until late in life, even when he was being acknowledged as the architect of India's Constitution convinced him that members of the Mahar community to which he belonged, and all others treated as Untouchable, could never get justice so long as they remained Hindus.

If leaders like Mahatma Gandhi wanted to keep Untouchables as part of the Hindu society, it was mainly to inflate the number of Hindus in India so that the community could lay claim to being a majority and thus secure greater representation in legislatures which alone could help them gain power in the parliamentary system which India had adopted after Independence. Even after untouchability was banned under article 17 of the Constitution, Ambedkar was convinced that the Untouchables would never be able to escape the stigma from which they had been suffering for ages. No wonder, he began seriously to mull over their plight and wonder if anything could be done to help them redeem themselves. Maybe, he thought, change of religion could help them gain a semblance of equality with the other members of the Indian society.

For long he considered Sikhism as an alternative religion. He even met prominent leaders of the community. But when he discovered that even this religion had a kind of caste stratification, he dropped the idea of embracing Sikhism. Many Muslim leaders wanted Ambedkar to lead his community into the Islamic fold. But it was plain that the chief motive on their part was also to inflate the number of their community and not any genuine concern for the Untouchables. Since there could be no improvement in their lot even if they embraced Sikhism, Islam or even Christianity, Ambedkar's attention turned towards other possibilities.

A book on Lord Buddha which he had read after passing the matriculation examination had impressed him. The book was presented by a well-wisher, K.A. Keluskar, a scholar and social reformer. Ambedkar started toying with the idea of embracing Buddhism. If turning to Buddhism as a remedy to gain equality in Indian society had not occurred to him earlier, it was mainly because Buddhism, although a dominant religion in several countries in South East Asia, is a religion without many votaries left in India. Of course, he could see Buddhist relics dotting the country and even a great admiration for Ashoka, the greatest Mauryan emperor, who had become a Buddhist after being horrified by the large-scale killings in the Kalinga war. But Buddhism as a religion was not as important as other religions in India.

What really appealed to him about Buddhism was the total absence of inequalities among the votaries of this faith. It was quite unlike the Hindu society which was governed by castes. When he seriously started thinking of Buddhism as the new religion of the Untouchables who had come to regard him as their messiah, Ambedkar first wrote a book on the life of the Buddha. The book titled, "The Buddha And His Dhamma", however, could be published only in 1957, after Ambedkar's death. It came to be regarded as a very authoritative account of the life and teachings of Siddharth Gautama, a prince of the Sakya dynasty, who later became the Buddha, the founder of one of the great religions in the world.

The fascinating story of the Buddha, as told by Ambedkar in his book, starts in Kapilvatsu from the moment he was conceived by Mahamaya, one of the two sisters married to Suddhodana, the Raja of the Republic of Sakya in the north-east corner of India. The child was conceived during the celebration of the annual midsummer festival. Just as Mahamaya lay on the royal bed she fell asleep and had a dream. In the dream a Bodhisattva, whose name was Sumedha, appeared before her, saying: "I have decided to take my last and final birth on this earth. Will you consent to be my mother?" Just when she was about to say, "Yes, with great pleasure", Mahamaya woke up. The following morning, when she confided her dream to Suddhodana, the king became very happy. He sent for eight learned Brahmins who were famous in the art of divination. Told about the dream, the Brahmins said: "Be not anxious, Raja. You will have a son, and if he leads a householder's life he will become a universal monarch. If he leaves his home and goes forth into a homeless state to be a sanyasi, he will become a Buddha, a dispeller of illusions in the world."

After some time, Mahamaya was on the way to her father's house in Devadaha for the delivery of the baby. She was being carried in a golden palanquin by couriers, and just as she was passing through the beautiful Lumbini Grove (on the Indo-Nepal border), she expressed a desire to halt there for a while. When Mahamaya alighted from her palanquin and was going towards the foot of a royal sal tree, a pleasant wind started blowing, swaying the branches in the breeze. One of the bows heaved down sufficiently low. She rose on her toes and caught the bough. Immediately she was lifted up by its upward movement and thus being shaken Mahamaya started having labour pains of childbirth. While she held the branch of the sal tree she delivered a son. That was the child, later named Siddharth born in the year 563 B.C. on the Vaishakha Paurnima day who was to become Buddha.

A great sage named Asita, who dwelt on the Himalayas, heard the gods in the sky shouting the word "Buddha, Buddha" just when the child was born. Asita beheld the gods waving their garments and coursing hither and thither in delight. Surveying with his divine eye the whole Jambudvipa, Asita saw that a boy was born in the house of Suddhodana shining with brilliance, and it was over the birth of that child that the gods were excited. At once, Asita set off to meet Raja Suddhodana and stood at the palace door. He asked the door-keeper to go in and inform the Raja that he had come to see him. Entering the palace, Asita met the Raja and told him: "A son is born to thee, O Raja! Desiring to see him have I come." Suddhodana asked the sage to wait as the baby was asleep. Then Asita said: "Not long, O King, do such great beings sleep. Such good things are by nature wakeful." When the Raja brought the baby for his visitor to see, Asita observed that it was endowed with thirty-two marks of a great man and adorned with eighty minor marks, his body surpassing that of Sakra, Brahma, and his aura surpassing them a hundred thousand-fold.

Asita knew that anyone endowed with the thirty-two marks of a great man, as the infant before him was, had only two careers open to him and no third one. "If he becomes a householder, he will become a universal monarch. But if he goes forth from home to a homeless life, he will become a fully enlightened Buddha." Being sure that the child would not remain a householder, the sage started weeping and shedding tears. When Suddhodana enquired the reason for his sorrow, Asita replied: "O king, I weep not for the sake of the child. There will be no misfortune for him. But I weep for myself. I am old, aged, advanced in years and this boy will without doubt become a Buddha and attain supreme and complete enlightenment and having done so, will turn the supreme wheel of the doctrine that has not been turned before him by any other being in the world; for the weal and happiness of the world will he teach his Doctrine. The religious life, the Doctrine, that he will proclaim will be good in the beginning, good in the middle, good in the end, complete in the letter and the spirit, whole and pure. O Raja! This boy will without doubt obtain supreme, complete enlightenment, and having done so, will take countless beings across the ocean of sorrow and misery to a state of happiness. But I shall not see that Buddha. Hence, O Raja, I weep, and in sadness I sigh deeply, for I shall not be able to reverence him."

Just as he was trying to fathom the full meaning of Asita's prophecy about his son, his wife Mahamaya suddenly fell ill and her illness became very serious. At the christening ceremony on the fifth day of his birth, the child was named Siddharth. Since his clan name was Gautama, he was called Siddharth Gautama. Realising that her end was near, Mahamaya called Suddhodana and her sister Prajapati to her bedside and said: "I am sure that the prophecy made by Asita about my son will come true. My regret is that I will not live to see it fulfilled. My child will soon be motherless. But I am not worried in the least whether after me my child will be carefully nursed, properly looked after and brought up in a manner befitting his future. To you Prajapati, I entrust my child, I have no doubt that you will be to him more than his mother. Now do not be sorry. Permit me to die. God's call has come and His messengers are waiting to take me. So saying, Mahamaya breathed her last. Siddharth was only seven days old when his mother died.

Siddharth grew up in the lap of luxury. He was eight years old when his education started. Those very eight Brahmins whom Suddhodana had invited to interpret Mahamaya's dream, and who had predicted his future, were appointed his first teachers. After they had taught him whatever they knew, Suddhodana sent for Sabbamitta of distinguished descent and of high lineage in the land of Uddika. He was a philologist and grammarian, well-read in the Vedas, Vedanagas and Upanishads. Under him Gautama mastered all the philosophic systems prevalent in his day. Besides this he learned the science of concentration and meditation from one Bhardawaj, a disciple of Alara Kalam, who had his ashram at Kapilvatsu. While everything for the cultivation of the mind was provided, even his education in the military science befitting a Kshatriya was not neglected. For Suddhodana was anxious not to make the mistake of having the mind of his son cultivated at the cost of his manliness. Siddharth was of kindly disposition. He did not like the exploitation of man by man. Though a man of learning, he did not despise manual labour. He belonged to a warrior class and had been taught the use of weapons. But he did not like causing unnecessary injury.

Yashodhara, a Sakya girl known for her beauty, chose to marry Siddharth Gautama at a Swayamvar attended by many young princes. So Siddharth was married when he had just completed his sixteenth year. But Yashodhra's father was not happy, for he felt that Siddharth, though a handsome prince, moved about in the company of saints and sages, preferred loneliness and therefore was not expected to be a successful householder. But he could not do anything since Yashodhara was determined to marry him. While the king was happy to see him married and thus enter the life of a householder the prophecy of the sage Asita continued to haunt him. He did not want his son to take sanyas. In consultation with his family priest Udayin, Suddhodana thought of providing a harem for the prince with very beautiful girls. But even with their brows, their glances, their coquetries, their smiles and their delicate movements the girls of the harem did not feel sure that they would be able to charm the prince.

However, egged on by the priest, they set upon their task to divert the attention of the prince towards sensuous pleasures so that he could forget the saints and the sages. The beautiful women made the prince wander in the woods like an elephant accompanied by a herd of females who looked like Apsaras and who seemed to have descended from the high heaven to seduce Siddharth. Some of them urged by passion, pressed the prince with their full, firm bosoms in gentle collision. Others violently embraced him after pretending to stumble, then leaning on him with their shoulders drooping down. Some with their mouths smelling of spirituous liquor, their lower lips red like copper, whispered sweet nothings in his ears. The nymphs tried all their enticements for several years on the prince. But they could not allure him.

Having lost all hope to get his son interested in the carnal pleasures, Suddhodana managed to get him initiated into the Sakya Sangh, which was a kind of supreme council whose members were committed to safeguard the interests of the Sakyas and to take important decisions concerning the welfare and well-being of the Sakya state. Taking interest in the affairs of the Sangh, Siddharth endeared himself to all, and it seemed that this would prevent the prince from spending his time with saints and sages discussing spiritual matters. When the prince had been a dedicated member of the Sangh for eight years, an event took place that altogether changed his life.

The Sakyas were involved in a dispute with the Koliyas, a neighbouring tribal settlement, over the use of the water of Rohini river which divided the two kingdoms. Every season there were disputes between them over the use of the river water. These disputes often resulted in quarrels and affrays. When Siddharth was twenty-eight, the servants of the Sakyas and the Koliyas clashed as a result of which both sides suffered injuries. The Senapati of the Sakyas called a session of the Sakya Sangh to consider the question of declaring war on the Koliyas. When all other members of the Sakya Sangh favoured war, Siddharth alone opposed it, saying that the dispute should be resolved with negotiations. He argued the Sakyas and the Koliyas were close relations. It was unwise that they should destroy each other.

But the Senapati and others were determined for a showdown with the Koliyas.[1] Since Siddharth was opposing the war, the Sangh took a decision by majority to punish Siddharth for his stand, which the majority of members in the Sangh felt amounted to betraying the Sakya cause. In the circumstances Siddharth had three alternatives to consider: he could join the forces and participate in the war; he could consent to being hanged or exiled; he could allow the members of his family to be condemned to a social boycott and confiscation of their property. Faced with these choices, Siddharth opted for the second and decided to become a Parivrajaka (he who renounces the world) and leave the country. It was a kind of exile for which he could opt under the rules of punishment for those who failed in their loyalty to the Sakya Sangh.

Actually, he was not failing in his loyalty to anybody. All that he wanted was to avoid war over a dispute which could be settled amicably. But Siddharth's decision to become Parivrajaka came like a bolt from the blue to his father Suddhodana and mother Prajapati Gautami. Siddharth told his father that he could not agree to the confiscation of their property for then nothing would have been left for the family. Suddhodana wondered what was the use of any property if his son was not to remain with them. His parents argued that they would also go into exile with him. But he persuaded them not to do any such thing.

When Siddharth informed his wife, Yashodhra, about his decision, he was totally surprised by the courageous stand she took, and instead of weeping over what he had done, she told him that in the circumstances he had no choice. Without betraying any emotion, Yashodhra said: "What else could I have done if I were in your position? I certainly would not have been a party to a war with the Koliyas. Your decision is the right decision. You have my consent and support. I too would have taken Parivrajaka with you. If I do not, it is only because I have to look after our son, Rahula. We must be bold and brave and face the situation. All I wish is, now that you are becoming a Parivrajaka, leaving behind all those who are near and dear to you, you will find a new way of life which would result in the happiness of mankind." Siddharth was greatly impressed by his wife. He realized as never before, what a brave, courageous and noble-minded woman Yashodhara was, and how fortunate he was in having her as his wife, and how fate had put them asunder. He cast a loving look at his son Rahula and left, never to return as a member of the Suddhodana family again.

Siddharth thought of becoming a Parivrajaka at the hands of Bharadwaja who had his Ashram at Kapilvatsu.[2] The next day he set off for the Ashram on his favourite horse Kanthaka accompanied by his servant Channa who walked along. A large number of men and women had already assembled before the Ashram. Many women smitten by his handsome looks yawned as if to swallow him, and fixing their eyes on each other softly sighed. They surrounded him and stood aghast thinking of his decision to renounce the world and move about like a beggar. Much to his surprise, Siddharth found his father Suddhodana and mother Prajapati Gautami already present in the Ashram. Seeing his parents he first went to them and sought their blessings. But they were so choked with emotion that they could hardly say a word. They wept and wept, held him fast and bathed him with their tears. Separating himself with great difficulty, Siddharth handed over his dress and ornaments to the servant accompanying him and had his head shaved, as was required for a Parivrajaka. Having thus prepared himself, Siddharth went to Bharadwaja and asked him to start the religious ceremony to confer on him the vocation of a Parivrajaka.

After the ceremony he was clad in the robes of a mendicant with a begging bowl in his hand. Then he left Kapilavatsu, still followed by a large crowd. He stopped and addressed them, saying:"Brothers and sisters, there is no use of your following me. I have failed to settle the dispute between the Sakyas and

Koliyas. But if you create a public opinion in favour of a settlement you might succeed. Therefore, be so good as to return. Hearing this the crowd started melting away. Suddhodana and Gautami also returned to the palace. People sighed for him saying: "Here was a Sakya blessed with high lineage, noble parentage, possessed of considerable riches, in the bloom of youthful vigour, accomplished in mind and body, brought up in luxury, who fought his kinsmen for the sake of maintaining peace on earth and goodwill towards men. His was an act of supreme sacrifice willingly made. There is no parallel to it in the history of the world. He deserves to be called a Sakya Muni or Sakya Simha." A Sakya maiden, Kisa Gotami, said: "Blessed indeed is the mother, blessed indeed is the father, who has such a son. Bless indeed is the wife who has such a husband."

When Siddharth's parents and his servant Channa returned to the palace without her husband, Yashodhra collapsed in total bewilderment. Although she had permitted him to go, she cried: "How has he abandoned me, his lawful wife? He has left me widowed. I have no longing for the heaven, my one desire was that my beloved may never leave me neither in this world nor the next. Even if I am unworthy to look on my husband's face with its long eyes and bright smile, still is this poor Rahula never to roll about in his father's lap? Alas! The mind of that wise hero is terribly stern, gentle as his beauty seems, it is pitilessly cruel. Who can desert of his own accord such an infant son with his inarticulate talk, one who would charm even an enemy?" Yashodhra wept and wept aloud. Self-possessed though she was by nature, yet in her distress she had lost her fortitude.

Leaving Kapilavatsu, Siddharth headed towards Rajagriha, the capital of the kingdom of Magadha, because it was thought to be the place where great philosophers and leaders of thought had their headquarters. Determined to meet the great sages, he crossed the Ganges, fearing not her rapid flow. Trekking 400 miles from Kapilvatsu to Rajagriha, Siddharth decided to settle down at the foot of the Pandava hill and put up there a small hut made of tree-leaves. As soon as the king of Magadh, Sreniya Bimbisara, heard about his arrival, he sent for Siddharth. The fact that sages had predicted that Siddharth, the prince of the Sakyas, would become a Buddha and lead countless people to a life of enlightenment was well-known in those days. King Bimbisara was a friend of the Sakya dynasty. Trying his best to persuade Siddharth to give up the path of renunciation and make better use of his faculties for the welfare of the vast populace, Bimbisara offered half of his kingdom to Siddharth so that he could become a king again instead of imposing upon himself inevitable hardships by adopting the life of an ascetic. Profusely thanking Bimbisara for his offer and advice, Siddharth declined and chose to search for enlightenment so that he could make people live in peace and not indulge in conflicts which lead to wars. "The conflict between nations is occasional. But the conflict between classes is constant and perpetual. It is this which is the root of all sorrow and suffering in the world. I have to find a solution to this problem of social conflict," said Siddharth to the king.

Soon Siddharth began the search for the sages in Magadh. On his way to meet Arada Kalam, who was thought to be the great master in the art of meditation, he passed the hermitage of Bhrigu and stopped there for a while to see sanyasis in meditation. There for the first time he saw different kinds of penances being practiced by ascetics. Well-versed in the technique of penance, as Bhrigu was, he told Gautama about all the penances and the fruits thereof. "Uncooked food, growing out of water, and roots and fruits – this is the fare of the saints according to the sacred texts. There are different alternatives of penance and different types of food ascetics live on. Some live like the birds on gleaned corn, others graze on grass like the deer, others live on air like the snakes. Many win their nourishment with great effort from stones, others eat corn ground with their own teeth. With their tufts of matted hair continually wet with water, some twice offer oblations to Agni with hymns; others, plunging like fishes into the water, were with their bodies scratched by tortoises. By such penances endured for a time –by the higher they attain heaven, by the lower the world of men, by the path of pain they eventually dwell in happiness – pain, they say, is the root of merit."

Thanking Bhrigu, Siddharth said:" I wish to learn the Sankhya philosophy and train myself in the Samadhi Marga, and see what help it can give me for the solution to my problem. I wish to go to Muni Arada Kalam. "Leaving the Ashram of Bhrigu, Gautama proceeded to Vaishali, where Arada Kalam had his Ashram. Arada Kalam was very happy to see the determination of the former prince of Sakyas to gain knowledge about the Samadhi Marga and he then expounded to Gautama the tenets of what was known as the Sankhya Philosophy. Gaining knowledge about the Dhyana Marga, Gautama practised the technique every day. To gain further knowledge about Samadhis, Gautama went to the Ashram of Uddaka Ramaputta and placed himself under his training. Having gained knowledge about whatever these rishis could teach him, Gautama went to Gaya and set up his hut at Uruvela in the hermitage of Negari, the Royal Seer of Gaya, for practising asceticism. The austerities and self-mortification practised by Gautama were of the severest kind. He visited houses with his begging bowl for food. Sometimes he had but one meal a day, or one every two days and so on up to once every seven days. He went to the extent of having a meal once a fortnight, on a rigid scale of rationing. He lived on wild roots and fruit or on windfalls only.

He plucked out the hair of his head and the hair of his beard, never quitted the upright for the sitting posture, squatted and never rose up, moving only squatting. He lived to torment and torture his body. To such a length did he go that there became accumulated on his body the dirt and filth for several years till it dropped off by itself. He took up his abode in the awesome depths of the forest, depths so awesome that none but the senseless could venture there without his hair standing on end. When the cold season brought chilly wintry nights, he dwelt by night in the open air and in a dark thicket by day. During the last burning month of summer before the rains, he made his dwelling under the baking sun by day and in the stifling thicket by night. When he was living on a single fruit a day, his body was emaciated in the extreme. Gautama went on practising austerities and self-mortification for six years. His body had become so weak that he was quite unable to move. His self-mortification and suffering was so deep now that it was becoming unbearable even for him, Siddharth Gautam, who had become a Parivrajak only to solve the problems of conflict and restore harmony and peace in the world.

"Can mortification of the body be called religion?" Siddharth wondered, because even after six years of penance he had not been able to achieve enlightenment. Then he reasoned: "New light cannot be attained by him who has lost his strength and wearied with hunger, thirst and fatigue; with his mind no longer self-possessed through fatigue. How could he who is not absolutely calm, reach the end which is to be attained by his mind? True calm and self-possession of the mind is properly obtained by the constant satisfaction of the body's wants." Just as he sat under the Banyan tree, a woman named Sujata, who had her wish fulfilled, left before him an offering of food prepared by her in a golden bowl. On the night of the day on which he partook of the food, Gautam had five dreams and when he awoke he interpreted those dreams to mean that he was sure to attain enlightenment. Fortified with hope and determination, he left Uruvela and went along the wide road to Gaya.

There he sat in meditation under a Banyan Tree, looking towards the eastern direction. He said to himself: "Skin, sinew and bone may dry up as they will, my flesh and blood may dry in my body, but without attaining complete enlightenment I will not leave this seat. To feed himself during the period of meditation, Gautama collected enough food to last him for forty days. It took Gautama four weeks of meditation to obtain enlightenment. He reached final enlightenment in four stages. In the first stage he called forth reason and investigation. In the second stage, he added concentration. In the third stage he brought to his aid equanimity and mindfulness. In the last stage, he added purity to equanimity. On the night of the last day of the fourth week light dawned upon him. He realized that there were two problems. Suffering in the world was the first problem and the second problem was how to remove this suffering and make man happy. Thus darkness was dispelled, light arose, ignorance was dispelled and knowledge arose. Before enlightenment Gautama was only a Bodhisattva, a person who is seeking to be a Buddha. And after reaching enlightenment he became the Buddha.

Before the Buddha formulated his Sasana, certain ideas had a firm grip on the minds of the people. They were beliefs in the infallibility of the Vedas, salvation of the soul, efficacy of rites, ceremonies and sacrifices as means of obtaining moksha; belief in Chaturvarnya, in Iswara as the creator of universe and in Brahmana as the principle underlying the universe; belief in Atmana or the soul and belief in Sansara (transmigration of the soul); a strong belief in Karma, i.e., the determination of man's position in present life by deeds done by him in his past life. The Buddha condemned indulgence in speculation as to the whence, whither and what am I? He discarded heresies about the soul and refrained from identifying it with either the body, sensations, volitions and consciousness. He discarded all the nihilistic views which were promulgated by certain religious teachers. He condemned such views as were held by heretics. He discarded the theory that the cosmic progress had a known beginning. He did not believe that a God created man or that he came out of the body of some Bramha. He ignored or denied the existence of the soul.

The Buddha repudiated the fatalistic view of life and other equally foolish ideas that a God predestined as to what should happen to man and the world. He discarded the belief that all deeds committed in some former birth have the potency to produce suffering, making present activity impotent. He did not accept the Karma theory and instead replaced it by a much more scientific view. He replaced transmigration of soul by the doctrine of re-birth and the doctrine of moksha or salvation of the soul by the doctrine of 'Nibbana'. The first distinguishing feature of his teachings lay in the recognition of the mind as the centre of everything. He said that mind is the fount of all the good and evil that arises within and befalls us from without. Whatsoever there is of evil, connected with evil, belonging to evil – that issues from the mind. And whatsoever there is of good, connected with good, belonging to good – it all issues from the mind. If one speaks or acts with bounded mind then affliction follows him as the wheels of the cart follow the feet of the bullocks pulling the cart. The cleaning of the mind is, therefore the essence of religion. He preached the avoidance of all sinful acts. He said real religion lies not in the books of religion but in the observance of the tenets of the religion.

After having attained enlightenment and formulating his views, the Buddha was not sure whether he should go forth and preach his doctrine or he should continue to devote himself to his own perfection. What troubled his mind were thoughts such as these:[3] "Mankind is intent on its selfishness and takes delight and pleasure in it. It is hard for mankind to accept my doctrine of righteousness overriding selfishness. If I were to teach my doctrine, and others did not understand it, or understanding it, did not accept or, accepting it, did not follow it, it would be weariness to others and a vexation to me." Then Brahma Sahampati, knowing what was passing through the Buddha's mind, appeared before him and with clasped hands said: "Thou art Buddha. Thou art the Blessed One who is blessed with the fullest enlightenment. Thou art the Tathagatha (the fully enlightened). How can thou refuse to enlighten the world? How can thou refuse to save erring humanity? Rise up, O hero, victor in battle, O caravan leader, free from the debt of birth, go to the world and not turn away from it." Knowing that there was so much unhappiness in the world, the Buddha realized that it was wrong for him to sit as a sanyasi with folded arms and allow things to remain as they were.

Having decided to preach his doctrine, the Buddha began searching for five persons who had renounced the world just as he had done, and who had met him earlier after he had left Kapilvatsu to launch his search for enlightenment. He found them at the deer park of Isipatana in Sarnath near Varanasi. Seeing the enlightened Buddha, they were deeply impressed by him and became the first to receive his sermon. Buddha's first sermon was very long and has been fully reproduced in Ambedkar's book, *The Buddha and His Dhamma*. Among other things he said: "Only when the self in ye has been conquered that ye are free from lust; ye will then not desire world pleasures and the satisfaction of your natural wants will not defile ye. Let ye eat and drink according to the needs of your body. Sensuality of all kinds is enervating. The sensual man is a slave of his passion. All pleasure-seeking is degrading and vulgar. But I say unto you that to satisfy the needs of life is not an evil: to keep the body in good health is a duty, or otherwise you shall not be able to keep your mind strong and clear and have the lamp of wisdom burning."

The Buddha told them that according to his Dhamma (the eternal law of the cosmos, inherent in the very nature of things) if every person followed (1) the Path of Purity; (2) the Path of Righteousness; and (3) the Path of Virtue, it would bring about the end of all suffering. He told them that the path of virtue meant the observance of the virtues called : (1) Sila (The disposition not to do evil, to be ashamed of doing wrong); (2) Dana (Giving of one's possession, blood and limbs and even one's life for the good of others; (3) Nekkham (Renunciation of the pleasures of the world); (4) Virya (Doing with all your might whatever you have undertaken to do with never a thought of turning back); (5) Khanti (Not to meet hatred by hatred is the essence of it); (6) Succa (It is truth. A person must never tell a lie); (7) Adhithana (Determination to reach your goal); (8) Karuna (Loving kindness to human beings); (9) Maitri (Extending fellow feeling to all, not only to one who is a friend but also to one who is a foe); (10) Upekka (Remaining unmoved by the result and yet engaged in the pursuit of it).

The fact that Siddharth Gautama, handsome young prince of the Sakyas, had renounced the world, leaving his young wife, a small son and his aged parents in pursuit of enlightenment to solve the problems afflicting mankind, was known far and wide. That he had now become the Buddha and started preaching his new religion by remaining a mendicant with a begging bowl in his hand, had created a sensation all over the country. No wonder wherever Buddha went, he attracted large crowds. The number of people willing to embrace his new religion went on increasing. In the Buddha's scheme of things conversion had two meanings. Conversion to the world of Bhikkus called Sangh or conversion of a householder as an Upasaka or lay follower of the

Buddha's Dhamma. An Upasaka remains a householder. A Bhikku becomes a homeless wanderer going around with a begging bowl in his hand and preaching Buddha's message. To become an Upasak, there is no ceremony. But to become a Bhikku, one must shave off his head and undergo a ceremony called Upasampad. All those who wanted to embrace Buddhism were welcome without any regard to their caste or creed. Barbers, scavengers, aristocrats and the rich joining the new faith were all equal without any graded inequality which was the hallmark of the Hindu society governed by Chaturvarnya. So impressed were the people by the Buddha's teachings that there was no stopping of conversions to the new faith. Even the king of Magadha, Seniya Bimbisar, became Buddha's follower.

King Pasenjit of Jetavana Vihara saluted the Buddha when he arrived in his kingdom to spread his message. Welcoming the Buddha, Pasenjit said: "Blessed is my unworthy and obscure kingdom that it has met with so great a fortune. For how can calamities and dangers befall it in the presence of the Lord of the world, the Dharma Raja, the King of Truth." Knowing the tendency of the king's heart, weighed down by avarice and love of pleasure, Buddha seized the opportunity and said: "Even those who have been born in low degree, when they see a virtuous man, feel reverence for him, how much more must an independent king, who by his previous conditions of life has acquired much merit, feel? There is no profit in vexing oneself by austerities, but meditate on Dhamma and weigh the righteous law. The tide of lust is a danger common to all; it carries away the world; he who is involved in its eddies finds no escape. But wisdom is the handy boat, reflection is the rudder. The slogan of religion calls you to the rescue of your self from the assaults of Mara, the enemy. Exhibit true superiority by virtuous conduct and the exercise of reason; meditate deeply on the vanity of earthly things, and understand the fickleness of life."

Buddha practiced what he preached. He not only preached against caste but also admitted the Shudra and the low caste to the rank of a Bhikku who held the same position in Buddhism as the Brahman did in Brahmanism. The Shudras who could not become Brahmins became peers of Brahmins by becoming Bhikkus. A similar change was noticeable in the case of women. Under Buddhism a woman became a free person. Marriage did not make her a slave as marriage under the Buddhist rule was a contract. As a Buddhist a woman could acquire property, she could acquire learning and what was unique, she could become a member of the Buddhist order of Nuns, and reach the same status and dignity as a Brahmin. The elevation of the status of the Shudras and women was so much the result of the gospel of Buddhism that Buddhism came to be called by its enemies as a Shudra religion (i.e. the religion of the low castes).

In the Aryan society women were placed in the same position as the Shudras and in all Aryan literature women and Shudras are spoken of together as persons belonging to the same status. Both of them were denied the right to take Sanyas, as Sanyas was the only way open to salvation. Women and Shudras were beyond salvation. Buddha broke this Aryan rule in the case of women as he did in the case of the Shudras. Just as a Shudra could become a Bhikku so a women could become a nun. This was raising women to the highest status then conceivable in the eyes of the Aryan society. Another issue for which Buddha fought against the leaders of the Aryan Society was the issue of the ethics of teachers and teaching. The Aryan society held the view that learning and education was the privilege of the Brahmins, Kshatriyas and Vaishyas. The Shudras were not entitled to education. They insisted that it would be a danger to the social order of the day if women or any males not twice-born were taught the Vedas. Buddha repudiated this Aryan doctrine.

As regards his own Order, over which alone he had complete control, Buddha ignored completely and absolutely all the advantages or disadvantages arising from birth, occupation and social status and swept away all barriers and disabilities arising from the arbitrary rules of mere birth. One of the most distinguished members of his Order, who was referred to as the chief authority after Gautama himself on the rules of the Order, was Upali, who had formerly been a barber, which was seen as a despised occupation. So Sunita, one of the brethren whose verses are chosen for insertion in the Teragatha, was Pukkus, one of the low tribes. Nanda was a cowherd. The two Panthakas were born out of wedlock, to a girl of good family after intercourse with a slave (so that by the rule laid down in Manu), they were actually outcastes. Kapa was the daughter of a deer- stalker. The percentage of low members of the Order was probably in fair proportion to the percentage of persons belonging to the despised jatis and sippas as compared with the rest of the population.

When kings, courtesans, commoners were becoming the followers of Buddha day after day, his fame spread far and wide. Having heard that the Buddha was residing in Rajagriha, his father, Suddhodana, sent word to him saying: "I wish to see my son before I die. Others have had the benefit of his doctrine, but not his father nor his relatives." The Blessed One consented to the request of his father and set out on his journey to Kapilvatsu. Soon the tidings spread in the Sakya country. Prince Siddharth, who wandered forth from home into homelessness to obtain enlightenment, having attained his purpose, is coming home to Kapilavatsu. This was on the lips of every one. Seeing his son after seven years, Suddhodana rejoiced, but sadness overpowered him when he realized that his son would never agree to be his heir. Seated in front of his father, the Buddha said: "I know that the king's heart is full of love and that for his son's sake he feels deep grief. But let the ties of love that bind you to the son whom you lost, embrace with equal kindness all your fellow-beings, and you will receive in his place a greater one than your son Siddharth; you will receive one who is the teacher of truth, the preacher of righteousness and the bringer of peace, and Nirvana will enter into your heart." The king trembled with joy when he heard the melodious words of his son, and clasping his hands, exclaimed with tears in his eyes: "Wonderful is the change! The overwhelming sorrow has passed away. At first my sorrow was heavy but now I reap the fruit of your great renunciation"

The following morning when the Buddha dressed as a mendicant with a begging bowl in his hand visited the palace of his father, all the members of his family greeted him with great reverence. But Yashodhara, the mother of his son Rahula, was conspicuous by her absence.[4] "Where is Yashodhara?" asked the Blessed One, and on being told that she had refused to come, he rose straightaway and went to her apartment. "I am free," the Blessed one said to his disciples whom he had bidden to accompany him into Yashodhara's chamber, "But Yashodhara, however, is not as yet free. Not having seen me for a long time, she is exceedingly sorrowful. Unless her grief be allowed to run its course her heart will cleave. Should she touch the Tathagata, the Holy One, you must not prevent her. When the Blessed One entered the room Yashodhara was, from the abundance of her affection, like an overflowing vessel, unable to contain herself.

Forgetting that the man whom she loved was Buddha, the Lord of the world, the preacher of Truth, she held him by his feet and wept bitterly. Suddhodana apologized for Yashodhara, saying: "This arises from her deep affection, and is more than a temporary emotion. During the seven years that she had lost her husband, when she heard that Siddharth had shaved his head, she did likewise; when she heard that he had left off the use of perfumes and ornaments, she also refused their use. Like her husband she has eaten at appointed times from an earthen bowl only." Then the Blessed One spoke to Yashodhara, telling her of her great merits and the great courage she showed when he took Parivraja. Her purity, her gentleness, her devotion had been invaluable to him as a Bodhisattva when he aspired to the highest aim of mankind to attain enlightenment. This, then, was her Karma, and it was the result of great merits.

Yashodhra's grief was unspeakable. The glory that surrounded her spiritual inheritance had increased by her noble attitude and had made her a unique person. She dressed her seven-year old son Rahula in all the splendour of a prince and said to him: "This holy man, whose appearance is so glorious that he looks like the Great Brahma, is your father. He possesses great mines of wealth, which I have just seen. Go to him and entreat him to put you in the possession thereof for the son ought to inherit the property of the father. Until then Rahula had always thought that Suddhodana was his father. But when informed by his mother who his father was, Rahula went to the Blessed One while he was taking his repast, and looking up in his face, said without fear and with much affection: "Aren't thou my father?" And standing near him, he added: "O Samana, even your shadow is full of bliss!" When the Blessed One had finished eating, he gave blessings and went away from the palace, but Rahula followed him.

No one prevented the boy, nor did the Blessed One. Then the Blessed One turned to Sariputta, a disciple accompanying him, and said:[5] "My son asks for his inheritance. I cannot give him perishable treasures that will bring cares and sorrows. But I can give him the inheritance of a holy life, which is a treasure that will not perish." Addressing Rahula with earnestness, the Blessed One said: "Gold and silver and jewels have I none. But if you are willing to receive spiritual treasures, and are strong to carry them, to keep them, I have plenty. My spiritual treasure is the path of righteousness. Do you desire to be admitted to the brotherhood of those who devote their life to the culture of the mind seeking for the highest bliss attainable." Rahul replied with firmness: "I do". Thus Buddha's son also became a member of the holy Order his father had founded. When Suddhodana heard that his only grandson like his father had also become a Bhikku, there was no end to his sorrow.

It was not only the tragic and moving life-story of Gautama Buddha that appealed to Ambedkar, it was also his message to the world. There was no caste system in the message he gave. The Hindu society is marked by graded inequality which causes discrimination, tension and hatred. In Buddhism all are equal regardless of the fact that they were formely Shudras, Kshatriyas,Brahmins or Vaishyas. There is no discrimination, no god, no recognition of soul in this religion. Buddhism is the earliest ethical system where man is called upon to have himself governed by himself. Like many other thinkers Ambedkar could see that among the world's religious teachers, Buddha alone had rightly judged the intrinsic greatness of man's capacity to work out his salvation without extraneous aid. If the worth of a truly great man consists in his raising the worth of all mankind who is better entitled to be called truly great than Lord Buddha. In no other religion are the values of knowledge and evil of ignorance so much insisted upon as they are in Buddhism. Buddha's doctrine is the doctrine of righteousness and his aim is to establish the kingdom of righteousness on earth. Ambedkar arrived at these conclusions after an exhaustive study of Buddhist scriptures and the writings of foreign scholars.

If most of his books are well-written and will remain readable for many many years to come, it is only because of the pains he used to take in preparing his manuscripts. It took him almost five years to complete *'Buddha and His Dhamma'*, which is easily one of the finest books he wrote. However, there was no money for its publication. He tried various sources both in India and abroad, but drew a blank. At last in desperation he thought of seeking Prime Minister Jawaharlal Nehru's help and for the purpose wrote him the following letter dated September 14, 1956.

My dear Pandit ji,

I am enclosing herewith two copies of a printed booklet showing the Table of Contents of a book on the "Buddha and His Dhamma" which I have just finished. The book is in the press. From the table of the contents you will see for yourself how exhaustive the work is. The book is expected to be on the market by September 1956. I have spent five years over it. The booklet will speak for the quality of the work.

The cost of printing is very heavy and will come to about Rs 20,000. This is beyond my capacity and I am, therefore, canvassing help from all quarters. I wonder if the Government of India could purchase about 500 copies for distribution among the various libraries and among the many scholars whom it is inviting during the course of this year for the celebration of the Buddha's 2,500 years' anniversary.

I know your interest in Buddhism. That is why I am writing to you. I hope that you will render some help in this matter.

Shri Jawaharlal Nehru, Yours sincerely,
Prime Minister of India, B.R. Ambedkar
New Delhi

But Ambedkar was again in for disappointment. On the very next day, September 15, 1956, Nehru sent the following reply:

My dear Dr Ambedkar,

Your letter of the 14th September.

I rather doubt if it will be possible for us to buy a large number of copies of your book as suggested by you. We had set aside a certain sum for publications on the occasion of the Buddha Jayanti. That sum has been exhausted and, in fact, exceeded. Some proposals for books relating to Buddhism being financed by us had, therefore, to be rejected. I am, however, sending your letter to Dr Radhakrishnan, the Chairman of the Buddha Jayanti Committee.

I might suggest that your book might be on sale in Delhi and elsewhere at the time of the Buddha Jayanti celebrations when many people will come from abroad. It might find a good sale then.

Dr B.R. Ambedkar, M.P., Yours sincerely,
26 Alipur Road, Civil Lines, Jawaharlal Nehru
Delhi.

Ambedkar could see Buddhist way of life is very different from that of the Hindu society governed by social stratifications which divide it into the four castes – Brahmins, Kshatriyas, Vaishyas and Shudras, without any possibility of upward or downward mobility. The Buddha felt that the caste system was a fixed order. Once a Brahmin, always a Brahmin. Once a Kshatriya always a

Kshatriya, once a Vaishya always a Vaishya and once a Shudra always a Shudra. Society was based on status conferred upon an individual by the accident of his birth. Vice, however heinous, was no ground for degrading a man from his status, and virtue, however great, had no value to raise him above it. As such, there was no room for worth nor for growth. Inequality exists in every society. But it was different with Brahmanism. The inequality preached by Brahmins was its official doctrine. Far from producing harmony, graded inequality, the Buddha thought, might produce in society an ascending scale of hatred and a descending scale of contempt. As its class composition was compulsory and arbitrary, it was a society made to order. No wonder, Buddha preferred an open and a free society. .

On a careful review of the rules of Chaturvarnya the Buddha had no difficulty in coming to the conclusion that the philosophic foundations on which the social order was reared by Brahmanism were wrong if not selfish. It did not serve the interests of all, much less did it advance the welfare of all. Indeed, it was deliberately designed to make many serve the interests of the few. In it man was made to serve a class of self-styled supermen. It was calculated to suppress and exploit the weak and to keep them in a state of complete subjugation. The law of Karma as formulated by the Brahmins, thought the Buddha, was intended to sap the spirit of revolt completely. He felt that the basis of the Hindu doctrine of past Karma as the regulator of future life is an iniquitous doctrine. What could have been the purpose of such a doctrine? The only purpose, felt the Buddha, is to enable the state or the society to escape responsibility for the condition of the poor and the lowly. Otherwise such an inhuman and absurd doctrine could never have been invented.

Brahmins maintained that revolt could not alter the state of suffering; for suffering was fixed by one's past Karma as their lot in this life. The Shudras and women - the two classes whose humanity was most mutilated by Brahminism - had no power to rebel against the system. They were denied the right to knowledge with the result that by reason of their enforced ignorance they could not realize what had made their condition so degraded. They could not know that Brahminism had robbed them completely of the significance of their life. Instead of rebelling against Brahminism they had become the devotees and upholders of Brahminism. No wonder the Buddha felt that such injunctions were harsh, and instead of accepting them he decided to opt for a social order which gave one freedom of thought. The Buddha repudiated the thesis of Brahmins that the Vedas are infallible and that their authority could not be questioned. In his opinion, nothing was infallible and nothing could be final. Everything must be open to re-examination and reconsideration. Infallibility of the Vedas means complete denial of freedom of thought. He felt that man must know the truth and the real truth. To him freedom of thought was the most essential thing. And he was sure that freedom of thought was the only way to the discovery of truth. For these reasons the Brahminic philosophy was obnoxious to Buddha.

The Brahminic sacrifices were mostly sacrifices of animals to please their gods. The Buddha condemned them as false sacrifices. He would not allow them even if they were performed with the object of getting salvation for the soul. The opponents of sacrifices used to ridicule the Brahmins by saying: "If one can go to heaven by sacrificing an animal why should not one sacrifice one's own father. That would be quicker way of going to heaven." The theory of sacrifices was repulsive to him. Thanks to the Buddhist influence during the Mauryan period and for quite some time later on, the killing of cows for sacrificial purposes or for food came to an end. While trying to regain their hold on the people who had come under Buddhist influence, Brahmins went a step further and resorted to the deification of the cow. They started preaching that the cow is a holy animal and killing and eating its flesh is a sin. But all this happened because Brahmins wanted to weaken the Buddhist influence.

Disgusted with Chaturvarna and the Brahminic injunctions which kept over sixty million Shudras in perpetual bondage, Ambedkar seriously started thinking that he and his followers should embrace Buddhism. Speaking at the Scheduled Castes Federation Conference at Ramlila Maidan in Agra on March 18, 1956, Ambedkar said:[6] "Unless we change our religion our struggle will not bear fruit. We are suppressed people because we don't have our own religion. The Hindus talk of us as their own. Their motive is just to increase their numerical strength and nothing else. Because of this fact I started the movement in the year 1917 that we are not Hindus and that if we had not been so we would not have remained Untouchables and would have also been Pujaris in temples. It is because of this that I started the temple entry movement in the year 1925. But the main motivation for it was not that we wanted to worship gods. The movement was launched because we wanted to assert our right. If I am a Hindu, I should also have the liberty and the right of worship and become a Pujari in the temple. But it is not so. On March 19, 1927, I started the Mahad Tank Satyagraha in Ratnagiri district to assert the right of Untouchables to take water from the tank. But again, attempts were made to coerce us, drive us away.

"So long as the Shastras of the Hindus exist and the Shankaracharya is in the saddle, they cannot emancipate anybody and their talk to emancipate us is nothing but sham. The religion that I am going to give the Depressed Classes is Buddhism. Everybody should be happy over it. There is no conflict of soul, God or even Gods in it. There is in this religion universal brotherhood, justice, equality and fraternity. All our problems will end only if we embrace Buddhism. Even amongst the depressed classes today, some sections do not have marital relations with each other. The Hindu religion is responsible for all these ills. I tried to stop it, but sad to say, some of our own people opposed me on this point. Unless we embrace Buddhism, caste struggle in our ranks and the middle classes will not come to an end."

Addressing a conference of Mahars, Ambedkar said: "The religion which does not treat you as a human being, which compels the ignorant to remain ignorant and the poor to remain poor is not a religion but a curse. The people who consider themselves holy and us unholy and who consider themselves high and us low, believe that this system of high and low is eternal and that they must always be regarded as holy and high while we must be regarded as unholy and low. As long as we are Hindus, we cannot resist injustice. For it we will require power – manpower, money power and mental power. Presently, we have none. The Hindu religion is based on the concept of castes. The Hinduism talks about how one individual should behave with another, but it does not teach what one individual must do to another one. The religion which wishes to keep one individual knowledgeable while keeping another one ignorant or illiterate, is not a religion but an intrigue to keep the people befooled. The religion which opens the way of acquiring wealth for one individual and teaches others to depend on others for their providence, is not a religion but selfishness. It is only Hinduism which considers one individual so degraded that the others would not even touch him. Why should we stick to a religion which does not value our humanity? Why should we stick to a religion which does not allow us to share even water? Why should we remain stuck to a religion which debars us from a job and insults us at every step.

In a talk on "Why I like Buddhism and how it is useful to the world in its present circumstances" broadcast in May 1956 by the British Broadcasting Corporation, Ambedkar said:" I prefer Buddhism because it gives three principles in combination which no other religion does. Buddhism teaches Prajna (understanding as against superstition and supernaturalism), Karuna (love), and Samata (equality). This is what man wants for a good and happy life. Neither god nor soul can save society. Marxism and Communism have shaken the religious systems of all the countries." He maintained that Buddhism was a complete answer to Marx and Communism and observed: "Buddhist countries that have gone over to Communism do not understand what Communism is. Communism of the Russian type aims at bringing it about by a bloody revolution. The Buddhist communism brings it about by a bloodless revolution. The South-East Asians should beware of jumping into the Russian net. All that is necessary for them is to give political form to Buddha's teaching. Poverty there is and there will always be. Even in Russia there is poverty. But poverty cannot be an excuse for sacrificing human freedom. Once it is realized that Buddhism is a social gospel, its revival would be an everlasting event."

On September 23,1956, he announced that his conversion to Buddhism would take place at Nagpur on the Dassehra Day, October 14, 1956. Consequently, Ambedkar, his wife and his private secretary, Nanak Chand Rattu, left by air on the morning of October 11 and reached Nagpur in the afternoon. Thousands of men, women and children, especially the Mahars, had arrived in Nagpur from the Marathi-speaking areas of Central Provinces and Berar and Bombay by trains and buses. Thousands who could not find or afford transport fare trekked hundreds of miles, shouting slogans: "Bhagwan Buddha Ki Jai, Babasaheb Ki Jai." At a press conference on October 13, when he was asked why he was embracing Buddhism, Ambedkar replied : "Why cannot you ask this question to yourself and to your forefathers as to why I am getting out of the Hindu fold and embracing Buddhism? Why do you want my followers to remain Harijans to enjoy only such benefits as those of reservations? Are the Brahmins prepared to be Untouchables to enjoy these privileges. I had once told Mahatma Gandhi that though I differed with him on the issue of untouchability, when the time comes I will choose only the least harmful way for the country. And this is the greatest benefit I am conferring on the country by embracing Buddhism. Buddhism is part and parcel of Bharatiya culture. I have taken care that my conversion will not harm the tradition of the culture and history of this land."

Wearing a white silk dhoti and a white coat, Ambedkar, his wife, also clad in white sari, and Rattu, arrived in a car at the venue where a vast throng of his followers had already gathered to witness his conversion to Buddhism. The ceremony commenced with a Marathi song, praising Ambedkar. Eighty-three-year old Mahasthaveer Chandramani of Kushinar and four saffron-robbed Bhikkhus, who had especially come from Gorakhpur, administered to Ambedkar and his wife in Pali three Sarans under Buddha, Dhamm and Sangh and the Panchsheel of five precepts of abstention from killing, stealing, telling lies, wrongful sex life and drink. Profusely garlanded by his devotees, Ambedkar then declared: "My social philosophy may be said to be enshrined in three words, liberty, equality and fraternity. Let no one, however, say that I have borrowed my philosophy from the French revolution. I have not. My philosophy has roots in religion and not in political science. I have derived them from Lord Buddha. There is hardly anything that I cannot achieve even while being an Untouchable. There is no other feeling than that of spiritual feeling underlying my religious conversion. Hinduism does not appeal to my conscience. My self-respect cannot assimilate Hinduism.

"By discarding my ancient religion which stood for inequality and oppression today I am reborn. I have no faith in the philosophy of incarnation; and it is wrong and mischievous to say that Buddha was an incarnation of Vishnu. I am no more a devotee of any Hindu god or goddess. I will not perform Shraddha. I will strictly follow the eightfold path of Buddha. Buddhism is a true religion and I will lead a life guided by the three principles of knowledge, right path and compassion. Hinduism believes in God, Buddhism has no God. Hinduism believes in a soul. According to Buddhism there is no soul. Hinduism believes in Chaturvarnya. Buddhism has no place for the caste system.

"It was not true that after the days of Shankaracharya, Buddhism was dead in India. It was going on for years together. In fact, Shankaracharya and his teacher were both Buddhists. Buddhism in its material form had disappeared. I agree. But the main reason for the decline of Buddhism was the invasion of India by the Moslems. Thousands of images were mutilated and destroyed, Viharas were desecrated and millions of Bhikkus were massacred. Terrified by these ghastly events, the Bhikkus fled to the adjoining countries. Some went to Tibet; some went to China; they spread throughout the world But as a spiritual force it continued to survive in India. Man cannot live by bread alone. He has a mind which needs food for thought. Religion instills hope in man and drives him to activity. Hindu religion has watered down the enthusiasm of the down-trodden. And I found it necessary to change my faith and embrace Buddhism. We have to consider ways and means of imparting knowledge of Buddhism to the masses who have accepted His Dhamma and many more will accept it on my word. Bhikkhus should become like Christian missionaries, social workers and social preachers."

But Ambedkar knew that it would not be easy for people, whatever their depth of degradation as Hindus, to answer the call for discarding their religion that had been their sole source of inspiration and survival for over 2,000 years and embrace Buddhism, which he wanted them to do. Consequently, instead of calling upon the vast crowd of about 5 lakh people to change their religion, he delivered a lengthy dissertation of his own thinking and philosophy about why a change of faith is necessary for them, for their very own bid to regain self-respect in society. He dwelt at length on their problems, all due to the fact that they were governed by the Chaturvarnya system and thus consigned to the lowest rung of caste ladder in Hindu society. He said any religion which cramped one's mind to such an extent that one could not even dream of having a better life because of the stranglehold of caste system could never allow them to come up in life and regain equality and respect.

For the lowest cadre devotees of the Manusmriti, there could be no possibility of inspiration for a better tomorrow or a sound mind which could view the problems of life objectively and try to find solutions. He said as part of Hindu society, which is founded on the ideologies of caste-based inequality and injustice, even their capacity to visualize a better future was hampered. "So long as the Untouchables continue to slave under the yoke of Hinduism - a diabolical creed - they can have no hope, no inspiration, no enthusiasm for better life. They might produce no more than a few hundred clerks - poor clerks who will do nothing except filling their bellies. What else can they do? Common masses of the Untouchables will not gain anything. The Scheduled Castes can never feel enthusiastic about anything in life and have to resign to their fate for they cannot derive inspiration from the ideologies prevailing in Hinduism."

"If you excuse me for citing my own experience, I may tell you how I got my education. Owing to the poverty I used to attend school with nothing more than a loin cloth on my body. I could not get water to drink in the school. I had to go without water for many days. My mother instructed me to address the strangers with respect. There was in our family discipline or "vinaya". Accordingly, I used to address the postman as postman mama. There was a lady peon, Maratha by caste, in our school. Even my satchel was Untouchable for her. When thirsty, I was not allowed to touch the tap myself. Untouchability was observed even in Elphinstone College, Bombay, where I was studying. What can be expected in this kind of circumstances. Untouchability cannot be removed by education alone. I once went to see Gandhiji. Gandhiji told me that he believed in Chaturvarnya. What kind of Chaturvarnya, I enquired pointing towards my hand with the little finger in the bottom and thumb on top. What do you mean by the Chaturvarnya? Where does it begin and where does it end, I asked. Gandhiji could not reply in a satisfactory manner. Besides the lack of congenial atmosphere there is also lack of equality among Hindus. This religion and this social order has ruined us. I do not accuse the Hindu religion in vain. This religion cannot save anybody.

"Why has our country lost her freedom time and again? Why have we been subjected to foreign domination so often? It is because this country as a whole never stood against the enemy. It was always a small section of the society, the Kshatriyas, and whoever overpowered it became the victor. This is mainly due to the pernicious caste system of the Hindus. The Second World War was fought in Europe during the period from 1939-1945. The soldiers who were killed in the battles were immediately replaced by fresh recruits. Whereas in our country in the past if all the Kshatriyas were done away with in the battle, there could be no mobilization or recruitment according to the Chaturvarnya since this abominable law stated that Kshatriyas and Kshatriyas alone were entitled to fight. This is what has been happening in the past. This is why our country has been enslaved many times.

"As soon as the wife of a Brahmin woman conceives she thinks of the High Court whether any post of a Judge has fallen vacant but when our woman becomes pregnant, she cannot think of anything better than a sweeper's post under the Municipal committee. This deplorable situation exists only because Hinduism has inculcated this kind of ambitions in the former and the degradation in the latter. No change in our status can be expected if we continue to be slaves of Hinduism. If we have any hope it is by renouncing the Hinduism and following the path of the Buddha. The fundamental principles of Buddhism is equality. There was only one man who raised his voice against the separatism and untouchability and that was Lord Buddha. In the beginning Lord Buddha got only ten or twelve Bhikkus. Out of these, nine or ten were Shudras. This is evident from the autobiographical "gathas" of the Bhikkus entitled 'Thera Gatha' and 'Therigatha'. Their writings bear testimony to the fact that Buddhism is the only religion which does not recognize caste and affords full scope for progress. My political opponents who observed my political activities very keenly say that I am a cunning fox. They say that I want to extract as many concessions for the Scheduled Castes as it is possible to get. On the other hand there are some who wonder as to why I have taken so long to take a decision in regard to the change of religion. The only reply I can give is this that the question of religion is the most difficult and a very serious question. It is a matter of enormous responsibility, really to educate the people in regard to the merits of this religion and to inculcate in the people the habit of behaving according to the principles of Dhamma.

"Some assert that the Untouchables will remain Untouchables no matter what I do in order to emancipate them. Many have suggested that it would not be wise on our part to leave the path that we have been following hitherto for ameliorating our condition. This kind of mischievous talk is likely to cause doubts and fears in the minds of the young as well as the older people belonging to the Scheduled Castes. Therefore I must answer this question. Removal of the doubts and fears will surely strengthen our movement. I would like to say many things on this question. Those who say we shall be left economically weak and backward are actually worried about the despicable occupations like scavenging, flaying and tanning. Their objection pertains to the removal of the dead bodies of animals once Mahars and Chamars stop removing the dead bodies of buffaloes and cows. If they don't do, who will do this? This is what worries them. Mahars and Chamars don't eat carrion was a slogan which was raised by me. Some thirty years ago I launched this movement. This somehow immensely offended our Hindu friends. I asked them: "You take the milk from the cows and buffaloes and when they are dead you expect us to remove the dead bodies. Why? If you carry the dead bodies of your mothers to cremate why do you not carry the dead bodies of your 'mother-cows' yourself?"

After explaining that Hinduism for them was nothing but a bondage of suffering, which made it imperative for them to do all the dirty work so that caste Hindus could live in peace and comfort, Ambedkar called upon those who wanted to embrace Buddhism to stand up. The entire assemblage stood up. He administered the three refuges and five precepts and different pledges to the vast gathering. Thus Ambedkar embraced Buddhism with several lakh followers in a typical Buddhist fashion. The spot where this conversion took place in Nagpur has come to be known as Deeksha Bhoomi. Thanks to large contributions made by his followers, a magnificent monument has been built over the spot where Ambedkar and his followers became Buddhists. On the occasion of his birth anniversarly on April 14 and on the day Ambedkar led his followers to the religion unfolded by the Enlightened Buddha, his followers take out processions. The scenes witnessed in Nagpur, Pune and Mumbai are so heartwarming and exhilarating as were the processions taken out by the Buddha himself from town to town accompanied by the vast number of his followers to preach the Dhamma he propounded to save this world from conflicts, tensions and wars.

At public meetings and functions, and at private gatherings, whenever Ambedkar was asked to expound his philosophy of Buddhism, Ambedkar said Buddha did not accept God as creator of the universe. Why he rejected the doctrine of the existence of God was because nobody has seen God. People only speak of God. God is unknown and unseen. Nobody can prove that God has created the world. The world has evolved and is not created. What advantage can there be in believing in God. It is unprofitable. The Buddha said that a religion based on God is based on speculation. A religion based on God, is, therefore, not worth having. It only ends in creating superstition.

Later, addressing meetings of Untouchables, Ambedkar said: "In your case change of religion is imperative for worldly as well as spiritual ends. Do not care for the opinions of those who foolishly ridicule the idea of your conversion for material ends. Of what avail is the religion that deals with life after death? A rich man's sense may be tickled by this idea in his leisure time. Those who are well-placed and prosperous in this world may pass life in contemplation of life after death. But why should you live under the fold of that religion which has deprived you of honour, money, food or shelter. I tell you, religion is for man and not man for religion. If you want to organize, consolidate and be successful in this world, change this religion. The religion that does not recognize you as human beings, or gives you water to drink, or allows you to enter the temples is not worthy to be called a religion. The religion that forbids you to receive education and comes in the way of your material advancement is not worthy of the appellation "religion".

"The religion that does not teach its followers to show humanity in dealing with its co-religionists is nothing but a display of force. The religion that asks its adherents to suffer the touch of animals but not the touch of human beings is not religion but a mockery. That religion which precludes some classes from education, forbids them to accumulate wealth and to bear arms, is not religion but a mockery. The religion that compels the ignorant to be ignorant and the poor to be poor is not religion but a violation. You must have a firm belief in the sacredness of your goal. Noble is your aim and sublime and glorious is your mission. Blessed are those who are awakened to their duty to those among whom they are born. Glory to those who devote their time, talent and their all to the annihilation of slavery. Glory to those who keep on their struggle for liberation; strive and meet dangers till the down-trodden secure their human rights.

"What is the Hindu religion? Is it a set of principles or is it a code of rules? Now the Hindu religion, as contained in the Vedas and the Smritis is nothing but a mass of sacrificial, societal, political and sanitary rules and regulations, all mixed up. What is called Religion by the Hindus is nothing but a multitude of commands and prohibitions. Religion, in the sense of spiritual principles, truly universal, applicable to all races, to all countries, to all times, is not to be found in them and if it is, it does not form the governing part of a Hindu's life.

That for a Hindu, Dharma means commands and prohibitions is clear from the way the word Dharma is used in the Vedas and the Smritis and understood by the commentators. The word Dharma as used in the Vedas in most cases means religious ordinances or rites. Even Jaimini in his Purva Mimansa defines Dharma as "a desirable goal or result that is indicated by injunctive (Vedic) passages." To put it in plain language, what Hindus call Religion is really Law or at best legalized class-ethics.

"Frankly, I refuse to call this code of ordinances as Religion. The first evil of such a code of ordinances, misrepresented to the people as Religion, is that it ends to deprive moral life of freedom and spontaneity and to reduce it (for the conscientious at any rate) to a more or less anxious and servile conformity to externally imposed rules. Under it, there is no loyalty to ideals, there is only conformity to commands. But the worst evil of this code of ordinances is that the laws it contains must be same yesterday, today and for ever. They are iniquitous in that they are not the same for one class as for another. But iniquity is made perpetual in that they are prescribed to be the same for all generations. The objectionable part of such a scheme is not that they are made by certain persons called prophets or law-givers. The objectionable part is that this code has been invested with the character of finality and fixity. Happiness, notoriously varies with the conditions and circumstances of a person, as well as with the conditions of different people and epochs. That being the case, how can humanity endure this code of eternal laws, without being cramped and without being crippled? I have, therefore, no hesitation in saying such a religion must be destroyed and, I say, there is nothing irreligious in working for the destruction of such a religion. Indeed, I hold that it is your bounden duty to tear the mask, to remove the misrepresentation that is caused by misnaming this law as Religion. This is an essential step for you.

"Once you clear the minds of the people of this misconception and enable them to realize that what they are told as religion is not religion but that it is really law, you will be in a position to urge for its amendment or abolition. So long as people look upon it as religion they will not be ready for a change, because the idea of religion is generally speaking not associated with the idea of change. But the idea of law is associated with the idea of change and when people come to know that what is called religion is really law, old and archaic, they will be ready for a change, for people know and accept that law can be changed."

References

1. See page 26, Vol. 11, which deals with the Buddha and His Dhamma, a book by Ambedkar.
2. See page 32, Vol. 11.
3. See para marked 5, page 111, Vol. 11.
4. See opening line page 166, Vol. 11.
5. See page 167, Vol. 11.
6. See page 73 of the book Last Few Years of Dr. Ambedkar by Nanak Chand Rattu.

18

Bid to Challenge the Congress

After resigning as Law Minister Ambedkar could clearly see that unless he enlarged the scope of his activities he would not be able to challenge the Congress party. He called upon his followers to think in terms of not only their own suffering due to the treatment meted out to them, but also the wider interests of the nation as a whole. All his life he had been struggling for the uplift of the Untouchables. But at some crucial moments in his life some of these Untouchables instead of expressing their gratitude to all that he had done for them, had betrayed him. Although he was a member of the Rajya Sabha (Upper House of India's Parliament), he had a great yearning to become a member of the Lok Sabha (Lower House). But he could never get elected to the Lower House.

Notwithstanding the fact that his relations with Gandhi always remained lukewarm and there was little love lost between him and the leaders of the Congress party, Ambedkar's name had become a household word all over the country. He wrote many scholarly books. He was frequently invited to address conferences in India and in Buddhist countries in Southeast Asia. But this did not bring him any prosperity. Following his resignation from the Nehru government, he was not well off financially. The 26, Alipur Road bungalow, where he shifted after his resignation, had been given to him by a well-wisher. His financial position was so bad that once even his power supply was disconnected for non-payment of the electricity bill. Nanak Chand Rattu, a Central government employee belonging to an Untouchable caste, typed the manuscripts of his books, attended to his correspondence, and very often accompanied him on various missions, and remained loyal to Ambedkar out of sheer devotion and admiration for him until he breathed his last.

All his life he was known as a leader of the Scheduled Castes. But because of the enormous fame and respect he had won, first as an architect of the Indian Constitution and later by drafting the Hindu Code Bill whose provisions among other things were intended to improve the lot of women to whatever class or community they belonged, leaders of several parties got interested in having an electoral alliance with him for the elections due to be held under the new Constitution in 1952. The Peasants and Workers Party of Maharashtra and the Praja Socialist Party led by Jayaprakash Narain and Ashoka Mehta initiated talks with Ambedkar's Scheduled Castes Federation for fighting the elections together. Ambedkar opted for the Praja Socialist Party as the other organization, although strong in Maharashtra, was reputed to be a communal body.

Addressing election meetings, he impressed upon the audience the need for an opposition party to keep the Congress in check. Underlining the importance of having a strong Opposition in Parliament, Ambedkar said that no party should have unlimited powers. It would be bad for the people if a stage came where the government could not be questioned by the Opposition. In parliamentary democracy, one very important thing is that the people should know the other side if there are two sides to a question. No democracy could do without it. In Britain and Canada, the leader of the Opposition was paid salary by the government. They regarded the Opposition as an essential component of democracy. People of these countries believed that the Opposition should be as much alive and active as the government. The government could suppress facts, resort to only one-sided propaganda for its own sake. But in these two countries the people were not going to be taken for a ride as the Opposition was fairly strong and well-entrenched there.

He said: "Numbers do not matter. It is the quality of Opposition that counts. I appeal to the people to elect the best if not all of the candidates fielded by the Socialist Party and the Scheduled Castes Federation, both of which are fighting the elections together in alliance, so that the opposition is of good quality. Free and fair election is one of the pillars on which parliamentary democracy rested. This is necessary for the transfer of power from one section of the community to the other in a peaceful manner and without bloodshed. In the olden times, if a king died, there was at least one murder in the palace. Revolutions used to take place resulting in murders before the new king would take the reigns of his country. This had been the history of India.

"No such thing happened under the parliamentary system of government which we have adopted. But elections must be completely free. People must be left to themselves to choose those whom they want to send to the legislatures. Now the question arises as to whether there is any desire on the part of the party in power to permit any opposition to be created. Unfortunately, the Congress does not want any Opposition. The Congress is attempting to gather people of sundry views under one canopy. But is this a desirable trend in the political life of the country? I appeal to the Congress to allow other political parties to function for the sake of parliamentary system of democracy and not to do anything to suppress the Opposition."

Ambedkar said when he had become a Cabinet minister in the Central Government in 1947 certain interested parties always keen to run him down had charged him with joining the Congress. "The fact is," he said, "I am like a stone. Wherever I may be, in whatever company I may find myself, I would never lose my separate identity. If anybody asks for cooperation I would gladly give it for a worthy cause. I cooperated with the Congress government for four years with all my might. But I never merged myself with the Congress. I would gladly help and cooperate with those who are sincere in their words and deeds for the interests of the Scheduled Castes. But I would never help those who are sweet-tongued but whose intentions and deeds are contrary to the interests of our people."

Expressing his unhappiness over the reluctance of the Scheduled Caste members of the Congress party to do or say anything for drawing attention to the plight of their brethren, Ambedkar's said that the 30 Congress Harijan members in the Constituent Assembly were nothing but stooges of the ruling party.[1] "Has any one of them," he said "asked any question, submitted any resolution, or proposed a bill? A foreigner reviewing the work of Parliament might very well draw the conclusion from the silence of these Harijan members that the Untouchables have no grievance of any sort. Really speaking, the contrary is the truth. We must have such representatives in the legislatures who will voice our grievances. But these Congress-appointed representatives of the Untouchables keep mum in spite of the harrowing tales of persecution and want of necessary amenities. We cannot have any position in the country's politics if we will have no strong organization. We should not wait till ten years to have a strong united organization. That organization must be built from now on. We will be doomed to a Manusmriti Raj after ten years if by that time we do not make any organization firm-footed. The organization is there, our Federation is our organization. We have only to strengthen it. The tree has been planted. We have only to water and nurture it. Our Federation has been accepted as an All India Organization by the Election Commission. We have not to build a new house; the house is there. We have only to maintain it tip-top. If we do not strive to do it from now on, the time will come when we will have to wander here and there and be subjected to all sorts of persecution."

Later addressing a session of the "Political Scientists' Parliament" of the D.A.V. College in Jalandhar, Ambedkar[2] said:" During my whole life, I have been, so to say, a wanderer from subject to subject, from profession to profession. I began my career as a Professor of Political Economics in the Government Commerce College in Bombay in 1919 after my return from England. But I soon felt that Government service was no good for a man who wishes to do public service. A government servant is bound by the rules of discipline. He is hampered at every stage in his work of public service. I then went back to England and qualified for Bar. After my return I practiced for a short period and then accepted the post of the Principal of the Government College in Bombay. I came back to the profession of teaching. I worked as the Principal of the Law College for five years. Then the 1935 Government of India Act came into being which brought the popular legislatures in existence for the first time. I then thought of taking a jump into the politics and I left the service and took to politics. Since then I have been alternatively doing legal practice and service for the public. Legal practice and public service are thus alternating currents in my life; and I do not know on which current my life would end — whether A.C. or D.C. "

He said there were innumerable references in Indian literature to prove that Parliamentary System of Government was not unknown in India. "Parliamentary government means negation of hereditary rule. No person can claim to be a hereditary ruler. Whosoever wants to rule must be elected by the people from time to time. He must obtain approval of the people. Hereditary rule has no sanction in the parliamentary system. Any law, any measure applicable to the people must be based on the advice of the people chosen by the people. No single individual can presume the authority that he knows every thing, that he can make the law and carry the government. The laws are to be made by the representatives of the people in the Parliament. There are pillars on which the Parliamentary System of Government rests. These pillars are the fulcrums on which this mechanism works. And these two pillars are (1) an Opposition and (2) free and fair elections.

"For the last 20 to 30 years we acclimatized to one single political party. We have nearly forgotten the necessity and importance of Opposition for the fair working of the Parliamentary Democracy. We are continuously told that Opposition is an evil. Here again we are forgetting what the past history has to teach us. You know that there were 'Nibandhkaras' to interpret the Vedas and Smritis. They used to begin their comments on Slokas and Sutras by stating first the "Purva-Paksha", the one side of the question. They used to follow it up by giving "Uttar Paksha", the other side. By this they wanted to show us that the question raised was not an easy question; it is a question where there is dispute, discussion and doubt. Then they used to give what they termed as Adhi Karan in which they used to criticise both the Pakshas. Finally, they gave the "Siddhant" – which was their own decision. Herefrom we can find that all our ancient teachers believed in two-party system of government".

After touring Punjab and other places, Ambedkar returned to Bombay on November 18. He was accorded a hero's welcome when he disembarked from the train at Victoria Terminus. He was taken in a procession to Siddharth College which used to be his residence during his stay in Bombay those days. Soon after his arrival he plunged into the task of organizing electoral campaigns of candidates he was fielding so that he could get his supporters elected in large numbers. Addressing an election meeting at Chowpatty, he declared that Subhas Bose's Indian National Army, which he had organized abroad to fight the colonial rulers of India, was mainly responsible for unnerving the British and hastening their decision to quit India in 1947. The Congress Party made tall claims for liberating India. Of course, Gandhi did a lot in the political awakening of the country. But what really clinched the issue for India's Independence was INA, stressed Ambedkar. He addressed a series of meetings under the joint auspices of the Scheduled Castes Federation and the Socialist Party in the Sir Cowasji Jehangir Hall, where he attacked the Nehru-led Congress party and charged the government with spawning corruption. Irritated by the Congress allegation that he was behaving like a mad man in attacking the Congress without any justification, Ambedkar left no stone unturned to demolish this propaganda aimed at tarnishing his reputation. .

But Ambedkar was up against heavy odds. Charges and counter-charges were traded thick and fast. The Congress went to the extent of saying that he was accommodated in the Union Cabinet mainly due to the efforts of the local Congress chief, S.K. Patil. This was very irritating to Ambedkar. He attacked Nehru's foreign policy, his handling of the Kashmir problem and at one meeting where the audience was mostly Muslims, he said they could not get justice under the Congress rule; there should be provision of separate electorates for them. He also charged the government servants with helping the party in power by influencing the electorate in its favour. He said even big business houses were trying to play a dirty role in the political life of the country. "It is a very dangerous thing," he said and added," If moneyed people try to influence the elections by contributing liberally to the election fund of any political party, what will result? "If the party which they have supported financially came to power, they naturally try to extract concessions for themselves either by seeking modification of the legislation to suit their ends or influence the party to legislate in such a manner as would be beneficial to their interests."

Actually, in contrast with the Congress Party, the Scheduled Castes Federation was a relatively very weak organization lacking both manpower and resources to fight the elections. Founded by the All India Depressed Classes Conference held in Nagpur from July 17 to July 20, 1942, for long the Federation was the central political organization of the depressed classes. Dr Ambedkar appealed to the Scheduled Castes and the depressed classes all over India to come together under the flag of the Federation. For quite some time, the Federation under Ambedkar's guidance remained an effective organization for focusing attention on the problems of the Untouchables. As the leader of the Federation which had a vast membership and widespread support, Ambedkar became a thorn in the side of the Congress. No wonder secret moves were made to sow seeds of intrigue and dissensions within the Federation. Due to his failing health, Ambedkar could not do much towards infusing a fighting spirit amongst his party cadres .

The elections to the Parliament and the State assemblies were held in January, 1952. Ambedkar, who had contested the reserved seat from Bombay north, was defeated, getting 1,23, 576 votes as against the Congress winner, Kajrolkar, who secured 1,37,950 votes. The Federation and the Socialist Party alliance was swept away. After the results were announced, Ambedkar said: "How the overwhelming support of the public of Bombay could have been belied so grossly is really a matter for inquiry by the Election Commission." Even the Socialist leader Jayprakash Narain was at a loss to understand how Ambedkar was defeated, because from all accounts there was an overwhelming support for the Socialist Party which was backing Ambedkar in Bombay.

His defeat in the 1952 parliamentary elections which he had contested from a constituency in Bombay greatly demoralized him. The number of Untouchables in this constituency was fairly large. Besides, he was being supported by the Socialist Party. Yet he had been beaten by the Congress. Elections to the Upper House or the Council of States were due to take place shortly. The Bombay state had 17 seats in this chamber. Kamalakant Chitre, who was the local head of the Scheduled Castes Federation, started lobbying with other parties in the Bombay state assembly for support for Ambedkar so that he could get elected as one of the 17 members representing the Bombay state in the Upper House in Parliament.

Ambedkar's wife, Dr Savita Ambedkar, also became active in mobilizing support for her husband. She wrote a letter to Kamalakant Chitre asking him to spare no effort to get her husband elected. She said although he was not keeping good health, his illness was more of psychic nature; he was deeply interested in politics. "In fact politics was like tonic for his mental and physical health." I dare say he will start running about if (and a very big if though) he were to be the Prime Minister of India. That is his desire and let us pray some day it will be fulfilled," she stated. Further, she said, "he had planned so many things to be done when returned to Parliament which was the only place for a man of his stature."

Feeling confident that Chitre and his other admirers in the Bombay legislature would not let him down, Ambedkar filed his nomination for one of the 17 seats. The elections were held towards the end of March, 1952 and Ambedkar was elected. Following his election he went to Delhi to attend the session of the Council of States in the last week of May, 1952. Without pulling his punches, he made a scathing attack on the defence budget. He said it was the greatest stumbling block in the development of the country. "The army is eating into the vitals of the funds that are necessary for the well-being of the country. If the defence budget were reduced by Rs 50 crore, it would do much good to the country. If India's foreign policy is aimed at maintenance of friendship and peace, who are the enemies against whom it is necessary to maintain a huge army?" he asked. Due to the enormous respect he had come to command from a section of the intelligentsia in the country, Ambedkar's utterances could not be dismissed lightly. However, the latest volley of criticism he had fired against the government's functioning with regard to defence and foreign policy estranged him further from Congress leaders. But he was not bothered and continued to plough his lonely furrow, worried only about the plight of the Scheduled Castes who had come to regard him as their saviour.

When there was little to cheer him in India, Ambedkar was informed that the Columbia University had decided to confer on him the honorary degree of Doctor of Laws at its convocation on June 5, 1952.[3] The Columbia University had accepted his thesis on "The National Dividend of India - A Historical and Analytical Study.", in provincial decentralization of imperial finance, which he had submitted in 1917 and for which he was awarded a doctorate degree. Now the University had decided to confer on him an honorary degree in recognition of the great work done by him in drafting Independent India's Constitution and also in recognition of the fact that he was a social reformer and a valiant upholder of human rights. He was to have received the degree earlier from General Eisenhower, the American hero of the World War II, who was President of the University. But on account of his preoccupation with Cabinet responsibilities, and, later electioneering, he could not go to New York. Although it was a great honour for an Indian to receive an honorary doctorate degree from a foreign university, the government did not take any notice. Only Dr. S. Radhakrishnan, Vice-President, sent a congratulatory message on May 26, saying: " I am very pleased to see in the papers that the Columbia University is conferring on you the honorary degree of Doctor of Laws. It is an appropriate recognition for your great work in regard to our Constitution. My warmest congratulations." In his reply Ambedkar said:" I am very glad to say that there are at least some in India who are prepared to appreciate the honour that is being done to me."

The Columbia University was reluctant to confer on Ambedkar such an outstanding honour in absentia. Even though his reputation had spread far and wide, Ambedkar could not manage enough foreign exchange for his wife, Dr Savita Ambedkar, to travel with him to America. The news that Ambedkar was being honoured by an important American University made his friends in Bombay, when he returned there from New Delhi on May 31, felicitate him at a dinner at the Cricket Club of India. The party was organized by Dr V. S. Patankar, and K.V. Chitre, Principal and Registrar respectively of Siddharth College, which was founded by Ambedkar. Speaking on the occasion Dr Patankar said that it was an irony that none of the Indian Universities had yet thought of honouring Ambedkar, the Chief Architect of the Indian Constitution. He added it was a pity that even Bombay University of which Ambedkar was a student had not taken any initiative in honouring him. Replying to the felicitations Ambedkar said that although he was credited with vitriolic temperament and on many occasions had conflicts with those in authority, he would never say anything harsh about India. He had never been a traitor and always held the interests of the country at heart. Even at the Round Table Conference, nobody could charge him with lack of patriotism, although his principle concern was the welfare of the downtrodden.

Ambedkar flew from Bombay to New York by a T.W.A. flight on June 1, 1952, to receive from a leading American University the highest honour ever bestowed on an Indian. The Columbia University Convocation was held on June 5. Honouring Ambedkar at its 198th Commencement function, the citation hailed Ambedkar "as a framer of the Constitution, Member of the Cabinet and of the Council of States, one of India's leading citizens, a great social reformer and a valiant upholder of human rights." Ambedkar received the degree at the function attended by a large crowd and where 6,848 graduates of Columbia's 17 schools and colleges also received their degrees. Lester B. Pearson, Canadian Secretary of State for Foreign Affairs and M. Daniel Mornet, the noted French historian, were also among those who like Ambedkar received honorary degrees from the University.

Following his return to Bombay, in a press interview he gave on June 15, Ambedkar again attacked the handling of external affairs by the government. He said public opinion in the U.S.A. was favourably inclined towards Pakistan mainly because Pakistan seemed to take great care in the selection of her foreign representatives and ambassadors while India sent abroad inexperienced persons who lacked diplomatic finesse. Also, he stated that American Professors visiting India had a poor opinion about the kind of education being imparted here. They felt that education here did not equip students for research and independent thinking. Despite the fact that Ambedkar by his outspoken utterances was becoming increasingly controversial, hated by the Congress and treated with contempt by the caste Hindus, Osmania University decided to confer on him the degree of Doctor of Literature honoris causa on January 12, 1953, in recognition of his eminent position and scholarly attainments. It was this university alone in the whole of India which had thought of according recognition to the sterling merits of a man who was easily one of the most brilliant Indians of his time.

But instead of resting content with academic honours and appreciation of his role as a messiah of the down-trodden, Ambedkar again plunged into politics, losing no opportunity to express his thoughts though not with a view to glorifying himself, but only with the burning desire of seeing India regain pride of place in the comity of nations. Poor Ambedkar! Not only the alienating attitude of the Nehru-led Central government was worrying him, he was also distressed by the increasing infighting and polarities which had started surfacing even in the All India Scheduled Castes Federation, which he had founded in July 1942 in the hope that this organization would act as a bulwark against the domination of the Untouchables by caste Hindus. The Federation had become a hot-bed of intrigue, group rivalries and growing indiscipline.

Unveiling the portrait of L.R. Gokhale at the Poona District Law Library in December, 1952, Ambedkar gave a talk on the "Conditions Precedent for the Successful Working of Democracy." He said: "Democracy is always changing its form, that it is not always the same in the same country and that it undergoes changes in purpose. The purpose of modern democracy is not so much to put a curb on an autocratic king but to bring about the welfare of the people. Democracy was a form and a method of governance whereby revolutionary changes in the economic and social life of the people are brought about without bloodshed. First thing required for the successful working of Democracy is that there must be no glaring inequalities and there must be neither an oppressed class nor a suppressed class. The second thing required was the existence of opposition to show whether the Government is going wrong. The third thing is equality before law and in administration. The fourth is the observance of constitutional morality. The fifth point is that the successful working of Democracy requires the functioning of moral order in society; for moral order is taken for granted in Democracy. The last thing is the requirement of public conscience."

His thought-provoking speech remained the subject of discussion for many days in newspapers and intellectual circles. Sometime later, addressing a rally of 50,000 people under the auspices of the Belgaum district Branch of the Scheduled Castes Federation, Ambedkar sounded a note of warning to the ruling party. Without making any bones about it, he said, if the lot of Scheduled Castes was not improved by the next election, the Scheduled Castes Federation would be forced to take stern measures which might create serious problems for the government. Anarchy might follow such a development. He recalled what had happened after the French and Russian revolutions and warned: "I shall wait for another couple of years or even till the next elections, for the alleviation of the misery of my people and if a new deal is not forthcoming through negotiations, I shall be forced to take recourse to stern measures."

Speaking on the Andhra State Bill in Parliament on September 2, 1953, Ambedkar attacked the government for its vacillating policy on the formation of linguistic states. He said it was wrong to believe that the linguistic reorganization of the country would lead to the disintegration of India. He strongly criticized the government for failing to provide in the Bill safeguards for the rights of the Scheduled Castes against the tyranny, oppression and communalism of the majority. When he said that no provision had been made in the Constitution for investing the Governors of the States with powers for the protection of the interests of minorities, Ambedkar stirred a hornets' nest. There were serious interruptions, some members laying the blame on Ambedkar's door by saying that he was the architect of the Constitution, others saying equally forcefully that anomalies in the Constitution should be set right now. One member taunted Ambedkar that he had himself defended the Constitution. The home minister added fuel to the fire by saying that Ambedkar had no right to criticize the Constitution for he himself had drafted it.

Unable to control his rage, Ambedkar burst out: "Sir, my friends tell me that I made the Constitution. But I am quite prepared to say that I shall be the first person to burn it out. I do not want it. It does not suit anybody. But whatever that may be, if our people want to carry on, they must remember that there are majorities and there are minorities; and they simply cannot ignore the minorities by saying, Oh, no, to recognize you is to harm democracy. I should say that the greatest harm will come by injuring the minorities. I fear sometimes that if the minorities are treated in the way in which they are being treated in our Bombay State - I do not want to be parochial, I do not know what will ultimately happen - I do not even like to call myself a Maharashtrian; I am fond of Hindi, but the only trouble is that Hindi-speaking people are enemies of Hindi."

All those who heard Ambedkar were really taken aback, because the acknowledged architect of the Constitution had made a virulent attack on the document he had himself defended so strongly earlier. Later on giving the reason for his attack on the Constitution, and even saying that he would be the first person to burn it, Ambedkar said: "The reason why I said so was this. We built a temple for a god to come in and reside, but before the god could be installed, if the devil had taken possession of it, what else could we do except destroy the temple? We did not intend that it should be occupied by the Asuras. We intended it to be occupied by the Devas. That is the reason why I said I would rather burn it."

Ambedkar's outburst against the Government ultimately succeeded in having some effect. In the last week of December 1953, the Government published a Bill entitled "The Untouchability (Offences) Act, 1953" and later introduced it in Parliament in March, 1954. The Bill prescribed for all those practicing Untouchability, punishments including jail, fine, forfeiture of the license for a trade, profession or employment, extending its jurisdiction, over citizens who were not Hindus. All the parties represented in the House or outside welcomed the introduction of the Bill. Dr Ambedkar himself felt much relieved of the anxiety and worry about the plight of the Scheduled Castes, and while speaking in the House made some suggestions to the government to make its provisions more stringent so that Untouchability could be dealt with effectively wherever it raised its ugly head.

But Ambedkar's failing health started ringing alarm bells. Kamlakant V. Chitre, who was personal secretary to Ambedkar for nearly 30 years, and several other close friends and admirers of Ambedkar got worried, seeing no improvement in the condition of their beloved leader. But they could not do anything because his wife would not allow him to be treated by any other doctor except Malvanker and herself. In February 1954, when Dr Ambedkar was on a visit to Bombay, one of his old friends, Mr Nair, who was one of the directors of the company publishing the Free Press Journal, took him to his bungalow in Juhu. Chitre and a couple of his well-wishers from the Scheduled Castes Federation met him at Nair's bungalow on February 12 and requested him to allow them to arrange to get him examined by a board of medical experts in Bombay. But Ambedkar's wife who was also present when this proposal was made opposed the move and started weeping loudly. When she was away from them for a while, Ambedkar expressed his helplessness, saying that he could not agree to anything without the consent of his wife. One of his friends said they would arrange for the whole expenditure to be incurred on his examination by a panel of outstanding doctors. But before this proposal could come through, his wife prevailed upon Ambedkar to go to Lonavala, a tourist resort near Pune. Later, she managed to persuade Ambedkar to dismiss Chitre, his son, Vasant, and several other fellows associated with the Siddharth College.

In order to wipe out the memory of his defeat in the 1952 Lok Sabha election and rehabilitate himself in the Lower House, he was always on the lookout for some announcement of by-election so that he could again contest. One such opportunity came in Nagpur where a by-election was to be held in a reserve Bhandara constituency in 1954. The number of the people belonging to his own Mahar caste in this constituency was fairly large. Therefore, he felt confident of winning the seat. In the last week of April 1954, Ambedkar came down to Nagpur to file his nomination. While campaigning he made a frontal attack on the government and the leadership of Nehru. He said Nehru's foreign policy had made India a friendless country, the government had bungled the Kashmir issue and had sheltered men who were dishonest. He was of the view that India was encircled by a kind of the United States of Islam on one side and Russia and China on the other, conspiring for the conquest of Asia in order to bring it under Communism. "If you want to be effective, then you must have guns and not mere soft speech. You must make up your mind. Do you want Parliamentary Government for you are trying to protect it against the attacks? If you do not want it, let us join with Russia and China tomorrow and make friends with them" repeated Ambedkar at his election meetings. Calling upon the electorate to vote for him, he said it was the duty of the people to replace a government which could not solve any problem. But even while the campaigning was going on, Ambedkar started receiving from his staunch supporters alarming reports which caused him a great deal of anxiety. The Congress had fielded against him an obscure backward caste nominee who was not even well-known in the constituency. But the Congress campaign managers obviously under instructions form their high command descended on the constituency with money bags to turn the tables against Ambedkar. They started bribing the local leaders to win over their sympathy for the Congress nominee in the fray. With money power they succeeded in winning over a Mahar sub-caste, called Manwar, and made it switch support to the Congress.

But Ambedkar and his supporters did not give up the battle as most members of this sub-caste were turning up in large numbers at meetings being addressed by him. However, the election proved that their presence at Ambedkar's meetings was nothing but sham. Even in a reserve constituency where most of the electorates belonged to his own Mahar caste, Ambedkar was defeated by the Congress nominee by a margin of over 8,000 votes. Nothing could be more disappointing for Ambedkar than the outcome of this election. He was in Rangoon, attending a Maha Bodhi conference when the election results were announced. He was totally heartbroken. But he had a premonition of his defeat. Before flying to Rangoon, he had written to his trusted colleague, K.V. Chitre: "Reports from other sources reaching here speak of my being eliminated in the by-election. This is not impossible, and I am quite prepared for it."

The defeat did not dishearten him. He took to task all those who had deserted the Scheduled Castes Federation and called upon those remaining in the Federation to work whole-heartedly. He said: "We suffer defeats because we are true to our principles and we are not out for sale. Nor will we shift from one party to another. If the Federation is liked by nobody, it is necessary to understand why. The Federation is disliked because it is a body of warriors out to fight. And what is the Federation fighting for? In the words of the Buddha, they are fighting for lofty virtue, for high endeavour, for sublime wisdom. But let not the dislike for the Federation discourage or unnerve the Federation. It should go on fighting without compromising with evil."

Analyzing the causes of his failure to win election despite his great popularity, Ambedkar could see that compared with the Congress, the All India Scheduled Castes Federation, which was a powerful organization for long after he had founded it, was now a weak body. It had become a hot-bed of intrigue, disruptive forces, group rivalries, growing indiscipline and insubordination. He was shocked to learn that things had come to such a pass that attempts were even being made to cause a cleavage between the Mahars and non-Mahar members of this body. There was no doubt that some of the problems cropping up in the federation were due to the machinations of the local Congress leaders who could seldom hide their jealousy of Ambedkar's popularity. Ambedkar's unbridled criticism of Nehru's policies only acted as a spur to some Congress leaders to run him down and cause him humiliation by any means.

Anguished Ambedkar wrote to Dadasaheb Gaikwad, who was acting as his chief lieutenant in the Federation, saying : " You must by now learn to take responsibility which after my death will undoubtedly be yours. I cannot remain a titular head of the Federation. For in that condition I get all the blame for the bad deeds by others which I am unable to check due to my inability to move about. I told you about your brother after receiving many complaints against him. Yet you insist he is innocent. I have been told that at Buddha Jayanti celebration held at Sholapur you condemned my move for conversion to Buddhism. You are reported to have said that Buddha was a Buddhu (fool) and people should think before they accept my proposal."

However, having become a political animal he was often at the receiving end of barbs of contempt and hatred aimed at him by caste Hindus. But he did not allow any opportunity to attack the government slip out of his hands whatever the state of his health. Speaking on the report of the Commissioner for Scheduled Castes and Scheduled Tribes in the Rajya Sabha on September 6, 1954, Ambedkar made a scathing attack on the government's policy towards the Untouchables and the attitude of the caste Hindus. He said if the government lacked sufficient resources to provide for the uplift of the Scheduled Castes, there should be no hesitation for the re-imposition of salt tax and the creation of the Gandhi Trust Fund. The fund could be utilized for the rehabilitation of the Scheduled Castes from slums to cleaner and better-maintained colonies. Also, Ambedkar charged the Prime Minister not only with apathy towards the Untouchables but also strong anti-Untouchable bias.

He said: "The Scheduled Castes are subjected to all sorts of tyrannies, oppressions and maltreatment at the hands of the villagers in the midst of whom they live. They are economically so subservient to, so dominated by the caste Hindus, that it is quite impossible for them to come forward to challenge the very people on whom they depend for their economic livelihood. They have neither the economic independence against their oppressors nor have they got the means to prosecute them. Ninety per cent of the police are drawn from the caste Hindus. Only a very small percentage being recruited from the Scheduled Castes for the posts of police sepoys. There are no officers amongst them. The result is that the upper grade policemen are in league with the caste Hindus. More often they refuse to record the complaints of the Scheduled Castes in their station diary when they go to the Thana, even though the offence may be cognizable. They throw them out, turn them out and tell them to go away.

"They do not record the complaint and, secondly, if they do, they probably would conduct the investigation in such a slipshod manner that ultimately the case collapses. In Rajasthan thirty Scheduled Caste people were shot down by the so-called dacoits. The real fact is that the Rajput and the high caste Hindus do not like the Scheduled Castes in Rajasthan to enjoy what are called fundamental rights which give them equality of status with the other Hindus. In order to terrorize them and to make them nervous, in the matter of exercising these fundamental rights, the high caste Hindus have organized themselves into a band of dacoits and they go on shooting the Chamars, who are trying to exercise and derive the benefit of the fundamental rights. Police parties have been sent there in order to give protection to them. But my information is that the police are in league with the dacoits.

"I ask the Home Minister whether the breaches of the law which are being reported and witnessed by Scheduled Castes or other people are not breaches of the fundamental law and the fundamental rights? Are not fundamental rights part of the Constitution? If you are allowing a large mass of bullies and hooligans to trample upon the fundamental rights are you not bringing the Constitution to contempt? Is it not your duty to create a special department either within the home ministry itself or separately for this purpose? The United

States has got a Judicial Department, the duty and the function of which is to see that the Constitution and the Federal laws are respected. I think it is high time that the Home Minister realized that if the Constitution is to function, if it is to be the law of the land, if all people are to recognize it, his duty is to see that it is enforced, and the only way in which he can enforce it is to take upon himself the duty of enforcing it and not leave it to even the State governments who can never do it, not even to the police who has no desire to do it, and not even to the Scheduled Castes who have no means to do it.

" In this country you find two nations - a ruling nation and a subject nation. The backward classes are all subject people. They have no authority in any place. None whatever. They have no place in Administration - they have no place in the Executive and the Executive and the Administration is entirely monopolized by the higher classes. They are monopolizing it by reason of the fact that they have been able to get the highest education. Why not examine all the Secretaries of Government departments. The son and daughter of every Secretary in the Government is to be found in Cambridge or Oxford. Twice and thrice they have made journeys in order to lodge their children there because they have the amplest means. The backward class man's son cannot get even primary education. This sort of revolution in the two different classes is going on for centuries - it is an intolerable business because we cannot allow one class to rule for ever. For some time they must see that the other classes also become educationally qualified in order that they too may hold the reins of government. We are not going to be subject people all the time. If you really want to unify the people, to bring all the people on level, then it is not enough that you should get the highest education and others should get the lowest and not even the lowest. It is from that point of view that you must introduce the system of foreign education. I struggled to get some quota from the government and asked to put the responsibility for university education upon the provinces. Personally for myself I think a sober man who is an ignoramus is not to be preferred to a man who is educated and who drinks a bit. I prefer the latter."

Ambedkar said that Nehru was against organizing even a conference of Harijans who were in the Congress party. The Congress propaganda for removal of Untouchability was a farce. He also drew the attention of the House to how C. Rajagopalachari, who had a knack of giving a pious look to an impious act, had abolished the system of sending Scheduled Castes students to foreign lands when he became the Education Minister in the Central Government. Ambedkar said Untouchability could not be eradicated unless a minimum sentence of imprisonment was provided. He said government should have sought to modify a number of state laws which were discriminatory against the Scheduled Castes and which prevented the Scheduled Castes and the lower classes from having permanent homes.

He denounced the government's eagerness to go in for the amendment of the Constitution, "every Saturday". He said there was no mandate from the people for doing so. The Constitution, he stressed, was only four years and some months old; but within that period it had been amended twice. He said he did not know of any Constitution in the world which had been amended so rapidly and so rashly. He wanted the Government to realize the essential difference between the Constitution and the law. They should treat the Constitution respectfully, urged Ambedkar, obviously trying to make amends for the criticism of the Constitution he himself had made in the House earlier. Surprisingly, Ambedkar's latest observations on the Constitution came in for high praise in editorials carried by several newspapers.

Worried as he always was about the problems of the Scheduled Castes, Ambedkar now really had no time to look into the problems of the Federation he had founded with high hopes. Depression caused by his failure to win the election even after an alliance with the Socialist Party was compounded by his failing health. His visits to Bombay for health reasons became more frequent from October, 1950. Actually now for over ten years Ambedkar had not been keeping good health. Partly, this was due to the enormous strain on him caused by extensive reading and writing, which had been a sort of passion all his life. He suffered from appendicitis, high blood pressure and even diabetes. His eyesight was also failing. This made him all the more sad and depressed.

That the Scheduled Castes Federation was really in a mess was clear from what P.N. Rajabhoj, general secretary of the Federation, wrote to Ambedkar. Calling upon Ambedkar to take serious note of the growing indiscipline in the party, he stated:[4] "Unfortunately, I cannot have access to you as I used to have in the former days. I make bold to say that since your marriage to Dr Savita Ambedkar you have not been allowed to interact with many sincere workers of the party. I consider it my duty to say so even at the cost of inviting your wrath. I write this with a bleeding heart. All these years I have done everything with the idea of serving you. I would have exposed many of the workers of the Federation who have tried to use the Federation for their own selfish ends. But I do not wish to wash the dirty linen in public."

It was of course true that Ambedkar's wife did not allow everybody to see him. In a book she wrote after Ambedkar's death, she justified her decision to keep a check on visitors because he was not keeping well. She said because of her great concern for her husband's health, she could not help keeping an eye on all those who would come to meet him. But this had turned all those who were not allowed to see Ambedkar against her. Preoccupied with his reading and writing, Ambedkar seldom came to know as to who had come to see him and sent away without any courtesy. However, one K. Krishnamurthy, a South Indian Brahmin, who was a great admirer of Ambedkar came to meet him with a French lady doctor who having heard of the deteriorating condition of Ambedkar felt confident that she could cure him. He said he was very much interested in Ambedkar's welfare for according to his astrological and spiritual reading if some urgent measures were not taken for his treatment, he would be doomed. On Saturday, March 17, 1956, when Savita was out for marketing, his private secretary, Rattu, permitted him to meet Ambedkar.

Ambedkar was impressed by Krishnamurthy's anxiety about his health and agreed to try the treatment of Madame Bastien, the French doctor, who he said could come and see him on the following day. Krishnamurthy and Madame Bastien turned up at the appointed time on the following day. She had a detailed discussion with Ambedkar over the causes of his ailments and the course of her treatment which was a process of irradiation of cosmic energy on his physical body in order to tone up the degenerated tissues of his legs and spine. She said plenty of energy was available in ether and if it was drawn in to the body's specific area, it could cure all diseased cells. While they were engaged in this discussion, Mrs Ambedkar returned from her marketing foray and seeing the French doctor chatting with her husband, she was furious. She called Rattu out and took him to task for allowing Krishnmurthy and Madame Bastien in. The visitors could sense Mrs Ambedkar's reaction to their presence and therefore soon took their leave, promising to come on the following day to start the treatment.

But when they came up again, they were not allowed to meet Ambedkar and asked to get out of the bungalow. Krishnamurthy and the French lady tried to meet Ambedkar three to four times again, but they were prevented from doing so by Savita, if she was at home, or by servants under her strict instructions if she was out. Krishnamurthy wrote a couple of letters to Ambedkar to draw his attention to the fact that his wife was not allowing them to see him. But these letters were intercepted by Savita and Ambedkar never came to know what had happened to Krishnamurthy and the lady doctor he had brought for his treatment. One of the three letters Krishnamurthy wrote to Ambedkar was dated March 22, 1956, but which was suppressed by his wife was as follows:

> Respected Doctor Sahib,
>
> Pardon me for intrusion into your precious time. On March 17, when Mr Bharadwaj and I met you, you had agreed to have yourself examined by a spiritual doctor and following this meeting we brought to you the Specialist, Madame Bastien of France, to get you examined and prescribe necessary course of treatment. Madame Bastein had a long discussion with you over the course of the treatment and the causes for your present ailment. As you agreed to try this treatment, we wanted to meet you again on the 19th. But unfortunately, we (Madame Bastien and myself) were told by your Personal Assistant (Nanak Chand), as your Mrs does not like the method of treatment and as she does not want any woman to come there (to your bungalow) and do anything with Dr Sahib, we were not advised to attend on you. Madame Bastien felt hurt at these words. In fact, it was her conclusion even at her first visit that the concentrated evil spirit around you is nothing but your Mrs. But we refrained from making this known to you as this may obstruct our anxiety to get you cured.

I tried in vain to visit your bungalow along with Mr Ujagar Ram of the Delhi Scheduled Castes Welfare Association. I had prolonged discussion with your father-in-law, who happened to be there, about the efficacy of such a course of treatment which costs nothing and which does not involve any oral or paraenetical administration of medicines. Though your father-in-law was quite convinced, he was afraid of his own daughter (your wife) in opening the subject with her. He told me categorically that she did not want any one else other than her family doctor to treat you.

Yesterday, the 21st March, I tried again to contact you in person and request you to continue the treatment at least for a few weeks and if you find it giving you some relief, you may continue it further. But your Mrs who saw both Ujagar Ram and myself sitting in the verandah awaiting an interview with you, told Mr Nanak Chand that we should not be allowed to sit there and should be asked to clear off the bungalow. She even added, insolently, that we had come there as the "agents" of the French woman who was attempting to seduce my husband and rob his property. I felt extremely wounded to hear such words. I have had no intention excepting to get you cured and thereby ensure your services to the people of India. If this is a crime I would gladly plead guilty.

I am now fully convinced and I concur with Madame Bastien, that if at all anybody is to be held responsible for your premature disability - and God forbid, your death - it will be only due to your own indifference to face reality — that is your Mrs who is the enemy of your welfare. You are a thousand times more intelligent than me. You have had a very wide experience in life. But, I am sorry to say — and I may be excused for my unpalatable words - that you are completely ignorant of the reality of the vicious forces around you. If we are fortunate—which I doubt very much — you will realize the gravity of the situation early, break off the shackles that chain you to be under advice of your Mrs and undertake the course of treatment suggested by Madame Bastien.

Yours sincerely,

K. Krishnamurthy

However, Ambedkar did make inquiries about her, but he was not told the truth. He was dissatisfied and agitated at the vague reply given to him, sensing something wrong. But he could not do anything except shouting at his wife one day that when she and Dr Malvankar had failed to cure him, why were not other doctors being allowed to treat him. Frustrated, Ambedkar had expressed many times his dissatisfaction with the joint medical treatment which Dr Malvankar and his own wife were giving him as he did not find any improvement in his health, although these two doctors had been treating him since 1946. Sometimes, Ambedkar was so irritated by the very presence of Dr Malvankar that he did not hesitate even hurling abuses at him. But Dr Malvankar did not take it all lying down and instead retorted in the same vein, saying he was there only because he had been summoned from Bombay. Following heated exchanges between the doctor and his patient, the doctor would depart in a huff. But again, Savita managed to keep her husband in check and after some time made him call Dr Malvankar for consultation.

Ambedkar became sadder on account of his failing eyesight. He said: "In the event of losing my eyesight, life would not be worth living, as I would no longer be able to read and write and accomplish the monumental task of writing my books." With his deteriorating health he desperately tried to get medicines from practitioners of Ayurveda and homeopathy but they failed to bring about any improvement. His doctor wife always insisted that he should remain under the treatment of Dr Malvankar, even if he had to be summoned from Bombay. Sometimes, she would send away other doctors brought for consultation by his friends and well-wishers. By January, 1955 he had become so weak, he could not perform routine tasks like taking bath or even a walk, getting in or out of his car, putting on his clothes and shoes without someone's help. At times, he would lie in bed with no appetite for eating anything and had to be persuaded to take something.

However, seeing the dominance of the Congress party in Parliament, Ambedkar had come to realize that there should be a powerful and strong opposition party to act as a peoples' watchdog. The imminent disintegration of the Federation made Ambedkar look to other alternatives to build a powerful opposition party in the country. He, therefore, came out with the idea of dissolving the Federation altogether and forming another political party to be named the Republican Party of India (RPI) whose membership would be open to all who accepted its three guiding principles viz. liberty, equality and fraternity. The RPI's objective was to rally all the Scheduled Castes, Tribes, Backward Classes and Buddhists besides Muslims under the banner of the Party to offer a credible challenge to the Congress. Ambedkar hoped that once the RPI was launched its image will improve with its dedicated, devoted and determined workers. With the passage of time leaders belonging to other minority communities would also join and mount the campaign for equality, justice and fair play in the country. No wonder, he enthusiastically prepared papers, encapsulating the philosophy and aims and objects of the proposed party, which he hoped would serve as the main Opposition party in the country.

Some of his followers called on him on December 2, 1956, just four days before he passed away, and apprised him with the destructive role of a few of the office –bearers of the Scheduled Castes Federation. They said they were in league with the Congress only to sabotage the Federation. Ambedkar patiently listened to them and then asked them not to get frustrated for he was fully aware of what was happening in the Federation. He said they should await his announcement regarding the formation of a new organization, the Republican Party of India, which would have a wider network of members and supporters. He said he had been working hard on the formation of the new party. Some of them gave him petitions for the redressal of their grievances. After meeting them he retired to his drawing room and asked one of his attendants to play his favourite Buddhist songs on the radiogram. In fact, whatever solace and comfort he could draw in the last few days of his life was from Buddhist songs which he had come to like very much.

With a view to giving shape to the proposed Republican Party of India, Ambedkar, despite his ill health, wrote letters to several political leaders like Dr Rammanohar Lohia, Ashok Mehta, Jaiyprakash Narayan, Acharya P.K. Atre and S.M. Joshi.[5] Dr Lohia welcomed Ambedkar's move and favoured the merger of the Socialist Party with the proposed Republican Party of India, as he thought this would be a befitting reply and challenge to the Congress. M.R. Chowdhury, a Muslim leader from Calcutta and his associates, convinced of the sagacious leadership, unwavering determination, clear vision and excellent qualities of head and heart of Ambedkar, felt confident that Muslims could look forward to succour under his leadership. On July 8, 1956, Chowdhury wrote to Ambedkar, saying: "The Scheduled Castes and other classes that total about 11 crore and together constitute the biggest cross-section of the masses are receiving a very raw deal at the hands of our administrators and are living at the mercy of the handful of caste oppressors. As the accredited leader of these castes and classes, you know better than any one of us how these unfortunate millions are groaning under the weight of political hostage."

On October 1, 1956, Dr Lohia informed Ambedkar that he was looking forward to meet him as early as possible.[6] "I only," Dr Lohia said," wish to emphasize the utter intellectual collapse that has overtaken our country, I hope only temporarily, and how necessary it is for a man like you to speak unreservedly." In an interview to the Press on October 13, 1956, on the eve of his conversion to Buddhism, Ambedkar revealed that his plans for the formation of the Republican Party of India had sufficiently progressed and the party would be formed before the general elections due to take place in 1957. He said the party would be broad-based and open to all who subscribed to its principles. The proposed Republican Party of India, at its formative stage, was gaining all-round support, leaders of many big and small parties hailed it and congratulated Ambedkar for initiating the move to challenge the Congress. But the entire exercise collapsed with Ambedkar's death on December 6, 1956. The RPI was formed but it could never get the dynamic leadership of Ambedkar and after some time went into oblivion.

References

1. See third para of the LFY of Dr. Ambedkar by Rattu.
2. See second para of 79 of the LFY of Dr. Ambedkar by Rattu.
3. See page 34 of the LFY of Dr. Ambedkar by Rattu.
4. See first para page 40 of the LFY of Dr. Ambedkar by Rattu.
5. See last para on page 48 of the LFY of Dr. Ambedkar book by Rattu.
6. See the opening para on page 52 of the LFY of Dr. Ambedkar by Rattu.

19

Titan Passes Away

Ambedkar was now nearing 65. For the past 10 years his health had been deteriorating. On medical advice he had his teeth extracted in the hope that this would bring about improvement. But what to talk of improvement, the new dentures caused him more pain. As he had trouble in breathing, an oxygen cylinder was installed in his house. He had been a teetotaller all his life. Yet on the advice of his doctor wife he had started taking sips of brandy in winter and some beer in summer with evening meals. In winter his body was given warmth by a heating apparatus. Sometimes he was also given an electric bath. That he was becoming very weak was kept a secret, known only to his wife and Dr Malvankar who had been treating him for a decade now. His private secretary, Nanak Chand Rattu, and some close associates also were aware of it. But so much was their dedication to Ambedkar that instead of spreading the news of his illness, they prayed day and night that Babasaheb should get well.

Western type of food to which he had been accustomed during his stay abroad was tried, but the attempt was given up as he did not like it. The medicines prescribed by his physician did not improve his condition. On the contrary, he started losing weight and looked gloomy and shrunken. He had become so weak that sometimes he could not even shave himself and had to ask Rattu to do it. Although he was using a staff to move about, he could not on his own walk even to his bathroom. While performing routine tasks like bathing or even walking he needed somebody's help. The change of climate did not help him either. Despite all this he would get engrossed in reading books brought from his library and lying on the table in front of him. Or he would start writing, dictating to Rattu chapters of the books he was planning to finish soon.

Although he had sacrificed everything to pull Untouchables out of the morass of hatred and contempt, the Untouchables, whether they were in his home state of Maharashtra or in any other state in India, had not succeeded in achieving equality or shedding the stigma of being born as low caste. The caste Hindus dominated society, whether they were in politics, administration, or privately engaged in their own businesses. The overpowering sense of the failure of his lifelong mission to bring about some change in the lot of the Untouchables made him more miserable. Ambedkar really did not know why his efforts had borne no fruit. Utter sense of failure of his life to achieve his goals on the one hand and his deteriorating health on the other added to his woes. He could not distrust his wife who always wanted him to be treated by Dr Malvankar despite the fact that all the treatment he had given him so far had failed to bring about any improvement in his condition. His wife not only wanted to supervise his treatment but also oversee that only those persons whom she could trust were in the orbit of his activities.

On a Saturday in March, 1956, he had asked his private secretary Rattu to come early the next morning. But when Rattu came as instructed on Sunday, he was surprised to find Ambedkar seated on the same table, writing on papers, just as he was doing the previous night when Rattu had left. Throughout the night Ambedkar had kept writing without taking any rest. He was still engrossed in his work and did not lift his head to see who had entered his room. To draw his attention, Rattu displaced some books on his table. Ambedkar raised his head and asked him in surprise why he had not gone home. When Rattu said he had spent the Saturday night home and it was now Sunday morning, Ambedkar realized he had been working long. "I thought you were still here and not gone home. I did not know that the day had dawned. I kept writing and did not move," said Ambedkar, pushing his writing table.

Unless he was preoccupied with something else or meeting visitors at home, or was unable to move about because of pain in his joints, Ambedkar maintained his daily schedule of visiting Parliament especially when the agenda included subjects on which he wanted to express his views. On May 1, 1956, he made a fighting speech on linguistic problems in the Rajya Sabha and strongly opposed the move to declare Bombay a Union Territory. In a talk on the Prospects of Democracy in India, recorded by the Voice of America, Ambedkar said, democracy could not be equated either with a Republican or a Parliamentary Government. "A democracy," he observed, "is a mode of associated living. The roots of democracy are to be searched in the social relationship, in terms of the associated life between the people who form the society. The Indian society is based on castes which are exclusive. Unfortunately, the voting and fielding of candidates is also guided by caste considerations. The caste-system is a descending scale of contempt and is the root cause of inequalities in Indian society. If you give education to the lower strata of the Indian society, which is interested in breaking social barriers, the caste-system will be blown up. At the moment the indiscriminate help given to education by the Indian Government and the American Foundations is going to strengthen the caste-system. Giving education to those who want to blow up the caste-system will improve the prospect of democracy in India and put democracy in safer hands."

By June, 1956, Ambedkar's condition had worsened to such an extent that his legs could not bear the weight of his body. His eyesight was failing. All this made him more desperate in seeking remedies for his ailments. He tried to get medicine and herbs suggested by his well-wishers. Some of the medicines were not allowed by his doctor wife. Sometimes he was provoked by his wife's attitude and started shouting: "Why should you object to others giving treatment to me, when your doctors could not cure me for these eight years?" In fits of anger he would decline to take his meal or medicine. And in such situations the help of his private secretary Rattu or some devotee who was on hand was sought to cajole him to take something. Having failed to fulfil his mission in life, he was sad at heart and sometimes, sitting alone, overcome by fits of despondency, started weeping like a child, much to the astonishment of his wife and servants in the house.

Ambedkar decided to attend the World Buddhist Conference at Kathmandu in Nepal in November 1956, as all his close associates wanted him to go there. Dr Malvankar, the physician in charge of his health, was summoned from Bombay to accompany him to Kathmandu. King Mahendra of Nepal inaugurated the conference in the Singha Darbar Gallery Hall on the afternoon of November 15, 1956. Invited to speak, Ambedkar said he had come to attend the conference only to declare that he found Buddhism as the greatest of all religions, as it was not merely a religion but a great social doctrine. On November 20 Ambedkar was requested to speak on "Ahimsa in Buddhism." But the majority of delegates pressed him to speak on Buddha and Karl Marx. Bowing to the clamour of delegates, Ambedkar chose Buddha and Karl Marx for his speech.

Ambedkar expressed concern over the fate of youngsters in Buddhist countries who looked upon Karl Marx as the only prophet for worship. He said the goal of Buddha and Karl Marx was the same. According to Marx, private property was the root cause of sorrow. Buddha also wanted to abolish Dukkha (sorrow), and the expression sorrow figured in the Buddhist literature in the sense of property. Buddha said that everything was impermanent. The Bhikkus were not allowed to own private property. Buddha did not lay the foundation of his religion on God or soul. So Buddha would not stand in the way of abolition of private property, if the principle of the denial of private property was applied to society. But Buddha and Marx differed over the means to achieve their goal. Communism adopted violent methods to abolish private property. Buddhism adopted non-violent means to achieve it. Marx's method gave quick results. Buddha's method though tedious was the surest way. The world could not be reformed except by the reformation of the mind of man and the mind of the world. There was no trouble once the mind was converted. Marxism was based on force. If the dictatorship in Russia failed, there would be a bloody warfare among the Russian people for appropriating the property of the state. The Buddhist system was a democratic system, whereas the Communist system was based on dictatorship. Therefore the Buddhist method was the safest and soundest. The Buddhist monks should follow methods adopted by Christian missionaries to propagate Buddha's teachings.

While returning from Nepal, Ambedkar visited Benaras Hindu University and the Kashi Vidyapith and made speeches in his usual challenging vein. It was clear from his speeches that he wanted to do for Buddhism what Shankaracharya had done for Hinduism. Ambedkar said that if the Brahma pervaded all, as asserted by Shankaracharya, a Brahmin and an Untouchable were equal. But Shankara did not apply the doctrine to social organizations and kept the discussion only on a Vedantic level. Had he applied it on a social level and preached social equality, his proposition would have been profound and worth consideration, notwithstanding his erroneous belief that the world was an illusion. Interestingly, Ambedkar asked the students whether they would follow Hindu scriptures which supported the graded inequality propounded by the Purusha Sukta and give religious sanction to social inequality or whether they would stand by the principle – liberty, equality and fraternity – preached by Buddhist scriptures. Ambedkar's speeches did not lead to conversion, but made many intellectuals ponder over what Hinduism stood for.

On his return to New Delhi on November 30, Ambedkar was tired and depressed. Although he remained preoccupied with his own thoughts, he was not indifferent to the plight of people around him. The first enquiry he had made on return from Nepal was about his pet dog, which had been admitted to hospital for treatment of some ailment He felt little better on the following day and in the evening visited the Buddhist Art Gallery on Mathura Road. When a close admirer asked him why Buddha's statues from different countries differed in features, he replied for 600 years after his death, there was no picture or statue of Buddha. Someone then made a Buddha statute according to his own imagination. In all Buddhist countries statues were made in accordance with the standard of beauty and style prevailing in those countries then.

On the night of December 3, he asked Rattu to escort him to the rooms behind his residence for he wanted to enquire about the health of his gardener who had not been keeping well for some time. Seeing his master inside his hutment, the gardener was overwhelmed.[1] He sighed, sobbed and said: "Bhagwan himself has blessed me with a visit. But sir, there is no hope for my life. What would happen to my wife, if I die." Consoling him Ambedkar said: "Stop crying, everybody is going to die some day or the other. I am also to die some day like any other person. Take courage. I will be sending you some medicine and you will be all right."

Ambedkar's last visit to Parliament was on December 4. He had a casual discussion with friends in the lobby and although weak his reflexes were normal. No one could say that he was going to breathe his last in two days. He had drawn up a programme to visit Bombay on December 16, 1956, for conversion of his followers to Buddhism. He made enquiries about the train reservations but later decided that in view of his weakness he would not be able to withstand a long train journey. Therefore, he decided to fly to Bombay on December 14. In the afternoon of December 5, Mrs Ambedkar left home at half past one to do some shopping with her guest, Dr Malvankar, without informing her husband who was already asleep after taking his lunch. A couple of hours later Ambedkar rang the bell two or three times, but no one responded. He enquired about his wife, and when informed that she had gone out with Dr Malvankar, he felt upset. The cook switched on the light and helped him go to the bathroom. A little later, Ambedkar again rang the bell for his wife to come. But since she had not yet returned, Ambedkar was very angry.

When she got back he started shouting at her as he had never done before. "Where have you been for such a long time?" He asked and unleashing a barrage of expletives on her, said: "You have cars at your disposal. You wander away and have lost interest in me. Remember if something happens to me, my people will not spare you." He went on hurling fire and brimstone on her. No amount of explanations she gave for her absence could satisfy him. Coming out of the room with moist eyes, she did not know how to handle the situation. She asked Rattu to go in and pacify him. It took him some time to calm down. But following this outburst in the house, her brother and two other persons, who were staying as guests, and who were to go to Bombay with the Ambedkars on December 14, felt rather uneasy and left the same day by the evening train. Even Dr Malvankar, who had been asked earlier to stay on, flew back to Bombay by the night plane.

On December, 5, when he was reclining on an easy chair in the lawn, a large number of his followers carrying party flags and raising slogans, "Baba Saheb Zindabad" tried to enter the bungalow, but they were prevented by the gateman. Ambedkar intervened and allowed them to come in and meet him. Soon after exchanging greetings and touching his feet, they departed leaving Ambedkar smug and satisfied with his life. Their visit was followed by one Bhagat Aminchand, President, Harijan League, Delhi. Ambedkar knew that the League had been floated by the Congress and Aminchand himself was one of those of his followers who had deserted him and jumped on the Congress bandwagon. After exchanging greetings and usual pleasantries, Aminchand was frank enough to tell Ambedkar that the more he attacked the Congress, the more he and others of his ilk benefited. Aminchand said that even for issuing a small statement as a rejoinder to his usual outbursts against the ruling party, they were rewarded. He said: "Sir, the more you abuse and speak ill of the Congress Party, the more we are benefited, cared and looked after. So much so that we need not run after anybody even for minor gains. These come to us in plenty without our asking. With your blessings, we are thriving and flourishing in all walks of life."

Ambedkar peered at him through his glasses, from top to bottom, from left to right, and then spluttered into what was probably his loudest laugh ever heard by anybody. "All right," he said, "goaded by your conscience, go your own way, enjoy the benefit you derive for Ambedkar-baiting from the Congress party and the Hindus. But do not also forget to be grateful to your benefactors, the bread-givers. Behave like a dog, who while relishing the leftovers thrown to him from a distance never forgets the kindness of his master and would wag his tail in gratitude."[2] Hiding his smile, Aminchand, stood with folded hands after listening to what Ambedkar had said, touched his feet again and left. Commenting on Aminchand's visit, Ambedkar said: "Just see, to what level these people have gone down. There is nothing like a sense of human dignity and self-respect left in them except feeding their stomachs with the morsels of food thrown before them and to praise and sing the songs of the ruling party. But for these blacklegs, who are bartering the rights and interests of the community for their petty gains, we would have won the battle for our political emancipation long ago."

In accordance with an appointment he had given, a delegation of Jain leaders came to see him about 8 o'clock at night. The delegation presented the copy of a book, "Jain aur Buddha" and requested him to attend a function the following morning and discuss some points about Buddhism and Jainism with their religious leader, Muni. Ambedkar accepted the invitation but said he would be able to come only if his health permitted. After the departure of the delegation, Ambedkar had his head anointed with oil by Rattu and felt relaxed. Soon he started murmuring a song he was fond of, his eyes shut and his fingers tapping the right arm of the sofa. Slowly, what he was murmuring became distinct and louder; its wording was "Buddham Saranam Gachhami." A little later, he asked Rattu to play this song on radiogram, and with devotion Ambedkar continued to sing with the recorded song. He was still under the spell of the song when his cook came to tell him that the supper was ready. Rattu helped him walk to the dining room, but just as he was passing by his library, he paused there and took out some books from different almirahs. He asked Rattu to keep the books on his table near his bed. He ate a little rice and asked Rattu to massage his head again. Getting up with the help of the staff in his hand, he started singing a Kabir song, "Chal Kabir Tera Bhav Sagar Dera." As soon as he sat down on his bed, he took up the books he had picked up from the library one by one, briefly glanced at them and kept them on the table. He lay down on his bed, asking Rattu to press his legs.

It was about 11.15 pm, when Rattu drew Ambedkar's attention towards him by moving books on the table and thus asked him leave to go home. Hungry and tired, Rattu wanted to go home, took out his bicycle but hardly had he reached the gate when he was summoned back again by Ambedkar. The master asked Rattu to leave on his table all the typescripts of the preface and introduction to the "Buddha and His Dhamma," the book he had completed, and the typed letters to Acharya Atre and S.M. Joshi, and also the letter to the Burmese Government he had dictated earlier in the day. Ambedkar said he would go through the typescripts at night, and read the letters which had to be posted the next day. As usual, the cook kept a thermos flask containing coffee and a dish of sweets near the table. But his doctor wife, who had nursed him for the past eight years, was not seen in his room, perhaps she was still sulking in the adjoining room because of the reprimands she had suffered earlier. Meanwhile, Rattu had gone home to return early the next day as Ambedkar wanted him to dispatch letters and attend to other work he had in mind for him.

But on the following day, December 6, instead of getting up early in the morning, as was his normal routine, Ambedkar remained sprawled on his bed with his one leg resting on a cushion. His doctor wife had a look at her husband, and thinking him still asleep, went out on a round of the garden in accordance with her usual routine every morning. But returning to her husband's room after the walk, she was shocked to find that he was no more. Obviously, he had died in sleep. She really did not know how to cope with the situation. In desperation, she sent her car to fetch Rattu from his house in Devnagar. Since he had never before been summoned like that, Rattu was stunned. He hurriedly got up, put on his clothes and rushed into the car. Mrs. Ambedkar collapsed on the sofa, weeping bitterly on seeing Rattu. She cried that Babasaheb had departed from this world. Unable to believe what Mrs Ambedkar was saying, Rattu immediately attempted to stimulate heart action in his master by massaging his limbs, moving his arms and legs, pressing upward the diaphragm and putting in his mouth a spoonful of brandy. But all his efforts failed to induce any sign of life in his master. Mrs Ambedkar started weeping loudly for her husband. Unable to bear the bolt from the blue, Rattu himself broke down. "Oh! Babasaheb, I have come, give me work" he lamented. One Chaman Lal Shah, well-versed in Yogic and mystic studies, who was close to Ambedkar and used to stay in the bungalow, joined in the mourning before the rest of the world heard that the messiah of the Untouchables had passed away.

News of Ambedkar's death spread like wild fire. His friends, admirers and followers, in thousands from all over Delhi, made a beeline for 26, Alipur Road, for a last glimpse of the great man. The news was conveyed to Bombay through Siddharth College. Although Mrs Ambedkar wanted the mortal remains of her husband to be cremated in Sanchi, where Lord Buddha had given his first sermon, she was prevailed upon by Ambedkar's well-wishers to drop this idea, and a decision was taken and conveyed to Bombay – that the body would be flown to Bombay for cremation after people in Delhi had paid their last respects. Prime Minister Jawaharlal Nehru, who always used to enquire with concern in Parliament about his health, called on Ambedkar's residence to offer his condolences and enquired about the funeral arrangements. The Union Home Minister, Govind Ballabh Pant, Jagjivan Ram, and many MPs who were among Ambedkar's great admirers called at his residence to have a last glimpse of the departed leader. Jagjivan Ram, another leader of the Scheduled Castes, who had cast his lot with the Congress, arranged for a plane to transport the body to Bombay. Traffic came to a standstill on Alipur Road, as all roads in the Capital led to the residence of the greatest leader of Untouchables, who had given his all for their betterment and felt greatly frustrated because of his failure to bring about a change in their lot in the caste-ridden Hindu society in India.

Ambedkar's body was put on a platform in an open truck and with cries of "Babasaheb Amar Rahe," the funeral procession accompanied by thousands of mourners started from Alipur Road. Passing through streets lined with weeping mourners the cortege took five hours to reach the airport at 9 pm. Wreaths were placed on the body on behalf of Jawaharlal Nehru and the Secretaries of the Lok Sabha and the Rajya Sabha. Many members of Parliament, leading lawyers and eminent scholars paid their homage to the great scholar statesman whose contribution to the uplift of the Untouchables proved a watershed in Indian society. The plane took off at 9.30 p.m. Shankaranand Shastri, Bhikkhu Anand Kausalyayan, Savita Ambedkar, Rattu, Sudama (the cook), Shankarlal Shastri and a few others accompanied the body. The body was received at the Santa Cruz airport in Bombay at 3 am by thousands of mourners who had been waiting for it for eight to nine hours. The body was carried to Rajagraha, Ambedkar's former residence at Dadar in Bombay, watched by lakhs of people who had been standing on the roadside for more than 10 hours only for a glimpse of Ambedkar. A pall of gloom had descended on Bombay. Factories, docks, railway workshops, textile mills, schools, colleges, cinema houses remained closed in the city in mourning for the great leader.

Since the early hours of the morning on December 7, all suburban trains, buses and trams moving to Dadar brought thousands of mourners from all corners of the city and nearby villages. Thousands trekked long distances from far-off localities in the city and suburbs, chanting mourning slogans and carrying black flags. The vast open square near Rajagraha was packed with mourners. There they stood or sat to have a glimpse of their saviour. Women beat their breasts, cried themselves hoarse, wept and sobbed. Scores fainted and had to be removed and given first aid. Many children got lost in the Hindu Colony where many of the narrow streets looked like rivers of human beings crossing each other. Several thousands rushed to Bombay from Pune, Satara, Nagpur and Nasik to participate in the funeral of their Babasaheb, as Ambedkar had come to be known because of his enlightened, deeply concerned leadership of the people who had been treated until he came on the scene like dumb driven cattle. By noon, the throng of people trying to reach Rajagraha had become so dense that the police had occasionally to intervene to prevent a stampede. There were spontaneous closure of markets in Sholapur, Nagpur and Pune in Maharashtra. The Ahmedabad textile mills were shut for the day. Ambedkar's death was the biggest blow to the people who had come to regard him as their messiah. Scores of people marching in processions taken out to express their solidarity and love for the great messiah fainted on roads.

Seldom before had Bombay witnessed such spontaneous scenes of public grief. The seething mass of humanity outside Rajagraha defied description. As preparation for the funeral, some of Ambedkar's close friends and admirers proposed that the body be given a hot water bath before cremation. But Mrs Ambedkar objected to the proposal. She did not allow even touching of the clothes to one Dr Mehta, who had been summoned to ensure that the body was in proper shape before being put out in the porch for the last glimpse by mourners. The body surrounded by a mountain of flowers and wreaths was kept in the porch near the iron fencing inside the compound for a last glimpse by thousands of this followers. Yashwant, the only surviving son of Ambedkar, whose eyes were red with grief, and was inconsolable sat near the head of his departed father. Mukand, Ambedkar's nephew, sat on the other side. Burning incense sticks created a haze over the body. The marks of tension visible on Ambedkar's face all his life seemed to have disappeared. The greatest Untouchable lying dead seemed at peace with his maker now. Men, women and children were in torrents of tears as they filed past his body. There was a sprinkling of Bhikkus in saffron robes who paid their homage to the departed leader. Two separate queues – one for men and another for women – were formed on two separate roads. While men saw their messiah through a fencing, women were allowed to enter the compound through a gate to have a last look at the body of a man whom they had treated like a living god all his life.

The body draped in a saffron coloured cloth was placed in an open truck loaded with flowers and wreaths for the last journey of the great reformer. An ivory statue of lord Buddha stood near the head of the body. Lighted candle sticks and burning incense were there on all the four corners of the truck. As the cortege moved, deafening cries of "Baba Saheb Amar Rahe" from thousands of throats rent the air. Immediately following the truck were Savita Ambedkar, Yashwant, Mukand, monks of the Buddhist order, besides lieutenants and close friends of Ambedkar. The monks chanted Buddhist hymns and carried earthen jars with burning incense. Placards carried in front of the funeral procession were inscribed with these words: "Parinivarna Procession of Babasaheb." Mourners carrying hastily drawn portraits of Ambedkar led the procession as it reached Parel. Except for occasional chanting of "Jai Bheem," mourners moved silently in their final tribute to the leader.

Every street and lane on the route to the Shivaji Park crematorium was lined with crowds of men, women and children. The funeral procession passed through Vincent Road, Elphinstone Bridge, Sayani Road, and Gokhale Road before reaching the Dadar Hindu crematorium. Traffic remained suspended for over 5 hours in Bombay. People showered petals and garlands over the body which was buried under flowers. Repeatedly, flowers covering the face were removed so that the crowds watching the cortege could catch a glimpse of their messiah. Hundreds of policemen had been deployed at the Dadar crematorium to hold back pressing mourners surging ahead.

As per his previous programme which had been finalized before his death, Ambedkar was to have reached Bombay on December 14, to preside over the religious conversion of a large number of followers to Buddhism. His mortal remains were here now in Bombay, a week before the planned ceremony. But his chief lieutenant, Dadasaheb B.K. Gaikwad did not forget Ambedkar's promise to his followers to convert them to Buddhism. When the body was placed on a raised funeral pyre so that the crowds could see their messiah being consigned to the flames, Gaikwad speaking through a microphone posed the question to his followers if they wanted to fulfill the last wish of their leader. The entire humanity gathered for the funeral raised their voice to obey their Babasaheb's call for conversion. It was the most spontaneous demonstration of loyalty to a leader ever witnessed in Bombay and probably in the country and served as a climax to the last journey of their beloved rebel against Hindu dogmas.

As Bhikku Anand Kausalayan, Buddhist priest, started chanting hymns to administer the oath of conversion to Buddhism to an estimated five to six lakh people, everybody listened with rapt attention. Tears glistened, lighted by dozens of gas lamps. Bhikku Anand Kausalayan then delivered a funeral oration in Pali. He made the whole assembly of men and women recite the sacred hymns of Buddhist faith after him. Before the funeral pyre was lit by his son, Yashwantrao, at 7.30 pm, the Bombay police honoured the departed leader by sounding the last post. Buddhist leaders from all over the country and from Malaya and Ceylon paid their homage. Acharya P.K. Atre's thundering speech moved mourners who had thronged the crematorium to pay their last respects to the greatest leader of the Untouchables in the 20th century. By a sheer coincidence Ambedkar's mortal remains were consigned to the flames on December 7,1956, when the eight-day celebrations of the 2,500th Buddha Jayanti concluded in Sanchi.

As soon as the Rajya Sabha assembled on the morning of December 6, 1956, Prime Minister Jawaharlal Nehru informed the House about Ambedkar's death.[3] He said: "I deeply regret to inform the House that Dr Ambedkar who had played a very leading part in many matters passed away a short while ago. For many years, Dr Ambedkar had been a very controversial figure in the Indian public affairs, but there can be no doubt about his outstanding quality, his scholarship, and the intensity with which he pursued his convictions, sometimes rather with greater intensity than perhaps required by a particular subject. But he was the symbol of that intense feeling which we must always remember, the intense feeling of the suppressed classes in India who have suffered for ages past under the previous social system, and it is as well that we recognized this burden that all of us should carry and should always remember.

"It may be that some of us thought, as I have just said, that he overdid the expression of that feeling, but I do not think that, apart from the manner of utterance or language, anybody should challenge the rightness of the intensity of his feeling in that matter which should be felt by all of us and perhaps even more by those who have not in themselves or in their groups or classes had to suffer from that. He was that. Therefore he became this symbol. But we in Parliament remember him for many other things and more particularly for the very prominent part he played in the making of our Constitution, and perhaps that fact will be remembered even longer than his other activities. I am quite sure that every Member of this House will join us to send our deep condolences and message of sympathy to his family and to express our deep sorrow at his demise."

The Deputy Chairman of the Rajya Sabha, Dr Radhakrishnan, who was presiding, said he would like to associate himself with the sentiments expressed by the Prime Minister. "I am sure every Member of this House shares the same sentiments. We have all heard with profound sorrow and a sense of shock of the sudden death of Dr Ambedkar. He was present in the House only the day before yesterday and was in his usual mood, talking and joking with his friends. Many may not agree with him and his political philosophy but he was one of our prominent members and he was listened to with respect. His speeches were marked by scholarship, erudition and deep study. He will, however, be remembered as one of the great architects of our Constitution. He was also very anxious to see that the Hindu Law was enacted and most of it has been enacted. It is a great loss to this House particularly, and as a mark of respect I request the House to stand up for two minutes." After this the House was adjourned.

Speaking in the Lok Sabha,[4] Nehru said: "Dr Ambedkar is often spoken of as one of the architects of our Constitution. There is no doubt that no one took greater care and trouble over Constitution making than Dr Ambedkar. He will be remembered also for the great interest he took over the question of Hindu law reform. I am happy that he saw that reform in a very large measure carried out, perhaps not in the form of that monumental tome that he had himself drafted, but in separate bits. But I imagine that the way he will be remembered most will be as a symbol of revolt against all the oppressive features of Hindu society. He used language sometimes which hurt people. He sometimes said things which were not wholly justified. But, let us forget that. The main thing was that he rebelled against something against which all of us ought to rebel and we have, in fact, rebelled in various degrees. This Parliament itself represents in the legislation which has been framed, its repudiation of those customs or legacies from the past which kept down a large section of our people from enjoying their normal rights.

"When I think of Dr Ambedkar, many things come to my mind, because he was a highly controversial figure. He was not a person of soft speech. But, behind all that was his powerful reaction and an act of rebellion against something that repressed our society for so long. Fortunately, that rebellion had the support, not perhaps in the exact way he wanted it, but in a large measure, the principle underlying that rebellion had the support of Parliament, and, I believe, every group and party represented here. Both in our public activities and in our legislative activities, we did our utmost to remove that stigma on Hindu society. One cannot remove it completely by law, because custom is more deep-rooted and, I am afraid, it still continues in many parts of the country even though it may be considered illegal. That is true. But, I have no doubt that it is something that is in its last stages and may take a little time to vanish away. When both law and public opinion become more and more determined to put an end to a state of affairs, it cannot last long. Anyhow, Dr Ambedkar, as I said, became prominent in his own way and most prominent symbol of that rebellion. I have no doubt that, whether we agree with him or not in many matters, that perseverance, that persistence and that, if I may use the word, sometime virulence of his opposition to this did keep the people's mind awake and did not allow them to become complacent about matters which could not be forgotten, and helped in rousing up those groups in our country which had suffered for so long in the past. It is, therefore, sad that such a prominent champion of the oppressed and depressed in India and one who played such an important part in our activities has passed away.

"As the House knows, he was a Minister, a member of our Cabinet, for many years, and I had the privilege of cooperating with him in our Governmental work. I had heard of him and, of course, met him previously on various occasions. But I had not come into any intimate contact with him. It was at the time of the Constituent Assembly that I got to know him a little better. I invited him to join the Government. Some people were surprised that I should do so, because, it was thought that his normal activities were of the opposition type rather than of the governmental type. Nevertheless, I felt at that time that he had played an important and very constructive role in the making of the Constitution and that he could continue to play a constructive role in government activities. Indeed, he did. In spite of some minor differences here and there, chiefly, if I may say so, not due to any matters of principle, but rather linguistic matters and language used, we co-operated in the Government for several years to our mutual advantage, I think. Anyhow, a very leading and prominent personality, who has left his mark in our public affairs and on the Indian scene, has passed away, a personality who was known to nearly all of us here, I suppose, and I feel sure that all of us feel very sad. We knew him well. He had been unwell for a long time. Nevertheless, the passing of a person is painful. I am sure that you, Sir, and the House will be pleased to convey our deep condolences and sympathy to his family."

Although Ambedkar at the time of his death was not a member of the Lok Sabha and therefore, according to the rules of procedure, the House need not have adjourned for the day, Nehru made a strong case that rules should be ignored for Ambedkar was an outstanding personality, and the House should be adjourned for the day. Nehru said: "Ambedkar was an ex-Member of this House. The rule says in such cases, a reference may be made in the House, there may be no adjournment unless he comes in the category of outstanding personalities. There can be no doubt that he comes under the category of outstanding personalities. According to this strict rule, it says, token adjournment may be made. I submit that, without doing any violence to this rule or to the spirit underlying this rule, the present case deserves for some reasons which I have mentioned and others which I have not mentioned that the House do adjourn for the day."

Echoing the thoughts of the Prime Minister all other members of the House who spoke paid him glowing tributes. Mrs Renu Chakravarti of the Communist party, said: "We, younger Members, never had the privilege of working with Ambedkar. But all of us cannot forget how he brought to the forefront of our peoples' conscience the disabilities suffered by a section of our people owing to our oppressive social system. Although we have passed the Hindu code Bill in parts, the principles which Dr Ambedkar had embodied in his original draft were wiser in many aspects. We pay our tribute to his outstanding intellect which rose against social inequality and narrow prejudices and he become one of those who were known as the architects of our Constitution." Asoka Mehta of the Praja Socialist Party, said: "I was privileged to be associated with Ambedkar on more than one occasion and in his remarkable and fascinating career, there were many facets. We who come from Bombay remember him as a teacher, as an economist, as a labour leader, as a political leader. Apart from the great work he did in the House, be brought a new awakening in my part of the country. It was because of him that large sections of people on our side were given a sense of social significance, they were given a sense of confidence. If he had not been there, perhaps my part of the country would not have been what it is today."

Frank Anthony, a Christian leader, said: "No adequate tribute can be paid to Ambedkar in the course of a few minutes. He was a versatile mind, a profound scholar. But he was a controversial figure. The dominant characteristic of the complex personality was the characteristic of being an indomitable fighter, which enabled him to triumph over personal disabilities, which perhaps would have crushed persons of less tenacious character. We did not agree sometimes with the way things were said by him, but having heard from him the bitter personal disabilities with which he was confronted from his earliest life, I would not presume to judge the fact that perhaps in some respects the iron had entered his soul and his bitterness to that extent, if not justified, at least was understandable. Dr Ambedkar started life from the humblest beginning, but his name will be writ large on the scroll of Indian history, and I believe not only his community, but the country has reason to be proud of a very great son."

V.N. Gadgil, Congressman from Poona, said: "Ambedkar was ten times dearer to us, Maharashtrians, than what he was to India as a whole. It was he who created a sense of self-respect and importance in the most downtrodden community in our area. Undoubtedly he was very bitter in his tongue, but his heart was sweet. His faults we all know, but his virtues outweighed them. He was thinking on much more progressive lines. Very recently, I had some discussion with him, and he said: "No more privileges to the Scheduled Castes. Now, they come into their own and fight against the injustice that is still there, along with the rest of the members of the whole Indian community."

Fully associating himself with the sentiments of the members, the Speaker adjourned the House after the members had stood in silence for a minute, praying for peace to the soul; the soul of not only the greatest leader of Untouchables, but also of a man the whole country would remain proud of for long.

Ambedkar's death was prominently reported by newspapers published from all over the country. Even newspapers outside India carried reports of his death and his contributions to Indian society. By the time he passed away, legal provisions were there on statutes in India for according equal treatment to the Untouchables. *The Hindustan Times* published from Delhi said: "In the death of Dr Ambedkar the Harijans of India have lost a champion who knew few peers and the country one of the greatest constitutionalists. For almost three decades, prior to partition, Dr Ambedkar strode the political stage of India as an indefatigable leader of the depressed classes to whom he himself belonged. Few men have overcome so quickly or so completely the disadvantages of birth and environment, but the memory of early wrongs appears to have survived the rich achievements of his later life. It gave an edge to action and utterance which often caused pain. That in spite of this, he was able to take a prominent part in the affairs of the country at a critical time, when it had just crossed the threshold of freedom, is a tribute to the quality of his mind and character. No one who battled so hard could emerge without leaving or receiving scars. Dr Ambedkar was a robust controversialist who hit hard and asked for no quarter. This estranged him from some of his close associates and he had sometimes to plough a lonely furrow. But to the last he remained a figure to be reckoned with in the political life of the country. Now that he is no more, the old scores will be forgotten. What will remain is a recollection of his great services to his country and the impression left on his contemporaries of a vivid, arresting and versatile personality."

The Times, London, carried a long obituary outlining his career from the beginning to the end. Among other things it said: "His name will figure prominently in any history of the socio-political evolution of India in the closing years of British rule. In spite of many handicaps and humiliations arising from the Hindu caste-system, Bhimrao carved his way to distinction and leadership, and was big both physically and mentally. The determination and courage of this thick-set, spectacled man were writ large upon his features; but he gave little evidence in manner and address of the wide scholarship gained by assiduous study in three continents, for he failed to acquire polish."

The Bombay Chronicle stated: "His influence in ushering a social and economic democracy in the country has been deep and profound. Whatever his apparent failings, which might be exaggerated in the heat and dust of current controversy, few people can deny that these were essentially human. Bitterness was almost ingrained in him due to the rigours of his early life and the later ill-health. He suffered for sometime from appendicitis and had blood pressure. In his declining years diabetes marred his health. Recently again, he underwent electric treatment for his legs which were unable to prop his heavy burden. Yet with all these misfortunes he had many endearing human qualities. Though a profound scholar he had a sense of rustic humour. His idioms were often hard, rude, grinding and rollicking. His rough and rugged exterior concealed many human emotions. The pathos of a picture made him abandon a show in the middle. When his pet dog fell ill, he enquired after its health, personally visiting the hospital twice a day and when news came to him that it had laid its bones, he rolled in his chair like a bereaved mother. He often gave legal advice free and conducted free of charge many cases when the interests of the poor were at stake. In his otherwise busy, studious and stormy life, he liked to hear music and draw pictures. Recently he was taking lessons in playing violin. In his death, therefore, India has lost a profound, pugnacious and picturesque personality of a rare kind."

But the people of the Konkan division comprising Thana, Kolaba and Ratnagiri districts of the erstwhile Bombay state, which for long had been Ambedkar's "Karmabhoomi," where he had grown up and where most of his near and distant relatives lived, could not reconcile themselves to his death. Partly, this was due to the fact that he had not been keeping good health for long was known only to his close circle of friends and admirers. The vast number of Mahars and members of other depressed classes who had come to regard Ambedkar in their hearts as somebody next only to God could not easily accept that their Babasaheb was no more.

The nominated representatives of the three Konkan districts made a representation to the Prime Minister, Jawaharlal Nehru, saying that Ambedkar had died in somewhat mysterious circumstances and therefore a probe should be ordered into his death[5]. Giving the grounds for their suspicion, the petition said the news about his death was not communicated to them immediately. "Why it was that we had to depend upon the All India Radio broadcast to hear about his death, when his own son was with us on December 6, 1956. What prevented Mrs Ambedkar from informing first of all Yashwantrao Ambedkar, the only son of Ambedkar. How is that the authorities of Siddharth College which is supposed to be the part of activities of Babasaheb, were not informed either telegraphically or on telephone till late in the afternoon on December 6. Besides these facts the grounds for our suspicion are as follows:

(1) Nobody was allowed to see Babasahib for a few days prior to his death on Decmeber 6, 1956, under the convincing reason of his ill-health or that he was very busy with the work on his book.

(2) Close friends and responsible persons of the Scheduled Castes in Delhi were not informed about Babasaheb's death till 9 a.m in the morning of December 6. On the contrary, some mysterious long distance telephonic call was booked by Mrs Ambedkar, which, it is believed, secretly gave the news of Babasaheb's death to somebody in Bombay.

(3) The family doctor of Babasaheb for the last decade or so was propagating in hysterical mood with the undertones of mockery in the early morning of December 6, that Babasaheb was enjoying the best of his health. It was later on revealed that the long distance telephone call booked by Mrs Ambedkar was for this doctor and he was the first to be communicated the news of Baba Saheb's death.

(4) The bearer of Babasaheb was prevented from taking tea for him in the morning of December 6, even though it was the routine to serve him tea at that hour. Ignoring his Memsaheb's protest bearer entered with tea into Babasaheb's room and found him dead.

(5) Mrs Ambedkar wanted to take the body of Baba Saheb to Sarnath for cremation instead of bringing to Bombay despite the fact that she knew that Bombay will be the central place for most of his devotees and relations to pay their last homage. She refused to pay Rs 5,000 for chartering the plane and shamelessly said that she had no money.

The petitioners said in view of the grounds mentioned above, there was suspicion that the death was pre-planned. Or did the act of mass conversion of the Scheduled Castes to Buddhism make the opponents of conversion take the life of our leader? An inquiry should be ordered into the circumstances of Babasaheb's death. About three weeks later the government made an announcement in Parliament that there was no foul play and he had died because of prolonged illness.

Unveiling his statue in the Parliament House compound on April 2,1967, the President of India, Dr S. Radhakrishnan,[6] said: "The people of India will ever remain grateful to Dr Ambedkar for devoting all his time and talents in framing a worthy Constitution. India can never forget such a great son. The Smritis or the laws written by Manu have no relevance today. There is no doubt that in the past all the laws of the Hindus and India were made by the Hindu Rishis and all of them were Brahmins by birth. But Dr Ambedkar has proved by his wisdom and intellect that great Rishis like him can take birth in any community. Dr Ambedkar was not only an eminent constitutional expert, he had also mastery over the Hindu philosophy and Hindu social laws. We have rightly honoured him by installing his statute in the compound of Parliament House."

Dr Zakir Hussain, a former President of India, said: "Ambedkar was a giant among intellectuals, in legal acumen and parliamentary skills he had few equals among his contemporaries. He will be remembered for ever as one of the chief architects of India's Constitution, as one of the ablest administrators of high caliber and integrity and as a founder of Neo-Buddhism in modern India."

Vincent Sheen, a well-known American writer, who had met Ambedkar in his lifetime, said: "Ambedkar was an Untouchable – aggressively so – and perhaps for this reason, perhaps by temperament, was an inveterate critic of all Indian society. He was bristling with barbed wire from the inside out, was no respecter of person and at times used sweeping terms to describe what he disliked. On one occasion we journeyed together on a train to Sanchi and back to Delhi, a long journey and spent our day at the Buddhist shrine down there. Even then (1950) Ambedkar knew a great deal about Buddhism and lectured me upon it at inexhaustible length; in the end he himself became a Buddhist.

"A big, brusque fellow with a most belligerent manner, he delighted me by his utter difference from any other Hindu of my acquaintance. It is a form of genius to be so individual and it is not much use explaining it by untouchability. I have known a fair number of other Untouchables, but nobody at all like Ambedkar. He enjoyed attacking me for what he considered my undue affection for India. If you like our Brahmin Government so much, Sheen, why don't you pack it up and carry it off to America? We don't need it and maybe you do. And off he would go on one of his hour-long diatribes about Brahminism and the caste-system and all the evils therein involved. He was perfectly capable of talking for three hours at a stretch on this and related subjects. He was highly irreverent about Mahatma Gandhi, to whom I believe he was (underneath this irreverence) genuinely attached. He was so obsessed by the caste-system, and untouchability in particular, that he could not possibly be fair to the government of India, of which he formed a part (he was Central Law Minister). His diatribes were a healthy corrective, just the same, and there was always some thing in what he said no matter how much he exaggerated. Few cabinet ministers I have ever seen could distribute such tongue lashings to their own associates.

"He was prodigiously educated. He had degrees from Columbia University and the University of London, had studied at Sorbonne and was a Barrister of Grey's Inn. His degrees were M.A., Ph.D., D. Sc and LLD. Degrees do not mean so much, perhaps, but in the torrential flood of his talk, there came up great chunks and whirling avtars of learning. He may not have been the greatest of Sanskrit scholars but he could plaster a text with dozens of references to early Hindu authorities. Critics of his caliber, so brilliant and merciless, are not to be found in public life today. Few politicians can possibly harp on the evils of the caste-system as he did, because the sober fact is that an overwhelming proportion of them belong to the higher castes. Many are indeed Brahmins. If the caste-system is the chief hindrance to progress, as Ambedkar believed, it badly needs another inveterate enemy of law of Untouchable origin who can fight it with all the unquenchable bitterness of personal experience."

References

1. See fifth para on page 104 of the Last Few Years of Dr. Ambedkar book by Rattu Amrit Publishers, 1997.
2. See fifth para on page 111 of the same book of Rattu.
3. See page 974, Vol. 15, Maharashtra Government Publication, 1997.
4. See from third para, page 976, Vol. 15, Maharashtra Government Publication, 1997.
5. See Memorandum to Prime Miniser on page 184 of the same book by Rattu.
6. See the opening para on page 147 of the LFY of Dr. Ambedkar by Rattu, Amrit Publishers, 1997.

Epilogue

Whatever improvement has taken place since Independence in the lot of Untouchables and other categories of people clubbed as Shudras is certainly due to the struggle waged all his life by Dr Bhimrao Ramji Ambedkar. But pity is that although the number of leaders swearing by Ambedkar, the number of statues installed in his memory, and the number of parties now trying to identify themselves with Babasahib all over the country have considerably increased, his tecaching have been being given the go-by, ignored or forgotten altogether. Until his dying day Ambekdar knew and shouted so long as Hindu society remained wedded to the Chaturvarnya system, there could be no redemption of the untouchables. But the new generation of leaders of the backward classes are reconciled to the caste system and whatever it entails. They raise Ambedkar slogans only to strengthen and expand their vote banks for winning elections. And once they are in power, they throw crumbs of comfort to the masses who constitute the depressed classes. But the main focus of their attention becomes lining their own pockets. When Ambedkar died he was penniless, but those who grabbed power in his name have become millionaires.

Even with the banning of untouchability under article 17 of the Indian constitution, the evil has not ended. The laws have provisions of penal punishments for those who mete out evil treatment to the depressed classes, deny them statutorily fixed wages or in any way treat them as unequal citizens. Yet cases of caste atrocities continue to happen. Those who are engaged in ignoble professions such as scavenging, removing hides of dead animals, burning of bodies at the cremation grounds and many other detestable callings remain untouchables. Even the offspring of liberated scavengers who are educated and, under reservation quotas fixed by the government, have been able to land respectable jobs in offices continue to suffer the barbs of contempt and reservations about them on the part of their caste Hindu colleagues.

Not long ago a TV channel showed a girl from a scavenger family near Bhuwaneshwar in Orissa being forced to dismount from her bicycle by the high caste villagers because they couldn't tolerate even the sight of a low caste girl becoming so well off as to pass through the village on way to her school riding a bicycle. She was made to walk on foot till she had crossed the village. Such incidents are happening at many places all over the country because of the centuries-old caste prejudice against the lower caste people. Honour killings are also more frequent now. Usually, they are the result of a low caste boy or girl falling in love or eloping with their friends who belong to upper castes. The community leaders can't tolerate any member of their clan should degrade themselves so much as to hobnob with people who are on the lower rung of the caste ladder

Unfortunately, the process of uplift of the oppressed classes has not worked smoothly. There is still a great deal of ground to be covered, because, having dominated for long the Hindu society by virtue of their superior status ordained by Manusmriti, the upper castes have not yet fully reconciled to the constitutional provisions giving to the lower castes privileges in the name of social equality. Although legally the upper castes cannot resist the concessions given to the Untouchables and other categories of people as they have statutory sanctions, they keep tyrannizing them, especially in rural areas. Very often they get away with blatant violations of the law because the law-enforcing administrative machinery is often dominated by the upper castes or is corrupt enough to connive at misdeeds of the influential and the mighty. As the downtrodden who are now becoming increasingly aware of their social and political rights, do not always take it lying down, sometimes it gives rise to tensions. The emergence of Naxalism as major law and order problem in India today is nothing but rebellion by the long suppressed down trodden against the system which does not do them justice.

When the Commissioner of the Scheduled Castes and Tribes in his reports submitted periodically to Parliament drew attention to the sufferings of the depressed classes, all due to the violations of law by the upper castes, democrats like the former Prime Minister, Jawaharlal Nehru, could not remain Ditent spectators to all that was happening. Immediately, measures for remedying the situation were initiated. Several laws were passed by the Parliament fixing stringent punishment for those who harassed and deprived the Untouchables and other weaker sections of their rights and dues without any provocation or justification. Even Police Stations for exclusively registering cases of atrocities against the Untouchables and for taking punitive measures against the perpetrators of such crimes were set up. There was some perceptible decline in the practice of untouchability in towns and cities. But the situation remained nearly unchanged in the far-flung rural areas.

Ambedkar was convinced that annihilation of the caste system alone could ensure justice for the depressed classes in the Hindu society. When he realized that the caste Hindus would never agree to give up the Chaturvarnya system which confers on them special advantages, he had sought to distance himself from the Hindu society by embracing Buddhism and making a large number of his followers do likewise. But unfortunately, he did not live long to make the entire population of untouchables embrace Buddhism and live as equal citizens. Ambedkar was a messiah. But after him there was no powerful or influential leader of the Scheduled Castes who could show them the right path. With opportunists coming on the scene, the social situation has remained as depressing as before though there has been marginal improvement here and there. The late K.R. Narayanan who had risen to be the President of India despite the fact that he belonged to a low caste remained convinced all his life that unless the caste system was ended inequalities could never go from the Hindu society.

What did Ambedkar personally gain from struggles against the caste system all his life? If he is being remembered today by the caste Hindus, who continue to dominate Indian society, it is mostly for his role as architect of India's Constitution. Every year they go through the motions of paying him floral tributes by garlanding his statue in the Parliament Compound. Whichever party is in power tries to identify itself with Ambedkar only to win the sympathy and support of the vast number of his followers for electoral purposes. The government they control issues commemorative advertisements on Ambedkar's birth and death anniversaries. The late VP Singh-led Central Government went to the extent of conferring posthumously Bharat Ratna, the highest civilian honour, on Dr Ambedkar. Ambedkar's birthplace in Mahow near Indore has a huge memorial built on it and even more imposing memorial is there at the site in Nagpur where he embraced Buddhism before his death. These memorials were built largely with funds from countries where Buddhism is still a vibrant faith.

The downtrodden who regard Ambedkar as their messiah and still swear by him with great fervour are swept with a consuming passion to take out big processions and dance on streets on his birth and death anniversaries in Pune, Sholapur, Mumbai and several other towns in Maharastra and Gujarat states of India. Ambedkar's statues and bust greet visitors at crossings and public parks in many towns in these states. Even Delhi has a vast stadium named after Babasahib. Although Ambedkar's writings on his searing experiences in life are there in books he wrote, and which were published by the Maharasthra government over 30 years after his death, none of his experiences finds mention as anecdote in text books though even little incidents connected with the life of other freedom fighters do so.

The social unrest caused by Ambedkar's ordeals and his lifelong campaign against the caste system because it was the root cause of the suffering of Shudras ignited sparks of protest in the minds of many. Having read and pondered over the life, achievements, failures and frustrations of Babasahib, Kanshi Ram, an employee of the Ordnance Factory in Pune, was deeply moved. Protesting against the cancellation of holidays to mark the birth and death anniversaries of Ambedkar, he started attracting attention. Gradually, as his will to fight for the rights of the downtrodden became stronger, Kanshi Ram's popularity graph started soaring. Many of the downtrodden who after failure of the Republican

Party founded by Ambedkar had reverted their loyalty to the Congress began to throng Kanshi Ram's rallies.

By recruiting a 21-year-old gutsy girl, Mayawati, as his lieutenant in 1977, Kanshi Ram virtually laid the foundation of a new polity in the country. She became a constant companion of Kanshi Ram, following him wherever he went like his own shadow. All over the country people were greatly impressed to hear her fiery speeches and vowed to follow her and her leader, Kanshi Ram. The basic aim and objective of the BSP was to establish a humanitarian social order so that people of *Sarv Samaj* (all castes) could be treated with equality and dignity. Seeing her growing popularity and magnetic charm, Kanshi Ram appointed her first as general secretary and later vice-president of the party.

Successive victories of BSP in elections in U.P started ringing alarm bells in other parties. The Congress which had long regarded the Scheduled Castes and the Muslim minority as its vote bank was taken aback seeing them switching their loyalty to the new party led by Kanshi Ram and Mayawati. The BSP achieved a grand success on June 3, 1995, when it formed the first Dalit government led by Mayawati in India's largest state of U.P. If a genuine and sincere attempt to revive Ambedkar's legacy was made in the country, it was only in Uttar Pradesh under the leadership of BSP, which was founded by Kanshi Ram and nurtured as a national challenge by Mayawati.

Notwithstanding Mayawati's alleged involvement in shady deals, there is no denying the fact that her admiration both for Kanshi Ram and Ambedkar has been growing by leaps and bounds. Under her leadership, Ambedkar's statutes have been installed at crossings, parks in almost every town in UP. She has also initiated proposals for setting up a museum and a university to be named after Babasahib. There is no doubt that Dalit uprising has received a shot in the arm with Mayawati shining in UP and having ideas and ambitions of making Ambedkar's presence felt all over the country which for centuries had been under the stranglehold of Manusmriti.

The Gandhi Centenary Committee in Bihar was very keen that as a homage to the father of the nation, they should be able to realize his dream of ending untouchability somehow. But how could they do it? The Committee advertised, propagated through word of mouth, distributed bills only to find some genius who who could put paid to this ages-old curse. About this time a struggling youngster, Dr. Bindeswhar Pathak, was knocking doors for employment. Engaged as a voluntary social worker by the Centenary Committee, Dr. Pathak was asked to explore ways and means for ending untouchability. Young Dr. Pathak accepting Committee's fiat as a gauntlet plunged headlong into his search for finding a solution to the problem. He could see that the stigma of untouchability was attached to people who had to remove night soil from dry latrines and carry it as head-load to deposit it at some other place. Unless they stopped doing this filthy job, there could be no redemption for them. Therefore the solution, concluded Dr. Pathak, lay in designing a system that could ensure end to physical removal of nightsoil.

At last the enterprising youngster hit upon an idea that solved the problem. He designed a twin-pit pour flush toilet the cleaning of which did not require the services of a scavenger. Instead of being manually removed, human waste was transferred to one of the pits through a connecting pipe with the flow of water used for ablution. When one pit was full, it was sealed and human waste was transferred to the other pit. After two years or so, when the first pit was opened, all it contained was rich dry organic manure which did not have even a whiff of bad smell or stink. Holes on the sidewalls of the pit had made the water to be absorbed by the surrounding earth. Thus, Pathak had put an end to scavenging, the root cause of untouchability. And the problem of untouchability was naturally solved. In this way Pathak not only realized Gandhiji's dream of ending untouchability, he also made the people at the lowest rung of caste ladder move about without any shame or embarrassment as equal citizens, just as Ambedkar wanted them to be.

All his life Ambedkar fought for getting lower-caste Shudhras respect and dignity, but could not succeed until his death. Dr. Pathak says with the widespread use of Sulabh toilets, at least those Shudras who are untouchables because they are scavengers now would automatically cease to bear the curse to remove which Ambedkar struggled all his life. " I say don't annihilate the caste system. Adopt and introduce my toilet system on a large scale. Untouchability which had been blighting Hindu society for ages would automatically come to an end," says Dr. Pathak.

Glossary

Adhyaya	—	Chapter.
Adi Parva	—	First chapter of Mahabharat.
Ahimsa	—	Non-violence, non-killing.
Apoorva	—	Unparalled, matchless.
Ashvalayan	—	Code of conduct established by hermit Ashvalayan.
Asuras	—	Devils.
Avtar	—	Incarnation.
Bhikku	—	Buddhist monk
Brahma	—	The supreme God
Brahmanas	—	First among the vedic Indian castes.
Chaturvarna	—	Four-fold ancient Indian caste system.
Chawl	—	Pertaining to the central top of hair.
Daityas	—	Devils
Danvas	—	Devils
Devas	—	Deities
Dharamshalas	—	Common places of serving people from religious point of view.
Dharma Sutras	—	Aphorisms for religion
Ekadashi	—	Eleventh lunar day mentioned inscriplures good for fasting.
Gotra	—	Lineage
Gotra Parivara	—	A sect of lineage
Harivamsha	—	One out of 52 purnas, clans of Hari, the God.
Hindu Mahasabha	—	Societal institution of Hindus.
Indira	—	Lotus
Itihas	—	History
Jambudvipa	—	One of the synonyms for ancient India.
Jayanti	—	Birthday Celebration

Kabir	—	A saintly Hindu poet of medieval period.
Kali Yuga	—	Fourth and the last era of Indian division.
Khandika	—	Part.
Khilafat	—	Pertaining to Khalifa.
Krita age	—	Third traditional Indian era.
Kusa	—	Pious grass used for performance in religious act, a sort of sacrificial grass.
Lord Shiva	—	God of destruction in Hindu mythology.
Mandala	—	Each of the 10 divisions of the Rig-Veda.
Matsya	—	Fish
Moksha	—	Salvation
Naradasmriti	—	Code of conduct by Muni Narada.
Nibbana	—	Pali language of the Sanskrit nirvana.
Nirvana	—	Salvation in Buddhism
Pali	—	Ancient Indian language of Buddhist scriptures.
Pandal	—	A huge tent.
Preya	—	Desired worldly happiness.
Puranas	—	Indian tradition of history, books of stories with sermons by hermit Vyasa.
Purohit	—	Forerunner of society, one who presides over sacrificial activity.
Purusha Sukta	—	Part of rigveda in praise of God (purusha).
Rakshasas	—	Devils
Rishis	—	Hermits, seers
Ryatwari	—	Tenancy
Sadachar	—	Good conduct
Sagotra	—	Belonging to the same lineage.
Sagotra marriage	—	Marriage in the same lineage.
Sakya	—	Clan of the Lord Buddha
Samadhis Marg	—	The way of transcendental attitude of mind.
Sanad	—	Certificate or a testimonial.
Sanatanists	—	One who believes in Hindu religion.
Sanghas	—	Buddhist Union
Sanyas	—	Renunciation.
Sapindas	—	Persons of the same lineage who perform sacrifices for their deceased ancestors.

Sapravara	—	Belonging to the same lineage.
Sattra	—	Session
Satya	—	Truth
Soma	—	Wine
Savalakh	—	One hundred and twenty five thousand Commentary on Vedas
Satyagraha	—	Passive resistance.
Samhita	—	Collection of scriptures.
Swaraj	—	Independence.
Sutras	—	Aphorism.
Savarna	—	Belonging to the same caste, upper caste.
Srutis	—	Vedas.
Shreya	—	Ways of desired sacrifices and renunciation.
Sippas	—	Influence, approach, chance.
Upanishads	—	Treasure of knowledge extracted from Vedas.
Uphnayana	—	A ceremony marking the investiture of the sacred thread.
Uttar Khand	—	2nd part.
Vana Parva	—	A chapter of Mahabharata dealing with forest.
Varna	—	Colour, caste and letter of the alphabets.
Vedas	—	Supreme Hindu scripture book believed to contain direct utterances from supreme God.
Veda Smriti	—	Veda and its commentary
Viharas	—	Buddhist monastery.
Yama	—	The God of death.

Bibliography

1 to 15 volumes of Dr Babasaheb Ambedkar's Writings and Speeches Published by the Education Department of the Government of Maharashtra.

Ambedkar, Savita – My Life with Dr Ambedkar

Ahir, D.C. – The Legacy of Dr Ambedkar (1990)

Ajnat, Surendra – Letters of Ambedkar

Bharill, Chandra – Social and Political Ideas of B.R. Ambedkar (1965)

Das, Bhagwan – Thus Spoke Ambedkar - Vol 1, (1963)

Gandhi, M.K. – My Experiments with Truth

Keer, Dhananjay – Dr Ambedkar – Life and Mission Popular Prakashan (1962).

Rattu, Nanak Chand – Reminiscences and Remembrances of Ambedkar Falcon Books, 1995. Last Few Years of Dr Ambedkar, Amrit Publishers, 1997.

Dr Ambedkar Papers – Columbia University folder on Ambedkar, New York

Kanshi Ram - The Chamcha Age, BSP, Central Unit, New Delhi (An era of stooges)

Microfilmed papers of Dr B.R. Ambedkar with the Nehru Museum Library, New Delhi.

A.K. Vakil – Gandhi Ambedkar Dispute (1991)

Index